C000154166

Narcissist and Empath

This book includes:

Narcissistic Abuse and Codependency + Cognitive Behavioral Therapy and Empath.
A Journey to Change Yourself, Overcome Anxiety, Narcissists, Stress and Shyness

Courtney Evans

© Copyright 2020 - All rights reserved.

The content contained within this book may not be reproduced, duplicated or transmitted without direct written permission from the author or the publisher.

Under no circumstances will any blame or legal responsibility be held against the publisher, or author, for any damages, reparation, or monetary loss due to the information contained within this book. Either directly or indirectly.

Legal Notice:

This book is copyright protected. This book is only for personal use. You cannot amend, distribute, sell, use, quote or paraphrase any part, or the content within this book, without the consent of the author or publisher.

Disclaimer Notice:

Please note the information contained within this document is for educational and entertainment purposes only. All effort has been executed to present accurate, up to date, and reliable, complete information. No warranties of any kind are declared or implied. Readers acknowledge that the author is not engaging in the rendering of legal, financial, medical or professional advice. The content within this book has been derived from various sources. Please consult a licensed professional before attempting any techniques outlined in this book.

By reading this document, the reader agrees that under no circumstances is the author responsible for any losses, direct or indirect, which are incurred as a result of the use of information contained within this document, including, but not limited to, — errors, omissions, or inaccuracies.

Table of Contents

Book 1 : Narcissistic Abuse and Codependency

How to End and Move on from Narcissistic Relationships, Survive in Today's World and Protect Yourself from Narcissism, Narcissists and Other Toxic People

Part 1 : Narcissistic Abuse

Chapter 1   Introduction to Narcissistic Abuse

Unless you live under a rock, you've definitely heard the word narcissism. In fact, the World Narcissistic Abuse Awareness Day, usually celebrated on June 1st, clearly shows that the world acknowledges narcissism to a high degree. Due to the increased spread of information among the public from every corner, the meaning of narcissism has become so diluted that even harmless people are labeled narcissists based on what they share on social media.

It is ironic that despite the popularity of the word, only a small percentage of the population understands what narcissistic abuse really is. Lambe et al. (2018) in analyzing how narcissism leads to violence and aggression, define narcissistic abuse as a form of psychological and emotional torture that is inflicted by people associated with a lack of conscience and who have antisocial disorders. Narcissism is a condition where one possesses an inflated sense of themselves. A narcissist seeks gratification from their unrealistic self-image; hence, they have trouble maintaining relationships. The same love and attention that they seek from others, they are unable to reciprocate. They lack empathy and have troubled relationships. Their idealized self-image covers a great vulnerability that is sensitive to the slightest criticism. Narcissism develops from a troubled childhood exposed to traumas in which one feels unloved and develops a deep sense of inferiority. Therefore, narcissists seek validation from people they identify as the most appropriate targets who will worship at their feet. They disguise their hidden motives with love for the would-be victim and after trapping them, they manipulate them to fulfill their selfish motives. Narcissism is real, and it has wounded many people in society. People who had their life together become off course and if one is not careful, they end up in great harm.

It is difficult to comprehend how someone professes to love you then goes right ahead to abuse you, but the truth is, love and loyalty do not always exist together. In an era where various people find their partners from social networking sites, it is easy to find yourself under the embrace of a narcissist because you can hardly evaluate their background or those of the people they've dated in the past. Online matchmaking businesses are on the rise and anyone not in a relationship seems interested. Those who want to love and be loved are being targeted by these businesses ready to hook everyone up with "like-minded" individuals. First, this boom of the business shows that people are increasingly and desperately looking for love. Second, it has greatly increased the risk of encountering imperfect matches.

This book aims at showing you how you can fully recover from the abuse of a narcissist and resume your original self. It equips you with the knowledge to understand when you are in a relationship with a narcissist and how to end it. Notwithstanding, you will be able to help other people you know who might be in such abusive situations. It brings to you the good news that most narcissists are predictable, and you can use their vulnerabilities to your advantage.

Thanks again for choosing this book, I'd really love to hear your thoughts about it, so make sure to leave a short review on Amazon (with a photo of the book if you enjoy it).

Chapter 2 Narcissistic Personality Disorder

It is important that people learn and become aware of this disorder. People should realize that this is one of the most significant personality disorders. It is a mental condition that makes a person lack empathy towards others, have troubled relationships, have a great need for excessive admiration and attention. These are people who put on a mask at all times to hide their true identity. It is agreed that narcissists have delicate self-esteem that is vulnerable to even a little criticism. Generally, they are unhappy people and do not feel emotions like remorse or real love. They tend to imagine and pretend to have these feelings. They construct an ideology; have strategies and plans for winning a person, which makes them better during the first stages of a relationship. They are able to study their victims and learn their strengths and weaknesses. That is why it is difficult for a narcissist to engage with a person that they realize lacks weaknesses or strengths that they can exploit.

You are not the only victim of a narcissist—millions of others have found themselves in the same situation. There are narcissists everywhere, at the workplace at school or anywhere you find a grouping of people. While both genders are affected, Women, compared to men, tend to be the easiest targets for these people. By nature, women are empathic which makes them more vulnerable. Because most people do not realize this, they then spend years of their lives in these relationships and in trying to make it work. It is so unfortunate that by the time one has realized that there is nothing they can do to make their partners happy; it is too late, and they have wasted a tremendous period of their life.

In modern society, the number of people with narcissistic behaviors has increased tremendously. It would be right to state that most of the domestic violence cases are tied to narcissist relationships. The issue is most people do not realize that their partner is a narcissist and assume that the violence they face is part of the normal family. Some relationships have unending issues that usually result in violence or rather a physical fight. For a normal family, it is easy to solve conflicts through mutual respect and cohesiveness. However, in the case where conflicts are unending and it appears that one of the partners takes pleasure in it, then it is not a normal or healthy relationship. As such, it would be helpful if people learned about narcissists and how they manifest various behavioral aspects in a relationship.

Narcissists have different cognitive aspects compared to other people. These are people who are preoccupied with fantasies such as ideal love, beauty, brilliance, power, and unlimited success. They lack a sense of reality in each of these things. They believe they're entitled to each of the noted aspects and they do not care about the people they hurt along the way. They are incapable of comprehending the negative emotions that they cause people. As such, they believe they are unique and special, which makes them think that they should get preferential treatment. These are unreasonable entitlements and expectations of proper treatment and automatic compliance with their expectations. Due to this, they will subject their partners to difficult situations without caring for the harm they are causing. For instance, they may ask you to quit your job, they may force you not to accept a promotion and expect you to adhere to it. They dislike things that are likely to improve their partner's position or those that are likely to give them freedom. Most people who have been with a narcissist will tell you that they had to give up their dreams with the intention of making their partner happy.

Additionally, these are interpersonally exploitative individuals. All their actions are calculated, they need to feed on their victim's emotions. They enjoy creating confusion in their victim's life. There is nothing that gives them more pleasure than to see their victims suffering for their benefit. For instance, they bring in another person in a relationship without regard for their partner's feelings. Normally, if a person starts seeing another person, or if they start getting back with their ex-lovers, they will hide this truth. A narcissist will do intentional things so you know, they want to generate jealousy and you start competing for them. They will stay and watch how you are struggling to please them. In addition, they do as much as they can to make it appear that it is your fault that the relationship is having problems. It is right to state this as inhumane, and because most people do not realize this, they are drawn into competition with the intention to prove themselves.

Generally, a narcissist is an arrogant individual. A person who does something manipulates you and those close to you and has a high level of arrogance. When you are in a relationship, he/she goes about telling family and friends that you have emotional instability. A narcissist is truly someone to avoid. They are boastful and pretentious, especially when they are relating to other people. Truly, a person who treats you poorly but treats other people with respect can confuse you. There will automatically be thoughts of being responsible for the problems and instability of the relationship. If you are in such a position in your life, the person you are with is a narcissist. The reason for this is that they want approval and need excessive admiration from other people. They will make you the 'bad' person in the relationship so that they can achieve what they need.

Being in love with a narcissist is more like being in a prison. They use different tricks and strategies to manipulate you. They discover the qualities that make us human-like compassion, love, and sentimentality and use them against you. It is true that partners of narcissists tend to feel betrayed that the romantic person they fell in love with disappeared over time. It is disturbing and one will have numerous questions as to what they did wrong or what they failed to do that made this person disappear. However, as we will discover, this is what they intended from the beginning; they cannot settle for a romantic relationship from its beginning to the end.

In a healthy relationship, partners are focused on building each other, they find a way for both of them to work. In this relationship, people tend to talk and listen to each other to find a solution to the problem they are having. To a narcissist they always take the lead, they want to dominate the conversation and make things about themselves. Their sense of importance makes them think that as their partner, you are there to serve them and whatever they do to you and for you is in line with finding their satisfaction. Thus, as the victim, it is difficult to express your feelings, needs, and rights. In another relationship, you will tell someone you are sad because they offended you in this manner. When you are with a narcissist, you will learn that there is no need nor room for you to express your feelings. They are quick to dismiss them and imply that there is no reason to feel that way and you are the reason why you feel that way.

Therefore, it is important that you watch for the noted things and don't fall for the fantasy. Narcissists could be charming and magnetic; they are experts in creating a flattering and fantastical self-image that will lure you. What you get attached to is their lofty dreams and confidence as they tease your self-esteem and employ a seductive approach that will leave you regretting meeting them. It is easy to be caught in their spider web thinking that they will always be there to satisfy your longing to feel loved, more

8

alive and more important. This is just a fantasy that, in the end, you will pay dearly.

Chapter 3 Who is Your Narcissist?

Understanding Your Narcissist

Just like a dark hole, a narcissist is able to get into your life, devour your health emotionally and physically. Most especially, a narcissist can take away your sanity and manipulate your sensibilities. The strangest truth about a narcissist is that they are attracted to empaths, yet the two are the extreme opposite of each other. There is a compelling pull that draws these two kinds of people together, which as many believe is the universe's way of maintaining equilibrium. For instance, as a typical empath, you have the intrinsic capability to place yourself in another person's shoes and exert deliberate efforts to help them heal. Whilst doing this for a good cause, you as the empath lack the ability to draw boundaries between helping such people and actually falling into being a victim of their condition through chronic self-sacrifice. On the other hand, the narcissist lives within great traumas and conditions; hence, they ideally hide behind an idealized version of themselves. This self-image comes off to you, the empath, as being highly attractive and charming, yet in the real sense, they are highly self-centered and indifferent. When these two extreme characters come together, they form a destructive bond that eventually harms the empath. Both characters collide as they attempt to learn and grow out of their conditions through trial and error. Therefore, it happens that your narcissist is the person who takes advantage of your empathetic nature when your characters collide.

Recognizing the Narcissist

While Narcissistic Personality Disorder is one condition, narcissists come in different forms and kinds. This categorization is based on how the narcissists behave towards others. For one to be known as a narcissist, they have to portray characteristics such as a lack of empathy, a dire need for admiration as well as a magnificent view of themselves.

In addition, most of the narcissists display some specific behaviors towards their partners. These include getting rid of people they no longer need or love-bombing their victims. However, narcissists behave differently depending on the severity of the disorder traits within them, and what their external environment has exposed them to. Therapists have for a long time attempted to separate these narcissists into distinct categories and understanding them helps you in owning up to your character traits that attract them. It would be pointless to be shown how to protect yourself from narcissists without first looking at how different narcissists act within their conscious limits, which will involve hurting you. The more you know them, the more you can consciously act and make decisions concerning your relations with them.

Healthy and Extreme Narcissism

One thing that most people do not know is that there is a continuum from healthy narcissism to extreme narcissism. Whenever we hear of the word narcissism, we associate it with all sorts of negativity. The explanation below changes the narrative and deepens our understanding of the entire phenomenon.

In their assessment of the concept of narcissism, Brummelman et al. (2015) described healthy narcissism (HN) as that which entails the possession of considerable degrees of self-esteem without necessarily being withdrawn from a shared emotional life. Extreme narcissism (EN) was described as that which denies people the ability to have a meaningful relationship because they lack self-esteem. Ideally, healthy narcissism makes one take pride in self-image, beauty and often times the triumph of a tough task. Although this joy in one's beauty and achievement can be momentary, it has a powerful sensation. This narcissism type has been considered helpful in managing one's relationship with others because if you can experience joy in being yourself and the impact you have on the world, then you can easily carry through difficult times. It prevents one from the burnout that most people experience after a series of failures. In the case of a romantic relationship, a healthy narcissist is able to take heartbreaks and disappointments reasonably, because they feel good about themselves. Usually, healthy narcissism mostly grows as part of child development where children at the young age of 2 begin to feel like the world revolves around them based on the love their parent gives them. As they grow up, such people realize that other people have needs as well, and they continue feeling good about themselves as they accommodate others.

Since extreme narcissism is what this book mostly focuses on, it is important to differentiate between healthy and extreme narcissism. First, as pertains to self-confidence, HN leads to high outward confidence that aligns with reality while EN leads to an unrealistic state of grandiose importance. HN enjoys power and admiration while EN seeks power at all costs without reasonable reserves. Further, HN has regard for other people's ideas and beliefs and does value them, while EN devalues people without feeling remorseful and has antisocial behaviors. HN has values and workable plans to follow while EN has no particular path and easily changes course due to boredom. HN develops from a considerably stable foundation of love as a child, while EN has mostly experienced a traumatizing childhood that conditions them to not be considerate of others.

Extreme narcissists are further put in the following categories based on how they manifest the narcissistic behaviors

Vulnerable Narcissists

Also known as, closet, covert, compensatory or fragile, a vulnerable narcissist is one who is shy by nature. Often, they dwell within an inferiority complex that develops from childhood; hence, they lack the capacity to trust, love or care for other people. Their emotional state is full of self-unworthiness and hatred. They tend to over-compensate these feelings by looking for other idealized individuals with whom they will feel special about themselves. They use techniques such as guilt-tripping and gaslighting to make their target empath give them sympathy and attention. Their main aim is to reclaim supremacy and command of their lives and to compensate for the traumas they have faced before.

Invulnerable Narcissists

Also referred to as the elitist, this is the conventional type of a narcissist, one who is bold and highly un-empathetic. They are the complete opposite to the vulnerable narcissists who suffer from a deep sense of inferiority complex since the invulnerable narcissists tend to believe that they are superior to other people. They seek glorification and pleasure, and they are constantly seeking this kind of attention from people they are in a relationship with. Usually, they can do anything to climb up and dominate another person. They can be described in simple terms as braggers and self-promoters that have a constant dire need to prove they are "superior."

Both extreme types use various narcissistic traits such as manipulating other people to fuel their delusions, unfaithfulness, lack of empathy and criticizing people.

Grandiose

Also referred to as classic or exhibitionist, the grandiose narcissist is a very familiar kind of narcissist, one who considers themselves more influential and important. They capitalize on their achievements and seek admiration from others. They often apply a personality that makes them look appealing and charismatic, and they attract their victims by matching their ambitions and energy with their achievements.

Through their know-it-all attitude, this narcissist is always eager to give their opinions even when it is inappropriate, and the opinions are uninvited. They believe that they are more knowledgeable and skilled than anyone else. They like to be the ones talking as others listen. Also, they are bad listeners because they are always thinking about what they will say next. It is difficult to hold a meaningful conversation with this narcissist.

In addition, they have a bullying attitude, which makes them want to build up themselves by humiliating other people. Some may appear more brutal in the way they emphasize their superiority. A grandiose bullying narcissist relies on contempt to prove they are winners.

Seductive

This is the narcissist who uses the technique of making you feel good about yourself, but with the main goal of making you reciprocate those feelings. They will idealize you to capture your attention and get you having that kind of admiration for them. When you have shown them great admiration, they can manipulate your thinking or give you the cold shoulder.

Vindictive

A vindictive narcissist is one who gets very irritable once you do not recognize the superiority that they try to assert. They are dangerous to be in a relationship with because they aim at destroying you and blackmailing you using your most precious belongings to prove to you that you are a loser. For instance, one may try to get you fired from work, trash talks you to people who regard you and even turn such people against you.

Malignant (toxic)

The behavior of this narcissist is highly comparable to sociopaths. They are never remorseful for their actions and have no regard for moral behavior. They are usually arrogant and have a highly inflated ego. They take pride in outsmarting other people and there is often a lot of chaos around them. If they are not caught by the law, they are a great disturbance to the peace of society. Not only do they seek attention, but they also want all other people to feel mediocre.

Amorous

These narcissists satisfy their worthiness by the number of sexual conquests they have had or how their victims help them elevate their status. Normally, an amorous narcissist puts on a pleasing appearance at first glance and will also use gifts to lure their victim. Once they have met their needs, mostly sexual needs, they quickly dispose of them. These ultimate heartbreakers lack remorse for abandoning people and not putting their needs into consideration.

Subtypes

In addition to the main types of narcissists mentioned, there are subsets of narcissists who are grouped not only by the way they manifest their narcissistic behaviors but also by how much they like to get out of their relationship with their victims and how hidden their behaviors are. Learning about them can help you identify them. All of the major types of narcissists mentioned above can fall into the following categories.

- **Somatic Versus Cerebral**

This category describes the typical feature of the narcissist who seeks to focus on self-gratification. Both types need to use someone else to look and feel better. Somatic narcissists focus on their physical appearance and like to feel beautiful above the rest, while cerebral narcissists like to be the informants because they feel they know everything.

- **Inverted Narcissists**

This refers to the narcissist who is co-dependent and has to get attached to other people to feel special. They feel fulfilled when they get into a relationship with fellow narcissists and they fear abandonment.

- **Overt Versus Covert**

This subtype of narcissists differentiates the nature of the techniques they use to manipulate people to meet their needs. While the narcissists mentioned above control others to their advantage, the covert narcissists will usually use methods that are behind the scenes and even have a ground to deny their actions. They tend to be more direct in pursuing their needs without worrying about being discovered.

Chapter 4   How the Narcissist Chooses the Victim

Narcissists are emotional predators and they normally experience emotional emptiness. To deal with this, they have to carefully select their victims: who they seduce, charm, and trap. The victim will then be providing what they lack. It is essential to keep in mind that narcissists are incapable of love, and most are characterized by deep envy of those who have that ability. The moral qualities that normal people tend to have include life projects, goals, creativity, sensitivity, empathy, and vitality. Narcissists are capable of switching their attitude from caring and charming to dismissive and ruthlessly critical, making their victims feel confused and full of self-doubt. If you are a victim of narcissist abuse, it is paramount that you understand that it is not your fault by any form, way or shape. They target individuals for simply being human and, therefore, vulnerable to them. It is in targeting their victims' that narcissists observe and learn to identify whether they have favorable qualities. Therefore, you were selected just because you have all or some of the following desirable traits.

A Person with a High Degree of Sentimentality

Narcissists are attracted to a person who loves deeply and are sentimental. It is easy for narcissists to appeal to such a person's needs and desires through the use of excessive praise and flattery, also termed as love-bombing. The narcissists tend to idealize their victims at the early stage of the relationship where they show a great deal of love towards them. At this stage, the victim will see their partner as loving, caring and charming because they are doing all things perfectly. In other words, a narcissist is able to secure the victims' trust through appealing to their craving for love. Their actions are a deliberate intent to create pleasurable memories that a victim will romanticize and that will create confusion in their thoughts during future abusive periods.

Sadly, a narcissist gets pleasure by toying with another person's emotions. A person who is sentimental becomes an easy target because they love easily and deeply. They will be drawn to the actions that a narcissist does at the early stage of the relationship to create the sense of a soulmate, which makes the victim addicted and dependent on them. When it comes to sentimental people, all the narcissists have to do is manipulate the desires of their target in having the most romantic relationship. A narcissist will carefully assess your personality and identify attributes that you value in yourself. They will then use these qualities against you because it is easy for them.

Resilience

People who have undergone difficult experiences in life serve as good targets for narcissists. It is of the essence to note that the quality of resilience means having the ability to withstand difficult situations with the hope of something better in the future. People who have had challenging experiences, such as abusive childhoods, are targeted because they are able to withstand enormous abuse without giving up. There are various aspects and understandings tied to this by psychologists where they state that when a person has been exposed to abuse for a long time, they grow into it such that they want it, argues Foster and Brunell (2018). There is another understanding of this whereby a person who has been under abuse will not give up easily and will take abuse from a narcissist for a long period, also argues Foster and Brunell (2018). They will make a good target because it means that the narcissist will have an unending supply of the benefits they seek. It is true that resilience is an invaluable quality when it comes to dealing with life's adversity, but in an unhealthy abuse cycle, it becomes easy for them to be ensnared within the narcissist's web of deceit. Resilient people tend to have a strong capability to detect threats in their environment. However, they still fall for narcissists and are subject to the same cycle of abuse that they encountered before. The reason for this is that they will opt to ignore their instincts and decide to fight for the relationship against all the odds. It is not surprising for a resilient person to compare love with the amount of faith one gets.

Low Self-Confidence and Low Self-Esteem

A person with these qualities could be highly vulnerable to a narcissist. One of the factors that make such a person vulnerable is that they crave acknowledgment from other people. They usually doubt their worth and capability to do certain things. Normally, a person with low self-esteem is not comfortable with the way they look, the way they do things and how they relate to other people. It is a quality that reduces a person's confidence such that they are not able to stand up for themselves. Upon noticing this, the narcissist will take advantage of the situation in a way that, during the idealized stage of the relationship, they employ excessive flattery and praises. In return, the person will feel appreciated and valued. Naturally, a person will be attracted to someone who assures them that they are good-looking, lovely and makes them happy. The praises and flattery will carry the victim to the point that they feel they have a purpose and that their partner cannot live without them. Unfortunately, none of this was true, and as time goes, they will be subjected to abuse. The same qualities of low self-confidence and low self-esteem will make them more vulnerable to the abuse.

Integrity

A person of integrity is faithful to his words and has high morals. To some extent, one can say that narcissists lack morals, but they find people who find them very attractive. Integrity can be termed as the basis of moral conduct because a person with it tends to have a wealth of attributes that a narcissist knows that they can exploit. Some of the aspects of a person with integrity are that they find that it is not within their moral code to lie, give up on a relationship defensively or cheat. It is desirable to have such a moral code, but when in a relationship with a narcissist only the narcissist benefits. They have no such moral qualities and will feel no remorse in hurting their victims. Subject to these moral codes, the victims will be reluctant to betray the relationship by stepping back. Integrity is a vital quality when in a relationship with like-minded or empathic individuals. However, when with a narcissist it is more of a weapon to be used against the person to end their sense of self and their trust.

Empathy

Empathy is an important quality among human beings as it allows them to connect and consciously feel what others are going through. It is the basis for emotions and that is why narcissists fail to have emotions and feelings because they lack empathy. The reason why narcissists prefer empathic individuals is because the emotional fuel that they provide is necessary for them to feel in control and power. It is an aspect that makes them continue seeking empathic people due to their abundant supply. Empathy is an empowering human trait but when it comes to relationships with an abuser, it serves to disempower (Wurst et al., 2017). The reason for this is that empathic people tend to see and try to identify with the narcissists perspective when they are being abused by them. The narcissists depend on this aspect to keep a continued cycle of abuse with their victims. A highly empathic person is an ideal and important choice of narcissists due to pity that they employ after abusive incidents.

In most cases, an empathetic person's reaction to a given situation is easy to predict. It is a major advantage to a narcissist because they know how they can manipulate their victims to act in the manner they want or to control them. For instance, a narcissist knows that if they give a simple sob story or a faux apology their victims will be quick to forgive. An empathetic person is quick to rationalize a narcissist's behavior with the excuses they make for abuse. As such, they depend on their ability to sympathize and forgive them even after they have been subjected to a horrific incident. They appeal to the victims' empathy and in so doing; they are not answerable for their actions. The challenge herein is that, as an empathic person, one always doubts their decisions in confronting their narcissist partner. They feel guilt and carry the burden as if they are the abuser in the relationship. Sadly, the narcissists take advantage of this as they count on an empathic person's compulsion to protect them instead of exposing who they are.

Conscientiousness or Dependability

The ability to be conscientious is an important quality and one that a narcissist will look for in a target. These individuals are concerned with the wellbeing of others. They are always ready and willing to help others in need. It is an important quality and makes a person more humane. However, narcissists look it as the way into a person and as a suitable aspect to exploit in their victims. A person with this quality tends to make decisions with their conscience and projects a high degree of morality on the assumption that other people will depict the same. However, it is not the case when it comes to narcissists who take advantage of the quality of the notion that their victims worry about the needs of others. The bad thing with this is that for a conscientious person they will readily give a narcissist a benefit of doubt; hence, granting them more chances. The care that they have in serving a narcissist's needs makes them sacrifice their own wellbeing.

Therefore, the analysis signifies that narcissists target individuals for their humane qualities. Normally, the noted qualities among others would play an essential role in enabling a person to properly relate with others and have a healthy and productive life. However, due to the lack of empathy in a narcissist, they tend to see the qualities as their enabling weapons to take control of their victims. They will manipulate and take advantage of their targets such that they forget their wellbeing and spend their time in trying to make the relationship work. The previously discussed qualities, and others such as intelligence, extreme perfectionism and personal accountability, will make a person take the blame on themselves as the reason why the relationship is not working.

Chapter 5 How a Narcissist Acts

A narcissist has been described above as a person who buries their true self and expresses themselves with a false self; a personality that often clashes with other people because the narcissist is highly conceited. The major attribute of narcissists is an extreme love of themselves, which they use to avoid being seen or always feeling wounded. Deep down the narcissists feel worthless and they painfully cannot admit this. Especially not in front of others.

Typical Behaviors

The following is a checklist of the behavior of a narcissist towards their partner.

Love-bombing

This is one of the most popular behaviors a narcissist employs when they realize that a person seeking love has let their guard down. Love bombing can be described as the deliberate attempts of influencing an individual by greatly endearing them. Moreover, true to the narcissists' sentiments, love bombing feels good, because it makes one create this perfect picture in their mind. Narcissists idealize their partner to get them to reciprocate these feelings and idealize them as well. Ranging from love notes in every place you visit daily, highly flattering comments, surprise appearances, and frequent messaging, the narcissists use these to manipulate one into spending more time with them and not with other people. They try to create an impression of themselves to you that they are the perfect partner, capture your attention and affection, and then shape up your role in the relationship as the support system.

Most people struggle with admitting that a person can be a narcissist if they say they adore them. However, they fail to differentiate between love and affection that grows gradually from the immediate love-bombing that a narcissist shows them. Simply put, love-bombing from a narcissist is affection and adoration that is just too good to be true.

Gas-lighting

Gas-lighting identifies as a consistent mode of encoding and it is among a narcissist's favorite tools. It refers to how a narcissist brainwashes their partner and gradually makes them lose a good sense of themselves. They are calculative and they know just how much a statement that they tell their partner will appropriately marginalize them and cause them to question their identity. To keep up with their gaslighting tool, narcissists are always lying, exaggerating things, become aggressive when criticized and hardly admit their flaws, and they always tend to cross boundaries. Exaggerations are used to elevate themselves while downgrading their partner and lies are meant to distort facts and leave the partner with questions at all times. They always intimidate their partner whenever they are accused of something and can even resort to fighting when their negative behavior is pointed out.

Discarding People They No Longer Want

In one way or another, a narcissist is bound to discard you. The one thing that you should know is that a narcissist is okay with or without you. Your feelings and values mean nothing to them. You can tell this by the way they lack remorse for their wrongful doings, and how they lack empathy and understanding.

In the love-bombing phase, you might be made to believe that you mean everything to the narcissist, not realizing that you are just an object of satisfaction and not a necessary partner whose package is a human being with a heart and soul. Whether it is the narcissist who ends the relationship, or you are the one who leaves or however the relationship blows up, there is always the next target waiting and being groomed to replace the object.

Further, a narcissist's mode of discarding is always brutal since they will accuse you of outrageous things, and even characterize you as if you are the narcissist yourself. They will discredit you to anyone who tries to listen your story. The worst part about the narcissist's desertion is that it tears our souls and humanity up and disorients our safe and valued place. Yet the narcissist has to use this tool to preserve their false selves by rejecting your real self.

Feeling Superior and Entitled

Whenever a narcissist is interacting with other people, even in a relationship, there is always a hierarchy, with themselves at the top of the ladder. At the top is their safe place and they cannot allow anyone to be above them. They have the dire need to be the most competent, owning everything and having everything done their way. At times, they even feel misused or injured and demand concern and apologies from you even if you truly did not hurt them.

They always want to get all of their partner's attention, always following you and talking to you to capture your attention. They need your validation and they want to get only positive words from you. Yet no matter how much you show them love, they do not believe that anyone can indeed love them. Hence, to keep up their fragile egos, they always want more because they do not believe that what you give them is enough.

Perfectionist Behavior

We tend to throw around the word "perfect" like it is some sort of an easy thing to attain. When placed under such expectations, it is easy for some people to reason out and say that perfectionism is logically not attainable. The worst happens when the voice of a narcissist takes away their logic and makes them believe in perfectionism. A narcissist has strange perfectionist expectations of the people around them, most especially their partners. Due to their false perfect image, they tend to expect that events should occur exactly as they deem fit, and that life would play out in alignment with their beliefs. Due to this, the narcissist is always dissatisfied with what you do and is always complaining.

Failure to Claim Responsibility but Deflecting to Others

Unless something goes exactly how they wanted it to, narcissists do not claim the responsibility of their mistakes. They do not like to feel imperfect or give others a window to criticize them. They have to blame someone to not appear as if they made a mistake. Sometimes the blame is generalized, for instance, blaming their boss, but most often, the blame will fall on their partner. They find their partner to be the best blaming target because the partner will most likely pardon them or leave them. Indeed, it is so obvious that someone who envisions themselves as perfect and superior cannot accept responsibility for their mistakes.

Lack of Empathy

Extreme arrogance and self-absorption rarely go hand in hand with empathy, and that is a behavior found in narcissists. Despite having the ability to detect how other people feel, narcissists fail to show compassion. They are interested in fulfilling their needs with little or no regard at all for their partner. They mightily struggle with being empathetic since their minds are full of how they can get you hooked into their needs and this inhibits their ability to be objective about how other people feel.

Emotional Reasoning

This identifies as some type of cognitive distortion through which a narcissist convinces themselves of something being true without facts and even while others convince them otherwise. They tend to interpret their emotional reasoning as the reality and the first problem that this causes is that it makes them believe that they are not worthy deep within them. It makes them never appreciate any form of love from their partner because they have convinced themselves that they are not lovable. They even overlook any form of solid evidence and instead rely on their assumed truth. The basic assumption that overlooks facts is "There must be a reason for how I am feeling right now." Due to this character, it is hard to reason together with a narcissist and make them see and believe your side of view.

Cannot Connect Emotionally

Narcissists lack the capacity to connect with other people emotionally since they have a constant need for self-protection. They cannot align their feelings with those of any other person and they cannot view things from others' perspectives. They want people to respond to their pain and not feel the pain of others. Yet it is impossible to effectively get intimate with a person who cannot compromise some of their standards or even trust you. Essentially, vulnerability requires trust, and this is something that narcissists are unable to develop with their partners. This explains why they engage in a one-sided relationship since they cannot see eye to eye with their partner. Even if they may be with you physically and showering you with love, in the real sense narcissists are not with you.

Cannot Work in a Team

Now, any collaborative work needs a good understanding of another person's true feelings. It requires a consideration of how the action you take might affect the other person and if any decision you make will make both of you happy. This is the kind of attitude that makes romantic relationships thrive because you strive to not do things that will have highly negative impacts on the person you love. However, a narcissist does not understand or try to give provisions for their partner's feelings. This way, they are unable to be a team player. Most importantly, they aim to control their partner and not be on the same level as them.

Chapter 6   How to Understand If You Are Caught in the Spider Web of a Narcissist

In most cases, people do not know that they are victims of a narcissist. They will confuse what they are encountering in the relationship to be a normal part of every couple. Even when the abuse is extreme, people live in denial that their partner is a narcissist. The main reason for this is the excessive flattery and praises that they received during the idealization stage. A narcissist knows how to properly initiate a relationship and make their subject drawn to them so that they will always romanticize their early times. The victims miss and wish to return to that time with their partners, thus, they will try to give the relationship their best. They even do not know when they are being abused because they are so tied to the hope of the relationship getting better. The following are some of the signs that may indicate you are caught in the spider web of a narcissist.

Frequent Threats

Most narcissists tend to threaten their victims with things that they know they would not want to happen. In response when a victim is threatened, they tend to humble themselves, which gives the narcissists more power to control them. If your partner keeps on threatening that they will leave you, that if it were not for them, you would not have achieved what you have, it is more likely that you are in a relationship with a narcissist. The reason why they use this approach is that it is more effective when it comes to instilling fear, self-doubt, and self-blame. Your partner is issuing threats as a way of showing that it is because of you that they are not comfortable with the relationship. Because they have laid down the threats, you will avoid bringing up issues because you fear they will take action. For instance, if they threaten you to leave and say they did not need you anyway, it will make it hard for you to leave because you know they won't beg you to stay.

You Have No Sense of Self

If at this point you feel that you have no goals and aspirations, it means that you have given up on yourself. At this point in your life, due to the person you are in a relationship with, you have put aside your desires and basic needs and sacrificed your emotional wellbeing to please the abuser.

At one time in your life, you may have been full of life; you were dream-oriented and goal-driven. But now, you feel that you are living to please and fulfill the agendas and needs of your lover. You have reached a point where your life revolves around them and you have nothing outside of the relationship. It then means that you have sacrificed your wellbeing for the sake of and to satisfy the abuser. A healthy relationship does not mean giving up your personal safety, friendships, hobbies and goals, but will mean driving you into realizing your full potential and living a happy life. Besides the sacrifices, you will later come to realize that you are incapable of satisfying your partner and the sacrifices were all for nothing.

You Have Health Issues

Most people who are in a narcissistic relationship live in denial and try their best to hide the challenges and difficulties they are going through. As such, they will struggle to maintain a good image in the society while deep inside they are suffering. If you are in that position, then you are caught in the web of a narcissist. When it comes to carrying weight as a representative of the psychological turmoil you are going through in a relationship, you may gain or lose a significant amount of weight, as argued Morf, Horvath and Torchetti (2011). Some people go to the extent of developing serious health issues that they did not have before they engaged in the relationship. You may look at yourself and realize that you look old compared to most of your agemates, which is known as premature aging. Morf et al. (2011) also suggest that the stress, anxiety, and depression that you are going through in the relations due to the chronic abuse is capable of overriding your immune system. At this point, it means that you are vulnerable to various physical and mental diseases and ailments. In addition, if you are having terrifying nightmares or you are unable to sleep, it is because you are reliving the trauma through visual flashbacks. Those people who are in a healthy relationship do not experience things of this sort.

Self-Isolation

One trick that a narcissist will use to ensure that they fully control you is isolating you from people close to you. If they know that your parents or friends could help you realize that you are being abused, then they will try to separate you from them. Some narcissists will use a smear campaign against you, as if you are the one who has a personality disorder. Your friends will stop trusting you and others deliberately avoid you. In other cases, it is you who is isolating yourself from friends because you are embarrassed about the abuse you are experiencing. In such case, you feel that you are a laughingstock among your friends. It is important that you realize that in doing so, you are empowering your abuser. However, due to blaming and misconceptions about psychological and emotional violence people will victimize you while it is not your fault. The misunderstandings that people have, including family members and friends, may invalidate the idea that the narcissist is being abusive as Bergman et al. (2011) found in their analysis of how a narcissist employs his manipulative techniques. Thus, because you fear that no one will understand you, you withdraw from the society rather than seeking assistance and to avoid retaliation or judgment. If you are in such a situation, it is important that you rethink your position because you are trapped in an unhealthy relationship.

If You Are Blaming Yourself for the Abuse

Narcissists' actions are indeed inhumane but they do not realize and instead enjoy doing these things to other people. They tend to employ what is termed as reverse psychology. In the idealization phase of the relationship, they will be on their best behavior. In a calculated manner, they engage in loving, caring and kind actions that are intended at winning your heart and love. In the late stages, they change and become abusive in all manners. They behave in a manner of hot and cold, which confuses you as to who they really are. Rather than realizing that their partners are doing this intentionally, most victims tend to take it as their fault. A narcissist is excellent in creating love triangles whereby they bring another person who could be a stranger or ex-lover in the relationship with the intention to terrorize the victim. If this is the case, then the victim tends to internalize the fear that they are not enough for them and results in competing with to win the abuser's approval and attention. Also, if you are comparing yourself with others in a healthier and happier relationship then consider why your partner treats other people with respect. Obviously, you will have such questions as 'why me?' leading to self-blame. The truth is you should not blame yourself. The abuser is the person who is wrong and the reason why you fail to doubt them is that they have trapped you in their spider web.

If You Fear to Achieve More Success or Do What You Love

Narcissists in a relationship flourish by denying their victims freedom. As such, they ensure that what their lovers are doing, they must approve or have a say. If you are in a relationship where you have to ask for permission from your partner to do certain things, then you have no freedom. If you feel that you will become a threat to your partner if you succeed, then it is time to leave that relationship. A narcissist will teach you to associate your areas of success, talents, interests, and joys with callous and cruel treatment. Then you are conditioned to fear success beyond what your partners approve because in doing so you will be reprimanded or face reprisals. The conditioning is what has led to your lack of confidence, anxiety, depression and most importantly hiding your capability. It is important to know that the reason as to why an abuser limits you from doing what you love to achieve more success, is because they know that if you do succeed, they will lose the control they have over you.

If You Feel A Disassociation

You are trapped in a narcissist spider web if you feel physically and mentally detached from your sense of self, consciousness, perceptions, and memory. Experts have credited dissociation as the essence of trauma. A person in such a situation has their physical sensations, thoughts, images, sounds, and emotions split and fragmented in a way that they have a life of their own. If you have emotional numbing even after a horrific event this is not normal. If repression, addictions, obsessions and mind-numbing activities have become your way of life, as they provide you with a way to escape the abuse, then your partner is a narcissist. It is not normal, but your brain has developed ways to emotionally block out impacts of pain so that you do not have to deal with the terrorizing circumstances. If this continues, you become disconnected from your loved ones, the abuser, your environment and your actual personality. At this point, it is necessary to find a trauma-oriented therapist. They will help you to evaluate the situation you are in by bringing the pieces together.

Chapter 7   Narcissist's Feelings towards the Victim and Vice-Versa

Narcissist towards the Victim

The most surprising thing is that narcissists focus on people who have their lives in order because they enjoy the challenge and the havoc they cause to someone who thought they had it all together. We have already established that whenever you exit from a relationship with a narcissist, you are damaged, and you do not have a clear route to where your former self was. This is the moment you realize that the victim was so toxic and that you should not have let them stick around for so long.

It appears as though a narcissist wants to make the relationship work, but their lack of empathy and emotional cognition denies them the chance to express true feelings. Yet to the narcissists, they cannot accept that it is their fault that they cannot get along with another person. They have to hide behind the explanation that it is another person's fault that they cannot love them. What they present on the surface is entirely different from how they feel deep within.

Since they spend their entire days and nights with their victim trying to fight off threats to their ego, they have negative feelings towards their victim.

Narcissists Are Jealous of Their Victims' Life

Narcissists are attracted more to a victim's strengths than their weaknesses. They simply recognize that you have a good life, but they don't want you to have it. They understand that you have a strong bond with your family and friends, and this is the first thing they want to destroy. This is motivated by jealous feelings. In the beginning, they are so friendly and even want to be in your inner circle but as time goes by, they start to shift their sentiments and criticize these friends and family. They do not like that you can bond so easily with others because deep within them, they are unable to create true bonds with their family members and they rarely have true friends. The other thing narcissists are jealous of is your job and money. They are not happy with the fact that you seem to be so flawless in something and this explains why they want to mess up your job. They also want to direct how you will spend the money you get because they do not want you to develop yourself. Furthermore, they are jealous of your physical and mental wellness, and they desire to change the state of affairs and make themselves feel superior to you even though they know deep within themselves that it is hard for them to attain this. Therefore, they resort to mean ways of degrading your wellness for them to appear and feel better.

They Do Not See Any Value in the Victim

Since they on chaos, narcissists keep attempting to find out just how much they can destroy their victims. They want to ascertain for themselves that they can impact your life, only this is not about influencing in a good way, but in a devaluing way. It is entertaining for them to see someone suffer and become poorer and at a lower level than they are.

In the mind of a narcissist, the social scene entails victors and losers. According to Bergman et al. (2011), the narcissist does not visualize a situation whereby one can make another better or use teamwork to achieve great results together, and for them, it is impossible for everyone's needs to be met. Due to the way they were humiliated or tortured in the past, the narcissist lacks value for anyone who has something that threatens their ego. They view other people as just objects for fulfilling their needs and cannot allow anyone to make them feel small under any circumstance.

Their Pattern of Abuse

Their abuse pattern is filled with thoughts that they like the victim at one time, but the moment they do something, they do not like them anymore. Every time they identify a target, they idealize this person and they know that it is easy to love them. Eventually, they discover that this person has flaws, which cause them to look for the perfect person whom they believe they can love.

Narcissists are unrealistic in what they look for in a partner. The shifting feelings of being pleased by a partner now, yet offended in the next minute, causes them to express the narcissistic abuse. They tend to be extremists with no equilibrium. Hence, at any particular time, they extremely love their partner or extremely abhor them. They enjoy the fact that they have found someone who will never disappoint them but then, they realize that

31

you are progressively getting out of reach and they are disappointed of you. Most especially, narcissists seem to use the traits they observed in the victim that attracted them to turn around the situation for their favor.

Once they divert their attention from their current victim, they are already trying to position a new one to be in line with their thoughts, the narcissist does not care about how you react to anything they do. They capitalize on fulfilling their interests and fantasies with you, using you as an object without remorse.

Victim towards the Narcissist

It is already established that it becomes difficult for the victim to speak up for themselves and characterize the betrayal experiences that they have towards their narcissistic partners. It is surprising that someone will fall in love with a person who does not value them, one who is jealous of their success, one who is not empathetic and one who does not show remorse for the wrongs they committed.

It is entirely not the victim's fault to be abused by the narcissist. Any person can fall prey to an emotional predator; hence, it is not useful to blame the victims but to establish their thoughts towards the narcissist and help them get out of the situation.

The feelings of the victims towards narcissists and which make them easy targets are:

Their Empathetic Nature

As aforementioned, most of the narcissists' targets are normally the empaths, mostly because the two groups of people exist in two different extreme ends. The narcissists seek people who will worship the grounds they walk on, while the victims have a lot of compassion and they always seek to understand everything a narcissist does. This is one of the most self-destructive thoughts of the victim. Even when the narcissistic partner is wrong, the victim will justify their actions and even blame themselves for the narcissists' wrongdoing.

Philanthropy

The victim is a philanthropic person who will offer to give anything to help their partner out of love. They cannot accept to see one suffering and they feel that as a person they adore, it is in their place to help them in any way they can. They are supportive and they want to help them grow in every way. They fail to realize that the narcissist only exploits them further and it is entirely upon the victim as to whether the relationship is worth it or not. In addition, they fail to understand that everyone is responsible for their own growth; hence, they are not obligated to help their narcissistic partners develop.

Placing the Narcissist First

The victim experiences a decreasing sense of self-esteem and puts their narcissists' needs more and more before their own. They almost believe that they do not have rights if those rights mean being against their partner's wishes. Due to this, the victim tends to sacrifice a lot for their companion without realizing that they are becoming more dependent on what their partner wants or needs to be done. They lose their independence and they think that it is okay to sacrifice and compromise for the person they love. In addition, this opens a window for their partner to pour more shame and fear into them. Due to the declining self-esteem, the victim buys into so much of what the narcissist says and feels, such that they believe it is acceptable when their pair does not approve of them. They give the narcissist so much power in their lives that they cannot do anything without consulting them. On the flip side, the narcissist enjoys being the one controlling how the relationship is run.

Respect and Being a Good Listener

Further, a narcissist's victim is a respectful person who believes in listening. This contrasts with the narcissists' urge to always be the one speaking. The victim is always willing to listen to their partner and courteously present their opinions when a chance presents itself. The worst thing about this is that the narcissistic partner will ensure that they are the ones being listened to, so that they can control how the relationship progresses. On the other side, the victim allows their partner to overstep their boundaries because they are afraid of saying no. Once they start to say no, they can take a step further into protecting themselves from the abuse, but they cannot co-exist peacefully with the narcissist because they do not want to be challenged.

Take the Narcissist at Their Word

In addition, the victim feels like the narcissist is true to their words. As aforementioned, most narcissists are able to present an idealized self in which energy matches the ambitions they have. Therefore, whenever the victim is promised something by the narcissist, it is easy for them to believe and even look forward to it, which is one of the reasons people keep holding onto toxic relationships. The victims believe in the intermittent hopes that the narcissists offer them. Whenever the narcissist is upset, the victim believes that if they behave better, they will be able to acquire the love of this person. Furthermore, having experienced the love-bombing in the beginning of the relationship, the victims rely on the hope that this ambiance can return in their relationship. They spend their entire time trying to make the relationship work by exerting more effort to please the partner and getting them to treat them special like they used to.

Further, the victim forms a bond that is highly difficult to break because of the push and pull kind of relationship. The victim falls for the love that the narcissist showers them at the beginning. They feel like it is impossible to leave the relationship despite causing them a lot of damage. It is more traumatizing to leave than to stay, hence, they prefer staying. Empathy arouses the aspect of looking at themselves and capitalizing on their faults, which is usually a perfect setup for the narcissist. They always think that they are the ones who are supposed to change because their characters are seemingly full of flaws.

Chapter 8   How the Narcissist Was Able to Get into Your Head

As a victim, you ask yourself how things turned out to be the way they are. Rather, how a person you knew as loving turned out to be an abuser. The important point to note is that when a narcissist is full of themselves, they leave no room for you. You should know that even when they were doing good things, these were deliberate actions to lure you. Narcissists operate in an extremely manipulative way even in a romantic relationship because they lack empathy and they have a tendency in being interpersonally exploitative. The following are the tricks and strategies that a narcissist uses to get into their victims' heads.

Idealization-Devaluation-Discard

A narcissist engages their partners in three stages within a relationship. The first phase is idealization, followed by devaluation and lastly discarding.

Idealization

This is the most critical in their endeavor to manipulate their targets. When the relationship is new, a narcissist puts you at the center of his world. They will shower you with unending praise and flattery to the point that you feel this is the love you have been waiting for your entire life. You will feel that they cannot live without you and you are convinced that you have met your soulmate. They will call and text or email and want to be close to you at all times. The technique of love-bombing, as used by a narcissist, is extremely effective in enabling them to win over their targets. You may be fooled into thinking that the narcissist actually has feelings for you, but this is not the case and what they want is to make you dependent on their attention and praise.

Devaluation

At this stage, the narcissist changes the way they treat you. It is the most confusing stage for the victims because they wonder what caused the sudden change. It is a period of hot and cold, which makes you more confused because at one time they may be good to you and at the other they are either beating or calling you names. Mostly, devaluation is characterized by things that narcissists do to overtly and covertly put you down; criticizing and comparing you with the others. It is more of emotional withdrawal that in most cases makes you think that you are the reason why they are treating you that way. It is no surprise that they will give you the silent treatment when they feel that you have not met the standards that they want. The fact that there are inconsistent idealization aspects makes you convinced that it is your fault that the narcissist is angry at you.

The narcissist sees you and treats you as an object. They are the ones who are jealous and possessive, but they will project the same onto you. During the early stage, the narcissist makes it appear that frequent contact will be there in the relationship, how they turn this and make you the needy one. Mostly the victim reacts by being jealous or needy, hoping that their partner will become more loving as they were during the beginning. The narcissist will use harsh words to gaslight the victims. They tend to blame you as a way of maintaining control over your emotions. Narcissists' show their true colors at this stage, but you may fail to realize this because you are still clinging to the person you saw at the beginning of your relationship.

Discarding

This is the final stage and as the name implies, you are abandoned by your partner. They tend to do this in a very demeaning way as much as possible with the intention to make the victims see themselves as worthless. They employ savage approaches, such as being physically aggressive, humiliating the victim publicly or leaving you for another lover. The core message or goal that the actions intend on communicating is that you are not important.

Making You Think You Are the Problem

They employ a technique known as 'gaslighting' to manipulate their victims and convince them that they are perceiving abuse in the wrong manner. They tend to make remarks that suggest that you have emotional instability, but in doing so, they are trying to displace the blame of abuse from them to you. In addition, if for instance, your partner slaps you, they will justify this by saying that it is you who provoked them. They will go ahead and discredit your emotions by stating that you are being too sensitive. Narcissists get you thinking that the abuse that they are subjecting you to happens solely due to your behavior. They strategically make it your fault and eventually you will buy into this line of thinking. You develop self-doubt, which then enables you to stay in the relationship even though you are being abused. It is surprising how they are able to turn you such that you cannot even trust your instinct and interpretations of things.

Making You Jealous/Triangulation

A narcissist enjoys playing with your psychology and toying with your emotions. They create a relationship that is characterized by infidelity, uncertainty, and provocation. They will deliberately create love triangles and even tell you what other people are saying to prove their actions. Triangulation has been pointed out as one of the most popular methods of how a narcissist controls your emotions. It entails bringing another person into the relationship they may be a complete stranger, relative, a current mistress or an ex-lover. They can engage any of these people in social media or in-person but make sure that you know what is going on. They are doing this so you can get jealous, which is a powerful emotion to getting someone to do what you want. They may go to the point of telling you that a certain ex-lover of theirs wants them back in their life. The obvious response will be you engaging in competition and feeling insecure about the position you currently hold in their life. Rather than having a productive conversation about the issue of jealousy a narcissist will dismiss your feelings and continue with their affairs without minding your concerns. As such, triangulation serves as an effective tool to maintain control and keep you in check.

Turning Other People Against You

Narcissists are egocentric and enjoy unending validation from the outside world. They need people to notice them and feed their great hunger of admiration and sense- of importance. Because they do not have emotions, it is easy for them to camouflage and engage different people in whatever personality that fits in the current situation. As such, you may see that your partner abuses you but treats other people with great respect. In so doing they will engage in smear campaigns that are purposely intended as tainting you as the 'bad' person in the relationship. They will tell other people that you are the one with emotional instability in the relationship and they will be quick to believe the same. If a narcissist has a reliable support network of empaths, people-pleasers and fellow narcissists then they will succeed in turning almost everyone against you. A smear campaign can effectively enter in your head through various aspects. It provokes you and the manner you react is more likely to prove that you are the one who is unstable. Then it is a technique that a narcissist uses to subject you to their relationship trauma making it difficult to reconcile the rumors spreading about you. The only way that you can deal with such a situation is by ending contact with your partner.

Hiding Their True-Self

A narcissist will present traits and qualities that they want you and the rest of the world to see. Due to this, it makes it hard to determine if someone is a narcissist especially during the early stages of a relationship. They will disguise their true self by being kind, caring and romantic, such that you won't see their lack of empathy and inhumanity nature until you are in the discard phase. There are some who belittle, invalidate and ridicule you on a daily basis and there are those who, after abusing you, turn into a remorseful, charming and sweet person. As such in most cases, people suffer from cognitive dissonance as they try to make sense of the personality their partner presented in the beginning and the one that they are showing now. To deal with this situation you may end up thinking that it is your fault that these things are happening and even try to change and improve yourself. However, the truth is you may have not done anything wrong. It is during the final stage that you will see their true self as sincerely abusive individuals (Back et al, 2013). You will realize how cold they are, and it may surprise you. A person who was charming is no longer there and has been replaced by a contemptuous individual that has been hiding from you all along. It is at this time that you will come to realize that they feel nothing for you.

Therefore, for a narcissist to get into your head it is something they plan through calculated moves. Thus, you do not have to feel bad that someone lured you into this relationship. The best course of action is to end it. There are numerous tricks that they will use but all tie to the aspect of controlling your emotions and putting you under their foot so they can determine what you do when you do it, and how you do it. Thus, such things as name-calling, monopolizing the conversation and brainwashing will serve this purpose.

Chapter 9 Developing the Mindset of Getting Ready to Take Back the Control of Your Life

It is bad for your wellbeing and quality of life to continue staying in an abusive relationship. Surprisingly people stay even when it is seriously affecting their body and mental health. There are various reasons why people opt to stay, but the truth is these are all the wrong reasons. If you have been abused for long and you are still in the relationship, it means that your partner has succeeded in manipulating you. You may think that you are staying to save your partner because they made you believe they cannot live without you. Truthfully, they are just saying things to make you believe you are still soul mates and to deflect the abuse. A healthy relationship does not work like that. To prepare your mindset in taking back control of your own life you will need to entertain new thoughts.

Now that you have learned that you are with a narcissist, there are two options: to stay and know how to deal with them or to leave. There are different types and levels of a narcissist and this will determine the extent of harm the one you are with can do to you. If you are with a person who is verbally abusive, manipulative and shows no sign of empathy or remorse towards you, it is high time that you leave now. The aspects such as denial, self-doubt, and self-blame are core to why you may continue staying in an abusive relationship. It is wrong to feel this way about yourself because the truth is you are not the reason why the relationship is not working or is having problems. Gaslighting by your narcissist is what makes it appear that you are the reasons they are abusing you. Thus, you stay trying to change so that you can be the person they want. Unfortunately, they never get satisfied and there is nothing you can do to satisfy them fully; this is the reason why it is important to think otherwise.

It is a trick to manipulate you, it is not that they care. You have to start thinking this way although you may not want to believe it, entertain this thought and you will see it is the truth. You see, in this relationship you are in a limbo where either you leave but then your partner draws you back again or they give you the silent treatment. At times, they will leave you confused over what has just happened when they return after a few days and start telling you how much they cannot live without you. Your mind takes you back to your first days in the relationship, you buy into these lies, and once again, you give them a chance. You believe that this time it will be better, and you even give up some of your needs, goals, and priorities to try to make it work only to be surprised later when the trend repeats itself. As much as you may not like it, let yourself consider that you are being used. It is a trick to manipulate you so that you can continue giving them the satisfaction of control and power. You have to accept that they have no empathy towards you, which means they do not care about your wellbeing.

Now that you have allowed this line of thought, how do you overcome the obstacles then?

Avoid Self-Doubt

It will be hard to overcome the obstacles of a narcissist if you have no sense of self-awareness. It is true that to this point you have given up doing what is best for you in trying to please your narcissist partner: your goals, dreams and even doing what you love to be more successful. It is bad enough that you do not listen and trust your feelings because you are all about pleasing and serving someone else. Even after making all these sacrifices, you should know that a narcissist will never honor your feelings. At one time, you may have told them that you are sad, but they dismissed this by saying that you are overly sensitive or weak. Narcissists are bullies by nature and when everything that you feel is being dismissed you will start dismissing yourself. As explained earlier, if you do not put yourself first and know that you are not the problem, then it will be extremely hard for you to overcome the obstacles. Thus, the first obstacle that you need to escape is self-doubt and self-blame. Disregard what they tell you. Listen to your body and what it tells you. There is nothing wrong with your feelings if you feel sad, disappointed, and angry or any negative feeling because of your partner. Trust what your body is telling you and do not consider any outside influence.

Disengage or Ignore

The narcissist takes pleasure in provoking you and enjoys any kind of emotion you portray; be it rage or love. Their key focus is your reaction to their behavior. For a normal person, they will determine that you are upset because of something wrong they did to you, but the narcissist will not. They are okay with the emotions you portray either happiness or anger and they think that this is love. For them it is a game and they use it to trap you. You are their victim and they need you to feed off of. What you need to do is deny them the satisfaction they gain from your reactions by disengaging. After knowing this and believing it, it will be easy for you to disengage. Do not be concerned with their annoyance, do not engage them about it and do not try to reason with them. Be concerned about you, what you can control and focus on that. All the other things you have been trying have failed, but by refusing to accept something they have done they will comprehend that they did something wrong. It is confusing when they use their 'hot and cold' aspects but it is advisable not to fall for it. In case of anything, pause and give yourself time to think, do not engage and do not take the bait. After doing this you will realize that, you have started feeling better and think about yourself.

Think About Boundaries and Set Them

In most cases, when a relationship has arrived at this point you have probably forgotten about boundaries. You have given up the boundaries that at one time you had and have allowed the narcissist to cross them. Think about boundaries, things that a person should not do to you. You can begin by writing these boundaries down, whatever they are and communicate them to the narcissist. It is true that they will not let you have them, and they will try by all means to disregard them. Setting good boundaries includes identifying steps that you will take when they are crossed. This is why it is important to be true to yourself. If you give a warning and they continue to cross, take the actions or steps that you had set to take. You should not suggest something that you cannot actually do, because if you fail to do it then it shows weakness. For instance, if you told them that if they ever hit you again, you will leave and you fail to do so, it will definitely communicate that you are neither serious nor ready to observe the boundaries. It takes incredible strength to adhere to the boundaries you set and take swift action when they are crossed to protect yourself.

Stop Using Words Such As "I'm Sorry" And "Fair"

Always remember that narcissists have no empathy, they lack emotions because it will help you in all decisions that you make. A normal person will understand what you mean by stating that they are not being fair and when you apologize. To a narcissist, 'fair' is not a real concept and all they care about is getting what they want. To them what is unfair is if they do not succeed in abusing you to feed their emotional deficiency. When they are calling you words, making you jealous, physically abusing you or even giving you the silent treatment, this is what is fair. Trying to make sense of things with them is a waste of time and will even worsen your psychological wellbeing. Thus, it is important that you stop apologizing because saying you are sorry sends the message that they are successful in whatever they are subjecting you to.

Acceptance

It does not mean accepting abuse; rather accepting they are a narcissist. Maybe the reason why you were with them is because you thought it could work like any other relationship. The truth is they are not going to change; they are not going to give up abusing you anytime soon. There is no sense in wasting your time and life on this. As much as you may not want to believe it, there is no happily ever after. It is important that you accept that you cannot change their personality disorder. If you do accept these things, it will be much easier for you and it will give you a high chance of doing what is good for you. The focus herein is to know that being in an abusive relationship is not good for you and whatever you are going to do is to strictly improve your wellbeing and not to compete or outsmart them. Do not make clear your intentions at this stage as you may end up fueling the fire. Acceptance gives you power over their attempts to manipulate you. It will add to your quest of taking back control of your life.

Chapter 10 Awakened from the Nightmare: Why You Should Not Waste Your Life on Certain People

At what point are you reminded that life is precious? Do you have to wait until you go through a near-death experience to understand this? The one awakening call you should consider is that no one knows what life is like beyond the human existence. Further, our days are numbered in this world until we're gone, and no one really knows about tomorrow. That alone should remind you to enjoy being human and existing right now. You are not going to live forever, so the best you can do is live in the now.

In making your life a worthwhile experience, you should seek to love yourself and not allow anything that threatens your peace have a chance in your life. One of the key principles you ought to apply is decluttering your life. Yes, you may have already accumulated so much in your life, much more than you need. You may have already allowed toxicity and negativity in your life, and you may be holding too much that you think you cannot get rid of. However, what do you do? Are you going to live your life stuck in the same mud that you got into long ago? For someone who loves their life, the answer would be No. Seek to say "No" when something bothers you. De-cluttering does not only refer to removing material clutter from your living space. It refers to so much more, including getting rid of fake friendships and toxic relationships. Appreciate the people that are there for you and get rid of the rest. You do not need everyone in your journey, and you cannot make everyone happy. With the myriad of distractions in the modern world, even people you thought loved you can forsake you and maybe using you strategically for their advantage. Nevertheless, realize that people who are real and true to you will never forsake you and neither will they maliciously take advantage of you.

A toxic relationship is among the greatest causes of a miserable life. It not only denies you peace of mind when you are together, but it also disorients your life once you have parted with your oppressor. Do not fret too much about minor things; most people care too much about this. Be reminded that life is so precious and insignificant things should not have space in your life. Cutting off on these small things will allow you to focus on the things that matter, including enhancing your livelihood, relationships with family and friends who matter, and establishing whether your romantic relationship is with your perfect match or you are in a relationship with the wrong person. No one is so important to come into your life to make you miserable. You have to brace yourself to face everyone as they come so you can identify what they are bringing into your life.

The worst mistakes you can do in the dating scene today are to not show boldness and instead show desperation. You cannot afford to be desperate. This is what will make you think that someone is coming into your life to fill in a blank hole, and that is where all the misery begins. The only person in a good position to manage issues in your life is you. You are the only one who understands you the best. You are your best cheerleader and you are the only person who can look out for you. Until you are an adult, your family exists to help and support you in everything you do, but in adulthood, you are expected to make your own decisions. Whatever decision you make has its consequences. However, the good thing is that we can always learn to eliminate the negative influence of people who do not wish us well and even protect ourselves from such influence by not allowing other people's idealism and thoughts to rent space in our minds and hearts.

You should be in control of your life. You should take it upon yourself to be the only person who decides what to take with you and what you should leave behind, starting now. Your ultimate goal in life should be to find your purpose and aligning with your purpose allows you to live a meaningful life where you are happy and fulfilled. Keep in mind that a meaningful life calls for careful planning, owning your own actions and being ready to defend yourself. Knowing where you are in life, where you aim at getting to in the future and whatever it is that you need to get there, you stand in the best position for living a rewarding life. The key to achieving a rewarding lifestyle is living the best way you can in the present and not procrastinating on doing something that is detrimental to your wellbeing.

Remember, your body is your best tool in going about your daily activities, and your mind is the best tool in showing you how to carry out your daily tasks and decisions. Therefore, take care of your wellbeing, both mentally and physically. Do not allow anyone to waste your time that could have been used in activities that count in your life. Realize that every moment counts. Most importantly, realize that you are important. No one can do you better than you, and thus no one has the right to dictate what you should do. Whatever makes you happy, go for it. Do not let anyone with a contrary opinion have space in your life. Always be reminded that you are unique and important.

Sometimes, especially when dealing with a narcissist, the lines may be too blurry such that you do not realize when someone has crossed them and is truly controlling your life, denying you the chance to make every day count in living a meaningful way. Therefore, watch out for the following things, which should let you know that you are in a place you don't want to be in.

You Complain About the Same Thing Over and Over Again

The basic rule of thumb you should know is that if you have complained about something about 2 to 3 times, you are in a position you do not want to be in. It is upon you to accept it or change it. Whether it is frustration at work or with your partner, you should not take complaining as a mere release of defeat. Rather, this should serve as a sign that you are subconsciously rejecting something in life.

You Are Made to Feel Ashamed About Your Past

Frequent reminders that you have been a failure in the past may get you feeling ashamed. Some partners are ever ready to remind you that you have made mistakes in the past. They make you forget that your past is who you were and that does not define who you are now or whom you want to be in the future. A narcissistic or toxic partner will make you open up about your past and will always use it to drive you to the corner and empower themselves. When you start feeling ashamed of your past because of your partner's constant reminders, this is when you realize that you are in a situation that is not good for your personal development and happiness.

You Are Beginning to Think That Changes Are Bad

Embracing change and leveraging opportunities as they come counts as among the most significant principles to thrive in this life, especially in today's world. If someone is influencing your opinion about changes and making you feel afraid of change, then you should not entertain them since this is not where you need to be. As long as you are taking calculated moves, change is what brings you where you want and need to be.

Your Partner Has Made You Abandon Your Favorite Hobbies

Whenever you do something that you deem important to you, it gives you joy. You know that you are headed in the right direction if you do something every day that makes you happy. However, if your partner criticizes your hobbies and makes you see how unreasonable or wasteful they are, this is not the ideal situation for you to be in. No one is justified to stand between you and your happiness.

You Barely Have Time for Yourself to Rest

You want to show how much you can achieve in a day, but you are always complaining about how unappreciated and exhausted you are. In all sense, we all have 24 hours and some of these are meant for sleeping, in which you rejuvenate your mind and go on with your work. If you are not able to get enough rest, you are always bitter and resentful. You are not a superhero that you should always be active. If you are in such a position, you are most probably trying to please your partner because they have conditioned you into this. Perhaps, it is your toxic partner who wants you preoccupied so you do not have time to alleviate yourself from their control. Clearly, you do not want to live in such a condition but to achieve a rewarding life.

Chapter 11   How You Can Get Better and Regain Your Original Self

One of the best things about life is that no matter how far you have gone down on the wrong road, you can still turn around and start to follow your dream. There never comes a time when you are too old to dream afresh and live your life. Whenever you feel like the path you are walking on does not lead you anywhere, do not hesitate to put a pause and establish the best direction to take. A new beginning in your life may take time, but it's all possible. Fortunately, our bodies and minds are filled with infinite power to direct our goals into whatever it is that we want to achieve. Life may knock you down to the point that you feel worthless and hopeless, but never can take your power of gaining your original self: the jovial, thoughtful, well-organized and smart person you are can always be activated.

Every day we live through this life in constant motion and there is always some kind of change that comes our way. Sometimes, this change is undesirable, and it leads us into a dark corner. However, sometimes, the change is what exposes us to rich pools of knowledge by teaching us through experience. What matters when we are this deep in misery is that we become too fixated and begin to imagine how we are not capable of regaining our original self. This is especially true if you feel like time has passed and your energy has wasted away, and you perhaps cannot regain your original glory. You feel like your best youthful years have passed on and you are now growing older, hence, you are better off continuing down the wrong road, wherever life takes you.

Fortunately, even the most successful people in history have made poor decisions, which have led them in the wrong direction. What they did is that they envisioned themselves as the winner and they did not focus on the time, effort and energy they had lost because of making the wrong decisions. If you are keen enough, you'll realize that after failure is when such people became rejuvenated and started following their dreams through calculated efforts. In the end, we all know that these people achieve more and become celebrated around the whole world. Be it the best athlete, the most successful businessman, and the richest man, these people have been through rough times in their lives, but they chose to not give in and instead carefully re-collect themselves and move on. For

47

instance, Steve Jobs has the most compelling story about huge mistakes. He hired a CEO who later came to fire him because their visions for Apple Inc., founded by Steve Jobs himself, differed. However, Steve did not give up in his life even after what he had envisioned for his entire adult life was taken away. He made various other successes, including starting up Pixar and NeXT, great companies in the technology world.

This same case applies to you whenever you have been through a miserable life with a narcissist. This malicious person used you for the betterment of themselves. They did not care about your dreams. In fact, they emphasized on crushing you and leaving a deep scar in your life. Abuse leaves you with low self-confidence and low self-esteem. It feels like you will never get your life together nor will you be able to achieve happiness and go back to fulfilling personal goals, needs and objectives. Altogether, it seems difficult to get your life together. The implication in this is that it is challenging to overcome narcissistic abuse and shift from pain of the past to gain momentum that will help you into a brighter future. The pain that you were exposed to broke your heart and destroyed your sense of self, which puts you in a challenging position. It is confusing how someone you thought as a soul mate turns out to be a heartless oppressor and this leads to massive confusion after the relationship. As most victims, maybe you are in disbelief where you ask yourself how you let all these things happen or how could they have done all those things to you while you thought that they loved you? You ought to know that your traits of forgiveness, compassion, and empathy are the ones that enabled you to give them the benefit of the doubt. Now that you have awakened to the harsh truth of abuse, you need to win and engage in true healing.

Due to all this misery that you have gone through and the pain of imagining where you would have been, you feel like all hope is gone and you can never be original, lovable and even achieve the success you had been aiming at before all this misfortune befell you. However, take it as a rule of thumb that experience is the best teacher. You have lived it all, you have seen it all, but most importantly, you have realized that this is the poorest version of yourself that you could imagine. Be reminded that life becomes meaningful when the series of learning opportunities are embraced well to make you a better person. It is the most painful experience that teach us the most if we are careful. The reason why they are considered the best teacher is that it gives you the real lesson and leads to deep personal growth. It teaches you to be calm and manage things in a better way in the future. Therefore, not only will you be able to regain your original self, but you are also in a better place to ensure that you don't fall to the same misfortune twice. Therefore, it is important to use this lesson for personal growth and to remember that you cannot achieve much in this world without experience. It sharpens your mind and is meant to give you the push you need to be successful. Maybe without it, you would not have been able to manage the success that awaits you in the future. Maybe, you needed to be folded and twisted in a turn of events for you to come out stronger.

Countless times people have said how they came to know who their real friends are when they were in deep misery. This is because experience teaches you the real lesson the hard way and you get to see the people in your life who are well-wishers and those who want to see you fail. For instance, the biggest lesson you learn is how a narcissist behaves and pretends to love and wants the best for you, while in the real sense they want to see you fail.

Being a self-reflective person allows you to access a richness of wisdom to help you understand what you have been through and what can be done differently going forward. That is the mantra of successful people. It is all about getting wiser and not wasting any opportunity to learn. We must never fear failure and painful experiences in life. We must know that experience is what shows that you have been tested but have not given in. You are now on track with more bravery and wisdom and you can face anything you want. Having been fooled the first time, you will not accept such tricks that they used in the future, and you will live a more meaningful life. On the flip side, the fear of failure is what holds us back from doing the things we can to achieve our goals.

Embracing the experience will allow you to set boundaries in your life such that no one, including your narcissist, should be able to invade your life. You will set the rules for your life and you will be able to tell who comes in and who goes out. Most importantly, you will be able to block negativity from coming your way, while only allowing the positive people and positive things in.

Most importantly, you will be attentive to inner awareness, an aspect that will take you to anywhere you desire to be in life. It offers you a distinguished opportunity to be re-born and grow. Most people do not get to this point of actually making the change they desire. Real change occurs as a result of dedication and hard work. Self-inquiry is an essential stride towards awakening from the prison bonds you have been subjected by a narcissist. Inner awareness will bring to light various issues in your life. You may uncover that the vulnerabilities that you had in your life can be turned around to avoid being made a fool of.

Essentially, you do not have to be afraid and see yourself as the worst failure. You can always be reborn as a stronger and wiser you, and with this, you will be unmovable. This experience will count as one of the most worthwhile experiences you have had in your life.

Chapter 12   How to Get Back Your Control

Getting back the control of your life after years of abuse might seem like a difficult thing to do. However, with the right guidance and using the right tools, you can effectively regain your control and find happiness again.

Yes, you have been abused. Yes, you have allowed this narcissist into your life for years. It will take quite a long time to regain control of your life after years of being isolated, stalked and monitored. Nevertheless, following the subsequent ways, you can remove the marks of abuse and get back to your original self as explained previously in chapter 10. These steps will help you to hold the control of your life and take revenge against the narcissist as discussed in the chapter 12.

Get the Negativity Out of Your System

Like it or not, there is a whole lot of negativity within your system by the time you are parting with a narcissist. This toxicity accumulated as you tried to appease them and in trying to make the relationship work. You tried to understand the narcissist as they took advantage of you more and more. It is now time to let go of all that darkness and allow space for your life to take shape again. Some of the things you can do to get this negativity out includes journaling or sharing your story with a friend, or even engaging a therapist. Talking out the story is so helpful, especially when it is with a listening partner since it helps in organizing your confused thoughts into place. In addition, it helps to empower you since you can finally be honest with yourself. Likewise, you can engage in mind and body exercises, such as yoga or dancing. This helps to discard the toxicity and clears your mind to accommodate positivity.

Compile a List of the Controlling Incidents You Have Experienced

Although it might seem trivial, compiling the experiences of control and abuse helps you realize what you have been through and appreciate your growth—the fact that you will not allow yourself to be in such situation again. Such remembrance gives you pride in your bravery of being able to leave such and look forward to a more rewarding life. You appreciate that you can now live as a free person and you cannot allow yourself to fall back in the abusive relationship.

Practice Listening to Your Inner Self

Your inner voice is the best tool you will ever have in dealing with any situation. It shows you how best you can do things and it never lies. Even amidst great pain and desperation, your inner voice can show you how to find your way out. The major reason why the narcissist was able to manipulate you was that they worked on the external stimulants of your brain, which in turn messed your internal stimulants as argues Morf, Horvath and Torchetti (2011). They were fulfilling their selfish motives by controlling how your brain responds to things. However, listening to your inner voice will help you make out a situation and you can learn when to move ahead, hold back or reject things being said to you. It will guide you in your newly acquired life, one in which you are free, and you understand yourself much better. It will help you to never fall for a toxic person again.

Organizing Time and Space

It is good to have a clean and organized space since this allows you enough time to absorb everything that comes your way. When your space is full of clutter, you feel overwhelmed because it registers in your mind that you have a lot to do. As aforementioned, decluttering allows you to organize your space and remain with only the things that matter to you. You will find that your brain will respond positively to living in an ordered place. You will feel more settled and you are energized to face every new day. In addition, clutter obscures your mind and your thinking. You can establish a good daily routine where your most significant tasks are allocated to the time of the day that you tend to be most active.

Connect with Family and Friends

As noted, narcissists usually isolate their victims from their loved ones and friends. They no longer understand you and they may even think that you hate them. They have judged you countless times because your attitude towards them has changed. There could be some of them who have tried to tell you that you are not okay in your relationship, but you have always denied their sentiments in the attempt to defend your narcissist partner, who has already conditioned you to support them against all forms of attack. Since you have been dependent on the narcissist for all your social contact needs, you find it difficult to associate with people. The truth is, however, that your loved ones are always eager to reconnect with you, spend time and share with you.

Be Patient: Take Your Time

The worst mistake you can commit is to judge yourself and think that you are not making fast progress regarding getting out of the pit and forgetting about your narcissist. You should not be hard on yourself. Instead, you should understand that healing takes time to be effective. Besides, everyone needs different amounts of time to be able to get over something. Based on the depth of your abuse or length of the toxic relationship, you might need more or less time to heal.

There is no time limit on healing. Remember, your abuser has already separated you from your most precious people and hobbies. They conditioned you into feeling lost and lonely without them. Therefore, healing might take time and it is upon you to be kind on yourself and be patient as you heal. Most importantly, do not jump right into another relationship. This will obscure your thinking and deny you time to heal. Consequently, you will carry the burden right into the next relationship and it will not be healthy.

Acknowledge What Has Been and Forgive Yourself

You might be tempted to beat yourself up for allowing such a toxic person to be in your life for such a long time. However, true healing and regaining power entails accepting what has been that you have associated yourself with a highly toxic person, who has consciously hurt you. Accept that you have been tricked and abused. Trying to please them and showing them that you understood them, denied you the chance to identify the red flags. Likewise, they used your strengths against you: that you were caring, that you had a good job, that you were highly organized, open to ideas, and that you were financially stable. You never deserved this, and it was wrong of them to abuse you.

After acknowledging this, know that it was not your fault and forgive yourself. Doing this is the most important thing you need to do right now. No matter how much time, energy, wellness, and cash you have lost, that is in the past. You have to forgive yourself and move forward successfully.

It does not matter why you stayed for so long, it does not matter why you were fooled. It already happened. So, forgive yourself.

Seek to Acquire Knowledge: Do Self-Inquiry

It seems so difficult to make sense of the abuse you have been through and what to do after this. For such a long time you have only learned to see the world through the perspective of your abuser. You are now confused and are wondering where to begin. Seek to be knowledgeable about emotional wellness. There are a myriad of articles and online courses that you have access to and that can help you in this.

Knowledge is power, and enhancing your power never goes out of fashion.

Shift Your Focus

Because you have been abused for a long period, it is easy to find your mind moving back to these thoughts. These are aspects of trauma and cognitive dissonance and are a hindrance to proper recovery. The reason why your mind may keep on pushing you back there is it wants to comprehend certain things and process related emotions. You should not entertain these thoughts about the past but capitalize on the present. You may find yourself making one-step forward and two steps backward. Train your mind to be in the present and the future you have chosen to make for yourself. To boost your motivation in this endeavor you need to resurrect your dreams and this time let them be magnificent. Remember the dreams and things you wanted for yourself before being drawn to a narcissist; think about how bad you wanted them and boost your desire to achieve them. This is what it means to shift your focus to look forward and change your status from a victim to a hero in your life. Even though you have been through pain, after healing you may be surprised by the self-loving person—aware, whole and integrated—you have become.

Regain Control of Your Life, Take Back Your Story, Realize Which Part of You Knew, Heal Your Inner Self

After doing all these things, it all boils down to taking control of your life back. You have already admitted that you were abused, and you have forgiven yourself. This is not enough. You need to now take the last step of being the driver of your life. The essence of this is to get your mind straight and in so doing you need to accept that you partner knowingly hurt you and is a toxic person. In addition, you have to accept that you did let yourself down because you allowed them to hurt you repeatedly. You failed to obey your instincts. They took advantage of your humane traits, used them against you. The truth is that you had a role in this relationship be it love or empathy. Besides accepting that they played a role in this you also need to acknowledge the role you played to be able to forgive. At some point in this relationship, you had a feeling in your stomach, but you disregarded any hints that you may have had. Maybe it is because you hoped it would work, you loved them, or you were empathic. After, identifying with the noted facts and accepting that this is the truth, it will be easy to forgive yourself.

To heal your inner self, you will need to eliminate any historic pain that you may be having. You want to have lasting results. In doing so there is a need to eliminate any unresolved pain, establish a sense of inner cohesion and restore the deeper connection to self-trust. Where you go from here depends on to what extent you intend to let go of any past pain. Know that this is the right path to healing and although it may take longer than anticipated, with a commitment to yourself and persistence, you will finally succeed.

Chapter 13   The Vulnerable Point of a Narcissist

Whenever we hear of the word "narcissist," we tend to imagine an authoritative and knowledgeable person who wants to make the world revolve around them. This is for sure how they want you to perceive them. Even though they ostensibly have a strong personality, narcissists do not have a core self. How they behave towards others and the image they portray is mainly for the purpose of validating their self-esteem. The worst thing is that they will never accept that they need help. They are never willing to change. Contrary to popular sentiments, narcissists can change. It is never too late or too hard to take a different course in one's life as long as one is willing to change. For one to change in anything, they must first admit that they have taken a wrong course in their lives but set their minds to the life to come. This is the most crucial aspect that the narcissists lack.

The vulnerabilities of narcissists are projected by their ability to love themselves only according to how others see them. They dread looking at themselves because they know the truth would overwhelm them. They are emotionally dead inside and they live for the fulfillment and validation of others. Unfortunately, they are unable to reciprocate the love they receive to those who give it to them.

As the victim for this miserable life of a narcissist, you realize that you are in a war where you have to fight for your sanity. Your self-absorbed and toxic partner uses some secrets against you. However, due to their inability to accept that they have a problem and to be open to the idea of changing, narcissists have various vulnerabilities that you can use to handle them. They have a frail egoistic nature, which makes them vulnerable. There are various things that scare them. Below are ways how you can use their vulnerabilities to feel empowered to disengage from the entire madness and make everything clear.

Handling Hypochondriacs

When you are a hypochondriac, you are in a condition of being overly anxious about your health. Due to their unending insecurities, narcissists are often anxious about their health and wellbeing. Due to this weakness, narcissists do not like anyone trying to put them down based on their looks. In addition, they would be willing to explore options, such as physical exercise and healthy eating habits as long as this would improve their physical wellness and appearance. Therefore, it is upon you to give them details on how they can spend their days to avoid losing their wellness, without necessarily pointing out that they have poor health. Direct them to activities that will keep them engaged and ensure that you can get your alone time to organize yourself.

Ask Rhetorical Questions to Get Them Thinking

Ask them how they would feel about what others would think about them. It is well established that narcissists never feel guilty but are always ashamed of what other people say about them. They are concerned about appearances because they do not want their real selves known or seen by others. If they believe that something might hurt their reputation, narcissists would stop to think twice. The trick is to not tell them directly how other people would react to things about them, but to ask them rhetorical questions and leave them coming up with ideas of how they think people would respond to facts about them. All they want is to look good in front of others. For instance, when they are charming your family or friends and making them turn against you, they want to look good. Therefore, rather than reacting to them with anger, emphasize how the community sees them. As they focus on looking good, they are able to do well, and you can leverage this chance to alleviate yourself. Remember that narcissists have a vulnerability point of emotional dependence. Their emotions are determined by what other people think about them. Given this awareness, you can get them talking and coming out with their ideas of what other people would think and involve you in addressing their perceived weaknesses.

Know What They Want to Achieve and Make Them Work for It

With a narcissist, you can never expect fairness. They are just all about themselves and they believe in getting what they want when they want it. You have to tread carefully around them because having them around is like having a pet lion. One day he will eat you.

Also, remember that you cannot be in a win-win situation with them. Do

57

not be negative around them and ask for favors directly. Manipulate their urge to get what they want and to achieve certain results by showing them that the only way they can get those results is by doing a certain thing. Make it look like doing that thing will make them look so impressive. Even when they are helping you in something that you would otherwise do single-handedly, make it look like they are the ultimate savior and they will always get you what you want before feeding into their ego.

Remember, a narcissist fears abandonment and they would not react well to the feeling of being abandoned by someone they have already identified as their target, one whom they have decided to shape to feed their ego. Therefore, never show the signs of withdrawal. In fact, you should tell them things such as that, you can never get enough of them and that they are the best person, taking care not to appear too desperate. Your words will win them. Your behavior should not directly show signs of withdrawing from them, while you are still under their cocoon, since they may get frustrated and even harm you.

Listen Up

Now, we know that whenever you are dealing with a narcissist you are in a less powerful position than them, and they are almost like a boss to you. However, the secret is that narcissists want to be congratulated, to be worshipped and to be admired. Therefore, you have to be keen on what they want and give that to them. They want to be adored, use words to tell them that they are the most powerful and best people. This does not require much effort. All you have to focus on is listening to them and appearing interested.

If you argue about their behaviors, they will despise you and can even harm you. Also, if you openly reject them they will freak out. On the flip side, show your weakness and they will continue to victimize you. Therefore, you have to be smart. You have to know how to play with your words in a way that you don't openly point out errors about them or play the victim. Most importantly, you have to keep your sense of humor. Laugh about their jokes and respond in a way that they will find entertaining.

Given their vindictive nature, it feels unfair to be candid with a narcissist. However, in case your integrity is not being overly compromised, feel free to compliment them, even more than they deserve. It is much better to pre-empt their deep sitting anger by constantly giving them the recognition that they crave the most. This is what they lacked when they were growing up and they felt like they were not lovable. Be reminded that narcissists are highly susceptible to sycophancy. Keep them flattered because this feeds their ego, and this gives you a strategic advantage over them.

Do not seek acknowledgment for doing them a favor. Remember, narcissists fear gratitude because they feel like they are handing over the control to you. They perceive this to be a sign of weakness and they feel like they are accepting owing you something. They do not want to let you feel like they might have needed your help to do something. Therefore, despite coming through for them in various circumstances, do not let the narcissist feel like you want to be appreciated.

Overall, remember that there is power in knowing how the narcissistic reacts to various things, what hurts their ego and what elevates their status. This helps you to be a smarter person and gaining a strategic advantage over them. With this, they cannot use you, but you will bear with them until you can completely detach yourself from them.

Chapter 14   The Seven Steps to Follow to Take Your Revenge

In this case, taking revenge refers to a full recovery from the abuse and having an improved wellbeing, socialization and quality of life. A narcissist feeds on your negative emotions; thus, when you stop producing those emotions, it means that you have embarked on doing what is good for you. Thus, making yourself better will be an act of adequate revenge towards them. They will not be happy to realize that you are now living well without them. Remember that the narcissist had conditioned you to believe that you are soul mates; they did not anticipate that you could break free. They would have wanted to be part of your life always such that even after discarded you will not get back to your old life before you met them. The following are suitable steps on how you will be able to fully get your life together.

Care for Your Appearance

The concern herein is to engage in activities that will help in improving your appearance. While in the relationship, the abuse may have resulted in you losing weight or gaining more weight. The stress, anxiety and in other cases depression negatively affected your physical and mental health. It is time to be more beautiful and be physically fit. Narcissists are attracted by beauty, but the issue is they want more; by the time you are parting ways, chances are you may have not been paying more attention to your appearance. When there is something that is disturbing you, how you look is not a major concern, especially when that something is abuse. You may have been trying to look beautiful for them but still, they were not satisfied. This time, the acts to improve your appearance are for you, to be happy with yourself, to be attracted by yourself and more so to have the best body that you can have. It is good to exercise, take yoga, go for a massage and even go for a run. Also, now you have to pay good attention to what you wear, get the best of your clothes or even shop the best in the market to be smart. In taking care of your appearance, it will obviously bring pleasure within you.

Learn to Be Confident About Yourself

In the course of the relationship, the narcissist fed you with insecurities.

When a person is being abused it is hard to relate well with other people because you fear that they know what is going on in your life. You think that people are talking negatively and laughing at you. At this point, you have low self-confidence and low self-esteem. Know that you can recover from this and you will ensure that you get your life on track. You will make yourself impenetrable to a narcissist's manipulative traps while at the same time you will be more brilliant. It is about supporting yourself, taking control of yourself, your behavior, your body, and your mind. It is concerned with self-perception and how you impact the world around you. Activities that will help to improve your self-esteem include exercising, setting small goals and achieving them, having positive people around you and avoiding comparisons to other people. You need to be nice to yourself, accept that everyone makes mistakes, focus on positives and listen to your guts. In addition, you will improve self-esteem by knowing your competencies and developing them. If it is academics, strive to excel more and if it is professionally, look forward to performing better. It is important to note that by demonstrating real achievement and ability in areas of your life that matter, you will begin to regain your self-confidence.

Keep Your Distance

It is more of putting a protective shield around you. If you can avoid any physical encounter with your ex-partner, this is best. Memories are a hindrance to a complete recovery and slow down the process, thus, what you can do is to avoid any instance capable of triggering those memories, such as social media, email, Facebook, Twitter or any other social network platform. You need to focus on complete recovery thus; it is not beneficial to care about what is happening in their life. Do not stalk their profile or ask any friends about them. Let them be, focus on your wellbeing. It may be a person you cannot avoid physically so what you will do is to mentally disengage with them. Learn to say no to anything that they may request; this is vital in building true confidence and self-respect. In certain cases, it may be hard to leave the narcissist behind especially when you are trying to raise a child together. You can set boundaries, inform them of those boundaries and be firm. In this situation, you may want to move on, but they keep on following you; give them a warning and if they break it again involve the police. You should not let them drag you down by invading your space and privacy. Now, this is your life and they are not allowed to interfere with it.

Always Put Yourself First

While in a relationship with the narcissist, you sacrificed significantly for the relationship in an attempt to make them satisfied. You gave up on your dreams and needs so that you could help them with theirs. Now it is your turn to do you, to do what pleases you and more important to achieve the best version of yourself. Now it means that you should not give up on yourself for the narcissist, no matter the kind of favor they may ask of you. Look at it this way, you are trying to recover the time you wasted with them, but do not be bitter about it. Know that you have emerged from all this strong and more capable of doing great things. What is more important to the priorities of your life, for instance, if you wanted to go on holiday to a certain country, this is your time to go and you should not give it up because they need your help with something. Especially if there are no commonalities, live your life and do not reach out to know how they are living theirs. If there are common prospects in the case of compromises, you should meet them halfway. Putting yourself first is vital and will prevent you from giving too much in any case.

Keep Busy

Keeping busy or rather, being active is vital in making progress in life. It is the most effective way of distracting yourself from thoughts, worries, and anger from the abuse. As a way of taking revenge, it is being focused on yourself and engaging in things that interest you. If you have hobbies engage in them, it will help you to develop new interests. Now that you are free to take advantage of this, you should stay committed and lead a satisfying life. They say that the idle mind is the workshop of the devil. Escape negative thoughts that may even self-harm or even harming the narcissist for what they did to you. For instance, if you like swimming you can just buy a membership and spend your free time swimming. There are other ways of being active: you can hang out with a person you know will be supportive, join a cooking class, art class, yoga class, a meditation group or a walking group. Just do anything, it does not require much to be active; it will enrich your body, mind, and soul. Avoid family, friends or people who will keep bringing things about your relationship. It is much better to spend the time with strangers that you will come across if you join any of the noted groups. It could be challenging to join groups at first because the friends you had were pushed away by the narcissist, but do not let these thoughts prevent you from a chance to build yourself.

The Fake Compliments

At this point, you have made significant progress in your life. You have managed to rebuild your self-confidence and your self-esteem is now high. In addition, you have other interests as in the previous step we noted that you are now engaging in activities that are interesting to you. A narcissist will not be happy to know that you now have other interests outside their world. To this point, you have made significant progress in taking your revenge, by getting your life together. You are happy and it is clear that you do not need them. You can now face them as if they never existed in your life, their words and actions have no impact in your life. They fear you because you are able to stand, defend, talk and act with confidence by yourself. It pains them. Giving fake compliments is much better than despising them—it will make them feel offended. It entails the use of fictional compliments, for instance, you can tell them "this shirt looks nice, the one you had last time couldn't be looked at" or any other but in such an approach. In telling them that, what you mean is that he has a good shirt, but he will not focus on that instead he will focus on the fact that the shirt he had last time was terrible and he will feel offended. It will make you feel better and in taking that approach there are no grounds for calling of names, it is a strategic approach.

Indifference

When they see that you have moved on with your life, they will feel bad. They would want to destroy that; they would want to take you back and prove that you are still under their thumb. In this case, they can begin to be good to you, sweet talk to you, invite you for a date; they may go to the point of requesting you to accompany them in important meetings. Do not be fooled; do not bite the bait or take it like anything important to you because it will add no value to you. Even when they offer to help it is sometimes more important to refuse that help as you do not want them to have leverage on you. They may even inform you of the progress they have made in life. For instance, he may come telling you that he has been promoted, he has made a huge sale, he bought a new luxury car, has a new business that is doing well or whatever titanic feats are happening in his life. Do not be tempted to belittle them it is not a good approach to revenge because it will show that you are still bitter with them. Instead, show no reaction at all, it is the most suitable way to offend them. They will know that the news has no impact on you; it is more like showing that you do not care.

If you adhere to these steps keenly and improvise where you deem appropriate, you will be surprised. The abuse will have played a pivotal role in not only shaping your character, personality, and ability but in making you resilient. You will get your revenge pleasantly. While you are now happy with your life making progress and accomplishing your dreams, they are now the ones who will be jealous. Note that doing any of these do it for yourself, have a self-interest in mind and more importantly, do not go to them showing what you have achieved, live as if they never existed.

Chapter 15   The Role to Play in Your Family/Friends Life to Help Them Realize If They Are in the Same Situation

Narcissistic abuse is the worst form of abuse that can be inflicted on someone, yet one that is highly misunderstood by the public. You may still be wondering why it is paramount to raise awareness about narcissistic abuse, especially in romantic relationships, while most people have not even heard about it. Research and statistics about this unfortunate phenomenon are hard to locate because of it being understudied. However, a closer look at staggering figures showing just how many people are associated with narcissism, which signifies the need to educate everyone regarding this phenomenon. The Institute for Relational Harm Reduction and Public Pathology Education found out in its analysis that the probability of people suffering from the Narcissistic Personality Disorder is 1 out of 25, notes Miller et al. (2010). Further, each narcissist will impact on 5 people at least, those whom they lure into romantic relationships. Further, this figure is considered conservative because there are unidentified kids who are victims of trauma; hence, they are exposed to the idea of being narcissists.

Worse yet, most people never realize when they are getting into a relationship with a narcissist until it is too late, and they have suffered a lot. A romantic relationship with a narcissist exposes people to a lot of trauma and confusion once it ends, since a narcissist manages to control what you do by engaging you in a friendly way. Yet the chances of encountering a narcissist in life are more than 70 percent since they are in society with us and they are always identifying targets.

There is need to pay great attention to narcissistic abuse because unlike physical abuse, the former does not leave clearly visible marks. Understanding the concept of coercive control is important, which is a relatively new concept for most of us. This phrase describes the kind of abuse that narcissists inflict on their partners because it does not entail physical abuse, but the aspect of the victim being isolated from their support system and being made reliant on the abusive partner, who uses the victim for their advantage. It happens when one begins to monitor your moves and takes away your ability to see your friends, and before you know it, you are reliant on them alone for all social contact.

In fact, this is one of the reasons why most people do not consider it a reasonable form of abuse and don't understand the need to raise an alarm until the damage is done. Describing something without proof has always been challenging and people fail to realize and acknowledge its presence and effects. In addition, it is challenging to describe categorically what narcissistic abuse is and to get people who have never experienced it concerned about it. People tend to feel like they are too strong to be tracked and controlled by a narcissist. Instead, they hold a myth that it is only the weak-minded and co-dependent types of individuals who are taken advantage of. Unfortunately, this kind of mentality is what gives most people a false sense of protection.

Therefore, this is why it is recommended that you should involve your family and friends, let them know about the disorder and how detrimental it is to a person's life. This can help you to further pinpoint other people who may be suffering from this abuse without knowing it.

It is important to let other people realize that is it not okay at all to be abused. Remind them that life is precious and that no one is warranted to stand in the way of enhancing their autonomy. Remember, there are various reasons that people stay in abusive relationships, including the threat of harm or for the sake of maintaining the social status, or for the hope that things will change for the better. Leaving from a relationship where one is heavily invested is not an easy thing to do. In fact, based on your own experience as a victim, you can tell that it took a lot of efforts and self-empowerment to get out of this. Therefore, you will be careful with your reactions towards the excuses other people give as to why they are unwilling to leave their abusive relationship. If at any time you make them feel embarrassed, they will get defensive and refrain from sharing with you. Therefore, you must use tactfulness to engage with them and be the most understanding person they can rely on. It is distressing to see your friend or loved one be abused. Yet they are always defensive when their partner is bossing them around. Rather than making them avoid you, be gentle and do not judge them.

Also, you should make it clear that even though the wounds are not visible, narcissistic abuse wounds count as abuse. Let them know that someone can appear so loving yet not wish the best for them. Narcissistic abuse is often disguised as great love, yet it is a series of evil deeds. It is a form of abuse meant at downgrading someone's identity and making them see the

66

world through another person's perspective and value system. It is the mixture of imitation love and emotional coercion that confuses one and makes them lack a way of interpreting their abuse. Therefore, let your family and friends realize that abuse that is emotional still counts as abuse.

Further, tell them how they can swiftly alleviate themselves from the abuse of the narcissist. As discussed in chapter 11, the way to untie yourself from the grip of a narcissist is not the use of force. Rather, it is the use of tactfulness of gaining a strategic advantage over the narcissist by observing their weaknesses and working around them. It is about being the smarter person, acknowledging that the narcissist will never care about your need and using effective techniques to tell them off. For instance, it would be unwise for a victim to panic and react with anger towards the narcissist once they realize that they are being abused. This would attract an even harsher reaction from the narcissist and the result would be injuries and great harm.

If possible, form a campaign and target people whom you feel are being abused yet are afraid to acknowledge it or get help. The worst thing about narcissistic abuse is that the victim hardly notices that they are being used, and they will continue holding on and hoping to get the initial spark of the relationship, without realizing that that was their narcissistic partner's bait to get them hooked. Therefore, it is important to call out the attitude of holding on even when you are hurting too much. Offer them a shoulder whenever they need someone to talk to or to cry with. Tell them that bad experiences happen to sharpen us and empower us to be better people in the future. Also, show them how to start improving themselves instead of giving up and concentrating on the amount of time and energy they have wasted in the abusive relationship. Most importantly, teach them about forgiving and being kind to themselves for having allowed the toxic person to take advantage of them: that they did not deserve such treatment, but that self-forgiveness is the first step toward healing and regaining full control of their lives.

Chapter 16   Reap Your Rewards

Now you have made tremendous progress in your recovery. The abuse from the narcissist is becoming part of your past and you have managed to recover a great deal of your old self. The advantage of the person you are today is that you have gone through difficult times and managed to emerge on the other side as a winner. The events, challenges, and abuse that you underwent will define you now as a person capable of facing anything that occurs in your life. Do not let it define you in a negative way, but in a positive way. As discussed earlier, forgiving yourself and forgiving the narcissist is crucial to you during your recovery period. At this point, you are neither bitter nor angry with the person who abused you. If this is the case, then you have made positive strides in your recovery. It is your time to reap rewards from it all.

You are now independent of the narcissist, something that makes them angry. You do not need them, and you are concerned with your own wellbeing. It will feel great to be free; you can now pursue your dreams and focus on becoming the best version of you. A narcissist wants you to be in a position where you believe the two of you cannot live without each other. They want you to give up everything for them. You are doing a great job, and nothing can hurt them more than by them seeing that you are succeeding in life.

Now that you are focused on building yourself, the narcissist has nothing to use against you. The position you are in now, what you have achieved will serve to discredit them even without talking. For instance, when you were with them you were overweight because of stress, now you have exercised, and you have a healthier body. Similarly, if you were underweight after leaving them now you look healthy you have gained weight uniformly. In addition, if you were a college dropout, you went back to college and now you have graduated. Also, if you were a poor performer at the workplace mostly because of the abuse now you have improved to the point that you got a promotion. It will hurt them more than anything else while it will bring you happiness that you did not think it would. Don't be surprised when they start checking you out and trying to reach out so that you can get back together. The only reason that they would want this is because they are jealous, they are hurt that you have made so much progress and you do not need them. The pain they are going through is the

68

best punishment, take heart and continue with your life.

To continue reaping the benefits and rewards of how far you have come, ignore them. A narcissist enjoys being the center of attention and wants to be under the spotlight; ignoring a narcissist is completely killing his innermost self. Even when they have discovered you, they want the impact to be lasting in your life. The fact that you have succeeded means that they did not succeed in leaving an impact in your life. Now you have the body you have always desired to have, you have a career you love, your dream house or car. However, you do not have just to focus on the major achievements. If you have inner peace, you have moved on from the memories and you are focusing on personal needs and goals, this is good enough progress. Narcissists are highly jealous people although they may not accept it. It is difficult for them to take the success of another person. If it is someone like your ex-husband and you have children together, it will be hard to separate physically. They will notice any progress you make in your life, although, they can fake happiness for your success they are experiencing intense jealousy.

Therefore, continue in this trend of being more successful. Continue improving yourself and the more successful you get, the more you hurt a narcissist. Be a success in everything and in doing so, you are subjecting them to more pain than you faced when they abused you.

Chapter 17   Conclusion

As established, narcissism is the condition where an individual possesses inflated regard for themselves. While most people have heard of the word narcissist or narcissism, a large part of the population is not aware of the concept of narcissistic abuse. This is the form of emotional torture inflicted on victims by narcissists; people who are associated with antisocial disorders and have high regard for themselves. It has become increasingly important to create awareness about narcissistic abuse because there are many in the society as well as several victims suffering under the narcissists' abuse. Also, due to the techniques such as love-bombing that they use to lure the victim, most people live in denial and continue to suffer because they think that the narcissists love them. More so, most people do not know how to alleviate themselves from the narcissist's abuse even when they realize they are in a relationship with one.

Therefore, this book has explained all about the Narcissistic Personality Disorder, how to recognize your narcissist by explaining the different types of narcissists, understanding how the narcissist chose you and how they were able to get into your mind by explaining how you were an easy target. Also, the behavior of a narcissist is explained to help you in identifying one and the feelings of the narcissist toward the victim and vice versa is discussed to show you that indeed the narcissist has no regard for you whatsoever. Most importantly, the book discusses about developing the mindset of getting ready to get back the control of your life and shows you that you can always start afresh, and that life is precious hence should not be wasted on a narcissist. Lastly, you are given the seven steps you can take to get revenge on your narcissist. You are shown that the narcissist has vulnerabilities that you can leverage to take revenge on them. Finally, the book discusses what you can do to help friends and loved ones who may be in the same problem and how you reap the rewards of leaving a narcissist and living a life of choice, stronger and wiser this time.

Narcissistic abuse disorients your life and moves you out of the path for achieving your dreams. However, the good news is that you can learn how to identify the narcissist, protect yourself from their abuse and launch strong boundaries. As explained above, there are various types of narcissists who behave in different manners, but all of whom are harmful to your life. Their sense of self-importance and exploiting people without remorse are remarkable traits. Also, narcissists have vulnerabilities, which can be employed by the victim to assume a strategic position to handle the narcissist. The first thing that the victim should do is to accept that it has already happened, that they have been abused and this has taken a toll on their lives. Then, one should develop the right mindset to help them deal with the narcissist and prepare to regain control of their lives.

Escaping the grip of a narcissist is a tough journey, which must be tactfully undertaken to avoid being harmed irrevocably. The one thing that one should keep in mind is that everyone's healing journey is different, and you ought to be patient with yourself. Also, one should take it upon themselves to generate awareness of narcissistic abuse and help out other people who may be suffering from the same silently. There may be some of your friends or loved ones who live in denial no matter how much you try showing them that they are not in the right relationship. Knowledge gained from this book gives you the capability to help such people. Overall, it is never too late to alleviate yourself from the abuse of a narcissist and resume your original self.

References

Back, M. D., Küfner, A. C., Dufner, M., Gerlach, T. M., Rauthmann, J. F., & Denissen, J. J. (2013). Narcissistic admiration and rivalry: Disentangling the bright and dark sides of narcissism. *Journal of Personality and Social Psychology*, *105*(6), 1013.

Bergman, S. M., Fearrington, M. E., Davenport, S. W., & Bergman, J. Z. (2011). Millennials, narcissism, and social networking: What narcissists do on social networking sites and why. *Personality and Individual Differences*, *50*(5), 706-711.

Brummelman, E., Thomaes, S., Nelemans, S. A., De Castro, B. O., Overbeek, G., &

Bushman, B. J. (2015). Reply to Kealy et al.: Theoretical precision in the study of

narcissism and its origins. *Proceedings of the National Academy of Sciences*,

112(23), E2987-E2987.

Foster, J. D., & Brunell, A. B. (2018). Narcissism and Romantic Relationships. In *Handbook of Trait Narcissism* (pp. 317-326). Springer, Cham.

Lambe, S., Hamilton-Giachritsis, C., Garner, E., & Walker, J. (2018). The role of narcissism in aggression and violence: A systematic review. Trauma, Violence, & Abuse, 19(2), 209-230.

Miller, J. D., Dir, A., Gentile, B., Wilson, L., Pryor, L. R., & Campbell, W. K. (2010). Searching for a vulnerable dark triad: Comparing factor 2 psychopathy, vulnerable narcissism, and borderline personality disorder. *Journal of personality*, *78*(5), 1529-1564

Morf, C. C., Horvath, S., & Torchetti, L. (2011). Narcissistic self-enhancement. *Handbook of self-enhancement and self-protection*, 399-424.

Wurst, S. N., Gerlach, T. M., Dufner, M., Rauthmann, J. F., Grosz, M. P., Küfner, A. C., ... & Back, M. D. (2017). Narcissism and romantic relationships: The differential impact of narcissistic admiration and rivalry. *Journal of Personality and Social Psychology, 112*(2), 280., J. *The everything guide to codependency.*

Part 2 : Gaslighting

Chapter 18   Introduction to Gaslighting

Here, we present gaslighting as a form of manipulation that seeks to sow the seeds of doubt into a targeted individual's mind, and as a form of manipulation that makes the victim question their memory, perception, and sanity.

By misdirecting victims, saying contradictory words and lying, gaslighting is done in subtle ways so that the victims do not realize what is done to them, as they are persistently denied of what is real.

Gaslighting is an attempt to destabilize a victim to gain total control over them, and we have already established it as a favorite tool for manipulators like narcissists who are control freaks.

Narcissists use gaslighting as a psychological manipulation technique for their benefit, by deliberately trying to alter other people's perception of reality, creating an imbalance of power and exploiting victims to serve their purposes.

There might be a chance you (or someone you know) are caught in a gaslighting situation if any of these things seems to be happening to you. If you find more than three of these scenarios valid for you, then it is time for you to take a step back and assess your situation. It is time to evaluate all your relationships at the moment, both personal and professional.

Mental manipulation can have damaging effects on victims. You must have noticed a particular person you relate with seemed to get whatever they want, whenever they want it. Have you looked at this person with admiration, and yet, with a bit of disgust because you feel they did not get the things they got in the right way?

All things considered, if you felt like they were exploiting you or other people, you are most likely right because narcissists are master manipulators who seek to control people at work, life, and relationships.

It is hard to spot the ways that someone might be using others for their own advantage, but there are ways to recognize it and even stop it before it happens. Mental manipulation allows abusers to take from others for their own benefit as it works in a way to make victims lose control of their minds and become vulnerable to the will of the abuser.

If you recognize a pattern of certain kinds of an anomaly in your relationships, and you are starting to see ways in which you are being manipulated to doubt what your reality is, then it's about time you take proactive steps to avoid further mental manipulation and emotional abuse because ultimately you might step down into a state of utter depression if you decide not to do anything about your situation.

So how do you avoid the mental manipulation and emotional abuse caused by gaslighting?

1. You have to develop an unwavering belief in your intuition.

It can be really challenging for someone who has been under the control of a narcissist to start listening to their intuition; this is because the narcissist has been telling them not to believe their intuition for some time.

Sitting in silence for a set portion of time in a day practicing meditation can help to silence the mind and still the body so that the truth of the situation can be sought out. By taking deep breaths, you had come to see how a narcissist has been gaslighting you and as time passes your intuition will come alive much more, and you will start trusting it.

When you listen to yourself and your feelings, and you feel self-doubt or confusion lurking around inside you, question why exactly you feel that way. Pay attention to the actions and words of the people you relate with daily. Then you will be able to notice the inconsistencies in their words and actions. It is necessary to develop an unwavering belief in your intuition as trusting your gut will help you to understand and be aware of what is going on around you.

2. You have to know your fundamental human rights

As long as you are not causing harm to others, you have the right to stand up for yourself. Some of our fundamental human rights as humans are the rights to:

Express our feelings and opinions.

Be treated with respect.

Set our goals and determine our priorities; and

Create our own healthy and happy lives, among others.

Of course, society is full of people who do not respect these fundamental human rights. Psychological manipulators such as narcissists, in particular, want to deprive people of their rights so they can control and take advantage of them but when you know your rights, you will have every right to declare that it is you, who's in charge of your life and not anyone else.

Be assertive for yourself. Start by choosing to stop responding to words and actions the way you did before, speak up, and do not be afraid to say no to things or people that seek to manipulate you.

3. You have to let go of self-blame

The narcissist's agenda is to look for ways to make you think you are crazy so that they can have their way and when you realize that you are caught up in a gaslighting situation, it is understandable that you may feel non-worthy, or even blame yourself for not satisfying the narcissist.

In situations like these, it is important to remember that you are not the problem; you are being manipulated to feel that you are insane so that you are going to surrender your power and rights. Self-blame can lead to more problems and give the narcissist an edge in the situation to abuse you more.

4. You can keep your distance

You have to understand that when you are in a situation with someone who is gaslighting you, you are never going to be able to convince them of your view of things. It is best that you get out with your brain intact and be willing to move on with your own life. Allow yourself to escape this situation with your sanity intact. A narcissistic person will not change, so it is best to keep your distance if you can.

You can take control of your senses back by confronting them if you do not believe you are in harm's way. You should know that explaining how you feel and what is bothering you is not doing something wrong. Make a request that the other person changes their behaviors and how they talk to you. Do not let them continue with the same actions. Take your power back and do what you need to do.

Also, know that people who manipulate others do not change easily. So, in doing what is okay for you do not try to change anyone who you suspect might be a narcissist or anyone you know to be a manipulator? Know that their behaviors are hard-wired to their brains and trying to change them on your own might well be a waste of your time and efforts. Leave such relationships if you can.

Chapter 19   What Is Gaslighting and How It Works

Gaslighting is a type of emotional exploitation where an individual continuously influences scenarios to convince the victim into doubting his or her views and memory. Gaslighting is a crafty kind of abuse which makes victims doubt the instincts which they have depended on their entire lives. In return, they are no longer sure of anything. Gaslighting ensures it is probable that the victim believes anything their abusers say to them even if they have personally experienced the same situation and have answers of their own. This form of abuse frequently comes ahead of other kinds of physical and emotional abuse. The reason for this is that the individual dealing with abuse has a higher tendency to stay in other abusive conditions as well.

Gaslighting is a word which was coined from a British play known as "Gas Light." It was showcased in 1938, and it was about a husband who tried to make his wife go insane by leveraging on a range of tricks which led her to doubt her rationality and views. "Gas Light" was developed into a movie in 1940 as well as 1944.

Any individual can be prone to gaslighting, and it is a technique commonly utilized by the narcissist, dictators, cult leaders, and abusers. It takes place gradually, so the victim is not aware of how much they have been brainwashed.

Gaslighting Techniques and Examples

There is a range of techniques used for gaslighting which can make it difficult to spot. Abusers use these techniques to keep truths that they do not want the victim to know hidden. Either men or women can abuse victims with gaslighting.

Below are some of the major gaslighting techniques a narcissist may use:

Withholding

Here, the abuser pretends he does not understand what the abused is trying to say. He or she also chooses not to listen and refuses to share how they are feeling with the victim.

Examples of these include:

- "You just want to get me confused."

- "Not again. I don't have time to listen to your nonsense today."

Countering

In this instance, the abuser strongly questions the memory of the victim, even though the victim has correctly remembered what occurred.

Instances of these include the abuser saying:

- "This is the same way you did not remember the last time."

- "You said something similar last time, and you were wrong!"

With these techniques, the abuser misdirects the victim from the subject at hand. Then, they begin to doubt what their views and motivations are as opposed to the problem at hand.

When this occurs, the abuser then begins to question the thoughts, experiences, and viewpoints more broadly via statements like:

- "You make things up in your mind way too much."

- "You don't see things positively. Why must you always be negative?"

Diverting or Blocking

Here, the abuser then diverts from the subject matter being covered and begins to question what the victim is thinking. This way, they begin to take charge of the conversation.

A few examples of this consist of:

- "Stop your whining."

- "I refuse to do this with you again."

Trivializing

This is another commonly used technique in gaslighting. Here, the abuser makes the victim start to believe that what they are thinking, or things they want are not vital.

For instance:

- "You are so insensitive. Why must everything be about you?"

Denial or Forgetting

These could be kinds of gaslighting too. Here, the abuser pretends not to remember events that have taken place. He or she may deny making a promise to do something which the victim finds essential.

Instances where this occurs include:

- "I don't remember making that promise. You are making things up again!"

- "What exactly are you going on about?"

There are gas lighters who then make fun of their victims for their misperceptions and transgressions.

How Else Does the Narcissist Gaslight Victims?

Now that we have covered the primary gaslighting techniques abusers take advantage of, let us delve further into how a narcissist uses these gaslighting techniques on his or her victims.

They Get Them Isolated

If the victim has a solid and extensive support system, it will be tough for the narcissist to take advantage and manipulate them. For this reason, they have to get them on their own and ensure they are unable to access their friends and family members.

When this happens, they become the only reference point of that individual. The moment they are able to do this, they begin to feed you wrong information regarding those you know and love, so you start turning against them. In time, they will start to believe that the manipulator is the only individual they can rely on. And this is precisely what the narcissist desires because isolation increases their level of control.

They Drop Little Secrets and Hints

A very crafty gaslighting technique used by the narcissist to get into the head of their victim is to tell them secrets that they alone know or leave hints about specific individuals they want to get the target isolated from.

They begin to say things like: "Is your friend really staying home tonight?" "I saw your best friend with that lady she asked you to stay away from."

They Are Very Nice to Their Victims

There are lots of studies which show that individuals who have been abused via gaslighting, still desire affection from those who abused them. Besides, if the abuser is nice to his or victims, their loyalty skyrockets, and they start to believe all the words that come out of the abuser's mouth.

Usually, the narcissist will start off by being nice to his or her target. Then gradually, they start to reduce this affection. At a point, they begin to mistreat them without due cause. The victim becomes disorganized and at a loss about what to do in order for the affection to return. The fact is, this is not possible because the love was never real from the start.

They Tell Obvious Lies

Even when the victim is aware that it is a lie, the narcissist keeps telling this lie without flinching. They do this as a way to set up the stage. The instant they tell their victims a blatant lie, they are not sure if anything the narcissist says is the truth. The goal is to keep the victim disorganized and unsteady.

They Deny They Made a Statement Even if the Victim Has Evidence

The narcissist says something to the victim, and the victim knows and even has proof. However, they deny they said it. For this reason, the victim begins to question what is actually true as well as their perception and begin to wonder: "Perhaps they never made this statement in the first place?" And the more the narcissist engages in this, the more the victim begins to question their perception and views and begins to accept what the narcissist wants them to believe.

They Use Something Close to The Victim

Narcissists use something important to their victims as a weapon. They understand how critical their victim's identity is to them and attack that first. The narcissist tells the victim that they will only be worthy if they did not have some specific traits, trying to break the victim down from the very foundation of their being.

They Wear Down the Victim Gradually

This is one of the craftiest aspects of gaslighting: it takes place in a gradual manner. A snide comment here and there, a lie, then two, and so on and so forth. Before the victim knows it, the narcissist begins to ramp up the frequency. Even individuals who are very self-aware can quickly be drawn into gaslighting. This is how efficient a technique it is, primarily when used by one without empathy like a narcissist.

It is similar to the analogy of the "frog in the frying pan." A frog is placed in a pot of cold water, then put on heat, which slowly goes higher and higher. This way, the frog dies in hot water without ever knowing what is happening to it.

Their Words and Actions Do not Align

When a narcissist is gaslighting, the words that come out of their mouths do not mean anything. It is only talk and nothing more. The way they behave fails to correspond with the things they say.

Chapter 20   What to Do to Fight Gaslighting and Narcissistic Abuse

Relationships where emotional abuse is a factor are inherently difficult, especially for emotionally sensitive people. Because empaths interact with others in a naturally sensitive, giving way, they have to work towards protecting themselves from narcissists since these individuals will use the empath's sensitivity against them. Everything you share with the narcissist is a potential weapon that may one day be turned against you since, as we have seen the narcissist regards the relationship as a competition where the role is to land on top. The following is a list of tips that empaths should take note of as part of mounting a defense against narcissists, both in their present relationships and in future ones (since they tend to attract narcissistic types):

- Always keep your guard up.

- Pay attention to your intuition in situations where something does not feel right.

- Learn to question your partner's intentions.

- Question the belittling, negative language of the narcissist.

- Make efforts to spend more time away from the narcissist (around other people).

- Question the idealized image that the narcissist coerced you into believing.

- Be aware of situations where you are doing things you do not want to do.

- Do not let the narcissist touch you or engage in other behaviors that attempt to establish false rapport.

- Be assertive.

- Consider when it might be time to cut ties with the narcissist completely.

Tip One: Always Keep Your Guard Up.

The narcissist does not recognize boundaries and, frankly, the empath is not very good at these either. Because the narcissist sees the world and all in it as an extension of their will, they will always be looking for ways to pump others for information that can be used against them later or for techniques that can be used for abuse. The empath, therefore, needs to keep their guard up. Be careful what you share with the narcissist in terms of information. Be careful of giving them clues as to your emotional state. The narcissist does not care. They will only use this information to hurt you.

Tip Two: Pay Attention to Your Intuition in Situations Where Something Does Not Feel Right.

Empaths are naturally intuitive, but narcissists are good at eroding the beneficial defenses of highly sensitive people. If the empath listened to their intuition, they would constantly be alerted to signs that something was not right about the narcissist. Something they said did not seem right. Something they did not feel right. Use your intuition as a guide in interpreting the behaviors of the narcissist and in directing your own behaviors.

Tip Three: Learn to Question Your Partner's Intentions.

The narcissist lacks empathy for others, so there is often a disconnect between what their surface intentions seem to be and what they really are. So, giving your narcissistic partner access to all the phone numbers of your friends and family may seem like a good idea for emergency purposes, but it may not be considering what the narcissist may choose to use these for when they have discarded you. The narcissist can use these to turn others against you, destroying you. As an empath, you have to start to question your partner's intentions. This is an important step in defense.

Tip Four: Question the Belittling, Negative Language of the Narcissist.

The narcissist uses belittling and demeaning language to lower the self-esteem of their partner and make themselves feel better. This also serves to weaken the empathic partner and keep them in the abusive language. For the empath, therefore, learning to question and doubt the negative language of the narcissist is extremely important. The worst thing you can do is internalize this negative talk as it will only leave you depressed and isolated.

Tip Five: Make Efforts to Spend More Time Away from the Narcissist (Around Other People).

Isolation is an extremely important concept in analyzing the narcissistic relationship. The goal of the narcissist is to isolate you, as in this condition, they can continue to abuse you, essentially using you to enable their mental illness. Empaths have to make a conscious effort to break free from this isolation, spending time with people who will enrich their emotional energy and teach them that they are not the inferior person the narcissist wants them to believe they are.

Tip Six: Question the Idealized Image That the Narcissist Coerced You into Believing.

The narcissist is able to hook the empath (or other highly sensitive person) by pushing an idealized version of themselves during the early stages of the relationship. This idealized image becomes something that the empath always returns to when times are bad, keeping them in the abusive relationship. The empath has to face this image head-on and tear it down from the wall. The narcissist has shown you who they really are again and again. Believe the truth of your eyes and ears, not the deceptive mind control of the narcissist.

Tip Seven: Be Aware of Situations Where You Are Doing Things You Do Not Want to Do.

Empaths naturally create dynamics where they function in alignment with others. All animals are capable of doing this, and it is the empaths in our species that help to keep us together. But for the narcissist, this is merely a tool to manipulate. The narcissist wants you to be in mental and emotional alignment with them so you will be their hapless creature, doing all that they want and working in their interest. As the empath, you, therefore, need to be aware of situations where you are doing the things the narcissist wants. Stop.

Tip Eight: Do Not Let the Narcissist Touch You or Engage in Other Behaviors That Attempt to Establish False Rapport.

This is a tip that comes straight from the mind control handbook. Experts in mind control teach others how to establish rapport with others in order to get them to do what you want. Empaths are extremely susceptible to these tactics because emotional rapport is natural with them. But the empath needs to understand that not everyone out there is a sensitive soul whose intentions are good. The narcissist or energy vampire will establish rapport in order to abuse you or drain you of your emotional energy. Do not allow them to engage in the characteristic ploys to establish rapport like touching you, mimicking your gestures, or ordering the same thing as you at a restaurant. This is nothing more than narcissistic trickery.

Tip Nine: Be Assertive.

Sometimes the simplest strategies are the most effective. Empaths frequently do not assert themselves because their personalities are dominated by a desire to get along with others and establish cohesion. Empaths highly understand and can make allowances for the bad qualities of others. But when it comes to narcissists and other energy vampires, the empath has to be assertive. The narcissist will abuse you if you let them, so a key to stopping this abuse is to exert your will rather than merely going along with the will of the narcissist.

Tip Ten. Consider When It Might Be Time to Cut Ties with the Narcissist Completely.

This is a tip that is easy for some but not for others. The narcissist may be a romantic partner in our lives, or it could be our parent, sibling, or best friend. You may not wish to cut ties with the narcissist because of a shared history or what they represent in your life. But an important step in healing is radical acceptance. The narcissist is never going to change.

You have to accept that no matter how much you may have a desire to help them. Protecting yourself, even saving yourself, may mean cutting ties with the narcissist completely.

Chapter 21   How You Can Avoid Falling for A Gas Lighter

Once gaslighting and manipulation are identified, the next step is to get through it. Overcoming manipulation can be very challenging. In some cases, a 60 year-old-man might realize just now that his 85 year-old-mother is manipulative. They might never get through their issues, but they should still be confronted. Manipulation takes a part of both the abuser and the victim. It can ruin people's lives, altering the direction they take and affecting the rest of their years. Manipulation can be hard to identify and even harder to overcome.

It can be done, and it should be attempted to get through. In a relationship based around manipulation, there might not be any coming back. Sometimes, people might just have to break up. You might have to get a divorce or stop calling your mom. It takes two people to partake in a manipulative scenario. Not both people will end up identifying it as a manipulative situation, however. In that case, the person that realizes what is actually going on might just have to move on, the manipulator never realizing the damage they caused.

This can be a challenging part of overcoming manipulation. Usually, some instance of codependency formed, making it even harder to break away. There are ways to overcome this, and we will cover.

Know Your Worth

The first step in overcoming manipulation is for the victim to identify that they still have value. A manipulator likely took everything from their victim. They belittled them, ridiculed them, and made them feel as though what they thought did not matter. In some situations, they might have even used gaslighting tactics to make their victims feel as though they are insane. It can be hard for a victim to then recognize just how much value they still have once they become aware of the manipulation.

It is important for everyone to know, no matter who is reading this, that you have worth. Everyone has value. No one deserves to be manipulated. No one deserves to feel as though they do not have any purpose, reason, or value. You have the right to be treated justly, and with respect from other people. You are allowed to express your emotions, feelings, wants, and opinions. No one else has the right to tell you how to feel. You set your own boundaries, and no one else gets to decide for you.

If you feel sad about something, that is completely valid. No one gets to decide if what they say hurts you or not. Not everyone might intentionally mean to hurt you, but that does not mean you are not allowed to still feel bad. You have the right to feel the way you do, and you have the same right to express those beliefs.

If you feel like you need to protect yourself, you are just in doing so. If you feel like your safety is being threatened, or someone is taking advantage of you, you have the right to remove yourself from that situation without guilt. No one gets to treat you badly, and though that can be hard for many of us to hear, it is the truth.

Manipulators aim to take these thoughts away. They want to deprive their victims of their rights in order to work towards getting what they want. This cannot happen anymore. It is up to the manipulator's victims to now recognize their worth and stop the cycle of manipulation.

Do not Be Afraid to Keep Your Distance

Many people that feel as though they are being manipulated end up being too afraid to do anything about it. They have been stripped of their own thoughts and opinions, their own feelings invalidated and instead focus on how other people feel. Those that have been continually manipulated might be afraid to leave those that have hurt them. They have depended on those that abused them for so long they do not know where else to go.

You are allowed to keep your distance. You do not have to feel guilty about protecting yourself. It can be hard to separate yourself from a manipulator, especially in a romantic relationship. You might see the very weaknesses that cause their manipulative behavior. Maybe in a relationship, a boyfriend's dad was an abusive alcoholic, and it greatly hurt him. It also caused his violent manipulative behavior that led him to hitting his girlfriend on a few occasions. It is true that he has his own pain, but that does not mean he is allowed to inflict it on others. The girlfriend has every right to leave her boyfriend and find her own peace and protection.

It is Not Your Job to Change Them

Once manipulation is recognized, the next step is to try to talk to the person about the manipulation. It is time to get down to the root issues of the relationship and figure out what can be done to help both partners get what they need, instead of just the manipulator. There has been an imbalance of power for far too long, and it is time to rebalance.

Unfortunately, not many manipulators are willing to admit their faults and later change their behavior. Instead, they will do whatever they can to distract others from their faults, placing the blame on their victims instead. When this happens, the victim has to accept that their manipulator is not going to change, and they must find the strength to leave.

There will likely be a desire to change the other person and help them improve their life as well. Not everyone will always be on the same page of their journey towards self-discovery. It can be hard to accept for some victims, but they have to realize that it is not their job to change their manipulator.

You can only help a person so much, and if they are not willing to change or improve themselves, it is not going to happen. Many people wait around for the other to change in their relationship, hoping their manipulation will get better. If a person is not aware of their behavior and is not actively trying to change it, nothing is going to happen in the end.

Hypnosis

If mind control is the best set of manipulation strategies for beginners to pick up and be able to learn quickly, then hypnosis is the next natural step in the process towards becoming a master of manipulation. In general, hypnosis lasts longer and is far more powerful than mind control is, although it also requires more skill to successfully pull off. While hypnosis has some concepts that overlap with mind control and brainwashing, it also has completely unique components, which can make it more challenging to learn. Hypnosis has a long rich history, and today it is used in a wide variety of fields and industries, including in medicine, sports, psychotherapy, self-improvement, meditation and relaxation, forensics and criminal justice, art and literature, and the military. Of course, all instances of hypnosis share common characteristics no matter what context it is used in, and these same characteristics can come in handy when attempting to manipulate someone else. Having a good understanding of the principles and concepts of hypnosis can turn you from a mediocre manipulator into a highly skilled one.

Chapter 22 Gaslighting in Relationships

When you get attached to someone you love the way they are and are also happily accepting them the same way. But there are times when it becomes important for you to change a few things in you and some in your partner for the betterment of your relationship. There are times in a relationship when you start thinking that your partner has stopped caring about you, has become self-centered or started imposing things on you. There are small things initially that you would think as cute such as cooking good food for your husband and telling him over dinner that you hit the car when you went out. At times it is fine, but slowly if these things turn darker and deeper it can be a big concern for you.

Manipulation starts from the ground level and can reach up to the sky. It is you who have to set the limits and understand when these small things turn into bigger ones. You should always have the confidence to speak up and stand against something which is not right and against your wish. You should always ask yourself a question - do you have that much courage to say no when you do not want to do something. Manipulative people particularly choose the partners who can be easily manipulated as they like things to happen their own way.

But these manipulative people are really wise and would not let you see these signs at the beginning of the relationship. You should always be vigilant in your relationship and if you observe that small threats are turning into bigger ones and if you do not agree to what they say, the big angry or aggressive, it is a clear sign that you are with a manipulative partner. And if your partner does not respect your decision even after you explain your reasons clearly to them and they still try to do things according to their wishes, it means that they are selfish and are not concerned about what you want from life.

Manipulators just do not change overnight. It is just that their small demands get bigger day by day and their tolerance of accepting 'no' gets smaller with each passing day. All of your time might pass by thinking whether you want to be in this relationship or not. The thoughts that come to your mind confuse you where one side you might think that love means giving and on the other side you might think that love should be unconditional. But believe me, if you want to spend your life happy, peacefully and according to your wishes, then coming out of the relationship is substantial for you. You might feel difficult saying no and staying without your partner, but it will make your life easy and you would be able to live it according to your own terms.

At times, people are just not able to say no because they have fear in their mind that how would they react when you will say no. Forget about your people-pleasing behavior, think about yourself, when you would stop bending over to make everyone happy, then is the time you would feel confident and be who you are. Now you know that is crucial to take a step when you got to know that your partner is manipulative. But let us first understand well about the signs of a manipulative lover-

- They provoke you- When they have nothing to say and are out of the argument, they would provoke you. They might do things which would make you angry and trigger your negative emotions. The only purpose to do is that they want you to indulge in a pointless quarrel so that they can use something in their defense. If you feel that they are unnecessarily exaggerating and poking you, the best thing to do is just calm down, and tries to stay on the topic. If you are unable to do that, then just try and end the discussion politely.

- They know how to use tricks- They are always ready with their dirty tricks to get what they want. They would request for you big things in such a way that they are asking for some small favors. They are very clever and know how to deal with different kinds of people. For example, they would say that if we cannot go to a far-off restaurant for dinner, then let us just go to a nearby restaurant for eating Chinese food. The only option they would leave for you is to select the easier one. But you should not come up in their tricks as it is not always important to help and you should help if you want to, not because they are providing with options.

- Gaslighting Technique- In this method they try to distort the past and twist the facts so that it would confuse you. They would ask questions like; Did I not call you? Why would I not call you when I know you need me? They would be so confident and sure that you start doubting your own memory.

They very well know which point is to be used when. To get rid of this wicked tactic you should always trust your memory and tell them that you remember what you said. This way they would either stop using this technique or at least beware that you remember very well what you say and do.

- Pressurize you- Everyone knows if you have less time to make decisions, you would not be able to see all the aspects of the situation. This is what manipulators do in a relationship. They would always push you to make decisions faster by giving you less time when they do not want you to think over something very much. So, it is always good to ask for some time, so that you can see the pros and cons of t according to you and check if it suits you. If they still want you to hurry, then politely just answer that you are thinking about it and need some time to take the decision.

- Emotional blackmail- This is a very common sign of a manipulator; they are really good at emotionally blackmailing you. They always try to you the weakest point of view and show insecurity by saying statements like, I will die without you or I cannot live without you, etc. They try to threaten their health and life but do not take it too seriously as it is just a threat. Also, if they say something like this, just tell them whatever they do, you would not be responsible for it.

- You are the one who is guilty, and they are the victims- Manipulators in a relationship would always show that it is your mistake and they are the ones who are the victims because of it. They would always make you guilt by saying- you know I have so much work in an office, stop being selfish, etc. which would make you feel guilty. But do not feel that way; stay calm and make them realize that they are responsible for their behavior. They avoid responsibility and just try to become victims by showing that are insecure and get benefit from you. They do such things to gain attention from you so that your love and concern for them increases. But you need to be prepared and know when to pay attention and when to avoid.

95

- Avoid discussions- Manipulators mostly avoid discussing common problems between both of you and family-related. They would always try to end the discussion before it starts or not even to listen to what you want to say. For this, you should always make sure that you stick to your point and make them understand that it is important and clear it out.

Changing a manipulator is very difficult as it is a trait of character. These people are difficult to change as they love sticking to it even if it costs you being separated. It is always good to take this step if you do not see any change in the person because it is always good to take trouble once rather than elongating it for your whole life. Separating, divorce or break-up are not small words. All these things take a lot of courage and time before making this decision. There are many things to analyze and see if your decision is right. It is just not simple to just ask yourself what you are being the victim of manipulation and you get the answer.

Chapter 23   Gaslighting in the Workplace, Home, and Society

Gaslighting at Workplace

The world of work is a competitive place. There are pressures to achieve our goals, meet deadlines, and get promoted. In this high-stress environment, it is very easy to ignore an incident of gaslighting or even continued manipulation by colleagues. Some gas lighters may be unintentionally driven to reach a once-off goal, such as achieving a promotion that you were also competing for. On a subconscious level (low level), you may wish to level the playing field if your colleague has got better qualifications than you. You may say to your colleague the morning before their interview, "Don't you think your outfit is a bit inappropriate for the position?" (And you may honestly think so.) However, your payoff is to undermine your colleague's confidence and sabotage their interview.

Gaslighting in the Home

Home is a place where we should be at peace, be able to let our guard down, and feel secure with our loved ones. Yet, it is also where we find relationships that contain narcissist traits and gaslighting. Any time that you want to make someone see something your way, you may be engaging in gaslighting. In fact, many people are "blissfully" unaware of the fact that they have been engaging in gaslighting themselves. Apart from messing around in their target's memories to instill doubt, gas lighters deny that they have acted maliciously. They will never own up to their abusive behavior unless it is to find another way to manipulate them by playing on your empathy (and sympathy).

On the low end of the spectrum, we might find a wife wanting to buy a new home entertainment center but needing to convince her husband to do so. She may say something like, "Honey, you like this brand. Remember that you said it is a reliable brand and that you think it is worth the money? You are so right!" There may be nothing apparently abusive or manipulative about this, but when we look closer, this is a moderated example of gaslighting. The wife establishes her power by pulling the husband in with endearing terms like "honey." She then lists the virtues of the brand she likes, but she falsely indicates that the husband had been in favor of it, and how can he not remember it? She sweetens the pot by flattering the husband—he is so wise. As a result of this gaslighting, the wife gets her home theater set while also feeling victorious in convincing her husband that it was his idea to get it. However, the husband feels manipulated, and he questions his memory since he does not remember having said those things, but surely, he must have since his wife (whom he trusts) says that he did? He doubts himself and willingly gives his power of choice to his wife.

On the high end of the spectrum, we may find a pathological narcissist who engages in intentional gaslighting to manipulate and disempower their family and, thereby, gain strength. An example of this may be a father who acts inconsistently towards his children. One day he might tell his children off for being noisy, while tomorrow he allows them to engage in noisy behavior in the house. He then tells his children that they made a noise on both days and that he will have to punish them. The father is in a position of power and gets the thrill of punishing his children, while the children feel uncertain about what was the right thing to do as they were punished. The children may refute the father and say that he gave them permission, which he will deny by saying that he is a strict father who has always avoided his children making noise. The children will begin to doubt that they heard their father correctly and fear the results of their displeasing him.

Gaslighting in Society

On the global stage, we will find many instances of gaslighting, where people have manipulated others to achieve their goals of self-empowerment and enrichment (emotionally and financially). Certainly, politicians are renowned for it, and it comes as no surprise to most of us that they would grandstand and manipulate, so why not gaslight? What is interesting to note is that what we would consider gaslighting in one culture may not be seen as such in another. Some cultures are more susceptible to gaslighting (and narcissism) than others. Webber (2016) indicates that cultures with a more collective identity such as some African cultures, where there is an emphasis on "we" and not "I" are less likely to engage in gaslighting and narcissism as power is shared among the whole tribe or family group. In large cities, there is also more pressure on people to reach individual excellence, which will encourage gaslighting, than in smaller towns or out in the rural countryside.

On the lower end of the scale, people worldwide will engage in gaslighting when it suits them and to attain a specific goal. They may do so to discipline and control their children by, for example, telling their child that they really do like going to school when the child hates it. The upper reaches of the scale for gaslighting globally may be best captured by referring to historical figures such as Hitler and Mussolini. They went from gaslighting (as Hitler did with his propaganda and speeches to draw in the crowds and convincing them of truths that they knew were false) before ending in a dictatorship. When looking at the strategies that Hitler used to gain prominence in German politics before World War II, it reads like the three stages of narcissist manipulations (or gaslighting) with Hitler wooing the people (idealization) and promising them everything their hearts desired, before suddenly changing to persecutions (devaluation), and, finally, death camps (discard). Granted, not all narcissists will engage in gaslighting to the point of being equivalent to Hitler; however, we may find the whole spectrum of emotional abuse in our lives if we look closely.

Chapter 24   Gas lighter in Politics, Society, Family, and Friendship

Many of the positive traits that are known to be part of the Dark Triad personalities have to do with confidence. There are many ways of describing confidence, but it is essentially the courage to be yourself in any situation that might arise. Being yourself might not seem like the classical idea of "confidence," but in fact, it is. Being yourself, whether it is vindictive, happy, or anything else, is what it takes to be confident. Emotions do not weigh down confidence; rather, it uses them for strength. It uses them as coal in the furnace of ambition – fuel for the fire.

A number of things can cause shyness. It could be coming from far back in a person psyche, or it could just be that they are feeling sick today.

Whatever it is, shyness is the state of not wanting to share what is going on with you to the world. It is a state of not sharing with the world, and not knowing how you will be received in the world. This is a state where you are hiding, within your own mind. It is a state of pride and a state of protectiveness.

You must be kind to yourself when you are a shy person. You have got to engage in polite and kind personal self-talk. For example, you can tell yourself, "It's okay. I am going to be okay. There will be a few awkward moments, and I will make it rough this thing alive." this is the attitude that will help you out. There are thousands, probably millions of shy people in this country. They each have to go figure out their own experiences, but you can know that you are not alone.

One thing to remember with social anxiety is that other people do not really perceive your social system as you think they do. You might be projecting how people see you, and you might think of yourself as a person who is awkward. The real fact is that everyone is awkward sometimes.

Social anxiety may make you feel like you do not want to do anything or go anywhere. A big part of learning to deal with this is learning about the anxiety state and learning to modulate your body. The number one way to do this is by breathing. By doing intentional deep breathing, you can cause a relaxation response in the body. Some actions are intentional, like riding a bike. Other states are more automatic, like breathing or blinking your eye. You can, however, decide to do intentional breathing, and you can affect your body's physical reaction by doing this. It is a very powerful tool for social anxiety. By employing this tool, you can recognize when your body is going to start to go haywire; you can do some breathing to calm yourself down.

If there is an event that you are scared to go to, like a party or a show, you can just notice to yourself as you are approaching the event, how you are feeling in your body, and keep checking in every couple of minutes. You will start to notice a tightening, and sometimes it will be in the chest, sometimes in other parts of the body. Usually, what is present with social anxiety is a tightening of the chest, a feeling of the heart rate going up, and a feeling of breathing being constricted.

If you are aware enough to notice that you are feeling the symptoms, just know that you can actually change that in that exact moment. You can start to breathe, and you will feel different. Once you start to take some deep breaths, you should notice that your symptoms decrease.

For some extreme cases, this might not be enough. Some people with this can be diagnosed with meds that help them to decrease these symptoms and to be healthier in the world. If you have extreme social anxiety, talk to a doctor, and see if there are options for you to take medication.

You do not have to share all of yourself all of the time. In fact, it would be quite strange if you did. You should look to being independent when it feels good to you, and you should know yourself enough to know when you are appropriate in your being shy. This is a natural tendency for many people.

Confidence is the opposite of shyness. Instead of wanting to close everything off and hide everything from the world, it wants to share everything with the world and make yourself known. When a person is confident, they feel that they have nothing to hide. It is a way of being out there in the world, sharing yourself for the benefit of others as well as yourself.

What it really comes down to is being yourself and not being afraid of being yourself. Essentially, we cannot change that. We can change behaviors in certain scenarios, and act a certain way around people, and we can make small modifications here and there, but what is truly down there deep within us is who we are. It is something that is at the core of each person.

So, what is it that keeps us from being ourselves, confidently? It may be that we do not trust ourselves. Some people hold thoughts about themselves that are negative, and they assume that they are not worthy or not as good as others. It might also be that they hold negative thoughts about the world, and they think that other people and the world are just going to punish them endlessly and that they can never be themselves.

Charisma is when a person is attractive, not just in a physical sense, but in a larger sense. Think about the most charismatic person you know. They are probably able to lead and be a leader. They are probably able to make people feel at home. The thing about charisma is that you are attractive. It means that people want to be around you because they think good things will happen when they are around you. Charisma is deeply tied to confidence because confidence is attractive, but it is something other than confidence. Charisma is a build-up of traits that are adaptive and healthy. People are able to sense a strong and healthy person, and charisma is that collection of attributes.

Chapter 25   How to Avoid Mental Manipulation

What Are the Traits of a Manipulator?

When we think of a manipulator or a person with the ability to use mind control techniques, our own mind may imagine someone with a specific look or style and spiel or script. If this were as easy as noticing a certain appearance or obvious clues, it would be fairly easy to avoid manipulative people and their practices altogether. Unfortunately, people who apply methods of mind control, manipulation, and persuasion for their benefit come from all walks of life and on the surface, they look, behave, and seem like anyone else. While it is not always easy to detect a person's intentions to manipulate, there are certain types of people who are more likely to use mind control techniques than others:

- The over-confident employer or boss. This person may show signs of superiority and contempt for anyone who does not agree with him or her. They may balk at any opinions or ideas that conflict with their own, even if it is for the benefit of the department or company. Their over-confidence is a mask to hide feelings of inadequacy, and they may use their position of authority to exert control over staff every chance they get.

- The possessive spouse or partner. The relationship begins on a strong note with heavy signs of affection and attention, only to later develop into a possessive and manipulative relationship where the manipulative partner seeks to control all or most aspects of their spouse or partner's life, including who they associate with, where they go and how they spend their money. These traits will escalate into abuse and will worsen over time until the relationship ends. Following the breakup of an abusive or toxic relationship, the ex-partner may cause more damage by stalking (online or in-person), contacting friends or family to spread negative information or rumors and trying other techniques to discredit and effectively "destroy" as much about your life as possible.

This can be specifically dangerous when a manipulative person has a history of violent or unpredictable behavior, and where there is a family (or kids) involved in a custody battle.

- Passive-Aggressive Behavior. This method is used as a punitive technique that involves getting back at someone in a covert way. For example, when a person is angry that their best friend showed up late, they may simply state, "What took you so long! Everybody is waiting!" This is considered a reasonable reaction in this instance, whereas the passive-aggressive tactic may involve the following:

- Instead of confronting the friend for showing up late, a passive-aggressive person will continue as if nothing is wrong, and may even dismiss the tardiness

- Later in the evening, a cup of wine or food might be "accidentally" spilled on the friend, or, they may be purposely ignored for the remainder of the evening.

- These examples indicate how confusing and ruthless passive aggression can be. It aims to punish someone in such a way, that they do not expect it to happen at all, or in such an indirect manner. When a person is confronted using passive-aggressive tactics, they may simply ignore the accusation or deny it. This can become very frustrating and lead to another technique known as gaslighting.

This occurs when a person is made to feel as though their suspicions, thoughts, or feelings are manifestations of their own mind and not based on anything legitimate. For the person impacted by gaslighting, they may feel that there is something wrong with them and their own perception, while the person convincing them of this is usually the one responsible for their suspicions in the first place.

How to Avoid Manipulation and Spot the Signs Early

Avoiding the trap of manipulation is easier when the signs are noticed early in a relationship, a friendship or upon being introduced into a group or organization.

There are often small, seemingly insignificant signs that can provide a good hint at what to expect later. There are also good practices to develop in order to prevent someone from manipulating you or choosing you as their next target. Always remember that manipulation is often aimed towards people seen as vulnerable, isolated, or "weak," even if this is not the case. Perception is everything, and maintaining a strong level of communication and circle of support can prevent manipulation and mind control from wreaking havoc on your life and other people in your life:

1. Keep close contact with family and friends If you suspect your new partner or friend is attempting to isolate you, watch for their reaction or signs of dismay when you make plans with family. Their possessiveness may be disguised as an excuse to spend more time with you and get more acquainted with you, though even in a new relationship, there are other commitments and people that play an important role in our lives. If you suspect there is a more aggressive attempt to keep you away from family and friends, make sure to discuss this concern with someone close, so they are aware of the situation and can be there for you in case, the relationship takes a turn for the worse.

2. Do not tolerate a lack of respect or manipulative mood swings. If you find yourself on the receiving end of an emotional or angry outburst, do not allow it to continue. Calmly explain that you will leave momentarily and return when the other person is in a better state to communicate more civilly. If you suspect this type of behavior will occur beforehand, make sure you are situated close to an exit, in case, the situation escalates very quickly and unpredictably. You have a right to feel safe and to find a quiet, peaceful place if things get out of hand.

3. Make your opinions and expressions heard. This might be easier early on in the relationship or experience with a manipulative person, as they may realize the need to approach with caution. In fact, if you make it clear that your opinions and thoughts matter, without any dispute about who is right or wrong, a manipulator may decide that your strong resolve is not worth their efforts, and they will move on. When this

happens, it may seem disappointing at first, though it can be a lifesaver in the long-term.

4. You have your own personal goals and priorities. Do not let anyone convince you that their personal goals or needs come first. In a relationship, both parties deserve equal consideration and respect. Anything less is not acceptable, as it tips the balance of power unevenly. For example, if you have a career goal or a long-term plan for your health, make it a priority and explain that it will remain as such. Anyone who attempts to discourage you from your goals by using demeaning comments and belittling as a way to make you feel less value is not worth the effort.

5. Do not let anyone convince you that it is "all in our head" This is how gaslighting begins, by gradually convincing someone that their concerns are a product of their imagination and nothing more. Any form of dismissal about a thought, feeling, or emotion should never be discarded by someone as unimportant or unworthy of attention. When we have a serious concern, it should always be considered as such.

6. Always assert yourself, when in doubt. If anyone tried to make you feel unimportant or that what you have to say does not count, it is a sign that they are trying to devalue your sense of self-worth and confidence. When you feel that someone is mistreating you or maybe trying to manipulate you, check-in with a friend or family member, and let them know what is going on. Sometimes, we internalize much more than we should and forget that there are people ready to support and help us when we need it.

Chapter 26   Narcissism and Gaslighting and Why This Is A Favorite Form of Manipulation of the Narcissist

Narcissists are not easily spotted because they have this special ability to mask their malicious traits, habits, and aspects of their personality. In the eyes of people who do not know much about them, they appear friendly, charming, and sometimes sweet.

Now, let us get to the real deal here. Frankly, when you are aware that you are with a narcissist, there is really one way of dealing with the individual—leaving. However, leaving could be tough, especially when you have a strong connection with the individual or you value some good traits in them, and you decide to stay in the relationship. I must tell you, staying with someone with narcissism does not come easy. It comes with a lot of challenges that you will need to cope with, so make sure you do not suffer abuse while in the relationship.

Finding yourself in this situation might not be your fault. Sometimes, you wouldn't know an individual is particularly high in their personality quality until you have gone far and deep into the relationship, then it dawns on you that what attracted you to the person are the narcissistic qualities that are now offensive. The narcissist in your life does not necessarily need to be a lover. It might be your parent, sibling, or relative. You need to confront that person's narcissistic traits but look for ways to cope and manage them while staying with the person. It might even be a boss, teacher, or a team member with strong narcissistic tendencies; and you also need to know how to cope with that situation.

Some people are narcissists, but that does not mean they are unlovable or should be totally isolated. In fact, people who have narcissistic traits could be the fun type. They could be charismatic and even good at the things they do. Sometimes, when you have them around, you derive pleasure and less pain, and if it is at the workplace, they bring success to the team as they are intelligent, and success driven.

If you have a choice in the situation, you may want to stick to the narcissist and try to reform the individual rather than packing your bags and leaving his or her life. Some narcissists are so vulnerable that their reaction to rejection is deadly, and you fear they might harm themselves if you decide to take a walk from their life.

Not all narcissists are the same. They are created differently, and the type of narcissist that is involved in your life will determine how you are supposed to treat him or her. Narcissists have been categorized into two types: vulnerable and grandiose (Egan et al. 2014).

People who fall under the grandiose type are the "darker" ones—darker in the sense that you can easily find the traits of psychopathy, Machiavellianism, and rudeness in them.

Vincent Egan and his team made it clear that people who show high traits of Machiavellianism are the ones who will easily get under your skin. People find it hard to live with those who have these traits, and these traits will always be a stumbling block between the narcissist and his or her goals. Narcissists have obviously mastered the art of one-upmanship by always trying to show that they are superior and by rubbing off everyone else's opinions and feelings.

Vulnerable narcissists use an outer shell of self-absorption and self-centeredness to mask their inner weaker core. Grandiose narcissists, on the other hand, have this total trust on their own greatness; and sometimes, they might be as great as they think of themselves.

If you compare the two types of narcissists grouped by Egan and his colleagues, you will realize that the grandiose narcissists are more emotionally stable, happier, and extroverted. The vulnerable narcissists are less emotionally stable and less agreeable, and they have a high tendency of showing psychopathy.

With this, if you have identified someone for who he or she truly is—a narcissist—and you might be wondering how you can deal with that individual, this part will be helpful to you. However, you should have it at the back of your mind that the only sure way of dealing with a narcissist is to prevent the individual from hurting you, and there is no better way of doing that than walking away.

Techniques for Dealing with a Narcissist

Walking away might sound impossible for some people because of the kind of relationship they have with the narcissist. To dodge the emotional, mental, and physical harm that comes with dealing with a narcissist, the tips below will be of help to you.

Identify the Type of Narcissist You Are Involved With

Before you embark on this journey, you should know that a lot of people have narcissistic tendencies but are not really narcissists. When you know what makes an individual a narcissist, you will be able to deal with them better. See if you have noticed any of these signs:

- Do they have the belief that other people get jealous of them?

- Do they take undue advantage of others when they want to?

- Do you notice the individual attaching too much importance to himself or herself?

- Do they show a little regard for how others feel?

- Do they constantly demand attention and praise from other people?

- Do they always act superior and arrogant to other people?

- Are they obsessed with attaining a lot of power, success, or love without getting satisfied?

Always remember that they are special and different from others, and people who can truly understand them are also special.

Vulnerable narcissists do not really feel good about themselves at heart. Grandiose narcissists, on the other hand, are less open with their emotions, making it difficult for you to realize that they are a stumbling block in your life or that they are trying to undercut you. However, if you are with a narcissist, the grandiose type will be easier to deal with and manage as long as you can get the individual on board with your overall set goals.

Know That a Narcissist Will Always Be One

Narcissists have this great gift of turning on their charm whenever they want to. If care is not taken, you might get drawn into their large promises and ideas. This narcissistic trait can actually make them popular in school or work settings, causing people who do not know their motive to easily fall for them.

Before you fall for this trait and get drawn in, make sure you watch how they treat others when they are not in the spotlight. If at all you catch them manipulating, lying, or disrespecting others, it shows they can also do the same thing to you. No matter what they say to you, know that your needs and wants are not significant to them, and when you try bringing up the issue, you might meet up with resistance.

The first step to take when dealing with individuals with a narcissistic personality is to see them for who they are and know that there is not much that you can change about them.

Expect a Pushback from Them

Individuals with a narcissistic personality will definitely respond if you stand up to them. If you start speaking up and setting boundaries, you should expect them to start making demands on their own.

Break Loose and Stop Focusing on Them

Being with someone with a narcissistic personality means you will have to focus your attention on him or her. Whether it is positive or negative attention, narcissists always succeed in keeping themselves in the spotlight. If you keep buying into their tactics, you will fall victim and realize that you have been pushing aside your needs to focus on them alone.

They derive satisfaction when they get all your time for themselves, so waiting for the time to break free from this bondage of theirs might never come even when you adjust your life just to suit theirs. If you want to deal with narcissists, you should not allow them to rule over you. Gain access to your sense of self and take control of your life. Always know that your needs are important too. Always remind yourself of your goals, strengths, and needs. Remember that it is not your job to take care of them, so break loose from them by taking charge of your life. Get yourself some "me time." Most importantly, take care of yourself.

Chapter 27   Effects of Gaslighting

Remember that you can get away from the abuse, but there are things that can happen if you're not careful, if you continue to stay in the presence of someone who gaslights you, and who abuses you.

What can happen though/ let us talk about what can happen if you continue to suffer at the hands of a gas lighter?

Memory Loss

This is what is so scary about gaslighting. When you experience gaslighting after a while, sometimes you will start to feel so guilty and have a lot of self-doubts that you will tend to forget things that happened. You may not know why it happened, and not remember things that happened between those time periods. Some people will even experience the abuser accusing them of something that happened, but they are unable to actually remember what happened.

Sometimes, what has scary about gaslighting is when you experience that, over a long period of time, you will begin to realize that you cannot remember the exact situations, because your mind and reality is completely skewered. You will start to realize that you cannot remember things that the abuser would accuse you of.

Sometimes, the abuser would accuse you of things that you are doing, but you do not remember doing them, and this, in turn, will lead you to wonder whether or not you did something. You will definitely start to realize this as well when you getaway.

You Feel Constantly Guilty

One-way narcissistic abusers take you down is making you feel guilty constantly. It is not a pity party "oh woe is me" concept, it is more of they will make you feel bad for even existing. That is the problem with narcissistic abusers. They will make sure that you feel guilty, constantly terrible, and you are the one at fault.

Narcissistic abusers will throw jabs at you, telling you how you are nothing. They will also say that you are just worthless, a piece of trash, and you are constantly not allowed to be anything more. That is the problem with many abusers. They will oftentimes make you feel guilty, to the point where depression, even suicidal tendencies start to come up.

Isolation from Help

This is what is scary about narcissistic abusers. Remember, they will claim that you are the one who is crazy, that others are lying, that you are not the one who is right here. They will tell you that you should only believe them, and never anyone else.

Over time, when you are with an abuser like this, you can develop a Stockholm syndrome, where you know that you need to get away, but you cannot. you isolate yourself from help, and oftentimes, even after you get out, you cannot really get the help that you need.

That is because you do not trust other people. They are all liars, remember? Your abuser would tell you that, and even if you have managed to leave, that can hang around in your head.

Self-Doubt

Self-doubt stems from how you were treated by your gas lighters. The goal of those who gaslight is to make the other person feel worthless like their own thoughts and reality do not matter. Sometimes, those who have been gaslighted will hallucinate, and sometimes they will see things that are not there in order to make the gaslighted happy.

But the self-doubt extends past that. When someone who has been gaslighted all their lives finally leaves, they are often scared of what is next. They have been living with the reality of their abuser for so long that they do not know how to wrench themselves away.

This causes self-doubt. It is the doubt of oneself, the doubt of what is really out there and the doubt of their own reality.

Social Life Issues

Sometimes, gaslighting does affect your social life. The abuser will try their very hardest to keep the one who is gaslighted away from their friends, or even family too. The constant lying and saying they are bad people will happen. Lots of times, those who have suffered from gaslighting might end up never seeing their family until years down the road. This is something that can happen for a very long time.

What is scary as well, is that the person might end up completely isolating themselves from anyone, only relying on the abuser and nothing else. It can make the person feel like they are not capable of being loved, and also make the person feel like they are not stable, which is the scariest part about it.

Difficulty Making Decisions

Decision Making was done all from the abuser, and not very much from the person who was gaslighted. So, if you have experienced a bit of hesitation in decisions and have a history of abuse, you can probably thank gaslighting for that.

Decisions were left to the other person, and whenever you did make decisions, it was oftentimes seen as wrong, or incorrect to do. So why make decisions then?

That is why many, who have suffered from gaslighting in the past, can doubt the decisions that they make, from there, may not believe what they are doing is right.

The Mental Health Side

There is also the mental health side of the effects of gaslighting. We did go over anxiety, but that is due to the confusion that the person makes the one who is being gaslit feel. The one who is being gaslit oftentimes does not know what is right and wrong, and they fear to do things. This can be a small occurrence, or this can be a major issue in their life that does need to be assessed.

The one who is suffering from being gaslit may also feel a lot of hopelessness, along with self-esteem issues. This can also lead to depression, and oftentimes, people who are survivors of this still feel like life is hopeless, that their feelings do not matter, and that they should never talk about it.

A Refusal to Show Emotions

This is a big one. This is due to the fact that survivors will always be on guard, always looking for the manipulation that is in any situation. Oftentimes, this can lead to people not trusting themselves, or trusting others either, or people do describe those who have suffered from this as always on guard.

They refuse to be vulnerable, for a good reason. They do not want to be hurt like that again. However, the problem with that, while it's a notable reason, it can be a problem for some people, since they'll refuse to show manipulation to the point where future relationships are stained, and they may have trouble holding a relationship because of this.

People Pleasing

On the other side of the coin, some people will become validation hungry after they have been abused for so long. That is due to the fact that they have been forced to experience this for so long that they do not know how to do anything else but look for validation, although it may not be in the healthiest of ways.

People-pleasing is not a good trait to have. It can make them outright refuse to change certain behaviors because they know that it pleases others. They might be seen as attention-seeking, and they will try to keep others around, even if it means sacrificing a little bit of themselves in the process.

Chapter 28   Signs to Understand If You Are Manipulated with Gaslighting

The problem with manipulation is that it is usually silent, and the person being manipulated often does not recognize it until a later date, perhaps until it is too late. In some cases, you might think that something isn't right, you might have an inkling that something is going on, but as soon as you begin to explore that idea in your mind, the manipulator spots the signs and goes back to his or her charming self.

That is the problem with a manipulator, they are almost like a chameleon, shifting skins to suit the situation and to make you think they are wonderful and loving when underneath it all they're exerting control in extremely underhanded and damaging ways.

Gaslighting is a very commonly used manipulation tactic. For that reason, we will not go into too much detail here, but gaslighting will make you feel like you do not know the truth. You question your own sanity, with part of you thinking you are right, but the manipulator using master tactics to cause enough doubt to throw you off course. As a result, you go around and around in circles, never really understanding whether it is you are imagining things or not.

Put simply, manipulation feels like extreme confusion. Manipulation can often be seen by those around you, e.g. a friend or family member has likely tried to warn you about what is going on, but you cannot see it. This is because they are not the ones being manipulated. They can see the change in you, they can see how your personality is dampening down, you are becoming quieter, you are spending less and less time with them, and you are moving ever close to the manipulator.

The problem is the person being manipulated is often so desperate to avoid thinking about it that they will convince themselves their friend or family member is lying. This can lead to further alienation away from their original support circle, completely playing into the hands of the manipulator.

This is a hugely common situation and one which often plays a part in a manipulative situation. It is also likely that the manipulator will tell the victim that the person is trying to cause trouble, perhaps they are jealous, and they do not want them to be happy. All of this is a tactic to alienate the victim away from those who care about them, and who may otherwise give them the strength to walk away. That means they are far more likely to stay within the manipulator's grasp.

What you have to realize is that anyone who uses manipulative tactics in a relationship or friendship is doing so because they have extremely low levels of self-worth and self-confidence. You might think from reading some of the advice that a manipulator is simply a very evil person, but it is often not quite that cut and dry.

Of course, someone who uses such tactics is not a particularly pleasant person to be around, but there are usually deeper issues at play, which cause them to use the tactics they use. This low self-worth and self-confidence push them to do anything to keep their partner in their lives, and they panic whenever any situation or person crops up who may pose a risk.

This may not be a realistic risk, but in their mind, it is something which could take their partner away from them. By using manipulation, they eliminate the risk at source, causing the victims to move closer to them, and twisting the whole situation in the mind of the victim.

It is messy, it is damaging, and it is deceiving, but ultimately, it is extremely effective.

Why is Psychological and Emotional Manipulation so Damaging?

When someone breaks their leg, you can see the damage. They have a plaster cast on their leg, and they are wincing in pain every time they move. They are given sympathy because of the visible wound.

When someone is injured physically by a partner, perhaps they have a black eye, you can see the wound once more. The fact you can see this abusive action makes it shocking, simply because it is there in front of you. You cannot hide from it, you cannot pretend it is not happening, and as a result, many people assume that physical abuse is the worst type of abuse.

117

That is not true.

Whilst we are not playing down the seriousness of physical abuse, we never assume that emotional and psychological abuse is less serious. In some ways, it is more serious because the effects are long-lasting, complex, and hidden away from everyone. Of course, physical abuse causes psychological effects too, but a slow-building emotional type of abuse is so invisible to the world, someone you work with, a friend, or a person you sit next to on the bus could be suffering at the hands of a manipulator and you would never guess. That is a shocking thought.

Psychological and emotional abuse is something you carry around with you for a very long time after the situation is over. Even if you find the strength to break away, and we pray that you do, the effects will still be in your mind for a while to come. Many victims require professional therapy, to extract the situation from their mind, unpick it, and see it for what it truly is - abuse.

This type of abuse also causes the victim to question every single thing in their life, even after the abuse is over. It is like a wound which does not quite heal properly; it slowly fades, but it leaves a scar, and occasionally that scar itches to remind you of its presence, usually at the strangest of moments.

Post-traumatic stress disorder, PTSD, is a very common condition after emotional abuse. This is something that can be treated and managed with professional help, but it is a very distressing thing to go through. Small events which occur in life can trigger memories of the past abuse, taking the victim back in time, almost to that very moment.

From these examples, you can understand why psychological and emotional abuse is so damaging. The mind is a complex thing and being able to understand what is going on in your life is a basic part of happiness. When you cannot unpick the details and see things, when you are constantly questioning yourself, being knocked down with remarks and negativity, life becomes very dark indeed. In the very worst cases, this type of abuse leads to extreme anxiety and depression, possibly leading to suicidal thoughts and actions.

For that reason, understanding the signs, finding the strength within, gaining support from those around you, and getting out of the situation, is the most important thing you will ever do with your life. It is also the bravest thing you will ever do, and probably the hardest too.

Chapter 29 Disarming the Narcissist during Gaslighting and Taking Control of the Situation

Depending on your situation, you may or may not be able to leave the toxic situation that occurs by being around a narcissist that uses gaslighting techniques. If you are simply friends or in a relationship with someone who is a narcissist, you will absolutely have the opportunity to walk away; however, if one of your parents or your caretaker is a narcissist that uses gaslighting tactics, it is less likely that you can simply walk away from them. This is especially true if you are not of legal age to go off on your own.

Learning how to take control of the situation and disarm the narcissistic abuser in your life gives you a better chance at maintaining a grip on reality and continuing to have a positive look at your self-worth. Learning these skills can make a difference in leading a happy and healthy life or living one that is a total nightmare. It can be hard to take control of the situation, especially if the gaslighting techniques and other manipulative patterns have been being used for an exceptionally long period of time.

In this chapter, we are going to look at a variety of different ways that you can disarm the narcissist in your life. These tactics will allow you to take control of yourself and your situation. It can ensure that you do not succumb to the negative repercussions that are caused by gaslighting. Not every one of these tactics will work in every situation; however, when you implement them, it is certainly going to help improve your awful situation with your narcissistic gas lighter.

You must understand that it is more than likely you will not be able to actually change the behaviors of the narcissist. Instead, you should focus on keeping yourself protected from the chaos that they like to cause in your life. When you realize what you are up against, you can then implement different strategies to combat the abuse that narcissists cause.

A great way to take control back for yourself is to disengage. Never allow your narcissist's bad behaviors to force you into engagement with them. You cannot reason with someone who is unreasonable. Instead of engaging, take the time to think about what you can control in the situation and focus on that. A narcissist will only be able to comprehend their wrongdoings when their counterpart refuses to accept their behaviors.

When you refuse to accept the narcissistic behaviors of any person in your life, it is likely that you will witness them going through a variety of different personality characteristics. From moment to moment, the narcissist will try and change their tactics. They will move from there charismatic self to the more aggressive and daunting version. This can happen in a split 2nd. They work through these different personalities to try and get some sort of reaction out of you, and the best thing you can do is to simply not engage. They are baiting you in, and you do not need to bite.

Another thing you can do to regain control and stop some of the narcissistic behaviors and gaslighting techniques of your partner is to set clear boundaries. Taking the time to figure out what your boundaries are in laying them out clearly to the narcissist in your life is advantageous. In fact, it works best if you write them down so that both parties have a copy that can easily be seen and reinforced.

At one point or another, it is guaranteed that the narcissist will crossover your boundaries. You need to send them a warning immediately so that they understand that lines have been crossed, and you will not put up with it. If you have set a consequence to crossing boundaries and they do it more than once do not offer them a warning, simply implement the consequence that you laid out to them.

It is imperative that if you set consequences for actions that you are willing to follow through with them. When you are trying to be strong and take control of the situation, you have to adhere to the boundaries that you set. How quickly you take action to protect yourself plays a major role, and the ability to follow through an even bigger one. If you are constantly bluffing, the narcissist will realize it and regain control of you and the relationship.

Another great way to disarm the narcissist in your life is to remove the words "that's fair" and "I'm sorry" from your vernacular. Someone that has narcissistic tendencies will not understand the concept of fair. When you use that word, they take it as they are winning. So, if you refuse to use the word and you are able to disengage, they will not feel as if they are in a constant state of control.

There are a variety of different reasons to stop saying I am sorry when you are dealing with a narcissist. When a narcissist hears an apology, it enforces their idea that they are perfect. Additionally, it helps them solidify the fact that you are always wrong. Attempting to reason with a narcissist or align your patterns of thinking through apologies is never going to work. So, stop saying you are sorry when realistically you have done nothing wrong.

Another thing you can do to maintain control of yourself and your wellbeing while in a narcissistic relationship is to accept the fact that you are not going to be able to change them. You do not need to accept their negative behaviors, but you do need to have an understanding that their ability to change is extremely small. You also need to accept that they are playing a game, and it is a game you can never win. By trying to outsmart them or get the upper hand, you will likely be adding gasoline to the fire. Simply accepting that they are who they are can give you the protection you need to remember your self-worth and the important role you play in this world.

There are a variety of different situations that will require you to continue maintaining a relationship with a narcissist. When you can accept that they have a psychological disorder and you can see the techniques they try to use to manipulate you, you will be much better off.

You are more apt to stand up for yourself by disengaging instead of feeding into old habits and patterns that enabled the narcissist to abuse you in the first place.

Another way to take control back for yourself and disarm the narcissistic person in your life is too respond to them the exact same way every time they exhibit unacceptable behaviors. When you do not feed into their lies and manipulation, they will eventually get bored with you and decide that they want to move on. When the narcissist decides to leave, it can be much easier than if the victim decides that they want to leave. By setting boundaries and being in control of our emotions, we will be able to disengage and respond consistently to the narcissistic abuser in our life. This will do an excellent job of disarming them and allowing you to control yourself, your future, and your happiness.

When you are trying to stay in control and disarm a narcissist, it is extremely important that you do not feed into their ego. Narcissists feel that they are more impressive than everyone else. They hold themselves on a pedestal that is almost impossible to knock them down from. When you offer verbal praise to a narcissist, it feeds his personal sense of grandeur. Instead of hearing what you are saying and taking it as praise, a narcissist is simply hearing how much better they are than you.

Unfortunately, when you praise a narcissist, it is likely that they are going to use your compliments to attack you and your person later. Narcissists, especially those that use gaslighting tactics, love to take the things that you say and twist them around to keep you confused. It is surprising that they would be able to use compliments and praise this way, but it is frequently seen, which is another reason you should avoid feeding the ego of a narcissist.

Gaslighting's narcissists love to try and put the responsibility for their negative emotions in their victim's hands. One way to maintain control of the situation and disarm the narcissist is by refusing to take accountability for their emotions. Oftentimes, people think that it is just easier to accept blame as it gets the narcissist to stop attacking; however, this is untrue. Realistically doing this is going to cause emotional harm to the person that is taking the blame.

When you continuously take the blame for a narcissist's negative emotions, eventually, it is going to take a toll. More often than not, this acceptance of blame will lead to the victim doing anything and everything the narcissist wants to ensure that they are not causing any negative emotions.

It is impossible to please the narcissist so, instead of taking responsibility for their emotions to allow them to work through them on their own without taking the blame.

While you should absolutely set boundaries, do be careful of using ultimatums. Realistically, no relationship should include the use of ultimatums as it is extremely controlling and degrading. Narcissists are known to use ultimatums frequently. If you decide to do the same thing, you are sinking to the level of the narcissist and maybe becoming just as toxic as they are. Taking the time to think about your actions and your words will ensure that you are not stooping to their level. When you do stoop to their level, the narcissist feels entitled to continue treating you negatively.

Chapter 30   How to Deal with the Effects of Gaslighting

Emotional abuse is always a traumatic experience. Recovering from emotional abuse means, first of all, starting to process it has undermined self-esteem. For that, you should avoid blaming yourself because who has trusted the other and gave everything for the relationship, has hardly done anything wrong in this sense. Rather, the blame should be sought on the person who has lied and manipulated and emotionally abused their partner.

Ending a relationship is never easy. Often enough, one cannot even say exactly why one did not draw a line promptly. Questions such as "why have I been so blind and have not left him before long?"

"The way is to calm the mind and make it realistic to look at oneself. A mature, balanced mind that learns to lose; a humble but not stunned spirit. A spirit that is open to the world, powerful and down-to-earth. "

Walter Riso

It is not that easy. Emotional abuse is rarely recognizable at first glance. After all, he is very subtle, but at the same time sophisticated. One should not underestimate the influence of love. He who loves is stubborn, trusts his partner and sticks to him. Therefore, emotional abuse is not visible to the naked eye. Even if you have already noticed it, you are still trying to hide potential doubts about the partner.

Sooner or later you cannot close your eyes and your heart to reality. At the latest, when you have the feeling that you no longer recognize your own reflection, it is time to act. After all, no one wants to end up as a shadow of himself.

Not everyone gets the chance to recover from emotional abuse

Emotional abuse is like an addiction. You are trapped in a cycle of punishments and rewards. In some moments you get a lot of attention and affection. At the same time, the partner is very passionate and makes a small present. However, this behavior can suddenly change, and you are rejected, blamed with reproaches and punished with disrespect.

125

Rewards and punishments are part of an endless chain that, as long as you do not free yourself, is always held by the offender. It is not easy to break away from her. One may even believe that even ending the relationship would not put an end to one's own suffering.

Many of those whose relationships are characterized by emotional abuse and who choose to leave their partner believe that this bold move should all be over. They believe that they have overcome their low point and now everything would be better. But that is not always the case.

Signs that you have not yet overcome your harmful relationship

- Guilt. One is angry that one did not recognize the emotional abuse prior and spent too much time with a person who only harmed one.

- The feeling of guilt mingles with anger. You accumulate so many negative feelings that you finally project them onto others.

- You become suspicious.

- In times of euphoria and zest for action, there are moments when you are completely exhausted and have no energy at all.

- Self-image and self-esteem are still damaged.

- Positive feelings are no longer experienced in the same way as before. You feel like you are stunned.

Emotional abuse and how to recover from it

As indicated at the beginning, it is good to reinterpret your own role. In this way, one can manage to recover from the emotional abuse by the partner, so that it no longer shapes the self-image. One should set aside guilt feelings along with that helplessness in order to regain the old self-esteem.

The following strategies can help.

Concentrate on yourself, be brave and take your life into your hands

You are not a victim but a courageous person who has to recover from a traumatic past. To do this, one should try to focus on the moment. To make life in the hand, after all, one is responsible for it. To free oneself from feelings of guilt and regain control over his actions.

Keep calm

To recover from emotional abuse means to learn to be responsible for yourself in this new phase of life. Anyone who dares to take this step may well be scared. However, this feeling should not prevail.

The healing of the wounds takes time. One may take some time to recover. After all, every process follows its own rhythm. If you accept his feelings, you will gradually regain control.

Control the reality positively

After a relationship marked by emotional abuse, it is common for one to congest his anger. You see yourself in a negative way because you are angry with yourself. In order not to lose yourself in negative thoughts, it is important to develop positive feelings.

- If you feel anger, you should seek the reason to break away from it.

- If you feel lonely, you can start a conversation with other people. It can also help to look for like-minded people who have experienced something similar.

- If you realize that there is no progress, that every attempt leads back to the starting point and you feel helpless, you should ask for professional help.

Emotional abuse should not be allowed to determine one's own life. You have to find a constructive approach where you can count on yourself as well as your personal environment. With the necessary support, the path to the old way of life is easier.

Anyone can break free from the cycle of emotional abuse. Maybe you will not always survive this process unharmed. However, building a resilient and dignified image of oneself can make you emerge stronger from a harmful relationship.

Chapter 31   The Correct Mindset to Use in This Situation

Most of our personality traits are carried from childhood. This is because the brain grows most in our formative years before the age of eight. That means that the connections that brain cells make in childhood remain with us all the way into adulthood and determine the personality traits we develop.

Most of the co-dependency tendencies you exhibit can be traced back to childhood experiences. Children who had to live with dysfunction will often develop codependency as a coping mechanism to help them deal with their environment. Unfortunately even after you are no longer in the dysfunctional situation, the codependent traits remain part of your personality.

So how do you get past the hand that fate dealt you? After all, you did not choose what kind of situation you were born into so should not you be free to break the hold your past has on your emotions and personality traits? Like everything else permanent change takes time and a willingness to confront your past.

Most codependents who were scarred by their childhood will bury the unpleasant experiences in an attempt to forget them. Unfortunately, all this does is leave you with unresolved issues. To be free of your past, you must be willing to acknowledge it and the role it has played in your life. Only then will you be able to really let it go and move on with your life.

Do not be afraid to seek help in the form of therapy or support groups to help you deal with codependency tendencies that are tied to your past. Therapy gives you a safe space to confront your inner demons and resolve them. It may not work overnight, but you will find that facing your past will slowly start to unburden you of emotional baggage that you have carried with you for years.

Ultimately, you can choose to not leave your outcomes up to fate by denying your past power over your future. Start by building your self-awareness using the techniques. Once you have identified where your codependency issues stem from, the next step is to seek help and start your journey to recovery.

EFT Therapy Techniques; Restore Broken Relationships

Codependent relationships typically cause a lot of emotional and psychological damage. Whether you are an enabler, caretaker, a rescuer or any other type of codependent, you will find that the effect of codependency leaves a lot of emotional damage in its wake.

Recovering from codependency is one thing but you also need to heal and repair your broken relationships. This is because not every codependent relationship ends with you cutting off the other person from your life completely. This means that you need to find a way to restore the broken relationship to a functional and healthy level. One of the most effective ways to do this is by using EFT therapy.

EFT refers to emotionally focused therapy. It is only natural that one of the most effective therapies for healing codependent relationships targets your emotional health. This is because emotions are the driving forces behind most relationships.

EFT therapy techniques focus on resolving issues in unhealthy relationships and restoring broken relationships. EFT is designed to help improve the nature of emotional attachment and connection in relationships. It is intended as a means through which the bonding and attachment processes that make up our relationships can be repaired and restored.

By using EFT therapy, couples are able to recognize their emotional responses as well as those of their partners. This helps them to not only identify the patterns that cause a relationship to break down, but it also builds intimacy and fosters strong bonds. The aim of this process is to help re-establish the emotional connection in relationships that had broken down.

EFT therapy uses a combination of the principles of attachment theory and person-centric therapy. It fosters reconciliation and mending of relationships by helping the two parties in a broken relationship to understand the role of their emotional reactions in the health of the relationship.

In EFT therapy, the main premise is that most problems that arise in relationships are due to codependency fears such as the fear of abandonment. This type of fear hinders an individual's ability to form healthy attachments to other people. The person then becomes emotionally unavailable which only leads to a breakdown in the relationship.

By restoring the ability of couples to meet each other's emotional needs, EFT therapy helps to foster healthy attachment between two people and mend broken unions. EFT therapy covers a wide range of issues that are common causes of conflict in relationships and teaches couples how to de-escalate conflict, address deeper feelings and uncover underlying issues that may lead to codependent tendencies.

Emotionally Focused Therapy occurs in different stages that are designed to address the emotional distress in relationships.

These are the key stages involved in EFT therapy.

1. De-escalation.

This step is intended to help couples identify the key areas of conflict in their relationship. It involves figuring out how negative emotions interfere with conflict resolution and hinder you from solving the issue amicably.

In this stage, the therapist will highlight your underlying issues and help you to see how reframing the conflict and looking at it from a different perspective can help to resolve it.

2. Altering interaction patterns

From de-escalation, EFT therapy moves on to altering or changing negative patterns of interaction between the two people in a relationship. Most relationships will breakdown due to negative interaction patterns such as blaming, shaming or controlling behavior.

Once a couple is able to successfully change from negative interactions to healthier ways of bonding, they have a better chance of restoring a broken relationship. In this stage, EFT focuses on teaching the partners to recognize and be mindful of each other's needs and emotions.

3. Consolidation and integration

The final stage of emotionally focused therapy revolves around developing new communication skills and interaction patterns. This is aimed at building healthy modes of interaction through open and honest communication.

The aim here is for the couple to change from old and dysfunctional ways of communication to healthier interaction patterns. Once these changes are successfully implemented, the broken-down relationship has a chance of becoming a healthy relationship that is free of codependency.

The Gift of Goodbye

Letting go is never easy. We like the comfort of the familiar and love to love what we have always known. However, sometimes goodbye is the best gift you can give yourself. The gift of goodbye is giving yourself permission to walk away from things that keep dragging you back and slowing down your progress.

A simple analogy that is used to elaborate on the importance of letting go is that of a boy who is trying to get some candy from his father. His arms are outstretched but he cannot take the candy because there is something else already in his palm. His father tells him, that if he wants the candy, the only way to get it is to empty his palms first.

At first, the boy is reluctant because he wants both what is already in his hand and the candy his father is offering him. Eventually, he comes to the realization that his hands can only hold so much so he has to choose one or the other. He drops whatever he was holding, and his father places the candy in his now empty palm.

This simple illustration just goes to show that we can only hold so much in terms of emotions within us. At some point, you have to spring clean and make room for better experiences. Yes, it may be scary but if you are unwilling to let go of the past you will never be ready for a new future.

If you are healing from codependency, there are plenty of old hurts and scars that got you where you were. Now that you have chosen the path to recovery, it is time to release your past and make room for the future. Sad as it may be, some relationships cannot be healed and the only way to move on from them is to have the courage to let them go.

Goodbye is not just about saying goodbye to relationships, it involves letting go of habits that drag you down, toxic values and self-destructive beliefs. At this point here, you have already self-analyzed and identified the toxic bits in your life and the strengths that will take you forward.

Shed the toxicity and the emotional baggage and prepare for a better future that is not bogged down by your past. Letting go is a gradual process, it is not something you can do overnight. However once you have made the first step, the rest will be easier, and you will find it easy to embrace the positive change in your life.

Effective strategies for letting go of emotional baggage

1. Identify your unresolved issues

This may be uncomfortable but be brutally honest with yourself. In most cases you will find that you already know what your main issues are, we just find it easy to camouflage or deny that they exist. List them all in order from the most prevalent followed by the not so major ones.

These could be things that happened in the past, like bullying in school or things that are happening in the present like being overweight or a bad relationship. Whatever the issue is, pick something that you realize your life would be better without.

List them down clearly in one column.

2. Who is to blame?

Look at the issues you have listed. Who is responsible for each of them? Do you blame yourself, a parent, your spouse? Whoever it is, mark the name next to the issue connected to that person. If you blame yourself, that is also okay, put your name down for the issues you feel you are responsible for.

3. What is the consequence?

You now have an unresolved issue and the responsible party; the next step is to answer what has the unresolved issue done to your life. Do you have low self-esteem, as a result, have you had bad relationships, as a result, are you chronically stressed?

Whatever the answer is, note it down next to the issue so that you can clearly see the unresolved issue, the responsible party and the consequence it has had on your life.

4. What opportunity are you missing out on?

What impact has the unresolved issue had on your life? Did you lose a job? Do you have a hard time having meaningful relationships? Whatever the unresolved issue has cost you, note it down. It could be one or multiple opportunities.

5. The fix

Now that you have a clear path from what the issue is and what it is costing you, what can you do to fix it? Does it involve forgiving the person and mending the relationship? Do you need to forgive yourself and let go of the past? Do you need to walk away from a toxic relationship?

At this point the solution should be clear; all you need is the courage to make the decision.

Chapter 32   Practical Tips to Understand If You Are Effectively the Victim of Gaslighting

The signs of gaslighting can be hard to see, especially for the person that is being manipulated by this tactic. Obviously, the effects of gaslighting are extremely detrimental. So, if you can recognize the signs of it as it is happening, it gives you an advantage and the possibility of getting out of this toxic situation before it completely destroys you and your life.

Oftentimes, people that care about you will recognize the signs before you will be able to. They may try and talk to you about the issues that they are seeing, but you may not be willing to hear them if the effects of gaslighting have already taken hold.

When someone you trust or once felt that you could trust comes to you and expresses their concern over signs of gaslighting, you should spend time reflecting on what they have to say to ensure that you are not a victim of this horrific abuse

In this chapter, we are going to discuss a variety of different signs that you may witness if you are being gaslighted. Becoming a victim of gaslighting can impact your life negatively in every way. By looking over the following signs, it may become easier to understand what is going on, which can, in turn, give you the clarity and confidence to remove yourself from your current situation.

If you find yourself doubting your own emotions, you may be experiencing the repercussion of gaslighting. Oftentimes people will try to convince themselves that things really are not so bad. They will assume they are simply too sensitive and that what they are seeing as reality is tragically skewed from actual reality. If you have never had an issue with doubting your feelings, it can be a very good sign of gaslighting tactics.

Alongside doubting, your emotions will come doubting your perceptions of the events that unfold in front of you, as well as doubting your own personal judgment.

Many people that are being manipulated by gaslighting will be afraid to stand up for themselves and express their emotions. This is due to the fact that when they do the gaslighting narcissist makes them feel bad or inferior for doing so. If you find that you are choosing silence over communication, it is a pretty good sign that gaslighting is present in your relationship.

At one point or another, we will all feel vulnerable or insecure. These are normal feelings; however, if you are in a situation of gaslighting, you will feel this way consistently. You may always feel like you need to tiptoe around your partner, family member, or friend to ensure that they do not have a negative outburst. Additionally, you will start to believe that you are the one causing problems for them instead of the reverse.

The gaslighting narcissist will do their best to sever ties between you and the people that you care about. This can leave the victim feeling powerless and completely alone. The narcissist will convince their victim that the people around them do not actually care. In fact, they will try to convince the victim that everyone thinks that they are crazy, unstable, or flat out insane. These kinds of comments make the victim feel trapped. It also causes them to distance themselves from the people that do actually care, which, intern, makes them in even less control than before.

Another sign that you are in the grips of the abuse that comes from a narcissistic gas lighter is feeling that you are crazy or stupid. The narcissist will use a variety of different words and phrases to make you question your own value. This can become extreme to the point that the victim may start repeating these derogatory comments. The sooner you can see the sign of verbal abuse, the sooner you will be able to make the decision to not let it deconstruct your sense of self-worth.

The gaslighting narcissist will do their best to change your perception of yourself. Let us say that you have always thought of yourself as a strong and assertive person, yet all of a sudden, you realize that your behaviors are passive and weak. This extreme change of behavior is a good sign that you are succumbing to gaslighting tactics. When you are grounded in who you really are and what your belief system stands for, it will be harder for the narcissistic gas lighter to get you to be disappointed in yourself. When you can recognize that the viewpoint of your worth has changed, it can give you the motivation to take back control of your own life.

Confusion is one of the narcissistic gas lighter's favorite tools. They will say one thing one day and then do something completely opposite the following day. The result of these types of actions is extreme confusion.

The behaviors of a narcissistic gas lighter will never be consistent. They will always try to keep you on your toes so that you are in a constant state of anxious confusion. This gives them more control. Finding that your partner, family member, or friend is exceptionally inconsistent with their behaviors should clue you in to the fact that you are likely in a toxic relationship with them.

If your friend, partner, or family member teases you or puts you down in a hurtful way too, then minimalize the fact that your feelings are hurt. It is a surefire sign of gaslighting. By telling you that you are too sensitive or that you need to learn how to take a joke, they are brushing your hurt feelings to the side. Someone who truly cares about you, even if teasing, will take the time to acknowledge the fact that they hurt your feelings. If you are constantly being questioned about how sensitive you are, be aware you could be succumbing to the abuse of gaslighting.

Another sign that narcissistic gaslighting is occurring is when you constantly feel that something awful is about to happen. This sense of impending doom starts to manifest early on in gaslighting situations. Many people do not understand why they feel threatened whenever they are around a certain person, but after further investigation and getting away from the narcissist, they understand it completely.

Gut feelings should always be listened to, so if your body is telling you that something is not right between you and another person, you should remove yourself from the situation before things get terribly out of control.

There are always times in our lives that we owe other people apologies; however, when you are in a gaslighting situation, you will spend a plethora of time apologizing to people. You will feel the need to say I am sorry regardless of if you have done anything wrong or not. You may really be apologizing for simply being there. When we question who we are and our value. It leads us to apologize profusely. If you notice how much you are saying, I am sorry is increasing, and the things you are saying sorry for are minimal; you may be in a gaslighting situation.

Second-guessing yourself or constant feelings of inadequacy when you are with your narcissistic partner, family member, or a friend are excellent signs that they are gaslighting you. If no matter what you do, it is never good enough, you should be aware that you may be being manipulated.

When it comes to 2nd guessing yourself, we are not just talking about second-guessing your decisions but second-guessing things like your memories.

You may wonder if you are actually remembering things as they happened because your narcissistic abuser constantly tells you differently. If you have never had a problem recreating and discussing your memories and all of a sudden you are trying to figure out whether or not what you are saying is true you may want to take a closer look at the person you are dealing with instead of looking at yourself.

Another sign that you are succumbing to the powers of gaslighting is functioning under the assumption that everyone you come into contact with is disappointed in you in one way or another. Constant feelings that you are messing things up are daunting and unrealistic; however, it is amazing how many people do not recognize when this is happening. They simply start to apologize all of the time and assume that no matter what they do, they will make a mess of things, which will lead to others being disappointed in them.

When someone that you are in close contact with makes you feel as if there is something wrong with you, it could also be a sign of gaslighting. We are not talking about physical ailments; we are talking about feeling as if you have fundamental issues. You may sit and contemplate your sanity and reality. Unless these were problems for you prior to entering into a new relationship, you should definitely pay attention to the sign.

Gaslighting can also make it extremely difficult for you to make decisions. Where you once made solid choices for yourself, you now have a sense of distrust in your judgment. This can make decision making extremely difficult. Instead of making your own choices, many victims will allow their narcissistic abusers to make their decisions for them. The other alternative is not making any decisions at all. Obviously, this could have extremely negative impacts on a person's life.

Chapter 33 Conclusion

In conclusion, here are a few common tips to help counter manipulation ad gaslighting:

Build Self-Awareness

One of the most significant reasons for many of us to become a victim of manipulation is that we cannot identify with ourselves. We have little or no idea about what is going on in our lives. We do not know what we want and simply drift along without a purpose.

Then, someone walks into our life, and inexplicably we take on their purpose as ours. If the person genuinely cares for us, then he or she will help us understand ourselves better. However, if the person is looking for a victim to manipulate and control, then we get stuck in the mire. Here are some reasons as to why building self-awareness is a critical tool to avoid being gaslighted:

Self-awareness develops your emotional intelligence - The more aware you are of yourself, your emotions, and how you react to them, the easier it is for you to preempt negative situations and work out ways to either avoid them or fight them. With a well-developed emotional setup, it becomes easy to identify manipulators and signs of manipulative tactics. In fact, with repeated practice, the power of your gut instincts improves considerably helping you recognize negative vibes that you might be getting from pretending charmers.

Self-awareness builds consciousness - You can act consciously and make intentional and informed decisions regarding all aspects of your life. You will be able to look at everything happening in your life objectively and rationally empowering you to see things lying underneath the facades that people are putting up to fool you.

Interestingly, despite knowing the importance of self-awareness, most of us find it difficult to become self-aware. The reason for that is that we are not taught to be present 'in the moment' and observe everything around us and within us, objectively and without judgment. We are all trained to react and respond to situations quickly (as it is considered efficient to act quickly), and therefore, we end up doing things impulsively. We do not give ourselves time to observe and imbibe the events and feelings in our lives and end up living like an automaton.

In fact, manipulators are more self-aware than the average person on the street because he or she needs it to survive and thrive in the world through control and manipulation. Therefore, building self-awareness helps you counter manipulators in a better way than otherwise.

Tips to build self-awareness - So, how does one increase self-awareness? Here are some suggestions that you can use. Practice if you want to get the full benefits of self-awareness.

Create some space and time for yourself - Regardless of how busy you are, you must make it mandatory to find some space and time when you can be with no one but yourself. Keep away from devices and their interrupting notifications. Just start with five minutes each day and do nothing but sit quietly and observe your thoughts. Do not react or respond to them. Simply watch your thoughts and follow them one at a time. You will notice that each thought increases intensity, reaches a peak, and slowly fades away to give way to the next thought, which goes through the same routine.

Every thought brings feelings too. Connect with the emotions of each thought. If your mind is on last year's family holiday, you could feel happy remembering it. Again, do not react. Simply watch your emotions, which also follow the path of the thought. They increase in intensity in proportion to the thought and ebb away as the thought fades.

Do this exercise on a daily basis. Initially, it is going to be frustrating because our thoughts are quite random. However, if you focus and practice every day, you will find it increasingly easy to hold a thought and stay with it until it fades away into oblivion.

Practice mindfulness - Mindfulness is the art of being 'at the moment' fully and completely engaged with your current activity. Mindfulness calls for complete immersion in the task you are doing. Do you think you are mindful? Here is an example of telling you that mindfulness has to be practiced and does not come naturally until you make it a habit in your life.

Keep a journal - Writing down your thoughts is one of the best ways to know what you are thinking and feeling. In a manipulative state, the more you write down your ideas and beliefs, the easier it gets to differentiate between imagination and reality. This power to differentiate gives you the strength to handle manipulation and use measures to counter it.

Build Self-Confidence

What is self-confidence? It is the ability to know your strengths and weaknesses with regard to the environment you are in so that you can leverage the advantages available to you at that point in time. Self-confidence is founded on self-belief, where you believe in your strength to do the things that are best for you. So, the more self-confident you are, the less likely you will be to fall prey to a manipulator's whims. Here are some recommendations you can use to build self-confidence:

Visualize yourself as being confident - Your mind is a powerful tool that can help you achieve your dreams. When you visualize yourself as being confident and strong, then your subconscious mind drives your body to achieve what you have dreamed. Low confidence is rooted in our belief that we are worthless and useless. Change this idea in your mind and gather the courage to convert it into reality.

Use confidence-building affirmations - Affirmations are excellent to 'install' thoughts into your heart and mind. When you say you are no good, then you begin to believe in your words. When you repeatedly say that you are good enough for yourself, then you begin to believe in these words. Therefore, use positive words about your self-image and repeat them as often as you can. Here are a few examples:

Enhance Your Friends' Circle

Human beings are social animals, and we need people to talk to and communicate with to survive. In times of need, it is people we reach out to, right? The larger your circle of friends, the more people you can seek help from. When you are under the mercy of a manipulator, you need multiple perspectives so that you can opt for the optimal solution. And for this, you need a lot of people who can give you numerous perspectives.

141

Additionally, a large circle of friends is a great deterrent to manipulators because they prefer to work on lonely people. Here are more advantages to having a healthy number of friends in your life:

Take Time-Outs Regularly

If you do not take regular breaks from your hectic pace of life, you are likely to be filled with resentment which, in turn, will lead you to become depressed, anxious, and unhappy, a perfect target for manipulators. You must always strive to be happy and to do that; you must find ways to unwind regularly.

Do the things you love during these breaks. Stay away from electronic devices that keep disturbing you. Connect with yourself when you take your breaks. You will return refreshed and rejuvenated ready to take on the challenges of the world. Breaks give you the opportunity to reflect on your life and find gaps that need filling up.

Reach Out for Help

It is almost impossible to live alone in this world. Being social animals, we constantly need to connect with other people, which not only keep you happy and energized but also help to get a different perspective of your life. Additionally, there are people out there who are capable of helping you out in times of need. All that is needed is to ask for help. Do not hesitate to do so.

Seeking help when in trouble is the wisest thing you can do because being a victim of manipulation can take its toll on your ability to think straight, and you need a professional or a trusted person to help you see things in the right perspective.

Manipulation Countering Techniques in Relationships

Other than the above common elements that help in building a strong character, here are some tips that will help you manage manipulation in different aspects of your life. Here, we deal with manipulation counter techniques in relationships, at the workplace, and in the family. So, let us start with relationships.

Part 3 : Codependency

Chapter 34   Introduction to Codependency

Codependency may be a relatively new construct but it has been in existence since the 1940s even though it wasn't termed "codependency" from the start. Research on codependency was first conducted on the wives and families of alcoholics who were formerly referred to as co-alcoholics. However, the first identification of codependency as a psychological construct can be said to be rooted in the theories of Karen Horney, a German psychoanalyst. In 1941, Horney proposed a theory about how some people adopt what she referred to as 'Moving Toward" personality style to get rid of their anxiety. According to Horney, people with this 'moving toward' personality tend to move towards others to gain their affections and approval. By doing this, they subconsciously try to control them by acting dependent. They are the type to turn the other cheek when slapped on one cheek. They would rather gain approval and acceptance from others than to respect or love themselves. Initially, the term 'codependency' was used to describe families of alcoholics who were believed to interfere with addicts' recovery in a bid to 'help' them.

To understand codependency, psychologist have referred to two important psychoanalysis theories, "Family systems theory," and "Attachment style theory." So, let's take a deeper look at each of these theories and understand how they explain codependency.

Family Systems Theory

A family is the most basic emotional unit in a society; it is probably where humans learn to develop feelings, bonds, and important human emotions. Although family relationships can be complex and no two families can be completely alike, the family systems theory suggests that all families have a similar emotional model or system. That is, emotions are learned in all families almost the same way.

The family systems theory aims to look at the family as a primary and unified emotional unit. Proposed by Dr. Murray Bowen, a psychiatrist, the family systems theory proposed that every member of a family is emotionally intensely connected to each other. Bowen proposed that the family is a system where each member plays a specific role and follows certain rules. Each member of a family interacts and responds to one another based on the role assigned to them. This leads to the development of a pattern in the family system; a pattern where the actions and behaviors of one member impacts the rest of the family in certain ways. Depending on the system, these behavioral patterns that have been developed, result in either a balance, imbalance/dysfunction, or both in the family.

What the family systems theory is saying is that the family has a massive impact on the actions and emotions of any individual and these could be negative or positive. It is also saying that when a certain member of the family system behaves in certain ways, it is bound to affect the behaviors of every other person in the system. When a person in the system experiences certain changes, it affects the family as a unit and the members in terms of actions and emotions. For instance, if a member of a normal family system where everybody plays their role and everything functions like it should, experiences a change such as a sudden addiction to alcohol, this sudden change will affect every other person in the family and how they act/play out their role in the system. Bowen further said that maintaining a certain behavioral pattern within the family system can lead to a balance in the system, but also cause dysfunction. Although the level of interdependence among families varies, every family has some degree of interdependency and that is how a normal functioning family should be.

For instance, if the husband in a family is unable to live up to his responsibilities probably due to being an alcoholic or addict, the wife has to stack up more responsibilities to her role to pick up the slack the husband's actions would cause. This addition in role of the husband to the wife, may help to ensure stability in the system. Still, it will also lead to a dysfunction by pushing the family toward a new equilibrium. This is since overtime, the wife will find it difficult to maintain playing two roles, thereby causing her to drop the husband's role she picked up, hers, or a substantial amount of both. An example is a family where the father is depressive, irresponsible, and lacking in his role. Let's say that the father is an underachiever, unwilling to work, or lacking in contribution of basic things in the home. Naturally, the mother has to assume the role of providing every basic need in the family while also playing her natural role of a caregiver such as getting the children to express their needs, providing the company they need, etc. When this continues over a long time, the mother eventually becomes overstressed from playing this overachieving role and subconsciously starts to drop some of the roles. For example, she may be so consumed with working and providing food, shelter, and everything else, to the point where she no longer has the time to care about or talk to the children about their needs, feelings, and thoughts. In an instance where the children try to reach out to her, she may even shut them up nicely or aggressively due to being overstressed. This causes the kids to recoil and shy away from expressing their feelings, needs, and thoughts in the future. This leads to an obvious dysfunction which affects the family overall and leads to something like "codependency." In a way, the mother is also showing codependent traits by enabling the actions of the father and struggling to pick up his responsibility.

The family system affects individual perception of self, emotions, feelings, and perception of the world, the most relative concepts that explain how codependency happens are: the differentiation of self, nuclear family emotional system, and family projection process.

Attachment Style Theory

In the simplest terms, attachment can be defined as emotional connection and bond with another person. However, in the words of British psychologist, John Bowlby, who is the first developer of the attachment style theory, "attachment is a lasting psychological connectedness between human beings." The origin of the attachment theory was to understand the distress felt by children when they are separated from their caregiver. This theory can be used to explain and understand codependency and why it is rooted in individual childhood and upbringing.

With the attachment theory, Bowlby tries to understand the relevance of attachment in tandem to an individual's personal development. Particularly, this theory proposes that an individual's ability to form a physical and emotional attachment to other people, produces a sense of security in self which is required for growing and developing the right personality. Bowlby argues that the earliest connection formed by children with their primary caregivers has a massive impact on the child's development of self and personality.

Children who were raised in proximity (emotional and physical) to their primary caregivers are likely to have a recognition of their inherent self and be able to protect themselves from any sort of problem or abuse. The main point here is that when there is a primary caregiver available in a child's life to protect all the basic needs from food to shelter, such child is very likely to develop a sense of security in him or herself. On the other hand, children who didn't receive support and care while growing up, whether emotional or physical, tend to experience more anxiety in their relationship with their parent and also future relationships.

Children who form an insecure attachment style with their caregiver are more likely to show codependent traits than children who develop a secure attachment style with their caregiver. For a child to develop a strong, secure and independent personality, he or she must have had a strong relationship with at least one primary caregiver which could be the mother, the father, or a guardian. For a child to have a strong relationship with a caregiver, the family must be a functional and normal one where the child is being provided with all of the basic needs. He can express himself without a fear of repression. In a dysfunctional family where either of the caregiver is probably an addict or an irresponsible parent, it is highly unlikely for the child to have a strong, dependent relationship. Therefore, a child raised in this kind of family will develop a lack of security in himself or the caregiver, thereby causing him to recoil from seeking new experiences, and sometimes relationships, that require intimacy. Based on the research conducted, there are four attachment styles children are likely to develop based on the sort of relationship they have with their caregiver. Still, people with codependent personalities usually have the avoidant attachment style.

Parents of children in dysfunctional families tend to be physically and emotionally unresponsive and unavailable to the children a whole lot of time. Knowingly or unknowingly, they disregard the children's needs and feelings, and most times do not take note of when a child is sick or hurt. These kind of parents also try to enforce premature independence in a child e.g. requiring an 8-year-old to look after her siblings. This may be due to marital conflicts in the family or a dysfunction with one of the parent which is affecting the family as a whole. As a result, the child learns right from childhood to repress or suppress the natural urge to seek out someone with whom they can share their feelings, distress, and pain or someone to seek comfort with. Due to the rejections he suffers when he tries to reach out to his parent, the child learns never to show signs of distress. It becomes even worse if the parent punishes the child when he expresses his feelings; the child resorts to keeping everything in, to at least remain in physical proximity with the parent.

As adults, people with avoidant attachment style become self-sufficient and self-nurturing and they develop a faux sense of independence in a way that deludes them into thinking they can take absolute care of themselves. This, of course, makes it difficult for them to seek support, love, and help from people, even the ones they share the most intimate relationships with. They never show an outward need of affection, warmth, or love, but they are willing to give out what they never received from their caregiver. That is, they make extra efforts to give out the love, care, and support they never received in childhood to people they choose to form intimate relationships with.

In conclusion, psychologists, based on research, believe that the kind of relationships people form with others be it family, friendship, or any other intimate relationship is influenced by the kind of attachment style they developed in childhood. Therefore, we can conclude that people with avoidant attachment style are more susceptible to codependency due to the kind of dysfunctional upbringing they had in childhood to develop an avoidant style of attachment.

Just a little break to ask you something that means a lot for me: Are you enjoying this book? If so, I'd be really happy if you could leave a short review on Amazon. I'm so curious to know your opinion! Don't forget to add a photo of the book if you can, thank you.

Chapter 35   What Is Codependency and What Isn't?

We all are born as unique individuals. We have an innate quality to feel and respond to our internal awareness as well as our external environment. This is how we can learn, plan, create and relate to others using our personal experiences. Co-dependency hinders the development of this unique sense of individuality thus restricting our engagement with the outside world in general.

It is very difficult to define the term self. It should be simply understood as the coalescence of all your unique individuality, your essential being. Co-dependents adapt and react to other's individuality and the sense of self, totally negating their unique being to cope up with life. This leads them to feel like a fraud and that they are cheating the world all the time. Co-dependents remain in an unhappy temperament owing to these facts.

Are You Addicted? Are You Ill?

Psychiatrist Timmen Cermak suggested that Co-dependency is a disease back in the year 1988. While it may sound morbid to term it as a disease, co-dependency should be seen as a condition with discernible, progressive symptoms that impair the regular or normative functioning of the individual. Like all other diseases or medical conditions, this can be treated, and its symptoms are reversed. Alcoholism became an illness in 1956 and the American Medical Association (AMA) clubbed alcoholism with drug dependency in 1991. The 1960 publication of The Disease Concept of Alcoholism by E.Morton Jellinick removed most of the shame revolving around alcoholism, branding it as a disease and not a behavioral issue. Ever since then, many medical and psychiatric practitioners have applied the medical model of treatment to various addictions such as gambling, sex, drugs etc. The same medical model has also been applied to the treatment of Co-dependency by medical practitioners and psychiatrists. However, some practitioners and counselors object to the classification of co-dependency as a disease. They argue that doing so stigmatizes, discourages and disempowers the person who is trying to recover. They believe that by labeling it as a disease, they make the patients see the futility of giving up on their addiction. People start believing that they do not have any power to put a stop to their addictive behavior.

The practitioners and psychiatrists on the other camp argue that, on the contrary, labeling co-dependency as a disease, it removes shame and the punitive treatment of any addiction. This makes it possible for the disease to be treated in a way similar to any other physical ailment such as diabetes, hypertension or blood pressure.

It has been intensively argued whether any biological component of addiction and co-dependency is required for it to be termed as a physical disease. Today by brain scans of addicts and co-dependents it has been revealed that there are defects in the patient's brain, primarily in the brain's pleasure center that process dopamine. It is still contestable whether the dopamine dysfunction predates the patient's addiction, or it is the other way round. Investigations into this area are happening as we speak, all over the world as they try and examine how a person's genes play an important part in the addiction. Researchers have also found out that environmental factors that include parenting and trauma play a part in the development of an individual's addiction later in their lives. Trauma and depression harm the chemistry of the brain, and they induce negative thoughts leading to depression. It is important to understand that label or no label, it is totally up to you to recover from co-dependency. You can call it a disease, or an addiction, only your efforts can bring you out of the trap of co-dependency.

Cross-Addiction

All addicts are dependent by default. They depend and rely heavily upon the object of their addictions. They end up spending most of their time and resources in and around their addictions. When these addicts choose to abstain, they may develop cross-addictions. Sober alcoholics take to smoking cigarettes, overreacting; develop sex addiction and so on. Food addicts who undergo bariatric surgeries become alcoholics or shopaholics.

This cross-addiction can result from a variety of factors. Neuroscience claims that when addicts stop practicing their addictions, they adopt other secondary addictions. This is at the same level as their primary addiction and can be just as harmful to the recovering patient. For an instance, an abstaining gambler can resort to drinking alcohol or chain-smoking cigarettes. The abstinence from gambling is of no use because the addict resorts to other addictions with as much passion as his previous addictions.

This happens because the patient does not recover from their addiction at an emotional level bringing in co-dependent traits in their behavior.

Cross addictions are easy to pick up when an addict starts abstaining from his or her addictions. Many new abstainers try and rush into relationships. This has become to be sometimes jokingly called as the thirteenth step of the twelve-step program! They are confronted with the relationship issues they have faced in the past. They have to address these issues of emotional insecurity, a problem that they have avoided or tried avoiding for long. Some resort to a newcomer in their life, which could be their newborn child and even 'obsess' about it. This again brings us back to the initial problem of co-dependency from where it all started. Sometimes it takes up years before a person addresses his or her co-dependency issues, contributing to frequent relapses into addictions. The mental obsessions through which most recovering addicts skim though redirect their means of controlling anxiety and addressing repressed feelings. This is an attempt to bridge the gap between the surfing addicts and their lost sense of self. There are no guidelines to dealing with specific addictions; however, healing the self is in the following. That plays a big part in the addict's recovery and in preventing relapses.

Feminine aspect of Co-dependency

Women comprise a large part of the co-dependents today. There are several reasons for this and some of them are the following.

Biological Factor

Women are wired for relationships naturally. Their limbic systems complement their ability to bond with others. Under pressure, the male hormones prepare for action. In contrast, the female hormones prepare them to tend for children or form relationships with others.

Development of a Gender(Ed) Identity

Generally, girls grow up depending more on their parents than the average male child. They are emotionally bonded to their family and are more accepting of the parental values. The rupture of their relationship with the parents is a constant source of anxiety for them. Autonomy is the biggest challenge for most girls and the lack of the same promotes co-dependent characteristics in their behavior. For the male child, intimacy is a challenge.

Political Reasons

Women have been subjugated politically and socially over the large part of the modern and pre modern history. They have been placed subordinate to the male on various levels and had to fend for the most basic of the rights such as the right to education and universal suffrage rights. Generations of oppression have made the women compliant and lower their self-esteem. They begin to seek identity from the established status quo and end up depressed and anxious.

Cultural Factors

In most cultures across the world, girls have had far lesser autonomy than boys. This autonomy has been restricted to girls in all walks of life from dressing choices to education choice and even matrimonial choice. They are seldom allowed to choose for themselves and thus do not have any sort of autonomy over their bodies.

Religion

Almost all of the major religions of this world have placed women in subservient roles to men. They are expected to comply with the male figures in their families for all their lives. Women have had lesser authority over household matters and even matters concerning their own life.

Social

A greater number of women suffer from personal insecurities and a low self-esteem, which leads to depression and anxiety troubles. It has not been established whether this is a direct cause, a byproduct or a concurrence of co-dependency. According to a Dove study, over 40 percent women are dissatisfied or unhappy with their appearance and about two thirds suffer from insecurities regarding their bodies. The airbrushed ideal models of how the feminine should look are to be blamed for promoting the severe anxiety in people regarding their appearances and bodies.

152

It Is Not Caregiving

Many people enjoy nurturing, caring and looking after other people. This characteristic is more prevalent in women because of the reasons explained. Mothers are naturally programmed to look after and provide for their children, starting even before the child takes birth. Co-dependent caregiving is different from looking after someone and the distinction needs to be understood. In the case of co-dependency, there would be more taking than any actual giving happening. So the disease should not be confused with the breast-feeding tendencies of the mother, which is not co-dependency. Caregiving comes from abundance that all mothers have but co-dependency is a result of degradation and insecurity.

Co-Dependency Is Not Being Kind

It is human nature to help others and display behavior of empathy and kindness towards all fellow beings. The man is a social animal in that respect. However co-dependent kindness stems from a sense of low self-esteem and deep identity crisis. Most co-dependents do not have a choice and they can't say no! The essential difference between kindness and co-dependency is determining whether the actions stem from a place of self-esteem or fear, guilt, and anxiety.

Co-Dependency Is Not Inter-Dependency

Most relationships fall in between the spectrum of inter-dependency and co-dependency. Here we would take a look at the two extremes to understand the nature of a relationship.

Co-dependency

It could be hard identifying co-dependent couple because they often appear to be intellectual, physically, socially and financially independent. In reality, they are two emotionally dependent and insecure adults. Often these relationships are marked by a power struggle or a power imbalance. There is no equality, closeness and faith. One person could anticipate the other's need and feel anxious, guilty or burdened about it. Such partners often directly or indirectly try to control the other to satisfy their ideas, needs, and demands. Such people experience lesser freedom in their relationships and end up fearing both intimacies as well as desertion. Such is the insecure nature of a co-dependent relationship

Inter-dependency

In such relationships, attachment develops at an early stage between the partners. It is natural for people involved in a romantic or any other serious relationship to be worried about their partners. They express concern and miss the other. However, inter-dependent couples structure their lives around that of their partners instead of encroaching in their lives. They enjoy helping each other out and are confident of the other being there for them in their time of need. They are not insecure about the other's presence and often do not see their partners as others but just a reflection of their selves. Their habits and interests may differ, and they give each other the space to pursue these different interests and inclinations. Their lives are inter-dependent. Such couples do not fear intimacy and neither fear abandonment. They are respectful and supportive of each other. They remain committed to the relationship.

Chapter 36   The Stages of Codependency

Different Stages of Codependency

It has been established by practicing psychiatrists and medical counselors that co-dependency is a progressive condition. People show progressively worsening symptoms paralleling that of an addict or an alcoholic. In the later stages, both co-dependents and alcoholics or drug addicts display serious mental or physical problems. If the condition is not treated properly and in time, it may spiral downward just like alcoholism does. Just like alcoholics, co-dependents show improvements when they receive treatment. Recovery can be initiated at any point in time for the co-dependent. It is never too late. However, the sooner the process begins, the easier it is to treat the disease. This part takes a look at the different stages of co-dependency in some detail. This might help the readers identify how far they have ventured in the lanes of co-dependency.

Early Stages of Co-Dependent Behavior

The early stage of co-dependency begins when the individual becomes overly attached to a subject. This subject could be a person, a substance or a behavioral pattern such as gambling. The overt attachment that soon reaches the level of obsessions makes the individual depend upon the subject in an unhealthy way.

It is possible to get attracted to a needy person or be extra involved with one particular family member. We would constantly want to help and please them. Gradually we become increasingly emotionally attached to that person losing focus on our own lives in the process. This turns the relationship into an obsession and begins to hurt both the individuals involved.

To recover from this point in co-dependency, you must confront the problem squarely and acknowledge the reality of the relationship. This is a prerequisite to changing this dysfunctional co-dependent reality of yours. The shift could get inspired by anything. Maybe a desire to lead a happier life with your partner could initiate your recovery process from co-dependency you must have a wake-up call. Change should become imperative and instead of ignoring or minimizing the facts, you must accept them as harsh yet true. Denial takes us nowhere. Recovery from codependency begins with collecting all the information you can and reaching out for help from professionals. Many people choose to join psychotherapy or a twelve-step program, which will be state towards the end. The process of recovery entails rediscovering your lost identity and shedding the weight of the various facades or disguises that we create around ourselves.

Middle Stages of Co-Dependency

In the middle stages of co-dependency, extreme symptoms such as denial, painful emotions, and obsessive-compulsive behavioral patterns begin to show in the individual. There could be occasional outbursts of violence and the person is just on the edge and needs to be rescued. Patients in this stage feel the obsessive need or the urge to control and seize power. Reclamation of independence, balance and peace of mind are intrinsic for the recovery of the patient suffering in the middle stages of co-dependency.

People progress into the middle phase of co-dependency due to the lack of support and a constant denial of the problem. People tend to minimize the problem and pushing it into the background to hide the painful aspects of their personalities from themselves and the world in general. Meanwhile, the person's addiction with seizing control keeps on increasing and poisons the relationship to an irreversible point. People in the middle stage of co-dependency begin to help more to control. They end up taking responsibilities that are not theirs and over burden themselves to the point of breakdown. It is common for mood swings to increase during this stage because of the increasing conflicts in the patient's psyche. Co-dependents often fall into cross addictions during this stage of co-dependency.

This is the stage where the most intensive recovery takes place. Patients begin to practice non-attachment and try to grasp the general sense of their powerlessness over the subject of their dependencies. The aim is to develop a focus on the self of the patient and take the focus away from the substance of dependence. As the focus develops around the self, so does the patient's self-awareness and self-examination. This is a part of both psychotherapy and the twelve-step program borrowed from the AA. AA stresses the fact that every alcoholic's success in recovery from alcoholism depends upon the rigorous self-honesty of the patient and this holds for all patients trying to recover from co-dependency.

It is a time when the patient needs to stop blaming others for his condition because passing the buck has no use in the treatment process. Even if the patient has been subjected to abuse and oppression, it should still become their onus to try and break free from the feeling of insecurity and inadequacy. Only they can restore their self-worth in their eyes and hence need to believe in themselves.

Final Stage of Co-Dependency and Recovery

In the final stage of co-dependency, the contrast between illness and health become the most pronounced. The world of the untreated co-dependent narrows down and their health declines. As co-dependency progresses and reaches its final stage, conflicts become very common. There is a further decline in self-esteem and self-care. The chronic symptoms of co-dependency include more progressed obsessive-compulsive disorders and addictions. Such compulsive behaviors might include monitoring the addict, enabling, OCD, dieting, having affairs, overeating and alcoholism. The recovery in this final stage of co-dependency depends upon the reinstating of the patient's self-esteem and confidence. The patient is encouraged to follow their own goals and pursue activities that specifically interest them. The patients express the desire to fully articulate and express themselves for the sake of the joy and freedom that they experience in doing so. The focus gradually shifts from the outside to the inside in the sense that the patient becomes less obsessed with the other and instead begins self-reflection and critical analysis of his/her behavior. As and by the focus shifts from the object of addiction or dependency, the patient gets to realize that they are way more desirous and capable of authentic intimacy. Recovery and treatment of co-dependency entail an ongoing maintenance to prevent any relapse in the co-dependent state again. It can take several years before the changes and the recovery becomes an integral part of you.

Chapter 37   Signs of Codependency

Codependent people tend to believe that they can't survive without their partners and are willing to do any kind of thing they can for the relationship's sustenance, irrespective of how much pain it causes. The persistent fear of losing their partners and being abandoned suppresses their other feelings. They feel unsafe and insecure when they think that they will have to address any of their partner's dysfunctional behaviors. It is similar to justifying or refuting a condition; therefore, they fear their partner's rejection.

People who are co-addicted will also seek to adapt themselves and their lives to the dysfunction of their partners. They may have given up hope that anything better is possible, rather than settling for the job of keeping the status quo. The thought of change could bring great pain and sadness to them.

Codependence functions in an identical fashion, be it the drug addiction or addiction to alcohol. It could even relate to issues like verbal or physical abuse or gambling. However, the worrisome behavior of the addict, which leads to the partner's problem denial and makes them more vulnerable to becoming codependent. The individuals who were abused as children face an even greater risk.

People frequently begin to think about where the codependent inclinations originated from, yet this takes place just after their awareness of the very same. 'Susceptibility to codependency in grown-up connections, reasons for codependency, and also liberating oneself coming from codependent connections are several of the inquiries which are raised quite often.

There is not a singular response to the above inquiries; nevertheless, what is recognized is actually that it normally starts in youth. Often, youthful little ones don't have the intellectual capabilities or even lifestyle take in to understand that the partnerships they are observing and also experiencing may not be healthy and balanced.

Greater than usually, little ones that mature in useless families consider all of them pointless or even keep them responsible for the issues of their family members. Some of the features of inefficient households are actually:

1. Unpredictable and chaotic

2. Extremely unsupportive

3. Unsafe and scary

4. Physically or emotionally neglectful

5. Prone to manipulation

6. Abusive or harsh

7. In a state of denial

8. Reject outside help

9. Are judgmental

10. Display inattentiveness

11. Make undue expectations from children

You Come To Be a Caretaker

If your parent was not able to carry out the activity of parenting, you might have handled the part of parenting to occupy the gaps. You handled your moms and dads or even household, footed the bill, prepared meals, and stayed up to be sure you were not sleeping with a lit up cigarette and burnt down your home.

You Learn That People Who Claim To Love You May Hurt You

Your childhood experience has been that your family physically and mentally abused you, deserted you, lied to you, insulted you, and exploited your goodness to profit. That becomes a familiar dynamic, and in adulthood, you let friends, partners, or family members continue to harm you.

You Come To Be a People-Pleaser

One way you prefer to keep in management is actually to make folks pleased. You offer, as well as you give.

You Struggle With Boundaries

For you, no one has modeled healthy and balanced limits, therefore all of yours are also weak (consistent delight and also treatment) or even too rigid (closed off and also resistant to trust others and also open).

You Experience Guilt

You may really feel bad regarding a lot of stuff you haven't caused. You are incapable of fixing your moms and dads or loved ones. Even when it's irrational, there is a strong impulse to saving and also mending it. As well, your failure to boost family creates you feeling insufficient.

You Become Scared

Childhood years have actually additionally been frightening. Today you always keep on getting sleep problems or aberrations, think on edge, and also are afraid of being alone.

You Believe Mistaken and Also Not Worthy

You have matured reasoning and being actually said to something is wrong with you. You have taken this as a simple fact, as it has actually been reinforced again and again since you have not known any other fact.

You Do Not Count On Individuals

Folks have repetitively deceived and injured you the negative impact is that you do not trust your pals or your spouse. This is a method to safeguard on your own versus potential personal injury, however it additionally restrains your means to relationships as well as actual affection.

You Will Not Permit Folks Help You

You were actually not utilized to delighting your needs or even creating others care for you. Giving assistance is even more soothing than getting it. You prefer to do it yourself than be indebted.

You Believe Loneliness

You presumed for a long period of time that you were the only one with such a household. You were experiencing being left alone and reproached by the lies that you must tell in your childhood years. By combining this seclusion along with unstable as well as troubled feelings, it's simple to find why codependents live as grownups in unhealthful partnerships, instead of being alone. Feeling alone also seems like an indication that you truly are turned down and also flawed.

You Become Excessively Liable

Your survival as a youngster, or the survival of your household, depended on you, leading in commitments that surpassed your age. You take responsibility for the notions and also acts of other people extremely.

You End Up Being Controlled

You try to manage individuals and likewise condition in a try to recompense for your emotions of helplessness when you feel that lifestyle has actually avoided command and also terrifying.

You split your understandings originating from what the mother and fathers' requirements suit the parent rather of your own self. You build up, acquire out of the residential property, however you still possess this gap. What presumes right is to find yet another specific with an identical split, and also then you 2 may conveniently display each various other?

Other things can simply bring about the crack exceptionally. It commonly calls for an adored one's secret. Perhaps a dreadful activity that may absolutely not be really mentioned, over which you must refute your extremely own feelings.

Signs that Denote Codependency

Low Level of Self-Esteem

The essential sign of self-esteem is that when you experience that you're not good enough or indulge in a comparison review of your own self along with others reviewing. The important element of self-esteem is that there are individuals who experience self-conceit, which is actually only a camouflage. They really assume that they may not be liked. Really, at heart, there are actually sensations of pity inadequacy. Perfectionism and also sense of guilt usually accompany low self-confidence. You don't really feel bad regarding yourself if everything is actually ideal.

People-Pleasing

There is actually nothing at all wrong using it if you desire to desire an individual you appreciate. Codependents usually do not think they possess a choice to create. "No" is actually a root cause of anxiety for them. There are actually codependents that consider it extremely testing to mention "No" to a person. They are going to compromise their personal requirements instead to feel free to others.

Poor Borders

Poor limits frontiers are actually even more like an unseen boundary in between you and others. It divides what yours and someone else's is actually, and that applies not only to your physical body, assets, and also properties, but to your emotions, notions, and requires too. Specifically, this is where codependents get involved in trouble. They possess poor ones or even blurry perimeters.

They think responsible for the feelings and problems of others or even point the finger at somebody else for their own. Lots of codependents have strong frontiers.

They are actually trimmed and also gotten rid of, making it difficult for individuals to receive close to them. Folks often switch over to and fro between possessing unsatisfactory as well as sturdy perimeters.

Sensitivity

The repercussion of unsteady boundaries is actually that you reply to the thought and feelings as well as sensations of intermittent person. When somebody states something about which you disagree, either you feel it, or even you become defensive. You absorb their articulations, and there is actually no restriction to all of them. Along with a perimeter, you may recognize it was actually merely their opinion and also not a representation of you and also not a sign of disharmony.

Caretaking

The repercussion of poor perimeters is that if an individual has a trouble or even an issue, you desire to support them to the point that you quit your requirements. It's regular for a person to really feel empathy and empathy, but codependents begin to place others in advance of on their own. Essentially, if another person doesn't desire assistance, they need to have to help as well as may feel rejected.

Management

Along with management happens a sensation of safety as well as protection for codependents? Our team all yearn for to be in control of some of the celebrations of our life. For codependents, command limits their ability to discuss emotions and also take risks.

Dysfunctional Communication

Codependents find it testing to correspond their thought and feelings, feelings, and necessities. It clearly is actually a problem when you are uninformed of what you require, believe, or fee. There will certainly be actually times when you will definitely recognize what you understand yet unwilling to share it. Considering that you do not wish to shame an individual, as a result, you don't disclose the fact.

Fascinations

Codependents prefer to spend their time paying attention to various other people or even relationships. That is caused through their weakness as well as anxiousness and anxieties. They might even obtain upset when they presume, they've created or might make a "oversight." Sometimes you might slip into fantasies concerning how you prefer traits to become or

163

somebody you enjoy as a method to get away the here and now discomfort. It is just one of residing in denial. Nonetheless, it avoids you from residing your life happily.

Addiction

Codependents get a really good feeling concerning them when other individuals like all of them for their actions. Others still like to be in a relationship, due to the fact that they experience depressing or even alone when they are extremely long through on their own.

Rejection

The very same goes for their necessities. They may be refusing their requirement for area as well as liberty. They reject their weakness and also need to have affection

Concerns Along With Affection.

Sexual problems are actually likewise a result of a concern encompassing affection. A close partnership can most ideal be called being actually near and open to one more. You may presume, due to the shame and also weaker borders, that you would certainly be disciplined, denied, or even abandoned. Alternatively, you can be afraid being actually smothered and shedding your liberty in a partnership. You may reject the need for closeness, as well as strongly believe the companion needs so much of your opportunity; your companion insists you are actually not available, but he or she denies their requirement for separation.

Agonizing Emotions

Embarrassment as well as low self-worth generate anxiety and also worry that they will certainly be actually reprimanded, denied, or even walked out on. They create oversights, become a complete failure, and also think stuck by being close or even alone.

164

Chapter 38   How to Understand If You Are In a Codependent Relationship?

Manipulative people tend to prey on those with low self-esteem issues. They know that if you do not have confidence in yourself, and that it will be easier for them to take advantage of you. It is not your fault that there are predatory people like this out there just as it is not your fault that car thieves exist in the world. However, if you want to protect your car, or in this instance, yourself, it is good to know the types of things that attract a coercive person to their prey.

Lack of family members or support is another characteristic that will draw a predator toward you. Whether it is a family member themselves, a roommate or a significant other, the pattern is the same. The person will usually guilt-trip you from spending time with others in order to alienate you from the other relationships in your life.

As mentioned before, and contrary to what popular media tells us, men tend to be the predominant manipulators in our society, whether it be in personal relationships or situations at large. The reasons are twofold. One, because they usually are in higher positions of authority, and so are in a better place to prey on those with vulnerabilities. And two, because men are predominantly raised in ways that nurture a sense of entitlement in them toward things that they do not have a right to. Men are taught to take when women are taught to give. If this idea seems ridiculous to you, think about how many times the women in your life, or yourself, if you are a woman, are in situations where they are serving food, doing the laundry or any other household chore (giving) while men in your life, or yourself, if you are a man, are sitting around playing a game or watching TV (taking). Even when both partners in a heterosexual relationship are working, women tend to do a predominant amount of the housework. This is all to say that if you are a woman, that is another target on your back from manipulative predators.

While there is nothing you can do, or should have to do, about being a woman, you should simply be aware of how some men operate. When you are interacting with a man, especially in the earlier stages of forming a relationship, notice whether he tends to speak with you or at you and look out for a tendency to keep unreasonably asking or expecting things of you.

While not all manipulative men pounce right away, if they are exhibiting those traits, these could be warning signs to watch out for something worse down the line.

Though it has already been mentioned several times, it cannot be stressed enough that another person's harmful actions toward you are never your fault. This part is only meant to make you aware of the possible characteristics that manipulative people seek out when preying on others. By having this information handy, you are better informed and in a better position to fend off any unwanted and harmful relationships.

The Daily Habits of a Mindful Partner

Here are the list of daily habits that I'd like to encourage you to implement in your relationship:

Mindful Couples Are Really Present With One Another

Living together makes it easy to assume you are always "with" one another - but unless your mind is actively engaged in the moment and your partner, you may as well be in different countries. Happy couples don't multitask or answer emails or messages during conversations. They listen. They are there, open and receptive, enjoying just being in the moment with their partner.

Mindful Couples Are Deliberate

They don't expect the strength of their feeling for one another to be the magic element that makes everything work - they know that if things work, it's because they make the work. By being constantly aware of the subtle changes in themselves, their partners and their environments, a mindful person is able to perceive more options, and make better choices. They take charge of their own emotions and actions, and never say things like "I just don't know what got into me".

A Mindful Person Doesn't Need To Manipulate Others And Also Will Not Tolerate Being Controlled By Someone Else

The need to control and dominate often stems from fear, and the mindful person bases their interactions with others on love and acceptance instead.

Mindful Couples Are Not Afraid Of Disagreement

Expecting that the ones we love always agree with us perfectly and on every topic is unrealistic, and striving to force ourselves into that perfection means we miss the beauty in the moment, the paradox, the humor, the bitter sweetness. A mindful couple can share love, acceptance and compassion for one another, even when they completely disagree with one another.

Mindful Couples Are Not Afraid Of Impermanence

In matters of the heart, many people are encouraged to think of endless, infinite love as the only standard to measure our connection, and anything less is not "true love". We celebrate 50-year wedding anniversaries and feel sorry for those who've never had a relationship past 3 months. However, a mindful couple is OK with any length of relationship, if it means that the connection was compassionate and honest. An amazing meal wasn't any less delicious because you got to the end of it.

Mindful Couples Don't Need Their Partners to Complete Them

Making another person responsible for your happiness means that you are using them as a means to an end, and not simply because you enjoy being with them. A mindful partner will have the courage to face up to his/her own "psychological work" and not expect to hash it out with someone else. Likewise, they'll have enough self-compassion to resist being put into the position of completing somebody else.

Mindful Couples Are Constantly Grateful

It's easy, once we have "won" someone over, to stop wooing them, to stop feeling thrilled that our attentions are reciprocated. A mindful couple never gets tired of those magical little things they fell in love with in the first place. They keep their minds, hearts and spirits fresh and thankful, knowing how much of a blessing it is to be intimate with someone, and they express their gratitude constantly. Little compliments, favors, saying thank you - these are all things that a mindful partner will keep up with, whether it's been 6 months or 60 years.

Mindful Partners Can Take a Step Back

When you meditate or learn to be mindful in your daily life, you learn that just because a thought drifts into your awareness, doesn't mean you have to cling onto it or identify with it. Mindful couples are able to take a step back in emotional moments, still their minds and come back to their partners with clear, open hearts. This way, nothing is said in anger.

A Mindful Couple Acts As a Team

In very real ways, we are all connected. A successful, happy couple work as one. Though they have their own separate lives as individuals, they come together as a couple and work on shared goals. There is no competition, only encouragement.

Lastly, Mindful Partners Are Compassionate, With Themselves and One Another

Perhaps nowhere else is it as evident than in a long-term relationship that people occasionally mess up and hurt one another. A mindful partner values openness and tranquility above holding onto grudges. They forgive not because they like the higher ground, but because they know that they, too, have also made mistakes. A mindful couple works through feelings of hurt, guilt, resentment and all the rest as quickly as possible so that they can get back to their connection.

Chapter 39   How People Become Codependent?

Codependency is the product of being exposed to dysfunctional beliefs about relationships and romance. Why do you stay in an abusive relationship? How could you believe that your partner who abuses you still holds the key to your happiness? Why can't you just pack up and leave?

Family Role Models

It all starts during childhood. If you grew up in a home that taught you not to reveal your true feelings and that you should just keep these to yourself, you are likely to develop codependency. It is also possible that you don't have a good relationship model to refer to. You might have witnessed this kind of relationship with your parents or with your friends or other relatives. Thus, you assume that this is the best relationship you can ever get and that if you continue to hold on, everything will eventually turn out fine.

People can often choose partners that mimic characteristics and dynamics of their mother and father relationship. It isn't unusual for a codependent person to marry or partner with someone who is controlling or dominating in some way. You might have seen your parents' abusive relationship. You might have witnessed how your mother stayed in and endured an abusive relationship with your father. You might have heard from your mom that she stayed because she was hoping that your dad would change. She can't leave him because she loves him and she can't let him destroy his life. These thoughts stayed with you and you believed that if you were to end up in the same situation, you would do what your mom did.

Codependency can also be the by-product of parents with extremely high expectations of their children. The result is a child that tries to earn love and people please. Nothing they do can ever feel good enough. They have this never ending drive to obtain their parent's approval. Unfortunately, they may never achieve this heart's desire. There are many stories of individuals that toil in their careers or personal lives in order to attain great success. Their sole purpose is to finally please their demanding parent and hear the words, "Well done" or "I'm proud of you." However, too many times these individuals reach the top only to be disappointed when they don't hear the words the so longed for. Their efforts were in vain because they fixed their eyes on the wrong prize. Rather than trying to chase after folly, we need to seek success for our own joy and fulfillment. We may never get the pat on the back that we hoped for, but in the end, we can be proud of our own efforts. This is true security and happiness.

Others Determine Your Personal Happiness

One of the reasons that you continuously opt to stay in an abusive relationship is that you believe that you cannot find your happiness without the other person. You believe that living alone is worse than being with your partner. You are convinced that if you live alone, away from your partner, you will never find happiness because you have convinced your subconscious mind that you need the other person to be happy and fulfilled.

Ultimately, only you can make yourself happy. You are the one who chooses to be happy, angry, sad, whatever. It's all a matter of perception. With the proper tools and practice, your emotions can be changed instantly. Realistically, at the end of the day, you are responsible for your own happiness. No one else can do it for you.

Fostering the belief that living alone is worse than being with your partner is your own doing. It is a wrong belief that you picked up somewhere along the way. You can continue believing this message and be miserable. Or, you can debunk this limiting belief and create a new truth that brings happiness. The truth of the matter is: the world would not end if you lived alone, away from your partner. It may be unbearable for a time, but in the end, you'd be okay. If you can imagine the worst case scenario, you'll realize that you actually have what it takes to make it through. So what's the new truth from your old limiting belief? The truth is that you can find happiness with or without the other person. In fact, sometimes you may be even happier without the other person – if you can believe it!

Low Self-Esteem

Lack of self-esteem is also one of the causes of codependency. You believe that you deserve this relationship because of who you are. You don't see yourself being able to find a more fulfilling relationship because you feel you are not worthy enough. You are convinced that you are fortunate because your current partner loved you even if you are not worthy. So, even if you hurt, you continue to stay. Low self-esteem causes you to not stand up for yourself; to not speak up when you don't agree; to sweep things under the rug in order to maintain peace; to put other people's needs above your own even at your expense.

There is a deep desire to be needed. You believe that the only way you can regain your self-esteem is to feel needed by your partner. You feel good and you feel fulfilled if your partner depends on you. Typically, people who did not receive unconditional love from their parents while growing up can struggle with feelings of low self-esteem.

A codependent person will do everything to make excuses for whatever wrongdoings other people are doing because that is the only time that they feel needed; it is the "savior" or "caretaker" attitude that is present in most codependent individuals.

An Unhealthy Relationship

A codependent relationship is an unhealthy relationship. You will never get true happiness and fulfillment, which are the very things that you have always wanted to have. If you are a codependent partner, you might be struggling with the fear of being rejected and being abandoned. You long for approval, validation, and appreciation. You feel that you are responsible for your partner to the point of setting aside your own needs and wants; the other person always comes first, even if it means that you have to suffer or go without.

You tend to bury the real problems that are causing the codependency. This behavior doesn't solve the problems; on the contrary, the problems will persist as new ones come in. It will not come as a surprise if you find drug abuse and alcohol abuse in a codependent relationship. The addicted person can often take advantage of the codependent person because they are easily manipulated and controlled. The codependent person will happily oblige in order to keep the peace and not rock the boat. This can create a vicious cycle that very quickly traps the codependent person.

Chapter 40   Recovery Goals

The number one rule of breaking free from a codependent relationship is to recognize that you can never change the other person. Only when you come to terms with this fact can you begin to take the measures necessary to liberate yourself from the influences and effects of a dysfunctional relationship. One such measure is to practice what is referred to as detachment. Simply put, detachment is the process of removing yourself from the codependent equation. This can be achieved by avoiding arguments, ending the role of being responsible for other peoples' happiness, or by stopping any other action that contributes to the codependent nature of the relationship.

Recognize You Aren't Responsible For Other Peoples' Happiness

The first step toward achieving detachment is to change your way of thinking. This covers a wide range of areas, so it is something that cannot be done all at once. Instead, it is a process that must be achieved one step at a time. While there is no wrong place to start as such, perhaps the easiest and most important place to start changing your way of thinking is in regards to other people's happiness. The bottom line is that you aren't responsible for how other people feel, no matter what others might say. Only when you come to this realization can you begin to move on with your life in a healthy and meaningful way.

This change in mindset will take a while to develop, as your current mindset is probably the result of years of conditioning. Subsequently, it is important that you don't look for immediate results. Instead, treat this the way you would if you were trying to develop muscle strength or lose weight. You wouldn't expect to walk into the gym one or two times and come out looking like a body builder. Similarly, you wouldn't expect to eat a salad or two and miraculously drop ten or twenty pounds of extra weight. Instead, you recognize that any meaningful results will take time. Therefore, expect these results to take the same time and effort. This way you can commit to the long game, allowing yourself the time needed to make the progress you desire.

The easiest way to begin recognizing that you aren't responsible for other peoples' happiness is to stop taking responsibility for all of their choices. If the taker in your relationship relies on you making the right decisions in order for them to be happy start demanding that they begin to share in the decision making process. This doesn't have to be an all or nothing scenario, rather it can be a step by step process in which you slowly turn over the burden of responsibility to the other person for finding happiness in their life. You might start by forcing them to choose between a few options rather than making all the choices yourself. For example, if you are planning to go out on a date, instead of making every decision yourself come up with a few options you think might work and make the other person choose one. This is a perfect balance that allows both parties to make decisions together, rather than relying on one person to be fully in charge.

Needless to say, there may be times when the taker puts up a fuss and refuses to play along. This is a classic attempt to maintain the status quo on their part, so don't allow them to hinder your efforts. Instead, expect resistance at first, but realize that once you cross the initial hurdle things will begin to get easier. Like it or not, the taker will have to adapt to your gradual changes or else face the possibility of more extreme changes, such as losing you altogether. They will only recognize such a choice if you stick to your guns, so don't let them bully you out of making this positive change in your life.

Recognize You Aren't Responsible For Other Peoples' Unhappiness

The next step toward detaching from codependent influences is to recognize that you aren't responsible for other peoples' unhappiness. Again, this is all about realizing that every person is ultimately responsible for how they feel, both happy and otherwise. Unfortunately, in the case of a codependent relationship you will be made to take the blame for when the taker is unhappy, no matter what the reason might be. Even if you aren't directly responsible for the action or situation that causes their unhappiness, the taker will still blame you for not protecting them more effectively from those things that brought them misery. Needless to say, this is about as unrealistic a mindset as you could imagine, one that usually creates a sense of hopelessness on the part of the giver. After all, you can't possibly protect a person from everything that might cause them to become unhappy, no matter how hard you try. Therefore, the mission is as impossible as it is hopeless.

In order to put this overwhelming hopelessness behind you once and for all you need to begin to change your perspective on things. Again, it is vital that you understand that no individual is responsible for someone else's happiness, sadness or any other state of mind. Therefore, don't feed in to the narrative that you are to blame when the taker in the relationship is angry, sad or depressed. Instead, take a step back and recognize the impact that the taker's choices had on their overall emotional wellbeing. The chances are you can trace their unhappiness to their past choices or behavior. Once you do this you realize that their unhappiness is the result of their own actions, not yours. After a while you will start to see a pattern, one that reveals the simple truth that the taker is solely responsible for their overall wellbeing. This will help you to change your perspective on things, thereby freeing you from the guilt for failing to protect others from being unhappy. The bottom line is that you didn't fail, therefore you are guilt free.

Begin To Make Decisions for Yourself

The basic lesson to be learned with regard to how a person feels is that it all comes down to the decisions the individual makes. When a person makes good, positive choices then they are likely to be happy and content with their life. Alternatively, when they make bad, negative choices they will be unhappy and frustrated with their day-to-day existence. That said, now that you have freed yourself from the idea that you are responsible for how other people feel the next step toward detachment from codependent influences is to start making decisions for yourself. This not only allows you to break free from the cycle of codependency, it actually enables you to move forward with your life, creating a life of happiness, fulfillment and meaning. By making decisions for yourself you can start to shape your life in a way you never imagined possible.

Another effective trick is to buy one thing at a time, spacing out the shopping experience in order to keep from feeling overwhelmed. You can choose to buy one thing a week, thereby curbing your spending as well as giving you something to look forward to. Once you have crossed off all the items on your need list you can create a list of the things you want. These can be purchased on an even more infrequent basis, such as once a month, thereby helping you to ease into the process of buying things for the sole purpose of bringing you pleasure. This same process holds true for any decision making paradigm. No matter what the decisions are the important thing is to start with your needs and then extend to your wants. This will enable you to develop the habit of choosing for yourself while maintaining some level of discipline that will keep you from losing control.

Become Self-Aware

When it comes to making decisions for yourself you might run into the common snag of not actually knowing what you want. This is something most victims of codependent relationships experience at first due to the fact that they never took the time to consider their feelings or desires before. Instead, they always considered the feelings and desires of others when making every decision or choice that they had to make. As a result, you may find it difficult to make choices for yourself since you may not actually know what things you like and what things you don't like. In order to overcome this obstacle you must become self-aware.

Once you have mastered the ability to determine your feelings in the safe space of your home you can start extending the practice into the other environments of your day-to-day life. While at work you can ask yourself how you feel at various points, thereby recognizing the impact different people or events have on your mindset. The important thing is to become self-aware so that you shift your attention from the thoughts and feelings of others to your own thoughts and feelings. Only then can you live your own life in a real and meaningful way, making the right choices for you and taking actions that serve to benefit you and bring you the happiness and satisfaction you truly deserve.

Accept the Truth

The final step to achieving detachment from codependent influences is to accept the truth. In this case the truth is summed up in the word "detach" itself. Don't Even Think About Changing Him/ Her. The most important lesson to learn is that the other person in your relationship is probably beyond changing, thus any time and effort you spend trying to fix them will prove wasted. In fact, the more you try to fix the taker in a codependent relationship the worse things will usually get. Takers don't want to heal, they only want to keep taking. This goes back to the example of the sick person never recovering in a hospital. Such a person doesn't want to get healthy since getting healthy means having to take care of themselves and losing the support of the giver. Therefore they want to stay

175

sick so that they can be cared for on a continual basis. Trying to fix them is ignoring the fundamental truth that they want to remain broken.

Furthermore, trying to fix other people is one of the main behaviors of a giver, making it a codependent tendency. If you want to detach from codependent influences you must eliminate any behaviors within your own life that would enable a codependent relationship, including the urge to fix other people. Therefore, rather than trying to fix the relationship and everyone involved the key is to fix yourself, thereby removing yourself from the equation and thus ending the cycle of codependency. Only by accepting this truth can you effectively let go of the codependent influences in your life and begin to move on, creating a life of freedom and happiness for yourself.

Chapter 41   Denial in Codependency

Denial is not inherently always a bad thing. It's actually an important tool for self-preservation. When encountering something emotionally overwhelming or physically painful, a little bit of denial keeps a person calm and collected. In the stages of grief, denial is the first, because it gives us time to recognize the other emotions we're feeling more gradually. However, denial can also be a dangerous roadblock on the road to recovering from codependency. You can have all the codependent symptoms we'll talk about in the following part, but fail to realize it because of denial. In this part, we'll describe what denial looks like, how to figure out if you're in denial, and what to do about it.

Denial a Blind Spot

There are actually four types of denial. Depending on the person, they might experience all four types at different times, or be vulnerable to one specific type. The first form of denial is when a person denies there's anything wrong at all. This is most likely because if the codependent accepted what was really happening, they would have to admit a change is needed. They might even need to imagine a life without their SO. In relationships with chemical dependency or abuse, a codependent would deny those issues existed.

"Things aren't really that bad."

The second type is when the person is willing to admit some problems, but they are in denial about their seriousness. They make excuses for their SO and rationalize a lot. The codependent acts as if everything was pretty normal, because if they admitted that things were serious, they would have to make room for some really scary possibilities. The denial ends up enabling bad behavior and causing it to get worse. In response, the denial also gets worse, to the point where everyone else sees the truth and can't believe you don't. With abusive relationships or relationships with chemical dependency, the codependent might agree that, yes, there's abuse or my SO does have an addiction, but it's really not that bad.

"Things are bad, but they won't stay that way forever."

The third type of denial is when a codependent admits that things are truly bad, but they deny the consequences. They don't want to think about the long-term effects of codependency or their SO's behavior. Instead of putting accountability on the SO or themselves, the codependent blames everything else around them. This way, they don't need to accept the consequences or responsibility of change. In a relationship with this type of denial, the codependent isn't happy with how things are (abuse or addiction, etc), but they stick around because they hope things will just get better. They deny the possibility that things could get even worse or never change.

"I don't need help."

The fourth type is when the codependent is able to admit the problems and their seriousness, but they won't get help. They believe they've got things under control, so therapy or rehab isn't an option. They close themselves and the relationship off from helpful resources, support networks, and more. Depression and hopelessness are standard results of this type of denial, because the person is able to see how bad things really are, but they're stuck. They don't want to "break" and finally admit that they need outside help.

"I feel...fine."

In each of the four types of denial, the codependent ignores their needs. They cut themselves off from their emotions so when someone asks how they are, they're always "Fine" or even, "I don't know." They don't go deeper than that. If the codependent were to acknowledge their emotions and needs, they would feel guilty, selfish, or too afraid to express them. It becomes more comfortable just to pretend those feelings and needs aren't there. As an example, let's say a codependent just heard that their mother was in a car accident. A typical emotional response would be fear, anxiety, or sadness. However, since the codependent is so used to shutting off their own emotional needs, they don't feel much of anything. Instead, they wonder how their SO will feel, because the codependent has to go to the hospital to check on their mom. Instead of looking inwardly, the codependent is always looking to their SO and wondering (and worrying about) what they are feeling.

How Do You Know If You're In Denial?

To figure out if you're in denial, you first have to get over the initial hump that prevents you from looking inwardly. If your denial is complete, you won't even want to know. However, let's say that you do. Here are some signs that denial is a part of your life:

1. You make a lot of excuses for your SO's behaviors.

2. You frequently tell yourself that everything is fine, even when people around you disagree.

3. You feel numb about things others would be upset or sad about.

4. Even though your SO keeps making promises they never keep, you always believe them when they say they'll change.

5. You know that your relationship isn't healthy (and maybe even that you have codependent tendencies), but you don't think you need help.

6. You hold out hope that eventually things will just "get better."

7. You really dislike talking about problems or other negative aspects of your relationship.

8. You know things aren't great, but you're always telling yourself it could be worse.

9. You believe you and your SO can fix things on your own.

The Problem with Denial

The biggest problem with denial is that it makes things worse. Imagine you had a rat problem in your basement, and kept insisting that it was okay, or that it wasn't that bad, or that you didn't need to call an exterminator. Those rats wouldn't just go away because you ignored them. In fact, they would keep multiplying until they were spilling out of your basement and taking over the whole house. That's what denial is like. It not only makes the situation worse by enabling your SO's problems, it makes other symptoms of codependency like the loss of self, painful emotions, weak boundary-setting, low self-esteem, and others worse, too. Depending on the severity of your issues, denial can be life-threatening for both you and your SO.

Dealing with Denial

Once you come to the conclusion that you are codependent and in some kind of denial, what do you do? There are four things to prepare for and remember when setting out on the road to recovery:

Accept All the Emotions

Denial numbs emotions. Once you realize the truth, you'll be hit by a wave of emotions. Shame is a widespread one. Before deciding it's time to really break from denial's shell, brace yourself. Accept that you are going to be feeling a lot, and most of it won't feel very good. However, you should also be prepared to accept whatever emotions come your way. Don't look at it with disdain or judgment - only acceptance. By being gentle and accepting all the emotions that come with letting go of denial, you are in a much better place to move on and make real changes in your life.

Consider why you're In Denial

With pretty much all of the symptoms of codependency, there are hidden layers. It's like an iceberg, with just a bit poking out that's clearly seen, while beneath the surface, the real stuff can be found. Think about why you're in denial about the problems in your relationship. Is it because of fear? Are you afraid that acknowledging reality will mean losing your SO? Maybe your denial stems from a long habit pattern originating with your childhood or a specific relationship. By examining the reasons for your denial, you can target the right source and prevent future repeats of your codependent symptoms.

Build a Support Network

It shouldn't be a surprise that a support network is an essential part of overcoming denial, since it's an integral part of dealing with all codependency traits. Supportive friends and family are essential, as well as a therapist and group like AL-Anon. Reading about codependency and denial can also be very helpful. All together, these people and resources can help you uncover the reasons behind your denial, how your specific denial manifests, and how to resist the natural temptation to retreat back into denial. You want a network that's supportive, but honest, and has your best interest in mind. They might tell you some hard truths, but at the end of the day, your support network should make you feel lifted up and not torn down. They will help build up your self-esteem and sense of self.

Be Patient with Yourself

Getting over denial is not easy. Your natural instinct is to keep shrinking back to it, where you don't have to face harsh realities about your relationship or yourself, and where painful emotions can be numbed. Instead of entertaining feelings of guilt or shame about this response, be patient with yourself. You can't change old habits in an instant. Give yourself some grace and forgiveness when denial creeps back in, and acknowledge that maybe that denial was necessary for a time, so you didn't feel overwhelmed by the journey. By being patient and not expecting massive changes all at once, you are more likely to progress and not get bogged down by negative self-talk.

Chapter 42   Symptoms of Codependency

Codependency generally occurs as your answer to the chemical dependency of another person. It's about your interactions in your lives with the individuals. It includes the impacts that these individuals have on you. Then you attempt to influence them and their behaviors in turn. You end up attempting to regulate their conduct as you start to see them spiraling out of control.

However, the co-dependence soul lies in you, not the other person. It's a silent war that you're starting within. Usually, it develops from low self-esteem. The individual who is codependent does not feel worthy. It's a dysfunctional self-relation. It manifests externally to others because you live a dysfunctional connection internally. You don't love yourself, neither do you trust yourself. You tend to be out of harmony and out of equilibrium. You may find yourself disconnected. You tend to live life in a reactionary way.

It is acknowledged that chemical dependency is a disease. Codependency may not be recognized in the same way, but it can make you sick, and won't help you or your loved ones to recover. Codependency is a progressive illness. As things get worse around you, your responses to these things get more intense. You may believe you're helping the other individual in the back of your mind. Maybe you have the best intentions as you watch them destroy themselves. You don't understand that this not only sabotages your connection with that individual, but it also sabotages yourself by continually having to react to their conduct. It is an exhausting way to live.

Codependents feel obliged to provide guidance to the other, to help fix what you see as their issues. You feel the other person is your responsibility. You're attempting to please them and are lost somewhere, wrapped up in that process. You want them to see you in their lives as necessary. You want them to see how important you are for their well-being. You're even going to give up your own routine to help someone else.

If your assistance is either brushed off, or not working the way you believed it would, you get upset. You blame others for the way things are. You blame others for feeling the way you do. You're feeling disappointed, used, and victimized. But you learn how to withstand it over time. You live with constant anxiety, hurt, and rage.

There is assistance if these signs sound familiar. Once you have determined that these emotions and tendencies do not assist you, or the other individual in any manner, you need to concentrate on correcting your tendency towards codependency. First, recognize the responsibility of all of us for our own emotions and behavior. Do not be afraid to let the other person live their life, and suffer their own consequences. Love the individual and be there for them, but do not attempt to regulate or manipulate their behavior's final result. It may be difficult at first, but they also have a lesson to learn - you won't always be there to rescue them from their poor decisions.

Second, understand that you deserve to be loved. Don't focus your life on others who think you don't also deserve happiness. Stop looking for interactions to make you feel good. Look inside, and begin to love yourself. Others around you will then see the radiance that you display, and gravitate toward you.

Third, start focusing on your own life. You probably let it fall to the wayside during your caretaking.. Look within yourself for your joy, not outward towards others. Think of your feelings and what happens to you. Then focus on the measures you can take to begin a happy life.

You may be codependent, but you understand you're an influential person. You've simply focused your attention in the wrong place. You have the ability to alter and begin recovery. While letting the other individual be who they are, you will be who you are.

For nearly four centuries, the word codependency has been around. Although it was initially applied to alcoholic spouses, first called co-alcoholics, studies discovered that in the general population the prevalence of co-dependents was much higher than had previously been thought. They actually discovered that if you were brought up in a dysfunctional family, or had an ill parent, you are more likely to be co-dependent. If that includes you, don't feel bad. Most of America's families are dysfunctional, so you're in the majority, covering just about everybody! They also discovered that untreated, codependent symptoms tended to get worse, but that they were reversible.

Low Self-Esteem

Not feeling good enough or habitually comparing yourself with others is a sign of low self-esteem. The problematic thing about self-esteem is that some individuals believe strongly that they are unlovable, or insufficient, but it's just a camouflage. Underneath it are feelings of shame, generally concealed from consciousness. Some of the things that go with low self-esteem are feelings of guilt and perfectionism. You don't feel bad about yourself if everything is ideal.

People Pleasing

It's okay to want someone you care about to be pleased with you, but usually codependents don't believe they've got a decision. Saying "no" creates anxiety for them. Some codependents find it challenging to say "no" to anyone. They are going out of their way and sacrificing their own needs to accommodate others.

Poor Boundaries

The boundaries between you and others are an imaginary line. It separates what is yours and someone else's, and that not only applies to your body, money, and property, but also to your emotions, ideas, and needs. So this is the reason why codependents get into trouble. They have blurred or weak borders with each other. They feel accountable for the emotions and issues of other people, or blame someone else for their own.

Some codependents have boundaries that are overly rigid. They are closed and withdrawn, making getting near to them difficult for other individuals. Though some will alternate back and forth, between weak and rigid limits, never reaching a healthy middle ground.

Reactivity

A result of poor boundaries is that you respond to the ideas and emotions of everybody. If you disagree with somebody saying something, you either resent them or become defensive. You absorb their words because no boundaries exist. With a limit, you would understand that it merely is their view, not a reflection of you, not a threat to you or personal attack.

184

Caretaking

Another impact of poor boundaries is that you want to assist if someone else has an issue, even to the detriment of yourself and your own wellbeing. It's natural for someone to feel empathy and compassion and sacrifice some of their own needs for others some of the time, but codependents put other individuals before them almost all the time. If an individual does not want assistance and does not request it the codependent person may feel rejected. In addition, they continue to try to assist, even if that individual obviously does not take their advice.

Control

Control enables you to feel safe and secure. Everyone in their lives requires some control over occurrences. You wouldn't want to live in perpetual uncertainty and chaos, but control limits your capacity to take risks and share your emotions. Sometimes codependents have an addiction that either helps them loosen up, such as alcoholism, or helps them hold down their feelings, such as workaholic, so they don't feel out of control.

Dysfunctional Communication

Codependents often have difficulty communicating their ideas, emotions, and needs. Of course, this becomes a problem if you don't understand what you believe, feel, or need. You understand, other times, but you're not going to own your reality. You're afraid to be accurate, because you don't want someone else to get angry. Instead of saying, "I don't like that," you might pretend it's all right, or tell someone else what to do. When you attempt to manipulate the other individual out of fear like this, communication becomes dishonest and confusing.

Obsessions

Codependents have a tendency to think about other individuals or interactions obsessively. This is due to their dependence, fears, and anxieties. They may also get obsessed when they believe they've created or made an "error." Sometimes you may lapse into fantasy about how you want things to be, or fantasize about someone you love as a way to prevent the present's pain. This is one way, mentioned below, to remain in denial, but it prevents you from living your life.

Dependency

Codependents need other individuals to like them in order to feel beautiful about themselves, and they're scared they will be either dismissed or deserted - even if they can work alone. Others always need to be in a partnership because they feel depressed or solitary when they are too long on their own. This characteristic makes it difficult for them, even if the relationship is painful or abusive, to end a relationship. They feel trapped.

Denial

One of the problems that people face in getting help for codependency is that they deny it, which means they don't face their issue. Usually they believe somebody else or the scenario is the issue. Either they continue to complain or try to solve the other individual, or they go from one relationship or task to another, and never own the fact that they have an issue.

Codependents deny their emotions and needs as well. They often don't understand what they feel, and are centered on what others feel. The same applies to their requirements. They are paying attention to the requirements of other people, not their own. They may deny their need for room and autonomy. While some codependents appear to be needy, others behave as if they are self-sufficient or in need of assistance. They're not going to reach out and get help. They deny their vulnerability and they need love and intimacy to keep doing so.

Problems with Intimacy

I am not referring to sex by this, although sexual dysfunction is often a facet of problems with intimacy. I'm speaking about an intimate relationship, being able to be open with, and close to, someone. You might be afraid of being judged, dismissed, or left because of shame and rigid boundaries. On the other hand, in a partnership you may be afraid of being smothered and losing your autonomy. You may deny your need for proximity and think your partner takes up too much of your time; your partner may complain you are unavailable, but he or she denies the need for separation.

Painful Emotions

Codependency generates stress and feelings that are painful. Shame and low self-esteem generate fear and anxiety

1. Being judged

2. Being rejected or abandoned

3. Making mistakes

4. Being a failure

5. Being close and feeling trapped

6. Being alone

These symptoms result in emotions of anger and resentment, depression, desperation, and hopelessness. You may feel numb when the emotions are too intense. Recovery is possible and help is available. The first phase is to be guided and supported. These symptoms are habits that are deeply ingrained and hard to define and alter alone.

Chapter 43   Codependent and Their Personalities

Codependents have an innate ability to attract other people into their life who aren't motivated or interested in participating in a give and take relationship. By continually choosing narcissists or addicts as romantic partners or friends, codependents tend to find their feeling disrespected, undervalued, and unfulfilled. While they likely complain and they feel resentful about the inequality of their relationships, codependents feel as if they are stuck and can't change.

The passive codependent will often be fearful and avoidant when it comes to conflicts. They will try to influence or control their partners through carefully executed strategies, and most of them will go unnoticed. This is because they have a fear of being alone, low self-esteem, and tendency to find themselves in relationships with people who are controlling, abusive, or dangerous. Since they make sure that they are hidden and secretive in their controlling actions, they tend to be viewed as the more manipulative codependent.

Then the active codependent tends to be more bold and overt with their manipulation tactics. They aren't as afraid of harm and conflict, and they have a bigger chance of starting arguments with their partner. These people are sometimes viewed as slightly narcissistic since they are open with their actions. While they are always in a cycle of trying to control others, who aren't interested in meeting their needs, they still don't feel any urge to end the relationship. They believe wholeheartedly that they can "fix" the other person. This never happens.

While both of these codependents may look different on the outside, they both have an "others" self-orientation. They will often stick close to addicts or narcissists while also experiencing feelings of unhappiness, resentfulness, and anger because the relationship lacks reciprocity. While active codependents will sometimes appear to be healthier, both have extreme insecurities. Neither one of them can break free from their relationships.

Codependency is not only booking into two subcategories of active and passive; those can also be broken down into five other subcategories.

Martyr

For this codependent, suffering is a virtue, especially when it comes to placing the needs of others before their own. At least these are things that some people will learn from the family, religious institution, or cultural heritage. At work, this type of codependent will pick up other projects and usually is the last person to leave at night, choosing to say no to drinks with friends. If they do go out, they will always pay without being asked, even if they don't really have the money.

When a person's being is wholly made up of sacrifices, it will often cause them to neglect their needs for love and care. Ironically, this is the same reason these codependents are trying to get the appreciation of others. This tends to backfire. Not only do they tend to resent those that they help, but the other person will either take everything they do for granted or will resent the codependent as well. Martyrs tend to be a type of active codependency.

Savior

The world is a scary place, but the savior is here to protect everybody. When their child is facing some type of problem at school, they are in the principal's office the next morning to fix the problem. When their friend can't make rent, again, they will give them some cash, again, so that they don't end up being kicked out.

Everybody is going to need help at some point. But when there is a person that feels personally responsible for providing other people with comfort, they strip that person of their chance to take care of their own comfort and wellbeing. The codependent will enable that person's self-limiting actions and will send them messages that they are helpless. With time, the other person may start to believe this. This is a type of passive codependence.

Adviser

To get a good idea of this type of codependent, take a moment to think about the Peanuts comic strip. Lucy is the perfect example. She sits from daylight to dark at a makeshift desk providing others with advice about anything and everything. This person could have a great skill in helping people through their problems and offering them some clear options. They too believe that they have great insight into the problems of others. Listening, though, may not even be the strength of theirs.

This is definitely a tango type of situation. This codependent tends to see people who seek advice as a person who doesn't have a lot of self-esteem. But the things are, the people who feel as if they have to control and advice others have just as much insecurity. This is what is called borrowed functioning. The codependent takes charge and tells others what they should do, and they are just as needy as the other person. They need to have a person allow them to be in charge to help give their self-esteem a boost. They are both dependent. This is a form of active codependence.

People Pleaser

This codependent will be the one volunteering at their children's school and helping all of their neighbors fix things. They are the ones that volunteer to make the coffee run. They love it when they get to feel the love and bask in all of the praise for their generosity. But there is darkness to all of this.

The codependent reaches the dark side when they start to no longer feel appreciated, or when the thoughts of doing something feels like a chore. They know they have reached it when they start to use their skills to control people. They have the belief that other people will like them for all of their favors instead of liking them for who they are. This is a type of passive codependence.

Yes Man

This is the person who says yes to everything even if they really want to say no, and they end up resenting them. They will fake a smile in agreement with others instead of telling the truth. They will always remain passive with their romantic problems and they won't tell them when they get upset.

Therapists will often hear comments like, "We never fight," from people in therapy. They will look at their therapist for some type of approval, but all this lets them know is that there isn't any honesty within the relationship. Not having any conflict within a relationship isn't a good thing. Look at it from a business perspective. In a business where most people are "fine" with their jobs and they don't complain tend to do so because they are afraid of losing their job. When you push away your real feelings, instead of trying to find a right way of sharing them, will create problems. This is a type of passive codependence.

Building Codependency in Childhood

It may be hard to think of a child as a codependent. As humans, we begin to form psychosocial problems from the moment that we are born. Children respond to people and things that happen around them from the get-go. Children are just starting to develop their personality traits up until they reach their teenage years, so it might be better to say that early programming could end up in causing codependency traits in life.

Adolescents

A person will reach their fifth stage of development when they reach adolescence. This usually is between the ages of 12 and 18. This is the time when they focus on Identity VS Role Confusion. Teens tend to struggle with fitting in and they try to figure out who they are. They create close ties, figure out how they should interact in intimate ways, and they think about their morals. This is the weird in-between phase of not being a child yet not being an adult.

Parents

Codependency is most often passed down in the family. If unhealthy patterns continue to live in unconsciousness, it won't be changed. If you aren't aware of something, how can you change it? As you move through this awareness, it's crucial that you don't start to feel guilty and beat yourself up when you begin to realize that you may have modeled codependent behavior for your children.

What parents want is for their children to grow up in a safe environment so that they can be healthy functioning adults. Parenting is incredible, but it is also daunting. A perfect parent does not exist and that is okay.

Friendship

Actions of codependency are most often seen within the most intimate relationship. This can create subtle codependent actions, or it can create rippling patterns. Codependency can be occasional or chronic.

Let's look at Tonya.

She has a friend, Rhianna, who she hasn't seen since they graduated high school. Rhianna e-mailed Tonya letting her know that she had just gotten a divorce as was moving to Buffalo where Tonya lives. Tonya has been there for 20 years now. Rhianna lets her know that she is afraid of moving there, so Tonya tells her that she will help her get settled in and sets up a lunch date.

Tonya is already at the restaurant when Rhianna rushes in. They hug, sit, and Rhianna immediately starts complaining about all the traffic. She hates all the crowds and asks Tonya why she didn't suggest a place that was closer to her house.

As the waiter comes up, Tonya smiles and greets him nicely. She frequents the restaurant and knows him. When he brings them their order, Rhianna is upset? She says the portions aren't big enough. The waiter asks if she would like more soup or bread, but the more careful he tries to be, the angrier Rhianna gets. Eventually, she tells him to take the salad away and asks for a burger. She eats the burgers, but fusses that it was "undercooked." For the rest of the two-hour lunch, Tonya has to listen to Rhianna rant about her ex.

Rhianna starts calling Tonya up every day to ask her for recommendations. When they meet up, Rhianna complains about the suggestions Tonya made. She is angry that Tonya's dentist caused her gums to bleed. Tonya leaves this lunch feeling tense.

Tonya is throwing her annual holiday party and invites Rhianna. After the party, Rhianna starts complaining about how the guests were rude to her. Tonya listens for a bit and then excuses herself. Tonya begins screening calls, so she doesn't have to talk to Rhianna. Tonya's husband resents the negativity that Rhianna has caused for them.

Tonya understands this, but whenever she sees Rhianna, she feels she has to spend time with her. She starts hiding the lunches she has with Rhianna from her husband.

Tonya doesn't know how to create boundaries with Rhianna. She doesn't like Rhianna all that much at this point, but she feels stuck. Tonya always feels stressed, and at home, she jumps every time the phone rings. She knows the things her husband says are correct, so now Rhianna is affecting her marriage. Tonya hides things from her husband. The problem is, Rhianna thrives on anger and Tonya is codependent on her and doesn't know how to end the relationship.

Chapter 44   Narcissist and Codependency

Much of self-explanatory literature describes co-dependency and narcissism as polar opposites. Co-dependency is frequently connected with surplus selflessness. Narcissistic personality disorder (NPD) is frequently linked to excessive selfishness.

Many narratives depict co-dependent individuals as victims that fall prey to people with real traits. This oversimplification fails a hard fact in the center of the two co-dependency and narcissism: equally co-dependents and narcissists can deficiency a wholesome sense of self.

Co-Dependency and Narcissism: Much Needs, Different Behaviors

Narcissism and co-dependency are linked to an itself. They frequently struggle to acquire a feeling of who they're. Therefore, they put a great deal of significance on what others consider these.

Individuals with NPD often create an extreme, almost exclusive attention on themselves. They may exhibit a lack of compassion or respect for others' needs. They might just care for others' feelings compared to themselves. Narcissistic individuals frequently require somebody else to match their self-esteem. They might require a constant flow of affection and respect to feel great about themselves. Some self-help sites refer to the flow as a "narcissistic supply"

Meanwhile, folks with co-dependency are usually hyper-focused others. They generally form an identity around serving the others' needs. They might attempt to control another individual's behavior, believing that they know what's ideal for the individual. Rather than praise, co-dependents frequently crave appreciation and also a feeling of "being required."

Virtually everyone needs to feel important or loved. Narcissism and co-dependency are two approaches to attain that objective. But, the two conditions can make an excessive dependence on the others' approval.

The Common Origins of Co-Dependency and Narcissism

The two co-dependency and narcissism are connected to adverse childhood experiences. A 2001 analysis of 793 moms and kids discovered a massive growth in NPD among kids whose moms were abusive. A 1999 analysis of 200 school students linked co-dependent behaviors to youth parentification. Parentification is every time a kid takes to a caretaker role because of their parent or parents, often because of abuse or neglect.

Individuals with NPD and co-dependency frequently have similar childhood adventures. They have just adopted different methods of adapting. By way of instance, say a set of twins develop failed. 1 sibling may create a very low self-esteem and find out they're just "worth something" when they're useful to other people. They could grow to a co-dependent adult who's accustomed to sacrificing their particular needs. The next sibling could create an inflated self-esteem as a protective mechanism. The negligence makes the kid feel immaterial, in order that as adult, they might crave continuous validation to show that their self-worth.

The co-dependent and exotic elephants can develop quite different behaviors and characters. However, in both situations, injury and also a fractured sense of self can be in the center of the issue.

Understanding the Dance of Narcissism and Co-Dependency

Individuals with co-dependency occasionally form relationships with individuals who've NPD. Typically the 2 partners create distinct functions to fulfill one another's needs. The co-dependent man has discovered a partner they could pour yourself in, along with also the narcissistic person has discovered somebody who puts their needs.

But this energetic can become more unhealthy. The co-dependent individual might attempt to live vicariously through their epic spouse. If their spouse does not show enough appreciation for their support, the co-dependent person could sense bitterness. The narcissistic individual often replenishes their spouse's people-pleasing trends for their very own narcissistic supply. As their self develops, their needs may grow, before the co-dependent person finally ends up.

Even should they create an abusive relationship, neither spouse might attempt to leave. Both individuals may remain in a weak position because of fear of being lonely. Without assistance, this energetic can develop increasingly hazardous.

195

Can Co-Dependency And Narcissism Overlap?

Narcissism and co-dependency are not necessarily opposites. The urge to feel needed isn't that distinct from the urge to feel significant. When many studies find lower levels of narcissism among individuals with co-dependency, many have really found more excellent rates of narcissism one of people that have co-dependent traits.

Someone who's co-dependent in 1 situation may be narcissistic in another. As an example, a individual could become co-dependent within their union, serving their partner's every demand. Yet the exact identical individual may sense a steady demand for compliments and respect in their kids. Inducing them to manifest significant tendencies.

Sometimes, an abusive person may attempt to gaslight that a co-dependent partner into thinking they're narcissistic. The abuser could undermine any series of self-confidence by phoning their spouse "egotistical." normal functions of self-care, like taking days spending some time with friends, might be labeled "greedy" the co-dependent person might think these accusations and attempt to correct the connection by ignoring their particular needs. Someone isolated from family members --that might provide a more objective opinion --is very likely to believe they're a narcissist.

How all people today display narcissistic or plagiarize traits on event could make it more difficult for an individual to choose if they are erroneous, co-dependent, or even both.

Co-Dependency and Narcissism: Treatment May Help

Co-dependency and narcissism can become pathological whenever they undermine an individual's quality of lifestyle or induce the man to damage others. It can be time for you to seek out assistance should you reveal these hints:

1. A record of connections where abuse has already been current.

2. Difficulty atmosphere close to other people.

3. Feelings of emptiness or very low self-esteem.

4. Feeling like your individuality is dependent on what others think about you.

5. Feeling like many others do not totally love you or admit your significance.

6. Feeling just like you're never adequately thanked for whatever you've given up.

A therapist may help individuals with narcissism or co-dependency know the origin of the insecurities. In treatment, you can discover how to replace faulty coping mechanisms with healthy behaviors. Talking through your adventures will allow you access to current methods of being.

Co-dependents deficiency a wholesome relationship. They're prone to place others before their particular needs. That can be unhealthy.

Narcissists also have a poor relationship. They place themselves over all else. They utilize the others in their endings and exploit relationships with no the feelings of guilt or guilt. They push blame on other people and cannot view their own role in wrong doing.

It's easy to view just how co-dependents and narcissists become hooked up. It's like two bits of this puzzle coming together. One might be the effortless mark for another. However, there's a more profound link.

It's discovered that you will find familial links to the interaction. In case you have a parent whose narcissistic you're very likely to become co-dependent or depriving yourself. In case you've got two adoptive parents the exact same holds true.

After a person starts to recover from co-dependency, they can start placing boundaries and standing to the narcissist. It's quite tough for many people to surmise of somebody who's completely bereft of their capacity to empathize and understand from prior mistakes. The main error that the co-dependent makes would be to provide the benefit of the doubt to this narcissistic partner as it's so tough to fathom someone may be so egotistical and unyielding. Thus the energetic starts.

The fantastic news for the stark reality is there is hope for healing when they completely realize that the narcissist lacks the ability of empathy that defines us as people. Because co-dependents are not easy to blame for issues they can work nicely with a therapist to produce changes. Not so for your narcissist. They're stuck inside their realm of non-attribute and are pathological unable to modify. How can you shift if they cannot realize there is something wrong together?

Highly recommend co-dependents anonymous for people that are trying to spare themselves for connections which are poisonous and violent. It's a program filled with special guidelines for healing from this kind of damaging relationship.

So far as help for that the narcissist well the ideal thing would be to shake off the dust off your feet and steer clear therefore that they do not get an opportunity to use one. The sole hope for your narcissist is they develop dependence and can seek out help for this where they may learn another method to link to the entire world. Alcoholics anonymous is now the best treatment modality for your millennial kind...but chances of recovery are slim.

Narcissist-Co-Dependent Relationships: If Addiction Is Not Just About Drug and Drug

Narcissist and co-dependent relationships happen when two individuals with complementary psychological imbalances start to rely on each other, resulting in a growing spiral of injury for the two people. Oftentimes, medication or other addictive behaviors are included, developing an extremely volatile situation where an unhealthy relationship centers on both spouses' destructive behavioral routines.

This kind of connection involves two different personality types. Narcissists will likely place themselves above all, use different individuals to accomplish their own endings, harness relationships without feeling guilty, and blame others when things fail, or perhaps look down on others just to improve their self-esteem.

For their own part, co-dependents have a tendency to deficiency self-esteem, enable other people to make decisions on their own put others ahead of themselves, feel that the necessity to maintain a connection, and are excessively determined by someone else -- their own narcissistic spouses, for instance.

After these relationships are shaped, it can be exceedingly tricky to let go of these. Guard yourself out of co-dependency is essential for lots of reasons, though it needs a fantastic deal of comprehension, self-examination, plus guts. Both narcissist and the co-dependent have the propensity to fortify one another in unfavorable ways, particularly in situations which involve alcohol or drug dependence. However, with the ideal measure of advice and service, it's indeed feasible to safely finish a relationship that is overburdened, to get your long-term advantage of everyone involved.

The Way to Finish a Co-Dependent Relationship

All human relationships are mentally stressful sometimes, and especially so when a individual breaks apart from another. People today need support from people closest to them through emotional moments, and also preventing yourself by co-dependency is a particularly stressful experience. Co-dependency involves real mental health problems on either side, which means that the choice to finish such a connection goes contrary to several deep-rooted customs.

Taking this daring step ahead therefore takes a solid conviction it is the correct and necessary thing to do. This belief has to be bolstered from the folks round the co-dependent, that assist them view their position with a clarity their particular emotions occasionally don't produce. The co-dependent must learn how to imagine a favorable result doesn't have to call their spouse, and their spouse also wants a type of help the co-dependent can't give.

The degree of comprehension and strength required to break loose from the connection will be evasive when the co-dependent remains within the connection. An appraisal from friends or family could be required, such as a physical separation from their spouse. Psychologists and therapists may demonstrate the co-dependent the road forward is really brighter as it might look initially. And through constant practice, reinforcement, and growth of psychological health, co-dependents can really rise above their current situation -- and also learn how to embrace a healthier way of themselves and others.

Chapter 45   Codependency in the Workplace

Have you at any point felt put upon in the work environment? However despite everything you volunteer to assist when there is something that necessities doing in a rush. The issue might be codependency yet it may not be adding to your profession prospects. Regardless of how hard you work and how much work you produce, in the event that you are mutually dependent upon a manager who uses you, the odds are that you additionally have an impact in the circumstance. Individuals who need certainty and who look for endorsement for the work that they do are regularly mutually dependent without acknowledging it. When they don't get recognition of any sort, they make a special effort to look for it. This doesn't make you a significant individual from staff, despite the fact that you may consider yourself to be being imperative. You may even find that you are underestimated so much that notwithstanding when you get away, you return to all the work heaped up prepared for you.

In a circumstance, for example, this, you are being utilized in light of the fact that you enable yourself to be utilized. You may not see it that way and may long for the endorsement that you have. Nonetheless, it's impossible that you will be considered for advancement, in light of the fact that your destitute nature implies that you don't have the stuff to be the board material. It might seem like somewhat of a killjoy to you that you have buckled down for little return, yet you are putting yourself in an endless loop and need to break free of it. Not just that, you may likewise be somebody who wants to work alone and are not an especially decent colleague. You don't have the foggiest idea how to designate and would prefer to be overloaded with work and feel required than offer what you have with others.

This is a circumstance that will in the long run lead to wear out and in spite of the fact that individuals may have cautioned you about that, your temperament won't cause you to trust it. You do what you do in light of the fact that maybe you don't get acclaim in some other part of your life. You have to assess your life and settle on the accompanying:

1. Do you have a decent work life/home life balance?

2. Do you appreciate the work that you do?

3. Would you appreciate it as much without the commendation that you look for?

To escape the endless loop that you have placed yourself in for reasons unknown or other, you have to think once again into your past and discover at what phase of your life you previously felt that you were not given acknowledgment for something that you did, in light of the fact that regularly this sort of codependence originates from youth.

Jan realized that she had issues however she didn't have the foggiest idea how genuine they were. Consistently she obediently got down to business and slaved albeit nobody had ever anticipated that measure of dedication from a representative in a moderately junior position. The issue emerged when she all of a sudden acknowledged during the nonattendance of her supervisor that nobody else appeared to give her the sort of input she pined for. She was lost. At that point, glancing through her past with an advisor, what she found was that during her youth, her mom never remembered whatever she did as being beneficial. Her mom would even leave the room instead of recognize that Jan could accomplish something that her mom was unequipped for. Every one of the long periods of youth, she had attempted her best to dazzle her mom − not on the grounds that she expected to − but since she felt dislodged and even had questions about whether her mom was extremely her mom. She couldn't comprehend why her mom couldn't recognize her. This pursued her into adulthood and in her first work, she was shocked that individuals really thought what she was doing was an advantageous employment. At that point she scrutinized their earnestness as far as she could tell, trusting herself not so much to be deserving of the recognition that she was getting. Hence the cycle started and she hungered for that criticism that solitary her supervisor could give her.

The issue with this kind of conduct is that she didn't really require that affirmation and was very equipped for doing a decent day's worth of effort however had slipped into the requirement for it feeling that it was the main thing that approved her. In the event that you feel that you are falling into this snare at work, you have to locate another path forward on the grounds that it is neither solid nor beneficial to be so needy upon another person to approve what your identity is. A supervisor who needs increasingly more out of you may really urge powerless individuals to accomplish increasingly more work on the grounds that typically individuals with low confidence don't approach much as a byproduct of their work. Regularly feeling approved is just as significant as getting a reasonable compensation for a decent day's worth of effort.

While it may not be the most beneficial thing for you to surrender your activity, particularly on the off chance that you rely on it to take care of your tabs, you have to adopt an alternate strategy. Watch individuals around you and perceive how they adapt to the remaining task at hand that they have. In the event that you don't request approval, the main approval you truly need is from yourself. On the off chance that you realize that you did an extraordinary day's worth of effort, learn not to request approval. Rather than that, treat yourself to something and salute yourself for what you have done. For Linda's situation, she figured out how to get things done to satisfy herself. You should do likewise. Within you, you have something many refer to as inspiration. Try not to give it a chance to be constrained by another person. Control it yourself and you become roused without requiring untrustworthiness and burning through the time looking for it. More often than not, damaging supervisor's heap on more work when you look for this sort of approval and you wind up inclination overpowered rather than satisfied that you had the option to deal with your remaining task at hand.

Try Not To Do It For That Person. Do It for You

Set little objectives for yourself that nobody else thinks about. Individuals who consistently give come a shot as victors. Trust me, it takes some time for this to soak in yet it truly works. For instance, in the event that you have twelve assignments to do in a day, work out which ones take need and set yourself little focuses on that are feasible. Increase your certainty inside yourself by keeping to your very own timetable. Obviously, need occupations complete first, however you have to switch the inspiration. It's not for the chief. It's for you. Make the challenge inside yourself adequately rousing that when you prevail at something, just you think about it. What other individuals think about your aptitudes and your objectives is irrelevant toward the day's end.

By doing this, you develop trust in yourself and needn't bother with approval from anybody. For Linda's situation, she was a splendid craftsman, but since her mom had never recognized it, she had taken care of her paintbrushes and had abandoned her energy throughout everyday life. Nobody should ever let another person direct their prosperity. When she at last developed her notoriety for being a splendid painter, she did as such alone terms and individuals rushed to approach her to do drawings for them. Actually, she experienced no difficulty making her energy into something very considerable, despite the fact that she additionally discovered that she didn't need to satisfy another person as long as she was content with the outcomes. She additionally figured out how to state "no" which is a hard exercise for somebody who has confidence and codependency issues.

Liberating Yourself

Give yourself some close to home objectives just as business related objectives and make them sensible. The explanation you start basic is with the goal that you can achieve those objectives. At that point, gradually, as you gain certainty, you can make the objectives somewhat harder. Keep in mind that you are just making them for yourself and for nobody else. You are the one in particular that you are out to please. When you have made your objectives for at home and you have kept them, take a gander at your face in the mirror and consider yourself to be the achievement that you are. Toward the day's end, the main individual's assessment of you that issues is your own. When you can recognize your very own triumphs, you don't should be needy upon your manager to approve you and you can go ahead in your vocation since you are never again a channel on individuals.

Chapter 46   How Improve Co-Dependent Life

The hardest but most fundamental responsibility that you will take on is facing your codependency and that of the people you are closest to. You will be taking a huge leap of faith, so you can become vulnerable with hopes of being a person who is more confident in the future. In order for this transformation to happen, you have to learn how to walk through your world with confidence and grace, set boundaries that are right for you, interact with people in a kind but direct manner, and be assertive when dealing with problems.

Learn To Be a Better Family Member

Once you have learned your codependency patterns go back to your family, you may have discovered there are some skeletons in your closet. If you have been denying any shortcomings or abuse within your family, this might have been a rather painful revelation. You need to explore your family's origins so that you can understand your codependency. Remember that you aren't perfect and this means that your family isn't perfect either.

Origins of Family

You have to use your journal and really think about your family. Try to write down any patterns or behaviors that might have caused you to become codependent. Make a heading for all your family members and try answering all the following questions:

1. What feelings do you feel the most when you are around this person?

2. Was this person around when you needed them?

3. From what you know now, are they really codependent?

4. From what you know now, are they really narcissistic?

5. Were the chronically physically or mentally ill?

6. Did this person express their feeling easily?

7. Did they yell or blow up at you when they got angry?

8. Did they make you feel loved?

9. Has this person broken any laws or engaged in dangerous or reckless activities?

10. Were they ever physically, emotionally, or sexually abusive?

11. Did this person push any mistaken beliefs onto you?

12. How did they deal with anger or handle conflicts?

13. Did this person ever get addicted to drugs, smoking, spending, alcohol, gambling, anger, etc.?

14. Did the person ever model any codependent behaviors to you? If so, what were they?

Once you have written about all your family members and answered these questions, see if you can find out or affirm what you know about your family and how they may have unknowingly planted the seeds of your codependency.

Now, take some time to look at what you have discovered and see if there are unresolved issued within your family. It doesn't help to dig up pain and hurt and leave it unattended.

Find out if you can resolve these problems by yourself, or if you need to address them with a certain family member. Your goal is to stop being a victim. What could you do to stop these ghosts from haunting you?

There are some ways you can look at all the information you found out about your family. One way is to find out how these things might be affecting your relationships now, how they could change your behavior with them. The second way is to find out if you need to confront the problems you have with specific family members. Will this help lessen their power over you?

Some people like working with just their current family meaning their significant other and children. Some people want to talk to their family members and parents that they were around while growing up.

There won't ever be a right or wrong decision when talking about family origin wounds. If they are still abusing you, you might need to decide to tell them to stop. You can stop spending time with them and put firm boundaries in place. You may decide to deal with any unwanted behaviors when they come up. It is totally up to you.

Being a Better Friend

Once you begin changing and moving toward a life without codependency, you will attract new friends. These friendships will be more interdependent and mutual. While working toward being an equal friend you are going to have two different aspects of friendship you will need to write about in your journal.

Getting to Know Your Friends Better

Just like you wrote about your family in your journal, you need to do the same thing with your friends. Don't worry about acquaintances, just the people you consider to be a real friend. Write their names at the top of the page. If you only have a few friends who are really close, this is totally normal. You could include friends that you think of as your second-tier friends. Now, you need to decide if your old friends still fit in with the new you. If these friendships are codependent, you can decide to move on, or you might decide to work on moving the friendship into a better place.

Answer these questions to help you figure it out:

1. If you aren't available when your friend wants you, do they get mad?

2. Are your friends very demanding?

3. Do your friends ever cancel lunch dates or they just don't show up?

4. Do your friends always ask for your advice?

5. When you talk to your friend, do they talk more than 50 percent of the time?

6. Is your friend unstable or fragile?

7. Do you have to walk on eggshells when you are around them constantly?

8. Are your friends not interested in what you are going through and don't realize you are struggling?

9. Do your friends call and expect you to stop whatever you are doing and talk to them right then?

You may realize that some friends are making your life better. You are the only person who truly knows if the friendship is hopeless and you need to move on. If you decide to try to help them, these friendships might be helpful in giving you opportunities to work on your codependency consistently.

Fixing Problems

Look at your friends closely by writing in your journal. Are there any unresolved problems that you have been too afraid to talk about with them? Make a list for all your friends and process everyone. You have to decide if you can get rid of the problems you can't control you just don't want to deal with them. If problems are still there, try to approach them. If you learn to be more honest and forthright with your friends and they get offensive, you now to have information that could help you make better decisions about your friendship.

Before you start talking with your friends, you have to know what you want to achieve. What motivates you? If you are motivated to strengthen the friendship and resolve things by being honest, go ahead. If you feel brave enough to let them know they are being a jerk, just save your breath and let them go.

Look at Your New Friends

While you are changing, new people are going to come into your life. They will see you are compassionate, well-adjusted, and assertive; a person who is honest about how they feel and know their expectations and boundaries. This might not be what they are looking for. They may want to fulfill some codependency needs. They may want a friend who is codependent and will take care of them.

You now know enough about codependency to see red flags in relationships and friendships. Take care of any concerns you might have immediately. Remember to put yourself and your needs first and you have the right to stop any friendship that doesn't feel healthy at any time. If a new friend begins to cancel all the get-togethers you have planned at the start of the friendship, this might show that they aren't really interested in you at all. If your new friends begin to ask you for favors, this might show they are extremely needy. If new friends begin to talk about themselves nonstop, this isn't good either. If a new friend is offended easily, gossips about other friends get moody, misunderstands you all the time, these are all big red flags.

There is an old saying that goes something like: "Partners come and go but friends are forever."

Yes, friends are important for our emotional well-being, and some friendships do last a lifetime. Just make sure you pick your friends wisely.

Becoming Free from Codependency

Every person you meet in your lifetime and all the situations you face will give you an opportunity to fine-tune your freedom from being codependent. How can this change happen and what can you do to help it? Each year research finds something new about human behavior. Psychiatrists used to think that personality disorders can't be changed. Now, they believe just the opposite. The things that people believe can influence their behavior. At first, it was thought to be a brain thing. Then it turned into an environmental/brain thing. Now, because of the advances in neurotechnology, research is newly excited about the brain. Many think neuropsychology will constantly evolve.

These changes that you have been trying to reach are very possible for you to achieve. Your goal is to develop and nourish your identity. Yes, you have an identity. Everybody does. You are only trying to remold your identity. Codependency traits are constant. You might be more or less codependent. You may show one or 50 codependency traits.

You have been given new insights, awareness, and tools that can help you fix your self-esteem, increase your sense of self, and be more confident. You will consistently be working on transforming by watching your behaviors, feelings, and thoughts. You make any adjustment you need to as you go along. You need to be present in your relationships and love.

208

You have to value yourself. You have to find your voice. You have to learn to love yourself with all your flaws. You just might find that you have all sorts of power to expand your happiness.

Chapter 47 How Changing a Codependent Relationship

If you or a loved one is involved in a codependent relationship, the mental (and potentially physical) ramifications of staying in that unhealthy pattern of behavior are far too great to continue going on that way. You run the risk of developing mental and physical exhaustion, and the effects can be both short-term and long-term. Moreover, you may become neglectful in other important areas of your life, such as friendships, family, work, or health. In order to achieve a healthy relationship and an overall sense of wellness, you must be willing to adapt and foster your relationship so that it can move away from a place of codependency.

The detrimental impacts of codependency can become deep-rooted issues in a person's relationship, but that doesn't always mean that splitting up or ridding that person from your life is the only solution. Yes, sometimes the best answer is getting out of the relationship, especially if there is physical harm that's been done. But if both parties are able to recognize the fact that there is an issue present, and the relationship hasn't reached the point of physical abuse or intentional emotional abuse, then there's a chance that conditions can be improved.

Thus, without any conscious knowledge of it, a person can be carrying around behaviors that will lead to codependency. These behaviors and psychological issues may be difficult to bring to the surface, but there are means of reversing destructive actions and patterns.

For one thing, if you or your loved one is suffering from codependency, you've already made a move in the right direction. Education is the most useful tool that you can use in combatting codependency, and by reading this, you're arming yourself with the power to improve a relationship.

You must make a very difficult decision and determine whether or not you can stay in the codependent relationship, or whether you want to in the first place. Oftentimes, people are afraid to leave codependent relationships, either because they're afraid of the loneliness that will come afterwards, or they're scared that their partner won't be able to live without them, or both. Nonetheless, these are not worthwhile reasons to stay in a relationship. This is the most crucial aspect you must realize when it comes to overcoming codependency: you are not responsible for another's happiness. That being said, you can control your own happiness. If, after doing some soul searching, you come to the conclusion that you truly want to end the relationship (or if you've known it all along but have been afraid to acknowledge it truly), then it's time to move on.

Again, terminating the relationship does not have to be the answer. Oftentimes, a relationship becomes codependent overtime, possibly because both parties have fallen into a set of destructive behaviors. It is reversible, though, and codependency can be conquered with some hard work and dedication. If both parties choose to stay in the relationship and are willing to fix it, then it's likely that you'll both be able to make a full recovery from codependency. Keep in mind, though, that while you can control your own behavior and how much effort you'll put in to overcoming codependency, you cannot control your partner's level of commitment. Realize up front that it will be his or her duty to take responsibility as well.

If you want to improve your relationship, discuss the option of therapy with your partner. Couples' therapy can be extremely beneficial for overcoming codependency; likewise, individual therapy may also help codependents to recognize their destructive behavior patterns and provide techniques for banishing them. In individual or couples' therapy, parties may be led to examine some of the family dynamics that they were exposed to growing up. While it may be difficult to work through some latent emotions, bringing deep-rooted issues to the service will make way for reconstructing positive behaviors. This may also help both parties in the relationship learn to express a full, healthy range of emotions once again.

If your relationship has reached a level of codependency due to addiction, then treatment should become a priority. How you go about initiating treatment is up to you - sometimes, family members choose to stage an intervention. There's no easy, foolproof way to initiate this kind of conversation with an addict. Most likely, the addict already knows that he or she has an issue; unfortunately, you may feel that the addiction has reached a point at which you can no longer continue on in the relationship if the addict chooses not to seek help. Your relationship has reached a state of codependency, and without change, you won't be able to return to a healthy state.

If you or your loved one wants to overcome codependency, consider seeking other additional resources. Mental health centers and libraries may offer programs or materials to the public.

Overcoming codependency within a relationship may require a great deal of strength, commitment, growth, and patience from a person. If you're trying to change your ways to overcome codependency, you'll have to commit fully to embracing your own emotional, physical, and mental needs or desires. You may have to learn how to say "no" and stand up for yourself, and quit relying on making others happy in order to find self-worth.

One way to stay in a relationship that has become codependent is by encouraging each party to take part in his or her own activities or hobbies. In order to move away from codependence, a person must be able to regain his or her own sense of independence. Freedom is necessary in a relationship; otherwise, if a person becomes suffocated by his or her partner, feelings of resentment can build up.

The goal in overcoming codependency in a relationship is to make small changes. There's no way that you and your partner will be able to change completely within one day; yet, change is necessary. To avoid becoming overwhelmed, start with small changes that you can implement and be persistent with every day.

You must be willing to consistently ask yourself if what you're doing is for you, or whether it's for your partner. If you're moving in the right direction, you'll most likely develop a firm resolve. Keep in mind that you can be both firm and loving - it's just a matter of implementing small changes to regain your own happiness and sense of self-worth.

Also, avoid the pitfall of resorting back to old behaviors, especially if your partner encourages you to "go back to the way you were." If your partner is on board with overcoming codependency, he or she will need to be supportive so that you both can make effective changes. With enough resolution, you can overcome codependency in your relationship.

Chapter 48   How Understand If You Are Codependent

This question seems like what we are supposed to address, but there can be a twist to it. Emotional and behavioral tendencies of codependency affect people of all kinds. But if you are the kind that avoids personal strong or uncomfortable emotions and instead switches to focus on your counterpart's needs, then you could be codependent.

Are you normally concerned about your partner's needs and welfare while you ignore yourself? If this is the case, you are codependent, and that is not good for your relationship.

Do Codependent Behaviors Exhibit in You?

Codependents have certain behaviors that can be pointed out in isolation. Throughout your life till now, have you exhibited any of the following behaviors?

1. Do you avoid conflict or extreme emotions, or control your genuine emotions with passive aggression such as anger or humor?

2. Do you like owning your partner's actions or sometimes offering excessive favors in return for their actions?

3. Do you confuse love for working to rescue your partner and focusing all your thoughts and energies on their needs?

4. Do you play the most part of giving than sharing in your relationship?

5. Do you keep sticking to relationships for too long in the manifestation of loyalty feelings to your partner even when they harm you because you fear being abandoned?

6. Do you oftentimes agree to what you would have preferably declined?

7. Do you concern yourself more with other people's opinions about you than your own?

213

8. Do you find it difficult to identify your needs, deciding over simple personal things, and communicating your thoughts to your partner?

9. Are you easily resented when your partner does not notice or appreciate your efforts, and sometimes feel guilty for not satisfying them?

These questions show how you try to act in a way that could please your partner in your hope that they will affirm your self-worth in return. You want to prove yourself to them so they can keep having you.

Have You Questioned Your Codependent Behaviors?

If you think your behaviors alone are not enough to tell of your codependence tendencies, then you need to question your behaviors further for sensible justification or revelation. Consider the following:

1. Has your counterpart abused you – physically, emotionally, or mentally?

2. Do you always find it hard withholding or limiting your help to your partner and other people?

3. Do you find it hard asking for help even when you get overwhelmed?

4. Do you doubt what you want to become in life, or are uncertain of your needs and wants?

5. Do you always find ways to avoid an argument?

6. Do other people's thoughts about you cause you anxiety?

7. Do you find your opinions less relevant compared to those of other people?

8. Do you live with an addict or underperformer and are okay with it despite your concerns about them?

9. Do you like sticking in familiar environments and routines and resist voluntary change?

10. Do you feel neglected or secluded when your partner communes or converses with others?

11. Do you find it perplexing receiving compliments or gifts from your partner or other people?

In considering the above questions, evaluate your answers and see if they are logical or reasonable enough for you to keep manifesting your behaviors. Are you being reasonable behaving the way you are behaving? Are your mannerisms rational, sound, and beneficial?

Are Your Feelings Caused by Codependency?

Codependents continually suppress their genuine original feelings and emotions and only display those that relieve their partner's anxiety or excite their partners and over time, lose touch with themselves and their identity. Ask yourself the following questions.

1. Do you sense a feeling of emptiness inside?

2. Do you have low self-esteem or feel inferior to your counterpart, falsely think highly of yourself?

3. Do you sense uncertainty about your personal needs, objectives, and feelings?

These three questions genuinely answered speak of one who has disregard for themselves and whose situation in life is deteriorating because they have lost control over their lives.

Is Your Relationship Susceptible to Codependency?

Codependency does not just commence in adulthood. It can originate from your upbringing in school or at home or from the previous relationships you found yourself in prior years.

1. Do you hail from a family whose historical background at one point existed in a codependent state, that is, all the needs of the family were suspended or put aside for the well-being of a certain member then?

2. Did any of your caregivers in school or previous childhood lover make you begin adopting codependency behaviors?

If you can trace happenstances of codependency in the people around you in your prior years, then you are likely to exhibit their influences on you in your adulthood relationships.

Does Your Partner Fit the Role of a Taker in Your Relationship?

Codependent relationships have two individual roles. You, the codependent individual, are the caretaker – taking care, and your counterpart, the dependent is the taker – receiving care or being cared for. Therefore, find out whether your counterpart is a taker.

1. Is your partner always trying to control attention, love, sex, and affirmations they can get or give?

2. Do they exhibit violence, finger-pointing, criticism, righteousness, irritation, neediness, invasive touching, incessant talking, or emotional drama just to show you or get you to give them what they need at any time?

If your partner displays such behaviors, then they are likely to affect you in such a way that you automatically take on the role of a caretaker, perpetuating codependence in your relationship.

Is There a History of Codependency in Your Family?

Do you recall in your past witnessing or participating in codependent relationships? Might you have been taught that you could express your needs and emotions only in specific ways? Do you remember being asked to serve others first and yourself later in your familial upbringing?

It is likely that even after you left that family environment, you persisted acting in a similar manner into your subsequent relationships, and this tendency might be passed on to your children.

Did You Have a History of Abuse Growing Up?

Did you begin to take on codependence tendencies in attempts to deal with traumatic situations earlier in life? Might you have begun suppressing your needs and emotions in favor of others' to keep your well-being and peace for yourself and them? Abuse in early life, if not intervened and stopped in time might make you adapt to it and rationalize other people's hostile behaviors toward you because you feel defenseless and powerless to stand up against it. Abuse is also possible to occur in codependent familial relationships.

If you have any unresolved historical emotional, physical, or sexual abuses, then you might be enduring the current situation as before – which is unhelpful.

Do You Recognize Your Prevalent Causative Situations for Codependence in Relationships?

In what ways or circumstances do you behave in ways likely to encourage your codependence tendencies in relationships? You probably go seeking people who exhibit signs of weakness and who need being taken care of or looking after. Think about the following:

1. Are you naturally drawn toward the suffering or addicts?

2. Do you consider yourself a passionate toward the mentally impaired persons?

3. Do you have a heart for those living with chronic diseases?

Being drawn toward such individualities, most of your interactions is likely to lead you into codependence with them.

Might There Have Happened a Divorce in Your Past?

Divorce can be a causative factor for codependency. If you witnessed your parents go separate ways and you stepped up to fill the gap of the missing parent for your siblings, then you might grow up with tendencies for codependency.

1. Did you avoid discussing the difficulties with the remaining parent because you did not want to upset them more?

If yes, then you began suppressing your emotions then, setting yourself up for codependent behaviors.

217

Have You Considered the Symptomatic Details?

Codependents manifest a myriad of symptoms that might hint toward their codependency motives. Do you often act with motives of controlling others, avoiding trust for others, attaining perfection, avoiding certain feelings, avoiding intimacy, caregiving, monitoring others, denying some realities, neglecting signs of stress-related illness, etc.?

1. How would you consider the family environment or structure or system that nurtured you during upbringing?

2. What kind of rules did you adhere to?

3. Did they slow down overall development or hinder flexibility and spontaneity in your thoughts and actions?

See If Some Of These Rules Applied:

1. It is generally not good to discuss your problems

2. Avoid trusting your instincts and other people

3. Do not express negative or extreme feelings openly

4. Keep and have your feelings contained within yourself

5. Avoid direct communications

6. Do not always approach some members directly or by yourself

7. Always be in your strong, right, good, and perfect form whatever the circumstances

8. Work hard the best you can and makes up exceedingly happy

9. Always be generous and share what you have, however little

10. Follow my instruction, not my actions

11. Playfulness is childishness and lack of seriousness

12. Avoid the limelight and do your things without expecting to be noticed or appreciated

13. Avoid extremes, either is bad and loss of grip or control on issues

14. Always be careful whatever you do; mistakes like spilled milk are forever regrettable

15. Do not share family secrets out there with other people

16. Do no ever decline responsibility

17. Learn to live with problems as if they were not there

18. The nice people most of the times are boring

19. Disagreement is bad, at all cost avoid it because it is personal in nature

20. Bully or sympathize and you will easily gain control over others

21. Speak loudly with exaggerated signals to get attention

22. Other people's feelings are your too – if one is not well everyone is not well

23. Take full control things and people around you to be assured of your safety today and tomorrow

Think Of The Following:

1. Is your family system rigid? Everyone has their roles, and they do not need to be helped to do their chores. No one gets involved in the welfare of the other hence everyone acts out in ways unfamiliar to the rest. There lacks versatility in what one can do.

2. Is there inconsistency in the way of doing things? Does the incapacitation of one party cause the things to be done in ways that are interconnected?

3. Is the system becoming unpredictable for the future? Are there signs of uncertainty where resources are likely to dwindle and render the family into crisis living, for instance?

4. Is the system impulsive? Are decisions being arrived at out of anxiety and in a reactionary manner rather than logically?

5. Is the system closed? If one acts in a manner contradictory to what is the norm in the family, they are reprimanded. Nothing comes in new; nothing comes out different.

Chapter 49 Codependent Patterns

How to Spot the Traits of Codependency

Many experts agree that there are three basic patterns of codependent behavior. These are the three most common patterns that can be easily seen and which can be indicators that a person is suffering from this condition.

The list of behaviors that follow is designed as a tool to help with self-assessment. It can be of great help to anyone trying to understand what codependency is. But it can also help those who have been in recovery for some time to determine which of their features still require attention and correction.

First Pattern: Denial

"I have difficulty identifying my feelings. I minimize, change or deny how I truly feel. I consider myself a selfless person, fully committed to the well-being of others."

Second Pattern: Low Self-Esteem

"I have trouble making decisions. Everything I ever think, say or do is rigorously assessed and never considered good enough. I feel uncomfortable when I receive compliments, awards, and gifts. I never ask others to satisfy my needs or desires. of what I think, feel and do, of my own. I don't see myself as a worthy human being, worthy of love. "

Third Pattern: Compliance

"I adjust and change my value system to avoid/reject and anger others. I am sensitive to the feelings of others to the point that I often feel the same as them. I am extremely loyal and stay too long in situations that are not good for me. I often hesitate to express my feelings and opinions if they differ from others. I neglect my interests and hobbies to do what others want. I accept sex as a substitute for love. "

Denial

The human mind possesses one very surprising ability and that is not very useful. Namely, it is a skill of our mind to distort reality to the extent that it believes that the distorted version of reality is true.

The phenomenon of denial plays a crucial role in bad habits and unhealthy behavior. People deny that they have a problem with alcohol, pills or drugs. The elements of denial are easy to spot: the girl convinces herself that her boyfriend is probably too busy, when he does not answer her for days, although she has called him repeatedly but has not received a response; a cancer patient hospitalized in bed convinces himself that this is just one viral infection and that he will be discharged home for the weekend; a man with an alcohol addiction problem, which diminishes his ability to concentrate and be alert, negates the cause, stating that he is feeling so tired and burdened with work; a man who has a problem with emotional attachment explains his insecurity and insatiability of meeting a girlfriend by the fact that the lack of money and lack of his apartment are a disturbing factor.

I know that by reading these sentences many of you are convincing yourself that it cannot happen that you ever fall into such a dramatic denial, you find yourself too conscious. But denial is pervasive; it is possible to be present in each of us. It can be very awkward. What is interesting about psychological functioning is that it is much easier to recognize denial in another than on one's own. Denial for each of us is a strategy of avoiding dealing with unpleasant content, with what we would most like to avoid, with an unpleasant reality, difficult events, with confusing reality.

How Do We Deal With Reality?

Increasingly, you hear comments like this: "I don't have time to deal with it, I'm too busy." We are constantly doing something, going somewhere, cooking, buying something, further planning what else we can do that we not have been finished before. It seems that over-employment is becoming a more respected phenomenon, which subtly provides us with an alibi for exclusion from reality.

People who favor denial as a defense mechanism in their language often use sentence constructions of the type: "I understand it should, but this is not the moment." We have examples like this: "I must check my health, but this is the period when I have a bunch of responsibilities at work." Certainly, these reasons are legitimate, but it is equally certain that they are justifications for distancing ourselves from something we should pay attention to.

Some people respond with anger when they are trapped in the face of the truth. A husband with an alcohol addiction problem is willing to vent his anger at his wife, insulting her and calling her derogatory names when she demands that he begin treatment.

People are angry when someone throws them out of a comfortable existence and they are forced to pay attention to something they avoid confronting. Then they feel attacked and quickly move on to attack. Denial with anger makes us blind to the truth, blind to the good intentions of others, and blind to seeing our stretch marks and desires.

In an attempt to avoid contact with the truth, we are not even aware of how much energy we invest in not being aware, not seeing, not feeling, not knowing. No matter how, why or how long we do something, one thing is for sure: "If you don't pay on the bridge, you will pay on a crossroad." When we use our time, energy and will to escape the truth, we are drawing on our physical, emotional and spiritual resources. Many of codependent persons are in the huge denial phase. So if you are reading this and you are neglecting the truth be sure that the truth will catch you eventually. No one ever managed to escape the truth. So if you are seeing the signs don't ignore them.

You can easily see this pattern of behavior in codependent persons and they tend to believe that they are just doing best they can. But with symptoms and these patterns, you will manage to recognize the person with this condition. Do you understand now?

Low Self-Esteem

People who have low levels of self-esteem are always too self-righteous. Sometimes they cannot honestly accept a compliment because they question the hidden motive of the people who give it to them.

The Most Common Symptoms of Low Self-Esteem

1. Inability to trust one's own opinion

2. Overthinking everything

3. Fear of accepting challenges, worrying that they will not be achieved

4. Austerity towards oneself, but indulgent towards others

5. Frequent anxiety and emotional restlessness

Some less Known Symptoms

Workaholic

At work, expectations are set. But even if there is the pressure at work, compared to private relationships where everything is more uncertain, work is more peaceful. It is easier to meet expectations at work. So some people with a lack of confidence can shift their attention to the work and invest all their energy into it.

Achievement: Too Much or Too Little

Many of us have already heard that people with low self-esteem do not achieve as well as they should because they are too afraid of the challenge and do not fully utilize their talents. However, there is another extreme. Some people with low self-esteem are too afraid of failure and rejection, so they strive to be the best at proving their worth.

What Are The Causes Of Low Self Confidence?

In most cases, everything stems from childhood. Early negative experiences lead to low self-esteem later in life, and they are:

1. Frequent punishment

2. Neglect

3. Abuse

4. Bullying at school

5. Lack of praise, warmth, and care

6. Belonging to a prejudiced group

Childhood is a time during which we form our "ultimate boundaries" and "rules for life" that affect the way we think and therefore all negative early experiences have a second-round impact on development.

What Is The "Ultimate Limit" And How It Affects Your Confidence?

The "ultimate limit" is how you feel about something, based on your previous experience. For example: how you felt when you first left home becomes the ultimate frontier for everything you have left in your life.

When it comes to self-esteem, the limit is how people around you treat you because we grow up with the voices of the people who matter to us. For example, did they say you were beautiful or were they never good enough to do what they did? Did you feel worthless? This greatly affects the way you see yourself and therefore your confidence.

This pattern is also very easy to see. It must be combined with symptoms of codependency we talked about. Did you find yourself by now?

Compliance

Conformity or compliance is the behavior of an individual that is following the norms and expectations of a social group. Such behavior goes towards uncritically agreeing with valid, generally accepted group norms and values, especially under group pressure. In practice, individuals and groups aspire to adapt to the environment fully and to do nothing that would be considered eccentric or unusual by the authority. Conformism excludes creativity, leadership, and activism and opposes change and progress. This term often has a negative connotation in terms of over-adjusting at the cost of losing one's self-esteem.

People often align themselves with a desire for security within a group - typically a group of similar age, culture, religion or educational background. This is often referred to as group thinking: a pattern of thinking

225

characterized by self-deception, the coercive production of conformity and conformity to group values and ethics, thus ignoring a realistic assessment of other courses of action. The reluctance to obey is accompanied by the risk of social rejection. Conformity is often associated with adolescence and youth culture, although it strongly affects people of all ages.

Although group pressure can have negative manifestations, conformity can be considered as good or bad. Driving on the correct side of the road can be considered a useful conformation. With the appropriate influence of the environment, conformity during the early years of childhood enables a person to learn and to adopt the appropriate behaviors necessary for interaction and development within his society. Conformity influences the formation and maintenance of social norms and helps societies to function spontaneously and predictably through self-elimination of behaviors considered opposite to unwritten norms.

Compliance is probably the easiest pattern to see. These persons practically don't have their personality. They can be very dangerous to themselves because they are very submissive and they will do pretty much everything for a little attention. For the codependent persons, the compliant pattern of behavior is the worst one. They have no limits when it comes to maintaining control. But they can be spotted very easily if you combine the pattern with the symptoms.

How many times have you agreed to something even though you knew you were right? Why did you do that? I'll tell you why. Because it's much easier for you to push problems under the rug than it is to deal with them.

But on the other hand, that's why you need control in the relationship. Through that control, you are replacing all that you have accepted and you shouldn't have.

Chapter 50 Why You Should Not Be Codependent?

Codependency is a dangerous trait to possess. Life has evolved at a blinding stage and our society right now is on the fast pace. We get bombarded daily with opinions, requests, offers of friendship and disappointments that it becomes simply too dangerous to tie your life inextricably with anybody else's own. What are the specific dangers that codependency may bring into your life;

Kills Off Self-Esteem and Confidence

Allison Pescosolido writes, "Nothing erodes self-esteem quicker than an unhealthy relationship". When you hitch your happiness to a need to be needed, you soon begin to forget that you have self-worth. Codependency teaches you that your life isn't worth much beyond that of your partner. Codependents think only of their partners and new ways in which they may care for him. You lose your own sense of direction and your work may even begin to suffer. Worst of all, a lot of dependents take advantage of your urge and consistently berate and force you to do acts that further shatter what little self-confidence you possess. Codependents may even suffer constant sexual and physical abuse and yet, believe they simply can't exist outside the realm of their partner's need and affection. There is a voice at the back of their head telling them they are just an extension of their partners. They constantly need to seek approval and acknowledgement from their partners and derive lesser joy from their personal achievements.

Turns You Antisocial

The inherent need to seek approval and feel loved makes codependents decidedly antisocial. Codependency can easily turn you into a social recluse outside your partner's presence. Feeling insecure and decidedly unable to assess if their efforts are worth extra praise, codependents often turn to staying off social encounters. They miss engagements with other people, can be quite boring and unable to focus on conversations and generally exhibit a wide range of actions that suggests they would rather be left alone.

Relegates Your Own Goals

A codependent individual may be genuinely successful. He may break records, achievements and produce huge strides in the corporate and business world but deep down, codependency often leaves a yawning gap in their hearts. No matter the scale of your achievements, codependency teaches you to cherish the needs of your partners above every other goal. As such, you may find yourself unable to commit the same amount of resources and drive to attaining personal business. Codependents have been known to give up their work and life goals to focus on a partner with needs such as alcoholism. Codependency takes away your goals and makes your partner the sole center of your existence.

A Helpless Mindset

Codependency makes you feel and act helpless. Codependent individuals become chained down by the weight of the expectations they have placed on their own heads. They develop a feeling of helplessness in the face of their relationship struggles. They hang on to their relationships because they can't seem to see any other option. They suffer neglect and abuse and still remain steadfast in their relationships because codependency tells them they have no option. An even worse aspect is that they see their partners as having no control over their actions. They treat their partners like children that have no control over what they do. They help them make excuses of not being in total control.

Can Affect Your Health Severely

Codependency can be a health threat. Anxiety, depression and stress are three major psychological disorders currently on the rise worldwide, and depending on another individual to provide you joy and relief is a short path to overloading your circuit. By taking on too much worries and making themselves open to so many problems, codependents pile more stress onto themselves and this can easily escalate into depression and anxiety disorders. Insomnia is also never too far away from most codependents.

Leaves You Firmly Vulnerable To Emotional Injury

Once you have taken control of your life and handed it over to somebody else's actions and inactions, you have set yourself up to be at his mercy. He/she can hurt you even unknowingly with the smallest of actions and you become extra sensitive to being hurt in any case. Opinions and criticism from any quarter also sting more. Your depreciated sense of self-worth and low esteem could also leave you in delicate quarters when it comes to emotions and feelings.

Makes You Open to Picking up Bad Habits and Addictions

Emotional injury and a loss of esteem aren't the only dangers that can arise from overdependence. A soft spot for a partner who has addiction problems could turn you into an enabler who helps him satisfy his addiction as a means of keeping him pleased. Even worse still, you could pick up the same bad habits in the hope of keeping him company. Addictions such as gambling, alcoholism and substance abuse can be easily picked up especially when your friend or partner already has a steady source. By becoming codependent on him, you could end up picking the same habits.

Refusing Help from Other People

One of the primary demerits of codependency is the way it draws you back from seeking help yourself. Codependents are so enmeshed in a control complex that they totally adore being in control and would not admit to things being skewed with them too. They grow to be emotionally flat and cannot bring themselves to show any form of emotion. They learn to exist independently of any help from the people around them and lose the ability to ask for proper help.

A Victim's Mindset

Codependents constantly feel cheated at all times. Their mind is a hodge-podge of conflicting emotions and they end up feeling underappreciated a lot of times. Codependency does not allow them pick faults with their partners and instead, they turn against the system. They help sympathize with their partners and teach them to look for conspiracy theories to absolve their partners of their misdeeds.

Stresses You Out Physically and Mentally

The human body has a threshold for the amount of problems and issues it can take at once. By adding more problems and issues outside of your own to your mind, you run the risk of maxing out your resilience and capability to withstand stress. Obviously, catering for a partner's needs will leave you with extra physical activity to carry out. Partners with problems such as chronic illness or alcoholism may need constant care that may task your physical capabilities beyond its limits. Of even more severe potentials is the risk of a mental overload. Piling up too many worries in your head can deal dangers to your psyche.

Chapter 51 Codependent Behavior and Different Types

The human mind has always been an enigma. The condition you have may be one of several types, and you need to learn what your "type" is. This will help you to focus your recovery on that specific type. This part will help you as much as the watchmaker's tale at the beginning. You need to find the missing part of the clock. This is the only way your clock will begin ticking again.

There are different types of codependent disorders and it follows there are different types of codependent persons. This is a very important part because you need to understand that this condition occurs in different forms. Codependency can take many forms.

According to most studies, there are three basic types of codependent persons. It's almost the same as a behavior pattern.

Codependent Addiction

Once codependence exists, it generates the dynamics of betrayal. You are convinced of your partner's love for you. When you learn the truth, you will feel, in some sense, betrayed. There may be lying, false promises, threats and everything else that results from dysfunctional communications. You will begin to provide an accommodation for the manifestation of another person in the relationship to preserve some sense of control. Over time, these adjustments will become a progressively unhealthy form of relating to someone. You can lose yourself in this vicious circle and not know what is happening.

Codependent Abuse

When abuse is involved in a relationship, it engenders a disproportionate controlling factor into the relationship as well. The abuse is typically sporadic, so you think "This is not always bad." But you are wrong. Interpersonal interactions are shaped in a manner designed to pacify the offending codependent person. This results in progressively shallow relationships.

Codependent Fear

Codependent persons will always feel fear, irrational of course but there, nonetheless. This form of codependency is marked by a tremendous lack of self-confidence, and is rooted in the ethics and beliefs of the codependent. This manifestation of codependency is frequently exacerbated by peer pressure, and feelings of insecurity. Codependent individuals will live their lives to please others, because they are in constant fear of losing the other person in the relationship.

These three codependent types always end the same—broken relationships and tremendous emotional suffering.

Codependency is a form of addiction, relationship addiction so that we will refer to it hereafter as an addiction. How painful and dangerous can emotional addiction be? Relationship addicts regard their desperate need for someone as a measure of true love. A disconnection for these emotionally unstable individuals, means endangering their identity, integrity, and personality.

Have you ever loved someone to the point of becoming addicted to that love? Have you ever so wanted to love that you couldn't control your emotions and surrendered to them? Although love is the most beautiful feeling, it can also be painful and devastating, not unlike a vice.

That is what it's like that for those who depend on it, and who do everything and anything to avoid being alone. Codependents may remain in a relationship for months, even years, in spite of the fact that they do not feel good about the relationship. It's as if you think you see, but you actually don't, or when you think you love, but you don't love at all. This is codependency—all kinds of love, for partner or friend—it matters not.

Being Too Busy Doesn't Mean You Will Never Meet the Right Person

Recent research has shown that relationship dependence is the most common type of dependency in the modern age. The reason, experts say, is the modern way of life, in which there is less free time for socializing and making new acquaintances. As a result, people are increasingly afraid of being left alone. Consequently, the codependent individual clings to each relationship vigorously.

Who Are Relationship Addicts And How Do They Perceive The Relationship?

People who are relationship dependent desperately seek love, and a partner who will always be by their side, and complete them. In stable emotional relationships, there is no needs based component, which means that it is possible to love someone regardless of what needs and desires are met or not met. Nor is there an obsessive need for the partner's constant physical presence. People who are addicted to relationships do not have an intrinsic connection to their loved one, but instead, define true love in terms of how desperately they need that person in their life. Regard it is a warning when you hear someone say, "I can't live without you", or "I would die without you". Codependency compels its victims to do many destructive and self-destructive things, largely to prevent the pain they would feel upon separation or, because they hate the partner they dependent upon, or both.

Loving someone doesn't mean that you own them. In a relationship where you constantly demand your partner to justify their whereabouts, no one will be happy. Remember, it usually better to let them off the leash. I believe that everything happens for a reason. You need to restore your self-confidence, and practice introspection. Remember just one more thing— if you don't respect yourself you will never gain the respect of others. Humans, like other animals, have a sixth sense—fear. They can feel it in you.

Addiction is synonymous with a desire for partner control, mainly manifested in possessiveness, which results in following, spying, or forbidding the partner to work. The codependent may also withhold any information that they believe may threaten the relationship. Nevertheless, these relationships are difficult to leave. It sounds paradoxical. It is preferable to accept the loss of a relationship than to struggle with someone who has a codependent condition.

When Does Relationship Dependence Arise?

The predisposition to future addiction is created very early—around the age of three. To establish our future emotional stability, our early relationship with our mother must comprehend her physical and psychological availability, her role as a "constant" in our lives, and the quality of her interactions. If these needs are met, the child can absorb their mother's positive image, and mirror it later in life. This solid foundation enables the child to distance itself from the mother, leave the nest, so to speak. This is only possible because of the emotional stability provided to the child in their formative years. The child does not feel powerless or abandoned, and they learn the ability to be alone, and to have fun when they're alone. However, this ability is guaranteed to last a lifetime. It is often tested in various stages of our lives.

Experts tell us that this emotional addiction is heavily influenced by the romantic fantasies of love we encounter in books, music, and movies.

Do romantic stories affect addiction? Do the authors of such works lack emotional stability in their creative expressions? As they say, art imitates life. Unstable individuals may build fantasies that are fueled by the descriptions they encounter in works of art. They may act upon them, assuming that these are normal relationships. They may expect that idyllic love is possible, or that pain and suffering does not exist— only "they lived happily ever after." Life is not a fairytale, but codependent people rely on these fantasies, because they do not have a healthy perspective on interpersonal relationships.

Were you aware that the brothers Grimm, who authored countless fairytales, found their inspiration in horror stories and medieval myths? Many of those stories did not originally have happy endings, they were re-written with happy endings. As I said, life is not a fairytale.

Psychologists tell us that such relationships are difficult to recognize, because many people interpret such behavior as normal and acceptable.

The truth is that many fail to recognize that they are in an interdependent, unhealthy relationship. However, some do recognize it for what it is, but cannot, or will not admit it to others, or to themselves. If they admit it, then they might be forced to make changes. They are extremely reluctant to do anything because of uncertainty and separation anxiety. So, their adopted philosophy is, "better any connection than no connection."

Why would anyone choose a relationship they don't enjoy from a fear of being alone? It's often said that a good divorce is better than a bad marriage. However, this is out of the question for the codependent, who cannot feel whole without them, because they serve as an extension of them. They feel as though they would fall apart without them. If such a relationship is broken, the inability to move on is a sure sign that the loss will not be accepted. Emotionally unstable and dependent people who lose their loved one's despair for years, and live for the day to come when they will, once again, find bliss with their partner. This fantasy, along with self-denial regarding taking blame for their partner's departure, leads them to the belief that "everything will be good."

Can Relationship Addiction Be Dangerous?

Relationship addiction goes hand in glove with other addictions. Drug addicts, for example, do not feel emotionally stable, lack control, and need something to complete them—in this case, drugs. Opiate addicts often report that they are complacent, and need no one. This is because the drug fills their emptiness. If one is codependent, then the partner is the drug, hence the statement "I cannot live without you." Relationship addiction can be very dangerous. For an emotionally unstable person, disconnecting means compromising one's identity, integrity, and personality. Such a person is prepared to execute various manipulations to prevent the connection from being broken.

How Can This Vicious Love Cycle Be Broken, Or Can This Type Of Addiction Be Cured?

Emotional stability is something that is built over time and maintained. Those who succeed in doing that have no concerns regarding the "vicious circle." Codependent individuals repeat the same patterns in all their relationships, continuing the vicious circle. Although friends and a supportive environment can be helpful, few can overcome their addictive behavior on their own, and then, psychotherapy is beneficial. In such situations, the client-therapist builds those abilities that the client failed to develop as a child sufficiently. It is a certain kind of "re-education" or "corrective emotional experience." The codependent, in some way, needs to be reborn.

They need to hit the reset button, and learn about the world and about relationships again—this time, in the right way. Believe me, it can be done and you will finally heal and be able to live a normal life in which people do not run away from you.

So, whatever type of codependent person you have a relationship with or, if you are that person, all these indicators of a dysfunctional relationship will materialize and, it is incumbent upon you to see, with the help of these examples, whether you are at risk or whether you are, in fact, a person that suffers from codependency.

Chapter 52   Complete Step By Step Cycle Recovery

Cultivating Self-love

One of the most powerful things you can do for yourself when finding yourself in a toxic or codependent relationship is to practice self-love. Self-love can be achieved and attained in many ways and some have already been explored throughout these part. Let's look at the many ways to cultivate self-love. You can use this as a guide and find a creative way to make sure you include some on a daily basis tarot-style cards, a self-love journal.

1. Take time for yourself. Do what you love doing!

2. Follow your passions. Stay committed to your goals, dreams and aspirations.

3. Lose the need to please and appease. Recondition your mind.

4. Meditate on self-love and incorporate daily mantras into your life.

5. Look after your physical health. Vitality and love for your physical body can help keep you strong and -end within.

6. Look after your emotional health. Put up healthy boundaries on your emotions and do not allow harm into your energy field.

7. Look after your mental health. Keep your mind focused and aligned to your truth, your inner knowing and your own peace of mind.

8. Look after your spiritual health. Remind yourself daily how wise, loving, empathic and connected you are; and that you are a beautiful, soulful being.

9. Spend time in nature. Connect to nature to help cultivate self-love and remind yourself of your personal power, beauty and greatness.

10. Strengthen your boundaries.

11. Be kinder to yourself. Treat yourself with loving kindness.

12. Remind yourself of your independence.

13. Develop your intuition.

14. Practice forgiveness.

15. Take time for self-reflection, journaling and explorations of yourself and psyche.

16. Balance your masculine and feminine energy.

17. Meditate on the moon. The moon relates to your emotions and divine feminine wisdom. Connect to her.

18. Let go of the need to compare yourself to others.

19. Self-care. Incorporate healing massage, self-pampering and other self-loving rituals into daily life.

20. Create a sacred space. Create a shrine, altar or sacred space with items that can help you connect to your inner nature and develop self-love.

21. Live intentionally. Apply meaning to daily life.

Cultivating Self-Compassion

Just like self-love, having compassion for self is essential when dealing with manipulative narcissists or any other toxic personalities. It is also imperative if you yourself are suffering from any codependent tendencies and destructive cycles of behavior. Without self-compassion, we would not be able to experience compassion for others. Compassion literally translates as 'the concern for the suffering of others' therefore being compassionate, for self and others, can have some profound effects.

Here Are 7 Things You Should Do To Help Bring Greater Compassion Into Your Life.

1. Charity or Animal Welfare

One of the most potent ways to increase our self-confidence and remind ourselves of our true intentions and compass is to help others.

2. Create a Vision or Manifestation Board

Linking with number 1 is our sense of personal goals, dreams and aspirations. A lack of compassion for ourselves primarily stems from an inability to put ourselves first, have self-love and follow our own inner desires.

3. Develop Healthy Boundaries.

This is essential and I cannot stress this enough. Having healthy boundaries is one of the most significant things you can do to help alleviate the strains of codependency.

4. Cultivate Compassion

Cultivating compassion through meditation, mindfulness or mantras is a highly effective practice to help break the cycle or chains of codependency.

5. Connect To Universal Symbolism

Connecting to universal symbolism can be very useful in reshaping and activating particular neurological activity and codons in the brain.

6. Learn To Laugh

Learning to laugh can be a very profound self-help when trying to overcome codependency and welcome more compassion into your life. This is because laughter literally releases emotions and blocked energy.

7. Recognize That Everyone Is a Reflection

We are all mirrors of one another and your partner is you in essence. When you recognize that we all wish to be happy, healthy and free from suffering, you will begin to treat yourself the loving kindness that you deserve.

Developing Awareness

Developing awareness is essential in the journey to recovery from a toxic or unhealthy codependent relationship (or if you are recovering from codependent tendencies yourself). Without awareness, we would not be able to feel, experience, see, observe, sense or understand life and all its many elements. If our judgment is clouded, our overall vision for life is blurred. This results in us attracting characters and situations that aren't particularly good for our health.

Binaural Beats

Because binaural beats are very influential and can have some real profound effects of developing awareness, increasing confidence and improving aspects of life in so many ways, we will explore all the various binaural beats in depth.

Journal

As listed in 'Cultivating Self-love' journaling and self-reflective measures are an effective way to overcome codependency and release yourself from limiting or self-sabotaging behaviors. When we write, we are free to express.

Intuitive, Psychic and Spiritual Development

Intuitive, psychic and spiritual development is a topic that is not explored on a mass scale or taught in mainstream education however thousands if not millions are recognizing the importance of developing their own inner intuition and awakening to subtle levels of perception. Intuition is not exclusive with spirituality and psychic phenomena however they are related. When one opens to their inner knowing and attunes their mind to higher levels of awareness, cognitive functioning and perception, this naturally opens them up to a more subtle and spiritual way of perceiving.

Learn About Astrology

Learning about the planets, stars and universe and cosmos as a whole can help to expand your psychic and spiritual awareness. This is because we are intrinsically connected to 'all that is' and life is not just limited to our one world on planet earth. Learning about and connecting to other planets, star systems and universal phenomena can help you feel more connected, safe and secure in your body and physical environments.

Practice a Healing Art

Learning and training in a healing art such as Reiki, energy healing or holistic massage can have a profound effect on your conscious awareness and general wellbeing. Feeling connected to others and the world around, and your own inner state of self-confidence and assuredness, is an effective way to help deal with any problems in codependent relationships. There are many healing systems and schools of thought to choose from so do some research and see what feels right for you.

Explore Your Subconscious

In addition to looking towards philosophical schools of thought such as yin and yang, Taoist philosophy and common issues regarding sexuality, explore the teachings of Carl Jung. Jung was a Swiss psychiatrist who went on to become one of the founding fathers of modern psychology. He came up with a set of universal archetypes which are inherent within every human being. These archetypes can be learned about and explored to understand the psyche and elements of our own human nature, beliefs, repression, shadow and self. Take time to reflect and do some soul searching.

Practice Mindfulness

Practicing mindfulness specifically on developing qualities associated with your third eye, intuition and spiritual perception can be very beneficial. Learning how to shift your thoughts, beliefs and viewpoints to one more interconnected and 'seeing' will not only bring greater awareness but also aid in your ability to put up barriers and protect yourself.

Decalcify Your Pineal Gland

Decalcifying your pineal gland can lead significantly to the ability to see and perceive subtle energy and therefore interact with others in a way more loving and harmonious to you. The pineal gland is a real gland which also relates to psychic and spiritual phenomena. When it is clouded, we are closed off from many extrasensory aspects of life. There are more than the five physical senses and those with an active and open pineal gland are aware of this.

241

Creating Healthy Boundaries Within

As you are aware by now, boundaries are essential when dealing with any toxic personality or attempting to overcome the destructive patterns of a codependent relationship. All of life on earth including ourselves is interconnected. We are not separate from one another.

Thoughts, feelings, emotions, beliefs, and intentions all swirl around in an energetic spiral rippling out to affect everything our intended awareness is directed at. When someone aims harm, anger, sadness, pain, suffering or any negative and harmful thought or intention towards you, you respond. We are transmitters and receivers of both consciousness and external sensory stimuli therefore when recovering from codependency, it is fundamental to take steps to protect yourself. This could possibly be the most significant lesson and most powerful thing you do for yourself on your journey to healing and wholeness.

As all life on earth is governed by unseen, energetic forces and science has shown nowadays how we ourselves have an electromagnetic energy field surrounding us responsible for our thoughts, emotions, feelings and overall state of wellbeing and energetic frequency (also known as the aura to some), the best way to develop healthy boundaries within is to practice daily exercises and techniques for strengthening your energy field and putting up a shield.

Strengthen Your Inner Chi!

Martial artists and many who practice hands on or energy healing are aware of the subtle yet powerful chi which flows through us. Chi flows through every living thing on earth -the trees, earth, plants, waters, sky, sun, sea, your hands, your feet and your entire body. It is in the crops we eat and the air we breathe. Without chi, we would not exist.

Chi is also referred to as the universal life force. It is an energetic force, similar to air and oxygen as both are breathed in simultaneously however chi also has metaphysical properties which can be tuned in to and embodied for healing.

When we create chi balls, this naturally strengthens our aura and unseen barriers (boundaries, electromagnetic energy field) as we are filling

242

ourselves up with more chi and strengthening many aspects of self. Due to the effect chi balls have on the mind, they also increase mental powers, calmness and clarity which can help in any situation when you need boundaries with a toxic person. It is so simple yet so effective.

Diet

As your chi is your life force, changing your diet to one high in life force foods will have an incredibly profound effect on your ability to protect yourself and put up better boundaries. Fruits, nuts, seeds, whole grains, vegetables, lentils and pulses, beans, herbs, herbal teas and organic wholefoods are all foods high in life force. As all food on earth whether that be vegetables, pasta or beef receive their energy directly from the elements of nature. These foods however hold a higher vibration. This is because a vegetable has primary life force, it has grown directly from sunlight, air, water and earth. Foods low in vibration or life force such as beef can be seen to hold a secondary or weaker life force.

Meditate

Meditation can be used daily to strengthen inner chi as you are literally filling yourself up with space. This strengthens your inner systems and has a range of effects, which ultimately result in your ability to retain your strength and boundaries in addition to your mind being on point. This will really help increase both your sense of self and your inner boundaries.

Chapter 53   Maintaining Recovery

Recovering from codependency is a long-term, almost never-ending project, and as such the recovered must be ready to keep at it for a considerable length of time. This part deals with tips to help you maintain the recovery process irrespective of challenges that may come your way.

Get In Control of Your Life

To engage something is to give it authority. Recuperation is tied in with making yourself your own position — what you like, what you need, and what you choose, instead of conceding or responding to another person. In any event, revolting is a reaction that weakens you. To give yourself authority implies you become a mind-blowing creator. That may feel like an overwhelming duty. It's putting your confidence energetically.

To Do This You Have To Take Cognizance Of Some Things:

What You Should Control?

Most codependents have an external locus of control implying that they think outer components are the reason for what befalls them and how they feel. Codependents expect and trust that change will originate all things considered or some other individual. Their concentration and power are outside of themselves. They look to others to make themselves feel better and affirm of them, particularly with regards to relationships. They likewise tend to rationalize or accuse others or conditions for their issues and when things don't go as arranged. As you quit doing that and start to take responsibility for your life and your feelings, actions, and inactions you're steadily taking your capacity back, and the locus of control becomes interior, on yourself. Every time you don't if it's not too much trouble respond, or control somebody, and you voice your feelings, conclusions, and cut-off points, you're fabricating your confidence and an inner locus of control. You quit being an unfortunate casualty. You quit spending your vitality attempting to change or control another person. In case you're despondent and get that commonplace unfortunate casualty feeling, you assume the liability to make changes to become upbeat, in any event, when you can't "fix" the issue. This is a procedure that includes building confidence, turning out to be self-supporting, defining limits, and mending your past. The last advance is showing that newly discovered confidence and fearlessness. Expressing your voice in your relationships as well as your abilities, abilities, and imagination on the planet. At the point when you discover some new information, when you take care of an issue without anyone else, when you're doing what you love, and when you're achieving your goals, you feel autonomous and confident and anticipate each new day. You realize you can take care of yourself, what's more, it's an extraordinary feeling.

People with an interior locus of control are increasingly fruitful in all angles of their lives. They accept that results are dependent upon their actions what's more, exertion as opposed to karma, out of line conditions, and things past their control. There are tests online you can take to decide your locus of control. Fortunately, you can change your locus of control. After you understand that you can have any kind of effect in claim life and feeling of prosperity, you start to take your capacity back.

Be Decisive

A great deal of codependents recognize what others ought to do yet have a last time settling on decisions for themselves, even little ones, similar to what to arrange off menu and how to manage their extra time. They may keep away from necessary leadership by and large and practice their habit, dream, and stress over somebody, or ask others their conclusions.

In the event that you experienced childhood in a family with strict principles, or on the off chance that one parent was controlling, you didn't have a chance to settle on significant decisions nor have the help of guardians to assist you with figuring out how to find your feelings about something and gauge options and results. Kids can rapidly figure out how to have an independent mind. High child rearing permits them to settle on age-fitting decisions. It incorporates tuning in and reflecting back to a youngster their feelings and needs and conceptualizing results of various decisions. Healthy child rearing assists kids with recognizing and trusting their feelings in request to build up an inside locus of control to what they need.

At the point when you don't have the foggiest idea what you feel and you're not talented in considering the results of your actions and likely results, small decisions can feel monumental. Instead, you act without thinking ahead as well as stay away from them what's more, build up a detached frame of mind toward your life. You may start seeking others for direction, and their suppositions can turn out to be more important than yours. In case you're a pleaser, you won't have any desire to disappoint them. Be careful not just of companions who disclose to you what you ought to do, yet of power figures too. In any event, when you're paying an expert for exhortation, investigate different choices and ensure the action you take is lined up with your values. It might be enticing to request that a psychotherapist settle on your decisions.

Instead, look for help in considering the outcomes of your choices, which enables you to settle on your own decisions and take care of your issues. In numerous useless families, kids are rebuffed for making honest botches. Now and again, discipline is dangerous, discretionary, and erratic. Those feelings of trepidation endure in any event, when you're never again living with your folks. That parent still lives inside you as your fault-finder and won't enable you to pardon yourself for botches. Perfectionism and the want to be faultless can frequent each choice with the goal that you need to investigate each buy, practice private discussions, and evade new encounters.

Another factor is dread of disillusionment. In vexed families, guardians infrequently set aside the effort to comfort kids when they're frustrated. Adapting to dissatisfaction is a piece of development, realized when guardians comprehend and identify with their youngsters' feelings.

Decisions aren't right or wrong; there are just outcomes. Usually, you won't know until you go out on a limb and settle on a decision. Give yourself permission to explore, alter your perspective, and commit errors. This is the means by which you develop and become more acquainted with yourself and the world.

Have Objectives and Work towards Meeting them

A good number of codependents recognize what others ought to do yet have a full time settling on decisions for themselves, even little ones, similar to what to arrange off a menu and how to manage their available time. They may stay away from necessary leadership out and out and practice their habit, dream, and stress over somebody, or ask others their feelings.

On the off chance that you experienced childhood in a family with strict standards, or on the off chance that one parent was controlling, you didn't have a chance to settle on significant decisions nor have the help of guardians to assist you with figuring out how to find your feelings about something and gauge options and results.

Youngsters can rapidly figure out how to have an independent perspective. High child rearing permits them to settle on age-fitting decisions. It incorporates tuning in and reflecting back to a youngster their feelings and needs and conceptualizing outcomes of various decisions. Healthy child rearing assists kids with distinguishing and trust their feelings in request to build up an inside locus of control to what they need.

At the point when you don't have the foggiest idea what you feel and you're not talented in considering the results of your actions and likely results, small decisions can feel monumental. Instead, you act without thinking ahead and additionally maintain a strategic distance from them furthermore, build up an inactive disposition toward your life. You may start seeking others for direction, and their assessments can turn out to be more important than yours. In case you're a pleaser, you won't have any desire to disappoint them.

Be careful not just of companions who disclose to you what you ought to do, however of power figures also. In any event, when you're paying an expert for counsel, investigate different alternatives and ensure the action you take is lined up with your values. It might be enticing to request that a psychotherapist settle on your decisions. Instead, look for help in considering the outcomes of your choices, which enables you to settle on your own decisions and tackle your issues. In numerous useless families, youngsters are rebuffed for making guiltless botches. Sometimes, discipline is extreme, discretionary, and eccentric. Those apprehensions endure in any event, when you're never again living with your folks. That parent still lives inside you as your fault-finder and won't enable you to excuse yourself for botches. Perfectionism and the want to be reliable can frequent each choice with the goal that you need to explore each buy, practice close discussions, and stay away from new encounters.

Another factor is dread of frustration. In grieved families, guardians once in a while set aside the effort to comfort kids when they're baffled.

Adapting to dissatisfaction is a piece of development, realized when guardians comprehend and identify with their kids' feelings.

Decisions aren't right or wrong; there are just outcomes. Ordinarily you won't know until you go out on a limb and settle on a decision. Give yourself permission to explore, alter your perspective, and commit errors. This is the way you develop and become acquainted with yourself and the world.

Know What You Are Good At

Everybody has an ability for something. You can improve your abilities and blessings with training. Do you see or have a talent for things in a region that others don't? Show improvement over your companions or take the lead in specific circumstances? Perhaps you know as of now what you're great at the same time, like many individuals, underestimate your gifts and capacities. Exercises and classes at which you exceed expectations likely use your gifts. You can adapt new abilities and enhance them with preparing and practice. On the off chance that you appreciate what you're doing, you're increasingly roused to adapt quicker.

Maybe you appreciate looking after children can comprehend and converse with youngsters. Not every person does. Is it accurate to say that you are regularly casted a ballot group commander? Do you keep spending plans, intercede companions' debates, fix things effectively, take the best pictures, engage people, or run the quickest? A few people can sing on any note, get familiar with a language, develop plants, win contentions, convince others, and draw what they see, make up stories, coordinate paint, structure garments, or make plans. I never speculated I had a high fitness for distant relationships until it was indicated out me. Yet, I realized how to gather a tight bag. I could generally tell whether pictures were uniformly hung or furniture would fit in a space.

Consider employments and positions you've held, including volunteering at church, club, and school capacities. Run-down the aptitudes that were required and those you learned. For example, on the off chance that you had a secretary activity, you utilized numerous abilities, composing, PC aptitudes, sorting out, altering, drafting letters, documenting, dealing with telephone calls, booking gatherings for your chief. On the off chance that you composed an award, you needed to inquire about, strategies, compose,

248

investigate, arrange, alter, make influential contentions, spending plan, facilitate with staff, and potentially arrange the proposition.

Chapter 54   How to Building Self-Esteem and Self-Love to Overcome Codependency

Positive self-esteem and the right perception of your self-worth can help to boost your recovery from codependent behaviors. This part focuses on ways to help you develop your self-esteem and shift your perception of your self-worth. If you adhere to the suggestions in this part, you will notice an improvement in the following areas.

1. A definite boost in your self-confidence.

2. Ability to make better decisions.

3. A significant improvement in your communication skills.

4. An obvious increase in positive self-esteem.

5. A significant reduction in trauma.

6. A general decrease in codependent behaviors.

Keep in mind that all these do not happen overnight and do not all occur at the same time. Habits take time to develop, so give yourself enough time for these characteristics to become fully formed.

Self-Esteem

People with codependent habits generally suffer from low self-esteem. A person with low self-esteem tends to feel unlovable, incompetent, lack confidence, not good enough, and is prone to be hypersensitive. The slightest form of criticism causes great damage to their self-confidence because they see almost every action and comment as a threat to their sense of self. They are quick to spot disapproval and if they are in an unhealthy relationship, they will spend most of their time trying to please the other person in an attempt to get their approval.

Low self-esteem can make the individual live miserably with the harsh voice of their inner critic constantly chiming off in their heads. Aside from a general lack of confidence, here's how to assess if you have low self-esteem.

1. Believing that others are better than you. This is not to be confused with a healthy respect for those in authority or superiors at work. It is a nagging sense of inferiority or not good enough.

2. Constantly focusing on your flaws and exaggerating your weaknesses while belittling your strengths.

3. Having a strong fear of failure that keeps you from attempting new things. You don't permit yourself to explore life because of your perceived incompetence.

4. Constantly feeling shame because you think you are unworthy. This can lead to depression and anxiety.

5. Inability to say what you want. You prefer to remain inconspicuous, so you refrain from expressing your true feelings.

6. Feeling pessimistic about life. Your actions are not from a place of positive excitement, instead, they are purely mechanical. Your outlook on life is rooted in pessimism.

7. Difficulty accepting positive feedback. Always thinking that people are merely flattering you or exaggerating when they praise you is a sign that you have low self-esteem.

How to Improve Your Self-Esteem

Develop Your Assertive Muscle

Learn how to say what you want especially in your relationship. Being assertive is not being rude or aggressive. Instead, it is firmly stating your views. Assertiveness is like a muscle. It gets stronger the more times you practice using it. Here are some ways you can develop your assertive muscle.

Use the Positive Inquiry Method

This helps you to accept positive feedback and also know more about the reason behind the compliment. For example, when someone says, "You are a good cook. I like your cooking," you can respond by saying, "Thank you and yes, I am a good cook. What do you most like about my cooking?"

People who have lost their self-esteem in a codependent relationship would usually respond with a weak, "It's just regular cooking."

Use the Negative Inquiry Method

This is used when you get negative feedback. You can use it to find out more about critical feedback. For example, when someone says, "This meal is terrible," you can respond by saying, "Yes, it wasn't my best dish. What was it about the meal that you didn't enjoy or like in particular?" A person with low self-esteem may respond harshly with, "If you knew all the efforts that went into preparing that meal, you wouldn't say such nasty things about my cooking!"

Use the "I Feel" Method

This is a great way to express unpleasant feelings to someone you love without sounding aggressive. The template for this is: I feel (your feelings) when you (say what they did). Could you please (request)? For example: "I feel worried when you come home very late, could you please not come home so late, or if you are running late, could you please communicate with me?"

Maintain a Positive Attitude

Whatever helps you to maintain a positive attitude can improve your self-esteem. Spend time inspiring people in your little ways. You can do that by sharing your ideas or new things you learn with others.

Engaging in physical activities is also a great way to change your physiology and to improve your overall mood. You can also take up new hobbies. Branching out of your usual routine is a good way to try new things, get you positively excited, unlock your hidden talents, boost your creativity, and improve your self-esteem.

Another good way to maintain a positive attitude is by setting goals and working toward accomplishing them. Start with small goals and achieving them. The more goals you smash, the higher your sense of accomplishment, which will, in turn, boost your self-esteem.

Remember and Apply the Following Tips

Take a Periodic Inventory of Your Strengths and Weaknesses

By listing at least five strengths and weaknesses you have, you should be able to have a fair idea of what areas of your life need more work. Doing this will prevent you from thinking of your entire life as a failure because you can see your strengths when you take inventory.

Stop Comparing Yourself to Other People

Being authentic means letting others be what they want to be while you be what you have chosen to be.

When You Catch Yourself in the Act of Using Negative Inner Narratives, Deliberately Create a Separation

For example, instead of saying to yourself, "I am feeling anxious and worried," say something like, "Audrey is feeling anxious and worried." This puts you in the position of an observer. You will begin to see and approach your situation as a challenge instead of being deeply involved in a situation you see as a threat.

Don't Be Afraid Of Failing

Instead, learn to fail forward by using your mistakes as stepping stones. Remember that you cannot fail forward if you don't attempt new things. Also, remember to keep things simple and not undertake huge risks.

Most Importantly, Learn To Hold Yourself in High Regard

If you don't treat yourself with the respect you deserve, you will inadvertently try to force it from others. Treat yourself the way you will treat someone you are in love with. Harsh talks and treating yourself poorly can dampen your spirit and diminish your self-esteem.

Self-Love

Codependents put in a lot of effort into trying to make their relationships work, they forget about themselves in the process. You cannot give what you don't have. You cannot give genuine love if you don't love and honor yourself, to begin with. Loving others more than you love yourself is not healthy. To help you improve the quality of love you put into your relationship, you need first to increase your self-love. The more you develop self-compassion and accept yourself completely, the more equipped you will be to share a healthy portion of that love with other people. Genuine self-love makes you feel worthy and whole. It doesn't depend on someone loving you back.

Here Are Some Simple But Effective Ways to Increase Your Self-Love

Practice Self-Care

Spend time with friends and family who genuinely care for you, get quality sleep, hit the gym a few times a week, take a walk in nature, drink plenty of water, get a massage, go for adventures, play like children, and find time for your hobbies. These are ways to show yourself that you care about yourself.

Honor Negative Emotions

It is not realistic to assume that you should remain in a positive state of mind every single moment of your life. There are times when events and actions of people around you will trigger strong negative emotions in you. Don't try to suppress these negative emotions. Remember the essence of the exercises in meditation and mindfulness. Simply observe these emotions and let them fade away with time. You don't have to act on them. You don't have to exaggerate them with feelings. But you shouldn't suppress them either.

Practice Gratitude for Who You Are

It is easy to focus on your minuses. Still, it takes deliberate effort to focus on the positive aspects of yourself. Instead of paying attention to all the wrong things in your life and your body, be intentional about shifting your focus to the things that are working well for you, the amazing things you do, and all the beautiful things you offer to the people around you. It doesn't matter how many flaws you have—we all have them—what matters is that you are grateful for your strengths. Take some time daily to write about the things you love and appreciate about yourself. It doesn't matter if it is a long list or just a few lines. The most important thing is that you are truly grateful for the things you write down. If you practice gratitude first thing in the morning or last thing before going to bed, you will discover that over time, your attitude and outlook about life will shift dramatically.

Express Your Uniqueness

You are not the same as anyone in the entire world. You are not like mass-produced products. You may look like everyone else, but you are one of a kind! Don't stifle your uniqueness. Don't be afraid to be different; you are meant to be different. Break free from trying to fit in or meet the expectations of others regardless of how important they are to you. And by all means, allow others to do the same. Show up in the world as your authentic self; that is the best thing you can do for yourself and those you love.

Connect With Your Inner Self

When you make time to connect with your inner self–your true essence– your appreciation for your whole self-increases. You can connect with your inner self using meditation, journaling, mindfulness practices, and yoga.

Remember That You Share a Common Humanity with Everyone

Realize that feeling insecure, vulnerable, anxious, and self-critical is common to everyone. Always keep that in mind and cut yourself some slack. You are not alone in your struggle against your flaws. Everyone you see, regardless of the appearances they put, has their challenges and problems. It is the common humanity we all share. Remembering that will ease away your feeling of loneliness.

Chapter 55   Where to Get Help

When you are in a codependent relationship, you are isolated from your family, friends and social circle. Recovery can happen only when you step out and seek support from your family, friends and also from professionals.

But this is not an easy thing to do, especially if there is addiction involved. The fear and shame can keep you from seeking help.

An abusive relationship will have the abuser wielding control over your actions and interactions. They will cut you off from outside influence. I had experienced this with my controlling husband.

However, you should develop self-esteem and confidence to ignore the fear and distrust. This will help you wake up and avoid attaching yourself to the negative thoughts of your partner.

Here are some ways in which you can seek support for codependency. You can choose any or all of these support measures to help you overcome your toxic relationship issues.

Why Support Is Key to Codependency Recovery

It takes tremendous effort on your part to achieve the self-discipline and focus to avoid being distracted or dissuaded from your efforts.

If the recovery efforts outlined in the previous chapters are not working for you, support is necessary.

It is also needed to sustain the efforts you have taken towards freeing from your codependent state.

Support will also help you focus on your objectives and help you move in the right direction.

And remember that you have to encounter plenty of discomfort as you face changes in your life such as a new outlook of your personality, your fear of people or circumstances, incompetence and confusion in facing issues and more.

Awkward, guilty and anxious feelings are natural in this situation, which can drag you back to your old unhealthy habits. With continuous and staunch support, you can avoid this.

Support can be in the form of

1. Twelve Step Meetings

2. Psychotherapy

The Comprehensive 12 Step Support Program

The main purpose of this program is to offer a comprehensive support. It helps you accept that you have an issue, helps you face it and find the methods that can treat and heal it. The meetings are of four types:

Speaker Meetings

These have a single person sharing his or her experience on codependency. The person may be undergoing recovery or fully recovered and offering help to others.

Topic Share

These meetings involved different facets of addiction recovery. The leader of the group discusses about the 12 steps or gives information related to sponsorship.

Open Share

In open share type of meetings, every attendee will be given a chance to share his or her experience on overcoming codependency or on the hurdles they faced in recovery

Tradition Study

Such meetings focus on the entire codependent recovery program and help codependents take the measures needed to help themselves.

The 12 Steps of the Program Include

1. Admit that you are powerless over others and that your life is not under your control

2. You believe that you require a greater power to restore your sanity

3. Decide to turn your life and will to God's care

4. Make a fearless and searching inventory of yourself

5. Admit truthfully to your faults

6. Gear yourself to allow removal of your character defects

7. Seek help from God to overcome your shortcomings

8. Write a list of persons you have been hurtful to and your willingness to make the necessary amends

9. Make the necessary amends as far as possible provided it does not affect others

10. Continue taking a personal inventory on your wrongs and admit to it

11. Use meditation and prayer to gain the knowledge and power to recover from the program

12. Experience spiritual awakening and help other codependents in their recovery process and practice the principles in all your efforts

Benefits of the Program

Irrespective of the type of meeting you attend you can gain benefits such as

1. Receive information from members with long time experience and also from books that are customized to your issues

2. The meetings provide you with success stories and lessons from previous experiences and positivity of other members

3. You can share your experience with other understanding people, get support and guidance via telephone or online meetings and also call a sponsor for support and advice between the meetings

4. Keep yourself motivated and encouraged so you can continue with the recovery and healing process

5. Attend meetings that are private and anonymous

6. The spiritual addition in the meetings help you recover more effectively

7. Daily meetings are held and you can choose a time that is convenient for you

Psychotherapy

This is a support system that is offered by a professional licensed in providing mental health support for codependency. The professionals include family and marriage therapists, clinical counselors and social workers. They possess doctorates or master's degree in their specialty. The professionals help with prescription and also perform psychoanalysis, if it is a psychoanalyst.

Advantages of Psychotherapy Include

1. Individual consultations that help address your specific issues.

2. Objective and expert guidance that focuses on your specific issues, reactions, thought patterns and behavior, and suggest new and healthy patterns

3. The personal therapy sessions help improve your intimacy skills

4. For individuals uncomfortable with group meetings, the one to one guidance of psychotherapy sessions offers better confidentiality.

5. Deep seated issues such as dysfunctional family, trauma, abuse, low self-esteem, shame, depression can be treated effectively by a professional

6. The counseling therapy sessions allows working out issues you have with your spouse such as communication, parenting, sexuality and intimacy.

Regardless of the type of therapy you prefer, the support you get from people who have experienced codependency will be the best.

Family and friends can also pitch in, but they do not have the perspective needed or may be the reason for your problem. Thus, they can further worsen your denial, shame, fear and other issues you are fighting hard to get rid of.

Chapter 56   Ways to Love Yourself

Perhaps one of the best things that you can do is to recognize the importance of becoming your own best friend finally. Our society teaches us in many ways to devalue true friendship with ourselves and to look for stimulation and stimulus from other people.

We are not talking about becoming an egomaniac and thinking that everything you do is simply wonderful. Nor am I discussing becoming a narcissist as both of these mindsets weave destruction in their wake with no apologies and lots of injured parties.

You may have heard the term self-love because it's very popular and many people toss around the term arbitrarily. You are told the importance of loving yourself. Still, nobody takes the time to tell you how to go about it or exactly, the best way to love yourself so that you don't become a flaming narcissist.

One key factor that you must keep in mind is that self-love is important when it comes to being able to live well. The way you feel about yourself influences many decisions in life like:

1. Who you choose will become your mate.

2. The kind of job and the work that you're capable of accomplishing.

3. How you cope with the problems that you have in life.

So the next question you probably have is what exactly should self-love mean to you and how do you project it and use it to grow as a person? How can it free you from personality disorders like codependency? How do you grow self-love when you do not like the person that you are?

These are all fantastic questions that show that you're on the right track. Self-love should become more than just an appreciation of yourself but a way of being that inspires you to become a better person.

This state of appreciation is for you to continue to grow based on the actions you choose each day. When the actions you choose are reinforcing, inspiring, and give back to your community, you strengthen your overall personality and make yourself much happier.

Self-love also reflects a type of acceptance that acknowledges your weaknesses but constantly strives to improve them to a point that they become super human strength.

Often, to find personal meaning in life one must have a true center that is focused on respect for oneself. You can grow self-love by first learning how to accept yourself for who you are.

Since our society teaches us to want to become like models and celebrities instead accepting who we are, this causes the average person unconscious distress. Yet the first step to freeing yourself from codependency is an acknowledgment of your shortcomings, that is, your weaknesses both physical and mental. No longer will you hide these.

You may feel that if you begin to acknowledge your shortcomings, you'll simply dislike yourself more. Yet this is shortsighted. When you begin to tell the truth to your subconscious, you are confronted with the reality that this is as bad as it will get. Once you cross this Rubicon you begin to realize that you have nowhere else to go but a steady climb upward!

I have put together what I call my seven steps to learning to become your own best friend and learning to love yourself in a way that will grow, strengthening everything you do in life. You really can change the way you think about yourself and begin to master your emotional, physical and mental domain.

My Seven Step Prescription For Becoming Your Own

Start Listening To Your Heart, Mind and Spirit

To accept yourself as you are, you must first understand who you are. That's logical, right? One of the best ways to do this is to begin to see yourself in absolute truth. I suggest that you disrobe and stand in front of a long mirror and simply look at your body. Then close your eyes and sit peacefully and quietly and listen to your thoughts and listen to what your heart is telling you. Don't allow yourself to say "that is bad", or "this is good" - just listen. When you do this, you will learn what you are thinking, how you are feeling and the pain that you currently are experiencing. Don't judge at this point but simply create a state of being and listen to yourself.

Act on What You Need Physically, Emotionally and Spiritually

I am not here to tell you what you should be experiencing. I don't have to. If you truly listen, in many cases your mind, heart and body will tell you what's happening. You may need more exercise, or you may need to stop thinking so negatively, or you may need to be grateful for the things you take for granted. You may need to connect with a higher power, God or the universe. Meditation and mindfulness at this point are your best friends, allowing you to sit quietly and hear what is going on. Still your mind.

Start Choosing Things That Strengthen You Physically, Mentally, Emotionally and Spiritually

When you do this, you begin to have higher appreciation for yourself because you may never have tried to become a stronger person. It is a process that can happen in tiny baby steps but if you work at it every day, your respect for yourself will continue to grow. A side benefit is that you will begin to like other people around you as well. If you doubt this, ask anyone who's lost a large amount of weight by putting forth a huge effort to become physically fit. Their self-esteem shoots through the roof and they begin to have a true appreciation and respect for themselves, as well as often becoming a source of inspiration and encouragement for others.

Confront Your Shortcomings and Accept Them - But Begin To Change Them for the Better

You will truly begin to like yourself once you confront your failures, shortcomings and issues with the mindset that you have decided to change. This is where the root of most disorders lies and when we discuss the subconscious, we will learn how to get rid of emotional baggage permanently. It is at this point that you are becoming your own best friend because you're getting the right advice from yourself and, finally, taking it.

Practice Intensive Care of Everything in Your Life

People who love themselves exercise, nourish themselves with healthy foods, practice meditation or positive thinking, get proper sleep and work to become a good friend to other people around them. They also have careers. Once you begin to do these things, not only will your self-esteem continue to grow but you will begin to have a deep appreciation for yourself to the point that you know you are worthy of love and respect.

Set Practical Boundaries for Everything in Your Life

You must learn to say no to people and temptation, particularly if the behavior they (or you) want you to engage in is self-destructive. People who love themselves understand the importance of not harming themselves physically, emotionally or even spiritually. Protecting yourself will bring the right people into your life and allow you to have quality relationships. If someone steps over one of your boundaries, that's a deal breaker and you must walk away. Respect for everything in your life is key.

Forgive Yourself but To Live Mindfully

You're going to make mistakes on your road learning how to love yourself. It's part of the process. But when you do make mistakes it is important to forgive yourself and stop being so hard on everything that you do. People that are most unhappy constantly judge themselves and believe that they are at the center of a huge volume of negativity. Yet the real truth is that most people are quite willing to forgive you if you can first learn to forgive yourself.

It is at this point that you must focus on living intentionally so that you will begin to forge the reality that you most want to create. If you follow the steps above, you will begin to make better and better decisions that will support the intention of redirecting your life in the direction you desire.

There is an axiom in psychology: "Where you put your focus and attention is where things will grow." Many ancient proverbs and sayings of the wise reflect this same idea. If you have a positive mindset, work hard and play by the rules and take the time to learn and live and love, life will begin to turn around.

It is amazing how fast you can transform negativity into a completely different pattern of positive affirmations that will continue to grow your heart, mind and spirit.

Take the time to work on the different things that you know are important to your future and focus on the positive. Before you realize it, your life will begin to change for the better.

It is impossible for you to love other people until you first learn to both forgive and love yourself. Still, you must do so in the right steps as mentioned above and with the right mindset. Learning to become your friend and to respect and love who you are is always the right direction. This will allow you to become an incredible person that is filled with love of life. Become this person and you will never be alone or have any need ever to be codependent again.

Chapter 57   Tips and Advice for Overcoming Codependency

As you do these small things more and more, they will eventually grow into habits. Once they are habits, they can help construct your emotional foundations. You do not need to do every single one of these things. Some of them may not even work very well for you. These tips are more intended as suggestions and guidance. Let them inspire you to develop your positive habits.

Keep a Journal

Writing a journal is an excellent way to make the whole process of self-reflection a lot easier. You can use it as a reference and memory aid. And reading what you wrote a few days after the fact will help you to better reflect on what happened and how you felt at that moment. This will prevent you from minimizing the pain you have felt in the past and from overdramatizing smaller events. So, as you write, remember to write down both what happened and what you feel. Getting in this habit will also help you to get better at identifying your feelings something that many codependent personalities struggle with.

Do Something Creative

Creative activities can be immensely therapeutic and relaxing. It can also help give your subconscious emotions a means of expression. When you don't know how to say what you are feeling in words (or aren't even sure yourself what you are feeling), doing something creative can help you process those emotions in alternate ways. Plus, you will end up with something cool in the end. So, whether it's arts, crafts, or some sort of DIY project, take the time every week to do something creative. Who knows? You may discover some hidden talents in yourself. At the very least, you will discover some hidden emotions.

Make to Do Lists

This might seem like it is coming out of the left-field, but To-Do lists can help more than you think. Each morning (or each evening before you go to bed), make a To-Do list for the day. Include big important tasks as well as the little things. As you complete each task throughout the day, mark it off your list. This is a positive habit that will help you better realize just how much you do get done in a day. It is a wonderful feeling to sit down after a long day and look at a long list full of completed tasks.

Whether it is expressing a thought, saying no, finding a new hobby, or working on any of the other steps, starting the day with the clear intention of how you plan to work on your recovery will not only help keep you on track but also help you notice the progress you are making. Think about it; after one week of doing this, you will have accomplished seven goals that are helping your recovery. Add those seven goals together, and you are that much closer to recovery.

Notice Something Beautiful

Take the time every single day to stop and notice something beautiful or pleasant. It could be the sunset, a cute dog, a particularly artistic piece of graffiti, or even just an extra well-made sandwich eaten for lunch. Just remember to stop and take a moment to acknowledge how wonderful it is and let yourself enjoy it without any outside pressure from anyone else. This is your small moment of enjoyment and peacefulness that you can have all on your own without anybody else.

Acknowledge an Accomplishment

Every single night, as you are going to sleep, think of at least one thing you accomplished that day. It could simply be accomplishing the small recovery goal you had set, or it could be marking off everything on your To-Do list. No matter how big or small, every accomplishment count. As you are going to sleep, you can use that time to appreciate what you have accomplished. If you can think of more than one thing, go for it. But always come up with at least one accomplishment from your day.

Keep a Dream Journal

Each morning, as soon as you wake up, write down everything you can remember from your dreams. This can be fun and enlightening. A dream journal will help you get more in touch with your subconscious and all those unexpressed emotions you are struggling with.

267

Plus, it can be an interesting way to pass the time to read through all the dreams you have been having the past few nights. As you reread them, look for any common symbols or themes. Alternatively, you can compare your dream journal with your regular day to day journal to see what in your life might be influencing your dreams. If you don't feel like an expert dream interpreter, you can take your dream journal (and your regular daily journal while you are at it) to your therapist to get his or her thoughts and opinions.

Startup Savings for Something You Want

Even if you do not have very much money to put away, this can be a very good exercise. Working toward a tangible long-term goal like a vacation or a new dress can help you build emotional strength and endurance. So even if you are just putting leftover change from the day into a jar, start saving money. And start saving it for a specific goal.

Even if you do not feel comfortable telling anyone what exactly you are saving for, you can still build up a savings and know for yourself what your goal is. Let it be a somewhat long-term goal, though, such as a dream vacation or even just a fairly expensive piece of jewelry or another item that you want. Part of building up emotional strength is learning to appreciate delayed gratification and long-term rewards. Saving up for things you want to get in the future can help you develop that skill. With these steps and tips in mind, you are ready to begin your journey to self-recovery. This is one of the most courageous and inspirational decisions you could have made, so congratulate yourself for coming this far and for deciding that it is time to change. This will keep you motivated and strong as you work through the process.

Chapter 58   Steps to Conquer Freedom

Healing Your Relationship with Yourself

Your primary and most important relationship is with yourself. If you cannot have a healthy relationship with yourself then it is impossible to be in a relationship with another that is not dysfunctional.

Healing the Wounded Inner Child

The most common causes of codependent patterns stem from childhood experiences of trauma and the inability to fully be a child at that crucial time in one's life. To go forward into the future, it is necessary to return to the past and heal the wounds and fill in the gaps that are holding us back in the present.

Essential Needs of a Child

1. Unconditional love

2. Feeling that they are being listened to and heard

3. Feeling safe and protected

4. Affection touch and physical expressions of care

5. Respect of your needs and opinions

6. The nurturing presence of someone who genuinely cares for them

7. Encouragement and praise

8. Guidance and mentorship

9. The freedom and space to play and explore their world

In dysfunctional families, children do not feel safe and unconditionally loved in a way that allows them to be their authentic selves and express their feelings naturally. As we have already stated, there are many ways in which children are shamed, neglected, abused, and made to suppress their true expression. This leads to children hiding away parts of themselves and taking on adult roles and responsibilities to survive. Very few people make it to adulthood without some wounds from childhood experiences, codependents often have more wounds that most. The scars from this wounding can dominate one's adult life, and the only way to truly heal these wounds is to revisit them and experience them again. However, this time you meet them with understanding and compassion so that you can finally be free.

Your Child Self

Some people scoff at the idea of the "inner child", but the fact is that we were all once children and still have those qualities within us. The happiest and healthiest people are those who have been able to grow into mature adults while still keeping those child-like qualities of playfulness, innocence, and wonder. However, many people are never fully allowed to be a child in the first place. On top of that, our society often places more value on making money and being serious rather than child-like playfulness and imagination.

An adult who has suppressed and lost touch with their inner child self is one who does not know how to be playful, be imaginative, and have fun. This is a great loss and causes depression and unhappiness. Many psychologists see the inner child as one's true, authentic Self and is vitally important to an adult being a whole and healthy individual.

Getting In Touch With Your Child Self

If you have identified that you have become estranged from your child self it can be difficult to re-discover it again and allow him or her to feel safe to express themselves. Your task now is to discover this part of yourself that you have suppressed and learn how to listen to it, discover what it needs, and begin to live the joy that is natural to your inner child.

There are many techniques and practices that one can try to awaken the child self. The common thread that runs through all of them is connecting with the intuitive, creative, and emotional part of yourself that is connected with the right side of your brain. In children this creative aspect of yourself is normally allowed freedom to express itself. Still, those who are forced to grow up too early are forced into a left-brained mode of being that operates out of logic and the concrete, real world.

270

Nurturing Your Child Self

As you may have done in the imaginative exercise where you dialogue with your child self, it is very helpful if you actively learn how to nurture yourself. You can fulfill the parental role that you possibly never had. Part of being free from codependency is learning that you can find the love, support, and compassion you require within yourself. A good parent is one who listens to their child, respects their boundaries, empathizes, and comforts them.

The following are a list of important parental actions that you can and should learn how to provide for yourself.

Understanding

Practice understanding the struggles and painful experiences that your child self was subject to. By offering this gift of understanding you allow your inner child to experience the all-important feeling of being understood.

Unconditional Love

Being able to bring unconditional love to even those parts of yourself that you have learned to hate is one of the most powerful healing processes.

Listening

It is important to take time out of your daily life to listen to the voice of your little child and hear what it needs to express.

Mirroring

A good practice is to repeat what the voice of your child self is telling you aloud. You can then name the feeling that you experience and state that you acknowledge what your inner self is saying.

Empathy

You can learn to empathize with yourself, empathy need not be for another separate person. It can be within yourself, or from your present self to your past self and vice versa.

271

Acceptance

Practice acknowledging what you are feeling and accepting that negative emotions are perfectly normal and acceptable.

Comfort

Provide yourself with the nurturing voice of comfort that tells the wounded self that this pain is temporary and things will get better.

Encouragement

Remember to give yourself encouragement and positive reinforcement.

Healing Your Shame

Shame is a common emotion that is very common in people who struggle with codependency. It is a very damaging feeling that can be ingrained very deeply in someone who has experienced what they perceive to be failures and the condemnation of their parents. Shame can be internalized to such an extent that an individual believes that shame is who they are. A person with this belief has a deep feeling that they are innately guilty, selfish, weak, unlovable, or responsible for challenging things that have happened in the past.

Unfortunately, codependent individuals tend to place the blame upon themselves for the abuse that they receive or that others they care about experience. It is important to realize that there is no need to feel shame or guilt for anything. Everyone makes mistakes and as a child you have no responsibility to be perfect and live up to others' expectations.

Allowing Yourself Feel Your Grief

Everyone, not just those who struggle with codependency, experience grief. There is nothing wrong with experiencing this as it is a part of life; however, it is common for people to try to avoid feeling their sadness. If your grief is not fully acknowledged at the time it occurs, then it will stick with you for the rest of your life. This is why it is very important to acknowledge your grief as it is happening. Still, if you have suppressed grief from your past you can heal it at any time you are willing to face it again.

Feel To Heal

It is important to learn that to heal you must feel. Just intellectually thinking about your grief and trauma will not allow the full experience of what has happened to you to be processed. As we already mentioned, that which is not fully experienced will stick around within you and resurface as physical or emotional pain and illness. The key is that you must feel to heal.

If you never allow yourself to feel your traumas then you will never be able to heal. It is that simple. There is never any easy time to allow yourself to feel your inner pains. Still, the longer you put it off the more pain you will experience in the long run and you will not be able to be free. Many people fear to feel their grief because they worry that it will destroy them and they won't ever be able to recover. It is important to know that this is not true, you are strong and have the power to face your grief and accept why it has happened and forgive yourself and others for the fact that it has happened.

Acceptance and Forgiveness

As you allow yourself to feel your emotions fully and therefore heal, the final step is to accept what has happened and then move on. At some point you must accept that in some way it was your fate to be born into the family and situation that you were. While you may not have consciously chose it, there is no use wishing for a different hand to be dealt to you. It happened and now it is in the past. You are free to drop the unnecessary baggage of the past and move on with your life free of that weight.

Forgiveness is a critical aspect of this acceptance process. With the distance of time and space from your trauma you can hopefully come to understand that those who hurt you or were not able to provide for your needs were themselves suffering. It is likely that in your parent or guardian's childhood they were not given the love and support that they needed. One thing is for sure – if you do not allow yourself to forgive yourself and others you will never be able to be free. Be careful, however, of not forgiving too soon or too late. If you try to forgive too soon then you will not allow yourself to feel your grief and understand why it happened fully. On the other hand, if you hold onto your resentment too long it will only hurt yourself and prevent you from moving on with your life.

Healing Your Trauma

Trauma can be physical or emotional, but it is the emotional traumas that leave lasting scars. The worst of traumas often occur when we are very young and are therefore extremely sensitive and feel things very deeply and without defenses. Adults have the maturity and ability to cope with traumatic events that children just are not able to handle.

The Following Is A List Of Some Of The Major Causes Of Trauma

1. The threat or intimation of physical pain or the threat of abandonment

2. Personal addiction or the experience of spending time around an addict

3. The death of a loved one

4. Abandonment, whether it is physical or emotional

5. Physical pain

6. The experience of being betrayed

7. Witnessing someone else experiencing trauma

8. Any type of abuse, which can range from physical harm and sexual abuse to seemingly minor criticisms that nevertheless cause trauma

9. Teasing and criticism

10. Neglect and lack of care

11. Experiences of helplessness

12. Chronic or extreme poverty

13. Loss of things you value, whether it happens or is threatened

14. Abandonment that is physical or emotional

Trauma is tough to pin down. While all of the above can cause trauma, there are many effects that a traumatized person may exhibit. Two children who have the same experience may have varying degrees of trauma. The symptoms of trauma can also vary and may not surface immediately after the event but for year's afterword.

Chapter 59   How to Stop Depending On Others

As people grow up, they learn to become more independent. Life events such as college, marriage, and having a family are trademark examples of a person becoming independent. However, codependent people struggle to reach the average person's independence. This can be problematic for many reasons because independence has major benefits. One benefit is independence can boost a person's confidence. When a person is learning to become more independent, this means that they are learning to rely on themselves. This leads to the person needing to become more sure and self-reliant in their decision-making. This, in turn, leads to the person building their confidence.

Another reason why confidence is important is that it can lead to a person to become less reliant on other people. The most obvious explanation for why this is true is that when a person becomes more independent, they do not need to rely on other people as much as they used to do. As a result, the person can learn that it is okay to be on their own. They are also more likely to appreciate another person's help when it does happen, especially when help is needed.

Independence is also a way to alleviate a person's stress levels. Once a person no longer needs to rely on other people constantly, they are less likely to be dissatisfied or stressed out when they are making plans. They only need to rely on themselves.

One other way independence can be beneficial is because self-value is improved. When a person becomes more independent, they can trust their instincts and themselves in general. Trusting one's self shows that they value themselves and their ability to make decisions. People also tend to feel accomplished when they work through something on their own.

For the people who struggle with independence, there are ways to improve reliance on one's self. It can be uncomfortable and overwhelming to take the necessary steps to independence. Still, the result is worth the hard times in the beginning.

The first way to improve someone's independence is to take the time to learn more about one's self. People can feel unsure of who they are. This is especially true for codependent people because their identity is usually attached to whoever they have become dependent on. A person might find that they tend to say yes or no to things that they do not necessarily want to do because they are so focused on appeasing other people.

A great way to learn more about one's self is to start journaling. The main benefits of doing this are that the person will begin to understand how they are feeling, why they make certain behavioral decisions, and why they act in certain ways. This will lead to independence because the person will begin feeling more confident in knowing who they are and understanding how their thought patterns work. Reflecting on how one feels and thinks about certain situations also leads to a new level of trust the person has in themselves and their instincts. The person will also likely learn more about what they want out of life that meets their own needs rather than someone else's needs. The result of understanding one's self is the person will also be able to reason about which areas of their life should take on more independence and when the independence should begin setting in.

Another way to become more independent is to stop asking other people for permission. While there are instances where a second opinion is welcome, people must learn to think for themselves and not rely on other people to do the decision-making. Once a person learns to stop asking other people for permission, then they can gain independence. This is because when a person stops relying on other people to make plans, they are, in turn, learning to trust that their mind and emotions can make the best decision for a given situation.

If a person is too dependent on getting other people's opinions or permission, then they have become overly dependent on the other person's ideas. This will not help a person gain independence; it actually hurts their chances of reaching independence. When people ask for someone else's opinion or permission, they probably already have the same idea in their head. Their goal is to gain the approval of the other person. This means that the next time a person is looking to ask for someone's permission or approval, they should look at their answer first and go along with their instincts. When a person can be more aware of their instincts, then their thoughts and emotions seem more reliable as well. There becomes no need to ask for permission, which means their independence is strengthened.

The next way to become more independent is if the codependent person learns how to be more assertive with other people. When a person becomes confident that someone will agree with them or not tell them "no," then they might start to become dependent on that individual. Codependent people are notorious for being agreeable with other people to avoid being abandoned or rejected. Once the codependent person can stop themselves from always giving in to what other people want, a newfound independence will take its place.

One's ability to learn how to be more assertive will actually allow them to know when to tell a person "no" and when it makes sense for them to say "yes." In turn, the codependent person can see when it is important for them to put themselves first.

Learning how to puts one's own needs before other people, when necessary, can lead to not only independence but self-value as well. Codependent people can become so dependent on helping other people and putting their needs ahead of one's own needs. This can lead to the codependent person forgetting about themselves and what they want to be doing.

It is important to be assertive in relationships and with other matters of life. For example, if a codependent person finds that a fellow employee is asking them to take care of work that is not the codependent person's responsibility, this may be because the fellow employee knows the codependent person says "yes" often. This can lead to unnecessary stress for the codependent person.

The codependent person should start saying "no" more often so that they can focus more on their own needs. They should also remember that the people who truly care for the codependent person will accept when they say "no" and want the codependent person to take the time to look after themselves.

Setting aside time for alone time and alone dates can also lead to independence. The codependent person can go about doing this by thinking about doing certain things that they normally do with others. It could be responsibilities such as grocery shopping or running errands. Still, the alone dates could also be going to a coffee shop and catching up on some reading over a cup of coffee or going to a movie.

The act of fitting in some alone time not only allows the person to increase their independence and feeling comfortable with one's own company, but it can also improve a person's confidence and self-esteem.

When codependent people set aside time once a month to take advantage of alone dates, then they can build up their sense of self-worth. This also means that the codependent person no longer needs to wait for other people to be available to do something; they only need to depend on themselves to be ready.

Alone dates can also be viewed as a form of self-love because the codependent person is showing themselves that they are comfortable being alone and with themselves in general. The act of being alone is great when learning to let go of the negative and shameful thoughts that often arise when a codependent person finds themselves alone.

One final way to build a codependent person's independence is to provide emotional support for one's self rather than seeking support from someone else. This is not just true for codependent people; non-codependent people also seek help from other people when they feel down or overwhelmed. The mind believes that other people can provide them with the comfort and advice that will lift their spirits. There is nothing wrong or abnormal about turning to other people for support. However, when a person becomes too dependent on receiving support from other people rather than turning to one's self for support, then this will only fuel their codependent tendencies.

It is extremely important to learn how to gain support from one's self because once a person is capable of getting emotional support from themselves then they will learn how to take control of their emotions and the course of their life. A person's ability to comfort themselves rather than relying on other people to do so is actually how a person can achieve emotional support from one's self.

The emotional support a person gains from themselves can prove to them that they are not only capable of physically taking control of their life, but they are capable mentally as well. This is especially rewarding for codependent people because their mind is the largest obstacle standing in their way of trusting in their self.

Once a person takes the necessary steps toward gaining independence, then they too can reap the benefits that independence can bring them. It will take time and effort to work through the mental barriers preventing codependent people from maintaining independence. Yet, it is important to push through the discomfort and fear to trust in one's self.

Chapter 60   Establishing Healthy and Happy Relationships

Have you ever made stupid errors that have destroyed major relationships? I have read many things about the psychology of how to have healthy, long-lasting connections—with romantic partners, family, or friends since I have been making my own mistakes in the past.

Below, I want to share some vital information for better relationships:

Be Truthful

Some problems you ignore or do not understand would possibly damage your relationship. It is better to face the facts straight away and fix them, instead of allowing them to undermine your relationship over the long run.

Be deliberate and understand the truth of your relationship. Therefore, think of everything like your feelings and thoughts, the feelings and thoughts of the other person, and their external environment. If you notice a certain aspect of reality is being flung away, it's time for the focus to double and get to the truth.

Avoid Failing in Their Mind

One of the greatest dangers in close relationships is to assume that the other person is just the same as you are in their feelings and emotions. Sometimes, our psychological selves just don't acknowledge the difference between the other person in our relationship and ourselves.

Use the Language Of Say

Say Culture is a social tactical approach in which you are honest and open about your emotions, opinions, and what happens to near people in your life. It makes you more honest and real. Tell them things you feel they'd like to hear about yourself. Be Expressive!

If, for example, you want to have a hug, tell someone else you'd like a hug. It is crucial, however, that you don't expect the other person to hug you for the Tell Culture to function. You just have to tell them your needs and wishes, instead. We can then act openly on our demands and desires as we choose.

Remove Barriers to Communication

To communicate openly and honestly, social barriers must be eliminated. Find your individual preferences for interaction and settle on something that fits best for you both.

Using Psychological Tuning

As you talk, don't hear just what the other person says, but also the feelings behind the words. Note if the person appears anxious, frazzled, sad, upset, confused, angry, happy, happy, etc.

Note the tone of the voice, the language of the body, and not the sentences, and the meaning of the words. This emotional accentuation will improve the ability to understand and respond in ways that will lead to healthy, long-term relationships.

Check Your Relationships

This is a magical solution to so many issues with relationships! Schedule regular meetings to address and strengthen the status of your relationship.

For example, every two weeks, my husband and I are checking in. In the last couple of weeks, we first thought about what we enjoyed the most. So, we discuss how our relationship should strengthen and how it can be strengthened. Eventually, we end up being grateful to each other for checking in and have some good chocolate to pay off. This has done great things to strengthen our relationship. It works!

Confide In Others

All of these techniques help you build trust that is essential to healthy, lasting relationships. Hold your relationship's confidence level in your mind, still individually assessed. How much trust do you have in another person acting in ways that suit your mental model? How much confidence do you have in this person?

Boundaries and Confidentiality Must Be Respected

It is so convenient for us to watch each other and to be in constant communication with technological developments. Moreover, it helps make us happy in relationships, because it increases mutual trust, and it does not force the other person to do something they wouldn't like to do.

Have Safe Disputes

Surprised? In relationships, disagreements can be good! If your first battle could lead to an end of the relationship, you're entering a relationship that expects never to fight. Instead, learn and talk to another person about strategies for healthy conflict resolution in advance.

Furthermore, when a conflict arises, start by stressing the importance of the other person and the relationship. Say the truth as well as your thoughts about them. Avoid the blame and be as forgiving as possible when understanding the actions of another person. If you find out that you have made a mistake and apologize quickly and thoroughly, be ready to change the mind. Do not dwell on the past and instead focus on improving future behavior. Focus on reconnecting and restoring conflict-stricken emotional links at the end of every conflict. My husband and I found such techniques helpful in resolving our tensions! You can benefit as well.

Fulfill Your Own Goals

Note that for yourself, you are not the other person in the relationship. Therefore, in any relationship, achieve your own goals first. If you judge it in your mind and heart, be patient and remember what you want from the relationship. Don't let others overshadow their needs and desires. Follow the Tell Culture Rules: be honest and open in your needs and wishes with the other person, and expect them to be honest and open with you. Otherwise, you face both anger and dissatisfaction, which reduces the likelihood of a healthy and lasting partnership.

Concession

Today's society stresses uniqueness, but we need to get out of the shell and place ourselves in another's shoes to make any relationship to work. This means that we need to consider their opinions, thoughts, and feelings.

Yet make sure that your interests are matched with the needs of the others. Seek a mutually advantageous solution in any conflict area. My husband and I always compromise— big and small — and this is the way we maintain strong relationships.

Don't Struggle With Transition or Diversity

Persons and interactions constantly change. This cannot be helped; it is only a fact of life, which can be remembered and celebrated. Often, for both partners to be content, a partnership must be more inclusive. Find, therefore, the possibilities for non-traditional interactions like polyamory and others. At other times, people who once were right are no longer compatible. It is necessary to let each other go at this stage to ensure mutual happiness. What counts is to be careful in your relationship and to follow your own goals. Unilateral sacrifices don't guarantee a healthy relationship. A healthy relationship secures the mutual interests of both the stakeholders.

Chapter 61   Developing Powerful Self-Esteem

The overall health of a relationship is dependent on the two individuals belonging to it. It is not its entity. If you're a deeply insecure person, you're going to carry those insecurities into your relationship. If you're jealous while you're single, you're going to be a jealous partner as well. These issues don't just disappear as soon as someone else is in the picture. Expecting a relationship to fix you is another way that codependency forms. Partners cling to each other with hopes it'll diminish their inner turmoil, led to believe it's the ultimate cure. When it doesn't seem to work, they cling harder until the attempt backfires entirely. To be in a healthy relationship, you need to work on being a healthy individual. One way to do this is by working on your self-esteem. Believe it or not, broken self-esteem is often the root of many flawed relationship dynamics. This is no less true for codependences.

Quit Codependency with These 22 Self-Esteem Affirmations

Positive affirmations are a proven way to improve one's self-talk. By reciting empowering mantras, your inner dialogue shifts and all self-sabotaging tendencies can be relinquished over time. To help build your self-esteem and solidify your inner confidence, try and make these positive affirmations part of your self-talk. Continued practice will rewire your brain to feel more personal satisfaction instantly.

1. Everything I need is already inside of me.

2. I am the master of my own emotions.

3. Today I will overcome obstacles with renewed strength.

4. I am my fortress. I, alone, am in control of what enters and what leaves.

5. I can easily supply whatever I need.

6. I am capable of doing great things.

7. I let go of my past troubles and welcome brighter days.

8. I can stand proudly and courageously on my own.

9. I am open and ready to experience my true power.

10. Every step I take leads me to success.

11. I am fueled by my inner magic.

12. I am inhaling powerful confidence and exhaling self-doubt.

13. I am stronger than ever before.

14. I am whole and I am enough.

15. I am buzzing with brilliance.

16. Everything I touch becomes infused with light.

17. I am an unstoppable force.

18. I am an overflowing cup of love and joy.

19. I am fire and I am blazing ahead.

20. The universe supports me and all of my dreams.

21. Beauty is all around me and I create it wherever I go.

22. Today is the beginning of my best life chapter so far.

Eight Exercises for Developing Powerful Self-Esteem

The greatest thing about self-esteem is that it can be built. How you feel about yourself now is not how you'll feel forever. The only reason you have low self-esteem is because your brain is used to creating negative thoughts about yourself – but it is in no way indicative of who you are. It's time to break the pattern for good and start looking at yourself with kindness. You possess many positive qualities and it's time you start recognizing that.

The Journal of Wins

Your days are filled with wins. You may not realize it, but it's true. The reason you don't notice them is because you're waiting for a big win to fall out from the sky, but you accomplish small and medium wins every single day! These deserve to be celebrated too. Thing is, it isn't realistic to accomplish a big win every day. No one does that! To rev yourself up for a big win, start a journal and fill it with your little victories. Every day, list three things that you did right – both the intentional and unintentional wins. Did you make yourself an delicious sandwich? Did you spend less time on social media today than you did yesterday? Perhaps you complimented a stranger and it made them noticeably happy? These are all wins to be celebrated!

Blame the Circumstances, Not the Individual

Whenever we make a mistake, we tend to blame our personality. This isn't always fair. The next time you fail or make a mistake, try blaming the circumstances instead. For example, let's say you forgot to pick up groceries on your way home from work. Instead of calling yourself forgetful or stupid, try calling out the circumstances that got you here. Attribute this mistake to how busy you've been lately and the stress you've been feeling. You would have remembered to do the task if you weren't so tired! It's not who you are deep down inside. Now, it's important to not dwell on the mistake. Start thinking of solutions for next time, should the same circumstances arise.

Talk to Someone that Makes You Feel Great

How we feel about ourselves is strongly influenced by the people we're around. If you spend a lot of time with people who speak negatively about you or the world in general, you're going to absorb this negativity into your self-talk. If you can't eliminate everyone that makes you feel bad about yourself, make a point to also spend time with people that make you feel great. Spend time with them without bringing your partner along, if you can. Do they make you feel funny? Smart? Capable? Insightful? Lean into these good feelings and have fun with your new friend. And recognize that you truly are all these wonderful qualities that you feel!

Get Physical

Getting physical may sound like an odd way to build self-esteem but believe it or not, it works wonders. When we go on a hike or jog a couple of miles, we are faced with real evidence of our ability to accomplish something. We are simply doing and then succeeding. When we sit and stew in our thoughts, it's easy for negativity and self-doubt to come flooding in. We need to get in the habit of simply doing and then looking back to see how far we've come. When we get active, we can put a distance to our progress or admire the view from our goal. It's a great way to remind ourselves of our power because we are using our power to give ourselves proof! The endorphins from getting active and the chance to remove yourself from your routine will also give you an immediate mood boost.

Respond to the Devil on your Shoulder

Some of us have an on-going relationship with the devil on our shoulder. It doesn't matter what we do, there's always a little voice telling us we're still not good enough. This voice may even convince us to stay away from any possible risk because we'll fail or we don't have the abilities to succeed. You've likely heard this voice before. However, I'll bet you normally listen and keep quiet when you hear it. From now on, you will not let this voice get away with making you feel bad. Even if it makes you feel crazy, respond to the devil on your shoulder. Fight, if necessary. Ask him what evidence he has to support what he's saying and throw conflicting evidence back at him. Think of how someone close to you would stick up for you in this situation.

Stand in a Power Pose

In a recent study, it was discovered that participants who stood in a power pose saw a decrease in their stress levels and an increase in their level of testosterone (which determines confidence). This is no surprise, of course, as body language is a known way of influencing our state of mind. The next time you feel disempowered, sad, or low-energy, get yourself into one of these power poses for at least two minutes:

1. Stand proudly with your legs apart and hands placed firmly on your hips. Make sure to push out your chest and straighten your back.

2. Lean back in your chair and put your feet up on the table. Keep your hands folded behind your head and open out your chest.

3. Lean back in your chair with your legs spread apart. Drape one arm over something next to you (such as a chair) feel free to do whatever you like with the other arm.

Try and avoid low-power poses by steering clear of crossing your arms, folding your hands, or hunching over in your seat. These will have the reverse effect. Choose a power pose and do it now!

Create an Alter Ego

Using an alter ego is a proven method for raising your confidence. In a study on mixed martial arts fighters, it was found that their creation of an alter ego helped to make them feel and perform better in the ring. Think of all the qualities you admire and start constructing a character that embodies all of these qualities. You can even think of a name for this character, if you like. The next time you're in a scenario where you feel shy or insecure, play this character. Ask yourself what this character would say if they were in this position and consider what they would do, how they would behave, etc. If you're taking this character out in public, try not to use their false name or give them a whole new life as it may be awkward if people find out you've been pretending. Make sure it's still you, but the 2.0 version of you. For a little extra fun, you can even play pretend that this character has a superpower. But this time, it's very important you don't try to show it off in public!

Treat yourself like a Loved One

The next time you catch yourself speaking negatively about who you are or what you've done, I want you to hold those thoughts. Now, instead of saying them to yourself, I want you to think of saying them to someone that you love. How would you feel if you heard someone speak that way to your loved ones? If it makes you feel angry or upset, this is the correct response. This should show you that negative self-talk is not the right way to talk to yourself either. If you want to give yourself criticism, think of how you'd give criticism to someone you care about. You'd make it constructive and gentle, wouldn't you? Perhaps, you'd even take the time to remind them of their strengths. Imagine forming this constructive criticism for someone else and vow only to criticize yourself in this same gentle way.

Another alternative to this exercise is imagining your negative self-talk being directed at your child self. Do you know what you looked like when you were a little kid? A toddler, even? Can you imagine speaking so negatively to that small child? I'll bet you'd instantly start to feel bad. Again, form criticism as if you'd be speaking to this child self. This is the only right way to criticize yourself.

Chapter 62 Conclusion

If you ever feel like you run towards codependency, then this is for you. If you ever feel like you cannot break this cycle, then this was definitely for you. If you feel like improving your relationships, then this will be for you.

Independently on what stage you are in or which one of these statements resonates the most with you, you should know that this was written to help you see, understand, and break the cycles that have led you to diminish your self-care, and self-love. It will also look forward to teaching you how to become more independent, how to love yourself, and how to overcome past issues that are still lingering in your present.

You must understand that stopping your codependency habits is not an easy thing to do, and you will probably have to work hard to find and maintain your life back and to recover yourself fully. It is not a fixed process that you get to do in six weeks. It is not bound by time.

It's a fluid process that should take you from A to Z, and at the same time, it will teach you and show you how you should act from now on. Like any other personal journey, you will have ups and downs, and you will probably end up confused by some of the choices you have made or by the fears you have developed. It is all part of the plan, and it should be welcomed during this time when you are healing.

If you genuinely want to overcome your codependency in the relationship you are in, and if you feel like you cannot do it by yourself, then hopefully, this will guide you through some tricky parts. If you still feel like you need to rely on more support, then you can always ask some relatives, friends, or a professional, to help you in any way you need.

Get all the information you can about this topic, especially if you have been living in codependency for a long time. But always remember that we are human beings, so our nature is to evolve as well, and one of how you can do this is by stepping out of toxic relationships that will damage yourself.

This book has probably (and hopefully) taken you on a different journey than what you are used to reading and feeling. And I hope you get to heal yourself with the help of these words.

You have now learned the truth about codependency, what the signs of codependency are and how you need to understand them so you can overcome them. This book has taught you the importance of self-esteem and our way of thinking; it has shown you some strategies you could implement to increase your self-esteem, it has proven that jealousy is a real feeling and that you need some strategies like the ones explained here.

And to achieve this, you will have to remain honest with yourself. How you have acted throughout your life, you need to be open about your consciousness and self-awareness. You need to be willing to try something new that has the potential to change your life completely for a better future.

There's no doubt that you may feel frustrated at some point during your journey, and you probably want to leave everything as it is. You would rather complain once again and feel the discomfort of being in a codependent relationship because that's easier to face all of your internal demons.

But just visualize yourself coming into terms with who you are, see the potential you have within you, embrace change and accept the new you, love the person you are finally becoming, believe in yourself for wanting to change, and create the happiness you deserve.

You can start today as this will be the best moment to open your eyes and become aware of your reality. Leaving things for later will only perpetuate how bad you feel and how unhappy you are at the present moment. I hope this can provide valuable insights into how our mind works, how we become codependent, and how we can overcome this to thrive in our lives.

Be assertive with who you want to spend your time with, but also become confident with your thoughts and how you canalize your feelings. No one else can do this for you. And once you start realizing how your mind works and the profound effect your words have on your overall well-being, you will also understand how important it is to have you and to love you as the first person in your life. No one else is more important than you, and you deserve this happiness and love; don't ever doubt it.

Start using your imagination to create your life that is filled with Equanimeous thoughts, positivity, and self-love. This doesn't mean that you are never going to have problematic situations again. Still, each time you do, you will solve them more peacefully because you have learned about the importance of being mindful. Therefore you will know that these situations come and go and you cannot change them.

However, it is up to you to react accordingly, so which one are you going to choose? Are you going to put yourself down again, or are you going to rise from these problems? You have got the right answer within you.

Lastly, being able to recognize your codependency, your jealousy, and your low self-esteem is only the first couple of steps, you will have to take on this journey. If you really would like to change your life then you must be willing to compromise seeing people who may harm your life, you may need to stop unhealthy lifestyle habits, and you will need to make a correct balance of how you are using your energy. Are you always worrying? Are you never happy anymore? Are you always taking care of others? Who is taking care of you, then?

Always listen to yourself, to your body, to your emotions, to your soul. Understand that the other person that cannot lie to you is yourself, so embrace your inner child and give him or her a hug and the opportunity to shine through this chaos you have created in your adult life.

Once you do this and your inner child has healed, then you will become aware of how your relationships will also start changing, evolving, getting better and overcoming all the problems you may face. You will stop getting stuck, and you will learn how to turn your problems into lessons that will, undoubtedly, teach you a lesson.

Each day is presented as a fresh opportunity for you to change your toxic patterns and to become your authentic self. Long ago were the days where you would always blame another person for your problems, now you have rediscovered the tools you have that will help you understand how you have been navigating this sea called life.

Make some changes that you won't regret, and start living the life you truly want and deserve. You are 1000% worth it - don't let anyone else tell you otherwise, especially if those thoughts come from your egotistical mind. And never forget this: once you start loving yourself and taking care of yourself, the rest will magically appear in front of your eyes, but you will still need to work hard for this. Be mindful and love yourself.

References

Beattie, M. (2009). *Beyond Codependency*. [Place of publication not identified]: Hazelden Publishing.

HOPE TOGETHER, H. (2019). *CODEPENDENCY*. [Place of publication not identified]: KENDALL HUNT.

Hunt, J. (2013). *Codependency*. S.l.: Aspire Press.

Sowle, J. *The everything guide to codependency*.

If you enjoyed this book, please let me know your thoughts by leaving a short review on Amazon. I will personally read it…Thank you!

Book 2 : Cognitive Behavioral Therapy and Empath

A Simple Cbt Guide For a Journey of Self-Care For The Highly Sensitive Person to Overcome Fear, Depression and Anxiety in Relationship. (Empath Healing)

Part 1 : Cognitive Behavioral Therapy

Chapter 1   Introduction to Cognitive Behavioral Therapy

Anxiety and depression are increasingly becoming hot topics for discussion today. Both in the media and elsewhere, there are ongoing discussions about the two illnesses, how they impact human life and productivity, and the best approaches for handling them.

The wave of discussions is not without cause. Of course, sometimes it happens that the media sensationalizes certain phenomena, but that is hardly the case in this situation. According to research, up to 18.1% of the population in America suffers from some kind of anxiety disorder every year (APA, 2000). The anxiety disorders may range from mild panic attacks to full-blown debilitating disorders. In fact, anxiety disorders have been cited as the leading cause of the reduction in workplace productivity. This is to say that employers are losing huge sums of money to anxiety-related events. In the family setting also, anxiety disorders can hamper relationships between family members.

Essentially, a person who suffers from an anxiety disorder can be unpredictable in their reactions to events and people around them, this sort of uncertainty can strain their relationships with others, and so individuals tend to keep a distance from those suffering the illness. Also, there is the emotional and financial toll that having to cater to a person suffering from any illness has on others. This is often increased in cases of mental illnesses.

Depression also has far-reaching consequences. A lot of people currently suffer from one form of depressive disorder or another, and in fact, one out of five sick leaves taken by an employee is usually because of a depressive episode (Sado et al., 2014). As you may know, depression can occur at any point, and often without warning. There are instances where certain situations act as triggers for depressive episodes, but in some cases, depression can occur without warning.

Although depression is easily identifiable and thus more well-managed than anxiety disorders, people still do not often ask for help even when it is glaring that they need it. There are many reasons people do not ask for help in these situations. For instance, there is still some level of stigma attached to suffering from a mental disorder. People tend to take a step back (both mentally and physically) when someone mentions that they are dealing with a mental health crisis. Of course, this can be linked to the depiction of mental health challenges in the popular media. Also, the cost of seeking help is often enormous. The average individual may not have the means to get the required help, attention, and medication that they need. Imagine a low-paid worker in a company who is battling depression, how will the person generate the funds needed to pay a psychiatrist to have a sit-down with them and offer the guidance needed to surmount the challenges the illness poses? It goes without saying that in the highly capitalist society that exists right now, employers are not incentivized to provide their employees with the healthcare benefits that they require.

It is for the reasons listed above that this book is very important. In this book, you will find a tested and trusted solution to depression and anxiety disorder. This solution is known as Cognitive Behavior Therapy (CBT). Cognitive Behavior Therapy provides you with the skills you need to manage the illnesses and to live a full, balanced life until the end of your days. At the start you may need to have to collaborate with a doctor in order to find out what works for you, however, for the most part, you can apply the skills yourself, which means that you do not have to worry about doctor's bills at the end of each month. What is more? The skills discussed are also practical; the scenarios discussed mirror human activities, and so you can apply the skills to your everyday life and still find out that they work. So, you need not worry that all that the discussion may just be theoretical. There is just the right amount of the theoretical and practical to provide balance.

You have to understand that this is not all just talk. A lot of research has gone into the writing of this book. Consultations were made, not just to doctors and other relevant medical practitioners, but people who suffered the illnesses at one point or another were interviewed, and they helped provide the solutions that were written down here, so you can trust that while we may not know the specifics of your problems, we have a fairly good idea of what they look like, and the solutions we have provided should adequately cover them.

You may be thinking that there is no need to read this book. Perhaps you have lived with the illness for years without having to go to a doctor or even to seek help. Well, what you have to realize is that when you leave illnesses untreated - especially mental illnesses - they pile on, and with the years, they become harder to resolve. Can you imagine how less burdened your life would be if you were to live without suffering from an illness of any kind? Can you imagine the changes you will experience in your relationships, at work, and generally in your day-to-day life? Illnesses should not be accommodated. More so when there is an affordable, tested and trusted solution right within your reach.

So, why put off until tomorrow what can be done today? Rest assured, the road to recovery is long, even though it is assured. It will take a lot of determination, diligence, and patience. That is why you need to start now. Begin by reading this book, then start implementing the ideas and suggestions you find within the book, only then should you even begin to nurse the idea of success.

The promises made within this book are bold, and that is because they have been tested and proven. The stories of success abound; some of them you will find when you keep reading. It is based on the strength of those results that the promises are made to you. As stated earlier, your particular circumstances may differ from the experiences given by the persons who have made use of this book, however, the solutions still remain the same. You may be skeptical, it might even be that you have read other materials like this that made lofty promises and none of them worked. That is understandable. Still, give this one last shot. Go deeper into the book. Read line by line, and observe all of the exercises that are given. There is no doubt that you will be so enamored and astounded with the results that you will be unable to put down this book until you have gotten to the end of it.

Thanks again for choosing this book, I'd really love to hear your thoughts about it, so make sure to leave a short review on Amazon (with a photo of the book if you enjoy it).

Chapter 2   What Is Cognitive Behavioral Therapy?

Over time, cognitive behavioral therapy has evolved to be associated with a variety of meanings, some of which we will consider for better clarity. On one hand, cognitive behavioral therapy or CBT can be seen as a form of treatment, usually psychotherapeutic based, which aids people in comprehending the feelings and thought processes that affect their overall behavior. On the other hand, cognitive behavioral therapy could refer to any method of psychological treatment considered to be efficient in the treatment of several issues inclusive but not limited to phobias, disorders (anxiety, depression, eating, etcetera), addictions (drug and alcohol abuse), as well as strong cases of cognitive ailments. CBT is used to change the behavior and attitudes of people towards the beliefs, images, attitudes, and thoughts they hold (basically their cognitive process), and how these processes are associated with their overall behavior, as a means of coping with emotional issues.

Many different researchers are of the opinion that cognitive-behavioral therapy is capable of causing a major improvement in the quality and functioning of a person's life. In many cases, CBT has been seen to be just as effective, if not more than, other contemporary types of psychiatric treatment or psychological therapy. It is imperative to place emphasis on the advances made by CBT in terms of both clinical practice and research over the last couple of years. In truth, CBT is a method for which there are enough scientific backings indicative of the fact that the developed approaches well and truly result in changes. In this vein, CBT is in itself distinct from many different types of psychological treatment.

Usually, cognitive behavioral therapy is conducted on a short-term basis in which focus is placed on helping clients handle a given problem. Over the course of the treatment, patients learn the ability to locate and alter disturbing or destructive patterns of thought that have negatively affected their emotions and behaviors. The basic ideology of CBT revolves around the concept of emotions and thoughts being fundamental to the general behavior of a person. Take, for instance, one who spends their time worrying about the tendency of a plane crashing or getting into a runway accident (among other accidents prone to air travel), might find they have a strong aversion to traveling by air. In recent times, cognitive behavioral therapy has grown to increased popularity among treatment professionals and mental health clients. Since CBT is largely a treatment option conducted on a short-term basis, it is typically less expensive and thus, more affordable than other contemporary forms of therapeutic treatments. CBT also boasts of empirical support and has been discovered to be efficient in aiding people in overcoming a vast array of maladaptive behaviors.

In a contextual sense, cognitive behavioral therapy can be regarded as a combination of both behavioral therapy and psychotherapy. While the latter covers the areas connected to the meanings people assign to things and the way thought patterns start during childhood, the former is concerned with the association between a person's thoughts, behavior, and problem. Many psychotherapists that specialize in cognitive behavioral therapy tend to customize and personalize their treatment models to fit the personality and particular requirements of every client.

The history of cognitive-behavioral therapy can be traced back to a psychiatrist of the '60s, by the name of Aaron Beck. At the time Beck was a psychoanalyst, and it was during one of his analytical sessions that he discovered how his clients were often inclined to have internal conversations in their heads like they were dialoguing with themselves. However, while the session lasted, usually, only a small fraction of these conversations would be relayed to him. Take for instance, during a therapy session, a client might be conversing in their mind: "Why hasn't she (the therapist) said much since we began? Could it be that she is not happy with some of my answers?" Thoughts of this sort would often tend to work up the client towards emotions like anger or anxiety. But the internal dialog doesn't end there, as there is usually a follow-up thought: "Perhaps she is just tired from seeing many clients, or maybe I am yet to pique her interest with an important subject." This second thought is capable of altering the emotions the client had about the first one.

Beck found out that the relationship between emotions and thoughts was a vital one. He coined the term "automatic thoughts" as a means of defining the thoughts filled with emotions that so often occur to the minds of people. It came to his realization that such thoughts were seldom ever performed to a person's awareness, although they could learn to locate and report them. If one had feelings of upset in any way, the thought pattern altered between negativity and unhelpful or unrealistic. Identifying such lines of thought was imperative in helping the patient comprehend and get over his or her problem. Beck, hence, named it cognitive therapy owing to the relative importance placed on thinking. Over time, the name changed to cognitive behavioral therapy (CBT) as we know it today as the therapy tends to utilize techniques of behavior as well. In use, the balance between the behavioral and cognitive elements tends to change across the diverse therapies of this sort, however, they all fall under the general term — cognitive behavioral therapy.

Over time, CBT has been put to the test in terms of scientific trial by different people in different places, applying it to a broad range of issues, most of which have garnered positive results.

Basic Principles of Treatment

1. The cognitive principle (indicative of the C): This principle is concerned with the interpretations, beliefs, thoughts, and the relative meaning that is assigned to them.

2. The behavioral principle (indicative of the B): This principle is concerned with the responses, actions and things people do in different situations.

3. The principle of interacting systems: Cognitive behavioral therapy emphasizes that psychological problems arise as a result of the relationship that transcends beyond a person's behavior and cognition to include their feelings, and even sometimes, physical responses like changes in breathing patterns, increasing heart rates, goosebumps, et cetera.

4. The 'vicious cycle' principle: Associated with the principle of the vicious cycle is that in cognitive behavioral therapy there exists a relative emphasis on how a problem in the principle of interacting systems can result in another quite immediately. Take, for instance, a person's cognition is capable of causing unrealistic behavior and vice versa.

5. The 'virtuous cycle' principle: In a positive sense, CBT places emphasis on the fact that making positive alterations in any element found in the interacting system can result in a positive alteration in the other elements, hence, aiding a person in getting over psychological issues, or lowering the severity of symptoms in the least.

6. The principle of "here and now": The general focus in cognitive behavioral therapy is usually placed on what maintains the present issues instead of the elements which may have originally triggered them. However, it is a common belief in traditional psychodynamic therapy that considering issues from a here and now perspective is shallow. Hence, the belief that any successful firm of treatment ought to uncover the unconscious conflicts, concealed driving forces, and processes of development which are considered to lead to the root of the problem. Approaches in psychodynamic therapy debate that treating the resulting problem instead of its supposed root causes would only result in a case of symptom substitution. That is, the resulting issue would again resurface, but in a much different form. Behavioral therapy proved that although such an outcome was as plausible as it is possible, the chances of occurrence are vaguely slim.

   Cognitive-behavioral therapy adopts this perspective shown by behavioral therapy. It provides theories relating to maintenance as opposed to the procurement of impractical coping techniques and poor beliefs.

7. The Psychological Interactionism Principle: This principle is of the opinion that the events people choose to place focus on, their inferences and interpretations of those happenings, as well as the beliefs they hold, the behaviors, thoughts, physical signs, and emotions they experience, all share a common interrelatedness and reciprocally affect one another in multiple, complicated ways.

8. The scientific principle: CBT provides scientific theories that have been and can be further rigorously evaluated by the use of evidential proofs instead of mere clinical anecdotes. It is vital for a host of reasons including;

- The treatment is grounded in theories that are both plausible and well established.
- Therapists can ethically tell clients in all confidence that the process is backed up by researched outcomes.

9. The Emotional Responsibility Principle: The fundamental element of any therapy concerning itself with matters that can be described as cognitive is that the behavioral and emotional responses of people are heavily affected by cognition. That is, the inferences and beliefs of people are the key elements at play in this therapy. If people were to be questioned on the things that induce emotions of anger, sadness, and anxiety in them, a good many would often resort to rendering accounts of certain scenarios or events. Take for instance that one finds that tests make them nervous while talking to a crowd makes them anxious, and bigotry makes them annoyed, among other samples. Try to recall any event of the past that elicited negative emotions in you such as depression or anger. If it is true that an event of the past triggered a negative feeling in you at the time, then the only possible method of changing how you feel about the situation is for the event to never have occurred. And if it was a person that made you behave or feel a specific emotion, then the only way of altering how you felt about that person is to undo what was done to you. And what are your chances of success on the off chance that the person is deceased?

Given this logic, it is imperative that there is something else occupying the core of our emotional reactions. In cognitive-behavioral therapy, this "thing" is the cognitive factor. What people believe in, what they tell themselves about it, and the meaning that is attached to it; all stem from your cognition. Let's consider a few model examples.

If you consider the late arrival of your spouse every other day of the week as proof that he or she is cheating, you would tend to feel depressed or hurt. But, alternatively, should you consider your partner's late coming as a result of the fact that he or she prioritized work more than your relationship together, your emotions would border between anger and sadness.

On the off chance that you think of their late arrival as nothing to worry about, you would typically be relaxed and calm about the whole thing.

Now, keep in mind that in all three model events, the late arrival of a spouse remains unchanged, although the different appraisals applied did result in diversity in emotional reactions. This principle consists of two sub-principles, namely the Specific Principle of Emotional Responsibility and the General Principle of Emotional Responsibility.

- The General Principle of Emotional Responsibility: According to Windy Dryden, everyone is largely, although not exclusively, responsible for how they act and feel as a result of the perspectives they assume on the events that occur in their lives (Ferriman, 1995). This principle lies at the core of many different psychotherapeutic models. It merely states that people are the ones highly responsible for how they feel and behave. Without accounting for this principle, it became rather challenging to approach change at some point within the course of therapy. Aiding the client to comprehend and accept this fact should be helpful in easing the approach to constructive workflow.
- The Specific Principle of Emotional Responsibility: This principle particularly specifies the type of cognition that takes center stage in psychological issues (CCBT). That is, it focuses on the ill-conceived beliefs such as "I'll never be good enough," "I'm not worth it," etcetera. Nothing else, neither thought nor cognition, triggers emotions but these specified above. This principle can be used in providing explanations that certain hard beliefs, rather than mere general thought processes, take center stage in influencing emotions. The field of study which concerns itself with identifying such beliefs and modifying them is REBT — Rational Emotive Behavior Therapy.

Chapter 3 What Is a Therapy Session Like?

In this section, we will be considering the structure of a cognitive behavioral therapy session. For better clarity, we will be exploring specific anecdotes that offer objective insights into how these sessions are held.

1. What is the duration of therapy sessions in CBT? The average duration of cognitive-behavioral therapy sessions ranges between twelve to twenty sessions, although there are chances of an extension depending on the type of issue a client has, as well as how complex and severe it may be in regards to the treatment. The duration of a single session usually ranges from about 45 minutes at the minimum to an hour maximum. The timing is usually as a result of the amount of concentration required by both the patient and therapist. As Simmons & Griffiths identified, there are a variety of elements that may influence the need for a much shorter therapy session duration. Some of such factors include fidgetiness or restlessness in the patient, anxiety, the inability to communicate adequately with the therapist, among other reasons.

2. Creating agendas, updates, and homework reviewing: At the start of every session in cognitive-behavioral therapy, the therapist and client join forces together in picking the goals and agenda for the meeting. The selection process should take roughly five minutes to complete. After this, another five minutes has to be spent on updates — the period in which both the therapist and client review the prior session. Within this time any emerging issues or emotions resulting from the session of the previous week are resolved satisfactorily. Since homework plays a vital role in effective cognitive-behavioral therapy, it is imperative that it is reviewed on a weekly basis as clients may tend to consider it insignificant to the process if treated otherwise.

3. Specific strategies in cognitive-behavioral therapy: This section serves a very important purpose in a therapy session, and maybe inclusive of a union of behavioral and cognitive interventions. The selected strategies often tend to vary with each session, depending on the client's issue and how it can be helped. Tools such as management or coping strategies play a key role in helping the patient understand the best ways they can handle their issues without letting it impede their progress.

4. Designing homework and reflections about the session: The final five minutes of the session are key and set aside for creating homework exercises, as well as discussing at length what is anticipated to ensure the client fully comprehends the importance of the activity. As a form of summarizing the final parts of the session, both the client and therapist should indulge in a moment of communicating how they felt about the session, the way it has worked, and the skills or issues that have been understood on account of it.

In conclusion, it can be seen from the structure of the sessions in CBT that this type of therapy has a well-defined structure aimed at both the client and therapist, ensuring both parties are united and create an efficient therapeutic bond.

Chapter 4   Understanding Anxiety

Contrary to popular belief, anxiety is a pretty normal phenomenon that is necessary for the survival of the human race. Owing to the presence of danger from predators, climatic conditions and environmental hazards, the senses of early humans evolved to adopt a system of raising alarms prompting an immediate call to action. Adrenaline coursed through the veins, prepping the body for a flight or fight reaction. The surge of adrenaline is usually associated with heightened sensitivity, increased heart rate, and sweating. In recent times, the growth of human civilization has diminished the fear of danger from predators. Albeit, in today's world, we still experience anxiety from different sources such as family, work, well-being, finances, social life, et cetera. The nervousness which dawns on us before a crucial appointment like an interview or meeting is a direct manifestation of the flight or fight response.

Anxiety is used as a general terminology in psychology to define feelings such as worry, apprehension, nervousness, and fear. These emotions are fairly normal to experience in everyday life, but they tend to increase in severity when they begin impeding a person's life. Severe anxiety is capable of leading to physical signs that require professional help.

Anxiety Attacks

It is best to mention that the term "anxiety attack" isn't exactly clinical, so it is not a medical term in itself. The term is used to identify emotions relating to terror, fear, and worry which comes upon a person instantaneously. In this vein, it is possible to equate an anxiety attack to a panic attack as they are quite similar in terms of signs and symptoms. Albeit, since there is a large variation in both contexts and their respective duration, it's best to consider anxiety attacks alone.

Anxiety attacks are associated with feelings of worry or apprehension about a potentially exhausting event. Signs and symptoms peculiar to anxiety attacks tend to manifest both physically and emotionally. The physical signs are inclusive but not limited to headaches, dry mouth, hot or chilly flashes, sweating, shortage of breath, among others. The emotional signs are restlessness, fear, and worry. Anxiety attacks are always linked to some sort of trigger believed to be considered stressful

310

by a person. There are variations to the intensity of anxiety attacks, meaning it can vary from mild to moderate to severe. For an anxiety attack to occur, the anxiety would have been present and growing in a person.

Symptoms and Signs of Anxiety

Anxiety is the defensive response of the body when a threat is perceived. The signs and symptoms of anxiety can be classified into three main categories outlined below:

Physical symptoms:

1. Rapid breathing

2. Hot flushes

3. Tightening in the chest

4. Racing heart rate

Psychological symptoms:

1. Fear

2. Catastrophizing

3. Worrying

4. Overthinking

Aside from these main classifications, there are other common symptoms of anxiety. They include the following:

1. Weakness

2. High blood pressure

3. Restlessness

4. Twitching in muscles

5. Lethargic reactions

6. Nervousness

7. Digestive complications

8. Heavy perspiration

9. Insomnia

10. Feelings of dread or panic

Types of Anxiety

There are different types of anxiety in the world today, but we will just be considering a few of them in this section:

1. General Anxiety Disorder: This type of anxiety is the most common of all, and is widely known by the acronym GAD. People with general anxiety disorder tend to experience feelings of worry and anxiety the majority of the time. It is like a state of nervousness and tension that never dissipates and occurs without any known triggers. Alternatively, it can also be triggered by elements that would not ordinarily lead to anxiety. GAD is typically linked to symptoms such as restlessness, negative thinking, trouble with concentration, lethargy, fatigue, reduced energy levels, among others.

2. Social anxiety: Social anxiety refers to any form of fear surrounding social situations, and is both irrational and inexplicable. Although some measure of shyness in public situations tends to be a natural occurrence, people with this form of anxiety usually experience emotions of anxiety and fear when it comes to social situations like public speaking, meeting strangers or figures of power, et cetera. To people with this type of anxiety, socializing is a distressing indulgence. Their anxiety typically stems from the fear of being rejected, judged or being spoken ill of. These fears make them keep away from social situations.

3. Panic disorder: Panic disorder is a serious case of worry and fear capable of having physical and mental effects on a person. The symptoms of panic disorders are manifested physically and mentally and tend to become so severe it can result in hospitalization. The common signs of panic attacks include increased heart rate, chest pains, profuse perspiration, digestive issues, light-headedness or dizziness, among others. Coupled with all these signs, people with this form of anxiety also tend to feel emotions of doom, helplessness, and anxiety.

Causes of Anxiety

Anxiety stems from many different complicated factors, a single element is seldom ever responsible for it. Below are some of the common causes of anxiety.

1. Personality traits: People suffering from anxiety sometimes tend to have some specific personality traits. For instance, perfectionists have very high chances of experiencing some form of anxiety owing to the nature of their personality.

2. Genetic inheritance: Anxiety can also occur from genetic predispositions. Recent studies have observed and suggested that certain families may have anxiety in the bloodline. Albeit, this inherent predispodition doesn't imply that it will be passed down to generations.

3. Stressful occurrences: Anxiety is capable of being triggered by certain occurrences in life. The most popular triggers include stress from work, abuse (sexual, verbal, psychological), childbirth, family problems, health issues, death, financial issues, et cetera.

4. Health conditions: Severe physical ailments can lead to anxiety. Health conditions like hypertension, asthma, diabetes, and heart problems are a few of the common ailments linked to anxiety.

5. Substance abuse: People who abuse substances such as alcohol and hard drugs are less likely to be able to handle their anxiety. As such, they usually wind up worsening the situation.

6. Mental health issues: Certain forms of anxiety are capable of being triggered on their own, however, some exist in combination with other conditions like depression.

Chapter 5   Understanding Depression

As a condition, depression can be defined in lots of ways. But the basis of the concept revolves around the experience of feelings of loss of interest in life or overwhelming sadness over an extended timeframe. To gain an in-depth understanding and be able to communicate effectively about depression, one will have to get a sense of what it feels like to be depressed, the things that trigger it, and how it is expressed in different ways. For a person experiencing depression, life is basically a cycle of exhaustion, despair, and anxiety.

Depression can be indicated by an overwhelming sense of exhaustion that leads to a deep sleep, which although long in duration, is in no way restful. Next, an overhanging sense of anxiety and dread ushers in the morning, making it rather challenging to leave one's bed. The emotional sense of exhaustion weighs heavily on the person, making the process of leaving their bed seem nearly impossible, if not altogether unnecessary.

Depression isn't always experienced as gross sadness. It is in feelings of emotional exhaustion that can lead a person to moody and irritable behavior. The behavior has its similarities, although it is experienced differently from person to person. So, while a set of people might find it difficult getting out of bed, others might choose to take a walk around the neighborhood in hopes of stifling an anxiety attack. Depression tends to not have a serious degree of consistency. That is, it is possible for people to experience a stretch of bad days or have their bad day stretch punctuated by good days. Alternatively, there is also the seasonal experiences in which depression occurs at a particular season of the year.

Causes of Depression

Although there is no single defined cause of depression, and its triggers remain much undefined, it occurs as an alteration of the chemical balance in the body and has a significant influence on one's mental state. There are certain elements indicative of depression in people. These elements include the following:

1.   Bereavement

2. Increased responsibilities (like in the birth of a baby or caring for sick relatives)

3. Financial setbacks

4. Separation

5. Changes in the brain

6. Conflicts in personal life such as disputes or divorce

7. Overwhelming life changes like retirement, change of environment or work, et cetera.

8. Burnouts from working too much

9. Abuse (physical, psychological or sexual)

10. Health issues like heart problems, AIDS, cancer, et cetera.

Although a degree of sadness is normal in terms of dealing with tough emotions or bad occurrences, if there are no improvements after a duration of 6 months, there is a likelihood of a much bigger issue being the case here.

Signs and Symptoms of Depression

The signs and symptoms of depression can range from severe to mild, and are inclusive but not limited to the following:

1. Feelings of sadness or moodiness

2. Loss of appetite; in some cases, change in tastes.

3. Disinterest in the activities that were once considered pleasurable or enjoyable

4. Unplanned weight gain or loss unassociated with dieting

5. Increased level of fatigue

6. Sleeping disorders like sleeping too little or too much

7. Continuous loss of energy

8. Feelings of guilt and worthlessness

9. Indulgence in pointless physical activities such as inadvertent pacing or wringing of the hand

10. Reduced speech and mobility (usually as observed by others)

11. Engaging in negative thoughts pertaining to suicide or death

12. Difficulty in focusing and thinking

13. Increased indecisiveness and inability to remember

14. Heightened sense of irritation

15. Feelings of hopelessness and pessimism

16. Consistent anxiety, sadness, and blank moods

17. Cramps, headaches, pains or aches, or digestive conditions without any related physical cause which does not let up even when treated.

For a symptom to be characterized as an indication of depression, it has to last for a duration of two weeks. In addition, medical conditions such as vitamin deficiency, brain tumors, and thyroid problems have similar symptoms to that of depression. As such, it is best to first rule out basic medical factors.

Risk Factors in Depression

Just about anyone can experience depression. As such, not even the most put-together of people who seem to live in ideal circumstances are exempted from it. For depression to occur, one or more of several factors come into play. Some of them are:

1. **Biochemistry**: Disparities between the chemicals found in the brain may be a causal factor in triggering depression.

2. **Genetics**: As was previously discussed, it is entirely possible for depression to be a genetic trait. Take for instance that one of a set of identical twins' experiences depression. There is a 70% likelihood that the other twin would experience depression at some point in life.

3. **Personality**: People who have a low sense of self, are easily flooded by stress, or generally pessimistic in their outlook appear to have higher chances of experiencing depression in their lifetime.

4. **Environmental elements**: A continued exposure to abuse, violence, poverty, lack or neglect can cause a person to become more susceptible to depression.

5. **Biological disparities**: People who experience depression tend to have some degree of physical alterations in their brains. The reason behind these changes is unknown, although it may be helpful in explaining the occurrence of depression.

6. **Hormones**: Any noticeable change in the balance of hormones in the body is capable of leading to depression in people. Changes in hormonal balance tend to happen during occurrences like menopause, heart conditions, thyroid problems, pregnancy (usually the period following childbirth — postpartum), among several other conditions.

Chapter 6 What is Panic Disorder?

Panic disorder happens when one experiences a repeated series of unprecedented panic attacks. According to the DSM-5, panic attacks can be seen as a sudden rush of extreme discomfort or panic which grows with the passing minutes. People suffering from panic disorders tend to have a strong aversion to panic attacks, and live in fear of them. Panic attacks are usually characterized by sharp feelings of overwhelming fright with no known or traceable source. Some common physical signs peculiar to panic disorders include labored breathing, profuse perspiration, and increased heart rate. Most people tend to experience panic attacks in their lifetimes maybe once or twice. According to the AMA, 1 in every 74 people will or may have experienced a panic disorder at some point in their lives (APA, 2000). A popular characteristic of panic disorder includes a constant sense of fear about having a panic attack, usually after about one month, at least, or more of continuously worrying about the recurrence of more panic attacks or their aftereffects.

Moreover, although the signs of panic disorder can seem terrifying and overwhelming in itself, it is possible to manage and improve on them with the right treatments. Seeking medical help is the most crucial aspect of combating the symptoms of panic attacks and enhancing the quality of life.

Signs and Symptoms of Panic Disorder?

The signs and symptoms of panic disorder tend to manifest in young adults under the 25-year bracket, as well as teenagers. If you have experienced four panic attacks or more, or live in a constant state of fear of recurring panic attacks after a prior experience, chances are high that you have a panic disorder. Panic attacks cause an overwhelming sense of fear that comes upon a person almost instantaneously, offering no warnings whatsoever. One would typically last between 10 to 20 minutes, depending on the case. Albeit, in extreme cases, the symptoms tend to manifest for even longer, reaching up to the one-hour mark. In all, however, the experience varies across a variety of people, as does the symptoms, putting into consideration factors like age and susceptibility.

Some of the ubiquitous signs and symptoms related to panic attacks are including but not limited to the following:

- Increased heart rate
- Heart palpitations
- Breathing problems such as shortage of breath and labored breathing.
- Sense of choking (usually like something is inhibiting your breathing)
- Vertigo (dizziness)
- Feelings of nausea
- Trembling or shaking
- Light-headedness as though drunk
- Chilly feeling
- Perspiration
- Tightening around the chest region or chest pains in some cases
- Tingling or numbness in the feet and hands

Causes of Panic Disorder?

Even now, there exists no well-defined cause for panic disorder, although studies suggest that there might be some genetic ties involved in its occurrence. Other associated factors that could result in panic attacks include major transitions in one's life, like getting married, getting pregnant, leaving for school, having your first child, among others. The reason is that these events lead to stress which is a contributing factor in the formation of panic disorder.

Sense or Fear of Dying

Alterations in mental state, related to feelings of depersonalization (the state of being outside of oneself like an out-of-body experience) or derealization (a sense of unreality — feeling surreal).

The signs and symptoms of panic attacks are usually tied to untraceable triggers. In this vein, it is factual that the symptoms are not a clear indication of the degree of danger the environment poses to a person. Moreover, since panic attacks are incapable of being predicted, they have the capability to affect the overall functionality of a person significantly.

The fear of recurring or remembering panic attacks can sometimes be the trigger element for another.

Who Is Prone to Developing Panic Disorder?

As was clearly mentioned above that there are no clear explanations regarding the causes of panic disorder, inquiries made about the condition shows that a specific group of individuals is more susceptible to developing panic disorder. According to the National Institute of Mental Health, women, more specifically, have twice the likelihood of developing panic attacks than men.

Treatment of Panic Disorder

In treating panic disorder, attention is usually placed on lowering or eradicating the signs and symptoms of the condition. This is achievable through therapeutic treatments by qualified professionals, and medications, in some cases. The form of therapy used in the treatment is usually CBT (cognitive-behavioral therapy). CBT helps the patient suffering from panic disorder to modify their actions and thoughts in order to understand the elements that trigger the condition, as well as how to handle their fears.

Medications used in the treatment of panic disorder are usually SSRIs (selective serotonin reuptake inhibitors) — a set of antidepressants. Some of the SSRIs that may be prescribed to treat panic disorder include the following:

- Sertraline
- Paroxetine
- Fluoxetine

There are a variety of steps that can be implemented at home alongside these treatments to lower the effects of panic disorder. They include:

- Steering clear of all forms of stimulants like caffeine (coffee)
- Getting adequate rest and sleep
- Regularly engaging in physical exercise
- Keeping a regular schedule

Chapter 7   Different Types of CBT and Their Purposes

Addressing Dysfunctional Beliefs Using Rational Emotive Behavior Therapy (REBT)

REBT, otherwise known as rational emotive behavior therapy, refers to a form of cognitive/behavioral therapy created by the psychologist Albert Ellis. In REBT, attention is usually placed on aiding the client to alter their dysfunctional beliefs. Let's take an in-depth consideration of the subject regarding how rational emotive therapy works.

How does REBT work?

To gain comprehensive knowledge about the outlook of REBT, it is imperative to first consider the entire therapeutic process through the following steps:

1. Highlighting the basic patterns behind dysfunctional beliefs and thoughts.

2. Identifying the dysfunctional beliefs, feelings, and thoughts which result in psychological stress is the primary step in the process. In most cases, these dysfunctional beliefs tend to be expressed in absolutes, such as the following: "I can't," "I should," or "I must." As Ellis hypothesized, the majority of many widely-used dysfunctional beliefs include the following:

   o Feelings of overwhelming upset about the misconduct or errors of other people.

   o Perfectionism and the belief that you have to be totally, 100 percent, successful and competent at everything to feel worthy and valued.

   o The belief that you stand better chances of being happy by avoiding the challenges or difficulties of life.

○   Feelings pertaining to lack of control over one's happiness, and that one's joy and satisfaction are hinged to external elements. (Thomas, n.d.)

The sheer act of having such dysfunctional beliefs makes it rather challenging, if not totally impossible, to react to events in a manner considered to be psychologically healthy. Holding such inflexible opinions of oneself and others not only leads to anxiety and regret, but it also causes recrimination and disappointments.

Combating The Dysfunctional Beliefs

After identifying all the underlying dysfunctional opinions, the next phase in REBT is to combat these erroneous beliefs. To do this, a therapist ought to challenge the beliefs by making use of methods that are both confrontational and very direct. Ellis was of the opinion that it was better if the therapist sounded logical, honest and unapologetically blunt instead of being supportive, welcoming, and warm. In doing this, the clients would be triggered by altering their behaviors and thought patterns.

Gaining Insights and Identifying Dysfunctional Beliefs Patterns

It cannot be overstated how the processes in rational emotive behavior therapy can sometimes appear to the clients as overwhelming. It is a difficult experience having to deal with dysfunctional belief systems, indeed, particularly because the mere process of accepting one's beliefs as unhealthy elements isn't as easy as it appears. So, when the client finally points out the problematic thoughts, the efforts involved in altering the belief system constitutes an even more difficult process. And although it is quite a natural phenomenon to feel upset when mistakes are made, the main purpose of rational emotive behavior therapy is to assist people in responding rationally to situations of this sort. When this sort of challenge arises in the future, the proper emotional reaction would be to discover that although it isn't an entirely bad idea to be perfect and be free of errors, it isn't a realistic goal to anticipate success in all areas of life.

So, if one makes a mistake, it doesn't imply the end of the world. All anyone can do is derive knowledge from the event and go about their lives freely and uncaged. Also, it is imperative to realize that although rational emotive behavior therapy uses many different cognitive techniques to assist patients, it is also focused on the emotional and behavioral aspects of these patients, too. Besides tracing and challenging dysfunctional belief systems, both the therapist and client tend to align as one to focus on certain emotional reactions that are related to problematic thinking patterns. It is also encouraged for clients to adapt and alter any behavior they find dismal using techniques such as guided imagery, journaling, meditation, among others.

Facing Fears Using Exposure and Response Prevention Therapy (ERP)

Exposure and Response Prevention Therapy or ERP can be regarded as the ultimate measure in the treatment of OCD (obsessive-compulsive disorder). In this form of therapy, the client voluntarily exposes him or herself to the objects of their fears repeatedly over a period of time without acting on the impulse to stop or neutralize the fear. By the constant exposure to the object of their fears, the brain would be compelled into the discovery of how irrational the fear is so that it stops sending fight or flight signals.

Take, for instance, a person who suffers from the Harm OCD and has a great fear of knives. In exposure and response prevention therapy, that person would be required to prepare a meal using a knife nearby. Once that challenge is completed, the person might be required to go about their business with a pocket knife on them. As time goes on, the overwhelming sense of fear surrounding knives will be eliminated when the brain discovered that there is no real threat to other people or themselves. And although harmful thoughts may not entirely be eradicated from the equation, there will no longer be any form of debilitation.

For best effects, exposure and response prevention therapy is best used both within and outside of the therapy sessions. The more a client learns to weave the techniques they learn into their day-to-day lives, the better their coping mechanisms grow with time. Some specific applications, such as OCD, makes it more convenient to access ERP. As the name connotes, exposure and response prevention therapy revolve solely around exposing clients to the causes of their fears. For example, a person with Contamination OCD might have a phobia for stinky socks.

However, the issues can sometimes be a little less obvious than the ones previously mentioned. Take, for example, a person suffering Relationship OCD might have fears, such as obsessing over the physical characteristics of their partners or the inability to be mindful during coitus rather than worrying about their rate of compatibility with their partners. In the case of people suffering from Harm OCD, the case might not be as simple as the fear of knives. It could be the fear of finding sharp objects in the house and harming others with it or the obsessive worry about harming a loved one randomly.

Obsessive-compulsive disorder is a highly complicated condition, meaning its therapeutic treatments have to be tailored to fit with the personality of the client as well as the fears peculiar to them, and how those fears affect their overall life. In exposure and response prevention therapy, the therapist works with the client in helping them understand the signs, triggers and coping techniques for dealing with the disorder, as well as how the OCD interferes with the client's life daily. The therapist proceeds to work with the client in developing a plan for conquering the fear.

This plan is known as the fear ladder, a sequence of tasks that will aid the client in slowly overcoming their fears. In creating the fear ladder, the therapist helps the client recognize the OCD-based problem challenging them. From then on, the client sets a series of goals they would like to achieve based on the identified OCD-based problem. The goal will typically be targeted and practical. Should it be too extensive, the client would be unable to devise a suitable plan for beating the problem. Take, for instance, setting a goal of avoiding anxiety at all costs seems both impractical and unconquerable, and doesn't exactly cover a given issue. A much better alternative would be, "giving a public lecture without getting too anxious." This alternative covers a particular issue facing the client and is a more practical goal that can be achieved.

Once identified, the therapist will be charged with designing the fear ladder, comprised of a set of activities in an increasing order to help expose the client to their triggers at a slow pace. The client will now be charged with undergoing each activity until their fears give way. After every successful activity, the client will rank their fears to keep track of their intensity and decipher whether or not they are ready to proceed with the next task.

Below is a common example of a fear ladder for a client with Contamination OCD who fears to eat with utensils in public cafeterias.

- **Fear**: Getting contamination from dangerous and potentially lethal germs at public cafeterias.

- **Aim**: To enjoy time with friends at cafeterias and not get overly anxious.

- **Fear Ladder**:

  o **First Task**: Begin by taking a trip to the cafeteria in your locale every day and try to focus on everyone who dines there.

  o **Second Task**: Take to YouTube or other video sites to see videos of people dining in public cafeterias that are crowded.

  o **Third Task**: Take a friend or sibling along to the public cafeteria and watch them sit for a meal.

  o **Fourth Task**: Take your friend or sibling to the public cafeteria and try walking around and just noticing the environment.

  o **Fifth Task**: Take your family with you to the cafeteria and try getting a meal on your own with the waiter.

  o **Sixth Task**: Take your family with you to the cafeteria and try placing an order on your own at the counter.

  o **Seventh Task**: Take your family with you to the cafeteria and try placing an order on your own for everyone.

  o **Eight Task**: Take your family and friends with you to the cafeteria and try placing an order at the counter for everyone.

  o **Ninth Task**: On your own, try signing up for a daily food plan at the public cafeteria.

- ○ **Tenth Task:** Go to a party with your friends and eat the food made.

Chapter 8   Set Your Goals

How To Carry Out An Evaluation Session?

An evaluation session in cognitive-behavioral therapy begins with the relationship between a client and the overseeing therapist. The treatment encourages a non-judgmental relationship that puts both client and therapist on an equal plane. The therapist takes charge of asking for the response and views of the clients about the experiences of the latter. The response of the client is what determines how the progress of the treatment is proceeding. Clients are encouraged to be collaborative during an evaluation session because the treatments provided would be based on their active involvement. The relationship between the therapist and client may prove helpful in assisting the latter to be open and talk about issues that bother them with the therapist.

Once a relationship is safely established between the client and therapist, an evaluation session in cognitive behavioral therapy will typically follow after the fashion outlined below:

1. Every evaluation session begins with the therapist and client exploring perturbing issues that the client wants to overcome.

2. When the client and therapist have reached an agreement about the problem that would be the sole focus of the session, they collaborate to plan the content of each session and discuss how best the client can deal with their problems.

3. Over the course of the session, the client can choose to work out a variety of exercises with the therapist in hopes of analyzing every behavior, feeling, and thought. The exercises would typically be provided in the form of worksheets or diagrams.

4. In the evaluation session in CBT, the client will often be given some sort of test (homework) to do during his convenience. So, at the end of every session, he can agree on a task to work on until the next session.

5. By the next session, the therapist begins by going over the concluding part of the prior session, as well as talking about how much progress has been made regarding any work assigned to him.

6. In the evaluation session, clients are taught to deal with distraction based on the following issues:

   o **Anxious feelings**: CBT teaches coping skills for dealing with different problems. Clients may learn ways of coping with different situations, thoughts, feelings, and behaviors in a manageable manner to produce faith in their capability to cope.

   o **Depressive feelings**: The clients would be asked to take a record of their thoughts and explore how they can be examined differently. Doing this can help in stopping mood from spiraling downward.

   o **Sleep issues**: A client may soon grow adept at identifying the thoughts responsible for making them fall asleep less fast, and learn to tackle them.

   o **Long-term problems with others**: It is usually best to find out one's assumptions regarding the motivation of others for doing something, instead of assuming the worst of them.

The structure of the evaluation session is quite straightforward. In the early stages of treatment, the first sessions, the therapist will indulge the client to ensure CBT is the right therapeutic treatment for their condition. Should CBT be right to treat the client, the therapist now proceeds to help the client settle in, because being comfortable is vital to building a relationship and correspondence.

To do this, the therapist will inquire about the background and general life of the client. Should the client have anxiety or suffer from depression, the therapist will inquire about how it affects their profession, social life, and family. Further steps will be taken to gather knowledge from events that may be associated with the problems of the client, the treatments they have undergone, and the goals the client would like to achieve in the process.

Should CBT seem appropriate after the initial evaluations, the therapist will alert the client regarding what can be expected from the treatment process, and what the experience would be like. Should the client find it inappropriate, or is uncomfortable with it, he or she will be encouraged to recommend other forms of treatment. Once the first evaluation period elapses, the client will begin collaborating with the therapist to simplify problems into their constituent parts.

In order to do this, the therapist could encourage the client to try journaling or keep a diary of their thoughts and behavioral patterns. The client will work alongside the therapist in analyzing the former's behaviors, emotions and thoughts to determine how realistic or helpful they are, and the general influence they have on the client. At this point, the therapist will begin devising ways of helping the client modify unhealthy behaviors and thoughts.

After a period of working on the parts that can be altered, the therapist will encourage the client to begin implementing the changes in their day-to-day life. This process would typically include:

- Identifying negative thought patterns, questioning them and substituting them with positive thoughts.

- Identifying when they are going to engage in an activity that would generate negative emotions rather than indulging in more productive endeavors.

- Clients may be given some homework from time to time to help enforce what is learned.

- At every session, the client and therapist will talk about how the former has begun putting into practice the changes learned, as well as the feelings that come with enforcing the changes. At this point, the therapist may offer guidance or some suggestions to aid the client.

- Facing anxieties and fears can be quite daunting for the client, so the therapist will not compel him or her into engaging in activities they don't want to do. The therapist will also proceed at a pace the client finds appropriate and will check from time to time to ensure the client is comfortable with how things are progressing.

Chapter 9 The CBT Experience

For a client, the first session in CBT can work up a lot of emotions which can be quite overwhelming. For this reason, this section has been put together on what to expect of your first CBT experience.

1. Expect your nerves to fly:

Whether or not you are already experiencing anxiety, expect to feel on edge and increasingly panicky the majority of the time. These feelings are usually a result of not knowing what to expect from your first experience. Keep in mind that these feelings are normal and do not raise any cause for alarm. So, keep calm; you aren't having an anxiety attack and your anxiety hasn't worsened.

2. Expect some degree of emotional exhaustion:

Both within your sessions and the days following them, you may tend to feel more tired, exhausted, and increasingly sensitive. These feelings are a normal effect of the process. As a matter of fact, CBT sessions considered more challenging and emotional tend to yield the best outcomes in the long term.

3. Expect to explore the present and future instead of the past:

It is a common process in some forms of therapy to spend time exploring the childhood of the client, their past experiences and relationships with family members. However, in cognitive behavioral therapy, the case is different. The sessions usually revolve around retraining the present thought pattern of the client and identifying new and better ways to help them manage their thoughts and feelings to progress. This experience can be especially relieving to clients who don't want to bring up their pasts or are tired of therapists digging up context clues from yesteryears. Although this approach is necessary, CBT doesn't implement it.

4. Expect a rollercoaster ride:

As it is in any other form of therapy, clients have to learn to expect ups and downs in the process. Cognitive-behavioral therapy is not without

331

this characteristic. In some sessions, the client is bound to feel like they are making major progress, while other sessions might leave them feeling not much progress was made. However, regardless of the feeling that accompanied each session of the treatment process, learning took place. And although it may not seem that way to the client, every one session of the whole process is important and cannot be done without.

5. Expect the process to be time-consuming:

Clients should not be naive in thinking that a couple of sessions will completely solve their problems and make them good as new. CBT doesn't work that way and requires a relatively long period and lots of practice for any significant progress to be made towards solving the client's problem. In a certain sense, the time seems befitting, because for a long period, the client has used one specific thought pattern, and any change in thinking habits will take time to be completely enforced.

What To Expect for Treatment?

The first part of the treatment process is entirely devoted to assessment and evaluation. It provides a platform for the client to communicate with the therapist about any challenges they are faced with, or how they would prefer to use the therapy to achieve. To get a grasp of the client's condition or goals, the therapist will make some inquiries pertaining to several key areas of the client's life. According to the results from the assessment process, the therapist will evaluate their skills and decide whether or not they are the right fit for the client's case. On the off chance that the client's case doesn't fit the therapist's skills, the latter would make a referral to another therapist better suited to handle the client. Sometimes, by the time the assessment or evaluation session is completed, the therapist and client should have come up with a suitable plan of treatment which outlines the type of interventions that will be implemented in the process. On other occasions, there might be added assessment sessions for the creation of a better course of treatment. Once the client has successfully agreed on a recommended plan of treatment, he or she will have a better knowledge of whether or not CBT is the best form of therapy for their condition.

Therapists in cognitive behavioral therapy make their assessments on the basis of the present state of the client, although they may tend to inquire

332

about the past sometimes. Therapists will usually seek answers from clients to the questions such as these:

What are the major factors that trigger the problem?

Does the problem interfere with your life? If yes, how?

For how long have you been experiencing these problems?

What is your driving force to seek change, and how motivated are you about the process?

In what way could your previous experiences, peers, or family have an influence on your present condition?

Once the evaluation/assessment session has been concluded, the next sessions that would ensue would be aimed at tackling the client's problem. These sessions usually involve more collaboration between client and therapist. The reason is that CBT involves more activities than other types of therapy and the majority of that time is used in the learning and implementation of coping skills.

Each session following the assessment session would be put to use in solving the client's issues, unlike in standard therapy where the majority of the time is used to talk about the problems of the client. All the sessions in the process typically follow a similar fashion to make sure that time is used judiciously. Every session starts off with a brief period dedicated to checking in, accompanied by a period used in reviewing the last session and going over any assigned homework. After this period, the client and therapist go-ahead to create an agenda for that session, and the remaining time is used in trying to achieve the agenda.

Studies about cognitive-behavioral therapy reveal that the treatment becomes increasingly effective, and improvement tends to be faster in clients when homework is integrated into the treatment process. For each session, there might be assigned homework to help the client enforce the skills necessary for the client to overcome their condition. In the early periods of the treatment process, homework would often involve keeping tabs on mood swings or recording specific behavioral patterns over a given timeframe, say, a week. Over time, homework could grow to include recognizing and correcting negative thought patterns, or putting into practice a behavior picked up in therapy sessions, like learning to be assertive with friends and family.

This next phase of treatment after the assessment period is the education stage. This stage is what follows in the ensuing sessions after the first one. At this stage, clients are enlightened on the psychodynamics of their problems. That is, how their present and past may be affecting or influencing their present condition. Clients may get to know how the brain is involved in the enforcement of thoughts and behavioral patterns even in cases where neither one seems productive. Clients would also be brought into the light about the cognitive behavioral therapy model, which they, in collaboration with the therapist, devised for the treatment process.

The latter stages of the treatment process involve the experimentation or implementation of knowledge learned. The treatment process will take a turn towards the cognitive component aimed at helping the client decide better-thinking patterns. Afterward, work will commence on the behavioral component involving performing activities to test the assumptions of the client, as well as the ability to recognize and learn better behaviors in the present and future.

As the treatment draws to its final stages and all the client's goals have been achieved, the time is right to begin turning down the frequency of each therapy session left. In other traditional forms of therapy, clients would be required to be in the system continuously for years unending. However, in cognitive behavioral therapy, clients are taught to be therapists to themselves.

In this vein, when the treatment process stretches towards the final parts, the sessions are scheduled in a less frequent manner so that clients can depend on themselves more in implementing the skills they have been taught. Doing this makes sure the client has faith in his or her capability to deal with any issue that arises after the treatment process rather than relying on the therapist.

The concluding part of the treatment process will be spent in practicing and maintaining the knowledge learned. Just as thinking and behavioral patterns have been ingrained in clients over the years, it requires lots of time and practice to reshape their actions and thoughts. The reason is that the mind will typically yearn to return to its comfort zone where the behavior and thoughts are unchanged, and only persistent practicing can be used to condition it into acting and thinking in a new way.

When clients finally feel comfortable enforcing their knowledge and coping skills, the treatment is now complete and the sessions terminated. However, it is helpful that clients book sessions from time to time for a professional viewpoint of their progress.

How to Devise an Initial Treatment Plan?

A treatment plan refers to a detailed outline created based on the assessment of a patient. It is a great tool used for involving patients in the treatment process. Treatment plans basically adopt a simple design and will usually contain the following information:

- Personal information about the patient, as well as their demographics and psychological history

- The diagnosis of their present issues

- High-priority goals for the treatment

- Treatment plan

- Timeframe for the treatment process

- Measurable objectives

- Space for recording progress

The first step of creating an initial treatment plan is to set goals for the treatment process. To do this, the therapist will have to assess the client and collect some information. Also, possible goals have to be identified and discussed with the client. Once the assessment and goal-setting processes are over, the therapist proceeds to devise a treatment plan which will be co-signed by the client. Creating treatment plans is a never-ending process, which requires regular reviewing and revising. As such, nothing is considered permanent or unchangeable. A template will be helpful in organizing the treatment plan, however, the information it holds is peculiar to a client and can be modified.

1. The Treatment Plan Template:

The treatment plan has to be specific, albeit, simple. And although variations may exist, the treatment plan template comprises the following information:

- **Patient information**: This field is located at the top part of the template and is filled by the therapist. It contains information about the client like name, date of the plan, insurance, and social security number.

- **Diagnostic summary**: This field is filled with a summary by the therapist about the diagnosis of the client, as well as the timelines of the diagnosis.

- **Problems & goals**: This section involves the goals and issues of the client, as well as some measurable objectives. Every issue area will contain a timeframe for completing the goals and objectives. Therapists ought to attempt to reach a minimum of three goals.

- **Signatures**: This is the final field, and is where both client and therapist sign their respective names. It indicates that the client is in agreement with the plan, and partook in its development.

2. The Treatment Plan Checklist:

To ensure that no important information is left out, this checklist can be used to remember every important detail:

- **Problems**: Are the problems reflective of any of the six problem domains, namely legal status, psychiatric status, medical status, social status, substance abuse, and employment? Are the problems detailed in behavioral terminologies and an unbiased way?

- **Goals**: Do the required goals appeal to the outlined problems? Can they be attained in the course of treatment? Does the client understand the outlined goals? Is the client ready to change and achieve their goals?

- **Objectives**: Are the objectives and goals complemental? Are they specific and measurable? Is the client capable of completing the objectives? Does the objective have a timeline? Are they plausible for the client's problem?

- **General**: Does the treatment plan appeal to the peculiarities of the client like goals, socioeconomic status, skills, culture, educational background, and lifestyle? Are their strengths included in the plans? Did the patient partake in the development of the plan? Is the plan agreed upon, dated and signed by everyone involved?

Identifying Automatic Thoughts

Thoughts are part of us. They are things that we come across every single day. Our thoughts are part of the reason we do all that we do, knowingly or unknowingly.

Automatic thoughts are not like any of the other thoughts that come into our minds because they have a way of making us realize the consequences of what we did in the past. They are the type of thoughts that are related to most of our powerful emotions. This is one of the reasons why they are not like every other thought that pops into your head. Automatic thoughts are sometimes referred to as hot thoughts. And sometimes these thoughts may come as a result of cognitive-behavioral therapy.

These thoughts can occur from time to time, and sometimes these thoughts can occur when you least expect, which means that you cannot plan when these thoughts come to mind. They may come in the morning or at night. Sometimes they may come when you are having a good time with friends and family, which means that you do not need to be involved in a particular activity or group of activities for your automatic thoughts to take control of you.

Identifying automatic thoughts is not one of the easiest things to do, especially at the earliest stages, but there are some tips that should help you identify certain automatic thoughts, and they include:

1. Travel back in time:

You do not necessarily need a time machine for this particular tip. All you need is your mind. You need to learn to go back in time and try to imagine the particular time you felt a certain way for you to understand what happened and why your mood changed. When you do this, make sure that you are not leaving any details out because the little details you could be leaving out can be the difference between identifying your thoughts and becoming confused.

For instance, you took a cookie that you were not supposed to, and when you get to your room or a different place, then you start feeling bad for what you did. All you have to do at that point is to sit down quietly and try to go down Memory Lane and try to find out the exact time you started feeling the way you are feeling. This is why identifying automatic thoughts can be difficult because when you start feeling some things as a result of your thoughts; sometimes you don't even know that you have started feeling it until you feel extremely uneasy. After doing all your best to go down Memory Lane and you find that moment in time when you started feeling like that, you need to ask yourself what exactly made you feel that way. Was it guilt, anger, or anxiety? When you can successfully put down all these possibilities on the table and work them out, there is a huge chance that you would be able to understand what you are going through, and you would be able to get over it.

Going back in time and trying to understand what happened is not very easy for a lot of people, In fact, some people cannot even do it at all, maybe because of the kind of experience or because of some reasons best known to them. The bottom line is these people find it hard to identify their emotions with this tip. If you are in that category and you don't like remembering because you do not like seeing yourself in that situation over and over again, you could use the power of your mind to your own advantage. How? All you have to do is to imagine someone else in the scenario and not you. When you can put another person in your place, it would be easier to put this tip to good use.

You must know that it still might not work for you the very first time you try it, but if you want to get good results, you must keep on doing it over and over again.

Going back in time can be difficult, but if you cannot imagine someone in your place as well, you could get help. Help from a friend or family member. You should never shy away from the help that may come from a friend or family member because that help might be what you need to be able to identify your thoughts. All you may need is just someone to hold your hand through all of this.

It may even be your spouse. When you do not have a proper support team to hold you through these trying times, there is no way that you are going to get what you want, which is to understand and identify your automatic thoughts completely. For those that feel like they cannot get the kind of help they need from their friends or family members, you can try to get help from a professional therapist or at least someone that has a lot of references that you trust. When you have someone like this, all you have to do is visit the person regularly, especially when you want to travel down memory lane. The only downside about getting a therapist is that they can be very expensive, especially over a longer period.

2. Let your feeling be the bait:

You need to use your feelings to get the exact thought that may find its way into your mind. It does not matter what the feeling is or what the thought might be. It is important that you do not rush this aspect for any reason at all so that you would be able to understand what happens to you when you have a particular feeling. When you want to start this exercise, sit down in a quiet place and pick a particular emotion. For instance, let's say that the emotion is "sadness," start asking yourself certain questions like "what does this emotion tell about me?" or "why is it that I have this kind of thought when I'm sad?" When you can do this for as long as you possibly can, you will notice that a lot of things would start becoming clear and very easy to understand.

When you can notice the emotions that trigger your automatic thoughts, you would be able to identify the thoughts even before they come. It sounds impossible, but it is far from impossible. This tip is supposed to help you be one with your automatic thoughts to the extent that you do not need to sit down for a long time thinking about what it is that is making you feel the way you are feeling. It will give you the power to identify your automatic thoughts with little or no stress at all. You should know that you do not get all this by sitting around. You get it when you practice and you work for it.

When you ask yourself all the questions that you want, you must stay true to yourself at all times because the main reason why a lot of people say that this technique does not work for them is that they do not tell themselves the truth. They sit all day asking themselves the questions but giving themselves lies for answers. You are the one with the thoughts, so even when you lie to yourself, you know it will make the technique futile. The bottom line to all of this is that if you know that you are not going to be completely true to yourself, just let it go because it's not going to work at all.

3. Keep track of stressful feelings:

This is a tip that a lot of people should know because it is one of the easiest ways to identify your automatic thoughts. There are a lot of ways to keep track of your feelings, but the easiest and most effective way is to write it down when it happens. When you feel something that reminds you of a particular automatic thought, all you have to do is to write it down in something that you are comfortable with. It is not compulsory that you must put pen to paper to keep track of your feelings. You could put it down on your smartphone or your tablet. You must put your notes down somewhere private. Something that you alone have access to because you do not want all your issues and feelings to be read by another person or by a group of people. This exercise aims to keep track of all your feelings. The feelings that trigger certain emotions and the same feelings that bring about certain thoughts.

When you do this regularly, you would be able to go back to your journal from time to time to check on what you have been feeling, and sometimes you can use your journal as a reference point for any of your other automatic thoughts. When you do this, it would be easy to identify all your thoughts without a lot of thinking. This method may be easy, but it is also difficult at the same time. How? If you do not do this over and over again, you would not be able to get the best out of it. It is one thing to write down what you feel, and it is another to keep on writing without stopping. The reason why some people would say that this method is bad for them is that they do not continue the process over a long period. They stop even before the process starts to work its magic. When you want to start something as important as this, you need time, and when you think that time is enough, then you need more time.

Identifying Intrusive Thoughts

Intrusive thoughts are those kinds of thoughts that come into your consciousness most times without warning or anything prompting them. These thoughts are usually things that you would consider as weird, disturbing, and sometimes very alarming. A lot of people experience this kind of thought and let it go, but some people let this kind of thought get stuck in their heads and find it hard to get it out, maybe because they are scared or probably because they do not want to face it. These thoughts can be part of a person for as long as the person allows.

Where do intrusive thoughts even come from in the first place? This is a question that a lot of people have asked but was never fully answered. This is because intrusive thoughts are somewhat difficult to understand. A lot of people do not know why they would sit down quietly, and certain thoughts would pop in and out of their heads for no reason. Believe it or not, some people experience this so much to the extent that they now find it normal. They put it in mind that these kinds of thoughts are part of them, and as such, they do absolutely nothing about them. Although intrusive thoughts have no vivid origin, some scientists believe that they come as a result of the difficulties that may appear in your personal life. When you have certain worries in your life, whether it is your work or relationships, they tend to secretly take a huge toll on you even without you knowing. You may think that they are not taking much of a toll on you because you are feeling nothing at the point, but they are, and your intrusive thought is a piece of good evidence that it truly affects you.

For instance, if you and your spouse are having some issues, even if it does not pertain to infidelity, there is a huge possibility that your intrusive thoughts would come with infidelity as the first reason why you guys are having problems. These thoughts would come and go from time to time, and sometimes they could make you feel really bad and make you want to end the relationship even when you do not have any proof that something like that is going on. This is how strong your intrusive thoughts can be. These thoughts may be alarming, disturbing and sometimes downright painful, but you cannot get them out of your head because you have been unable to straighten the things that have gone crooked in your life.

You must know that the more things go wrong in your life, the worse your intrusive thoughts will become. If you have problems in your home or office, you need to straighten them out as soon as you can because they will not just go away. They are one of the main reasons you have intrusive thoughts, and they are eaten deeper than you think, so if you want to get rid of intrusive thoughts, you need to get rid of your problem first.

This is one of the main reasons why identifying your intrusive thoughts can be very difficult at times. When you struggle to find what is causing them and you have no idea what it is, how can you get rid of it? You need to find out what exactly is wrong with you before you can think of tackling the problem.

Chapter 10   Problems Associated With CBT

Cognitive-behavioral therapy has been known to help a lot of people around the world with their different problems, but cognitive behavioral therapy has also been known to have its issues.

1. You need to commit a 100%

One of the main reasons why cognitive behavioral therapy does not work for a lot of people is because they don't commit at all in any way, and this is one big problem that comes with CBT. You need to put in all that you can before you can get CBT to work for you. The CBT process is known to be very long and sometimes very unpredictable, but if you do not prepare your mind and body to undergo that kind of stress, there is no way that you are going to get anything done at all. Commit to the process 100% without looking back or without going back when you feel like it.

Sometimes you may think that the whole process is not working and that the process is not even for a person like you, but it is far from the truth because the process would only work for those that want the process to work for them. Some people would go out of their way to get theirs done by excellent therapists, but you must know that no matter how much you spend on therapy, it would not work if you fail to put in all your efforts and commitment to it. If you know that you are not going to be able to put in your all when it comes to cognitive behavioral therapy, you mustn't even try it in the first place because you would only be wasting your time.

2. A lot of money is involved

Because this process takes a long time to be completed, it usually takes a lot of money to get it done. When you decide to get into something like this, you need to be ready to spend a lot of money, especially when it comes to getting the therapist that would help you with the whole process. Therapists these days do not come cheap, especially if they have a lot of references and are respected by a lot of people.

You could choose to get a cheaper therapist to help you, but you must know that you are going to be paying that therapist over and over again until the procedure is complete. For instance, the average therapist gets

343

paid by the hour, and we are talking about months of therapy here. You are going to be spending so much money and, at the end of all that, might not get all you want. If you want to get more out of all of this without spending a lot of money, commit with all that you have, but if you can't, just let it go.

3. Everyone cannot use it

Although CBT can be very useful at times, it cannot be used by everyone. CBT is a procedure that helps people, but not if they have a complex mental case. It is easier to get rid of minor mental issues using CBT, but it is not easy to get rid of the major ones. You may want to use CBT to get rid of a mental problem, but if you know that the case is serious, CBT is probably not the way for you to go. You should probably get better help if you want to get rid of bigger mental issues.

This is why it is difficult to see a doctor or a therapist prescribing CBT to people with severe mental issues because it would do them more harm than good. It would only make them waste their time and make the procedure even more difficult. You may have heard stories of people with mental issues that go for help and come back home worse than they left. This is because these people were not given the right kind of treatment at the right time.

When you want to get something done, especially when it comes to a mental issue, it is important that you get it done the right way and with the right tools because if you don't, it would only harm the patient more, and you do not want that. Some people even go out of their way to make this procedure work for them or a friend maybe because they have been hearing about how the procedure works but these people fail to understand that if something was not meant to work for you, it would not work for you. It is as simple as that because you cannot take drugs for headaches when you have a stomach ache.

4. It takes up a lot of time

Time is something that a lot of people have and something a lot of people don't have enough of. If you are the kind of person that feels that you do not have a lot of time to do certain things, CBT is not the way for you to go at all. CBT requires time and effort to get it done and if you

344

cannot squeeze out some time to get it done there is no way that it would work for you and you must know that squeezing out a little time would not work as well because you need to make sure that you get the procedure done the right way.

This means that you have to put in a lot of your time in order to ensure that you complete the procedure which means that you would have to drop some certain things that you normally do in order to get it done properly which means that you may drop things like your yoga, morning workout and many more. The bottom line to all of this is that if you do not look for a way to make out time for the procedure, it is not going to work.

5. **It usually makes people feel bad before making them feel good**

By now, you should know that there is absolutely nothing easy about cognitive-behavioral therapy at all, but it tends to give good results. It is important to know that these results can only come as a result of great suffering to an extent. Before you feel good about CBT, there is a huge chance that you are going to feel bad at first for so long. CBT encourages people to face their fears and problems head-on, and this is something that a lot of people are running away from in the first place, and no one feels good the first time they are facing their fears. This is why they find it extremely hard to finish the procedure sometimes.

This is one of the reasons why some people do not even consider the procedure in the first place. It would only make you want to drop it. When you start this procedure, that is, if you do, you need to put it in mind that there is a high possibility that you might feel like dropping the whole procedure because, at that point, you wouldn't care anymore. Why? This is because this procedure is going to push you to the limit.

Yes, the limit. It is going to take you to places that you do not want to go to. It is going to stretch you, and when you think that it cannot stretch any further, it is going to surprise you and stretch you even further. You are going to feel terrible about all of this, but you should know that according to research, the pain would only be a bad memory when you start getting better.

There are stories of people that feel bad to the extent that they leave the therapy even when they are halfway into it. This is why it is important to know what you are getting into before you actually begin because if you do not, you might regret it for the rest of your life. There is a possibility that you could get through these without stress, but that can only be done with help from friends and family members.

6. It focuses only on the initial problem

Problems are things that almost everyone experiences and the CBT is a procedure that is used to solve certain kinds of problems, but there is something that the CBT does that is not so great. It focuses on the problems alone, but it does not focus on the things that cause those problems. For instance, if someone is suffering from anxiety, CBT may be able to help them get rid of it, but it would not get rid of the thing that caused the anxiety in the first place, which means that there is a possibility that it would come back.

When you attempt to tackle a problem without actually finding out the root of that problem, there is a huge possibility that you are not going to get rid of that problem completely. You can try to avoid the root of the problems over and over again, but you are only going to be killing yourself slowly. If you want to get rid of a problem completely, CBT is not the way to go because your problems would resurface immediately the effects of the procedure wear off. This is a problem you must look at.

You should keep in mind that these problems do not affect everyone that goes into CBT, so it should not be a reason not to go into it. If you know that you have the money, time, and commitment to go on with a procedure like that, you can go ahead and get it done, but you must get it done only with the prescription of a doctor or a therapist. All you really need is people or a group of people that can help you through all that you need and when you have that, you are more than halfway to your final destination. Therapy is also something that a lot of people try especially if they are not close to the ones that they trust or love because at least with a professional therapist you can rest assured that what you say there stays there and would not be heard by anyone else.

Chapter 11 Automatic (Negative) Thoughts

On average, a person has between 70,000 to 100,000 thoughts per day. And those are quite normal. Thoughts are our way of interpreting the world around us and assigning meanings to people's words and actions. Through the thought process, we analyze activities in our immediate vicinity and assign meaning to them, sometimes even without realizing it.

One key thing that you must bear in mind at this point, however, is the fact that thoughts are not facts. If anything, they are our assumptions of the world and our interpretation of them. Thoughts are automatic and often flow from the experiences we've had, our culture, socialization process, etc. Thus, your thoughts on a particular subject are often not objective.

Automatic thoughts can be words, sounds or memories that come up without any conscious effort by the individual. One of the key features of automatic thoughts is that they are believable. Generally, we do not always stop to question our thoughts because that would be akin to questioning our reality and thought process. Also, automatic thoughts are persistent. They pop up at the slightest and may begin to follow a pattern if consistently indulged.

Automatic thoughts are normal. They become harmful when they become negative, in that sense, they cause harm to the individual through inducing stress and stress-related diseases. Thus, primarily, automatic thoughts, whether negative or positive, occur as part of the natural thought process of a person. They also occur as a result of habit. This is where a person has consistently indulged in negative thinking that the brain and thought process becomes accustomed to that.

Humans are creatures of habit. This means that if a person does something often enough, it becomes part of them. That also can be said of the thinking patterns of a person. Once they indulge in negative thinking consistently over a long period, they get accustomed to it, and it then occurs more out of habit than as a result of any conscious efforts. If the action gets repeated often enough, stronger pathways are created in the brain and it gets easier for the person to do so, and becomes harder to resist the impulse not to.

Automatic negative thoughts are problematic for a couple of reasons. Chief amongst them is the way it impairs the functioning of the brain. It reduces the volume of serotonin in the brain. Serotonin is the enzyme responsible for feeling good. When it gets depleted, the individual finds it harder to derive pleasure from the simple acts around him. It also enlarges the amygdala, which is the fear center of the brain. This will make the person feel that harmful thoughts are keeping them safe. Automatic negative thoughts also increase the likelihood of the person getting a neurodegenerative illness. Thus, negative thinking will not only be affecting you in the moment, but it will also open you up to having other illnesses in the future.

There are different types of Automatic Negative Thinking (ANT). Some of the examples are fortune-telling. Here the person nurses the certain belief that something negative will happen in the future and that the person or their loved ones will suffer harm as a result of that negative action. They are almost always having a negative outlook towards any new idea brought to them.

As previously stated, this sort of reaction may not even be conscious. They may have so structured their psyche that their default response is always negative. Another such example is mind-reading. Someone who does this might claim to know what the other party is thinking about them and, in the vast up majority of those cases, such thoughts are negative ones.

Here, the person does not even bother to check the validity of what he is feeling at any point or how rational it is, all things considered. So of course, it just takes a little time for the person to no longer believe that the other party harbors negative thoughts about them, they also begin to see such thoughts as true.

Another automatic negative thought is blame. A lot of people immediately search for someone to blame when something bad happens. Even in situations that do not warrant any blame being placed on anyone, they would want to pitch the blame on someone else. Mostly, this acts as a coping mechanism and enables the individual to make sense of the particular event that occurred.

In some other cases, they do not channel the blame outwards but inwards. They would blame themselves for whatever negative event that occurred, thinking that somehow they caused it, or that they deserved it. As earlier mentioned, this is mostly a coping mechanism but it acts to prevent the eventual resolution of the problems.

Finally, there is labeling. This is a situation where the individual attaches negative values to themselves. The labels such as *fat, loser* or *stupid* are just reproductions of how the person feels about another person, or about themselves. The labeling can become so strong that they seem like self-fulfilling prophecies.

Of course, in all of the cases previously mentioned, what is being worried about might even eventually happen. However, worrying about it will hardly change the outcome. This is coupled with the fact that negative thoughts can have dire consequences for the individual - as already pointed out. Thus, in every sense, negative thoughts should not be encouraged.

How to Challenge Automatic (Negative) Thoughts

Generally, when you notice a negative thought creeping up on you, the first thing is to examine if it is true. Thus, you first need to ask yourself whether that thought is true or whether it is a false reality being pitched to you by your brain. After that, you then examine if the thought serves you any purpose at all. Then you consider if there is another way of looking at what is being thought about. Essentially, you will be considering whether your perspective is correct. It may be that your thoughts are being clouded by certain things which you are not even aware of. Finally, you need to honestly ask yourself what you would tell someone else in a similar situation as you. If someone were to walk up to you with the same thoughts, how would you guide the person to abandon such thoughts? What would you say? We often have better perspectives speaking to others than speaking to ourselves so this process should be able to help you put things in a better perspective.

Apart from the above, here are some of the steps you can take:

1. **Maintain a mood diary:**

A mood diary is like a journal. It is a book (it could be an actual hardcopy book, or if you prefer, it could be a soft copy) where you record your moods at each point. The idea is to help you keep track of your emotions and also for you to notice when your mood has changed.

A mood diary also further helps you realize what thought is influencing your behavior. If you are acting a certain way and you are not sure of the reason for that, a mood diary can help you check for the root of the feeling, and also further help you take care of such. The diary helps you detect patterns. What a lot of people do not acknowledge is that their negative thoughts arise from a pattern. However, if you write them down, you will be able to track them and if there are changes that need to be made, you will be better equipped to make them and improve your life generally.

You must understand that it may not be easy writing down your thoughts using this process. It may seem like you are naked - and in a way, you will be. It does take some getting used to. You will get used to it with practice. However, if you consistently stick to it, you will begin to see the benefits in no time.

2. Challenge hot thoughts:

Hot thoughts are the thoughts that elicit the strongest reaction from you. They hold emotional significance for you and that might be because you have held on to them for a long time. In this sort of scenario, you would have ceased trying to rationalize them because of how long you've held on to the belief. However, when you take the time to challenge the thoughts you will discover that there is a balanced way to look at the thoughts that would bring about better results for you.

The process of challenging thoughts is simple. Simply, you need to find out if you are looking at the thought cohesively, whether there is some evidence which negates what the thought is presenting to you. Then you need to consider if there are better ways of looking at the thought; here you will just be considering whether you could think more realistically and whether this could lead to a different outcome for you. Finally, you need to consider what a trusted friend or loved one will say in that situation and concerning that thought.

350

We are sometimes blinded by sentiments but our friends and those closest to us are usually able to point out inconsistencies in our thought process and harmful thought patterns. You should consider asking your friends. They can provide better insight; more than you even realize you need at that moment.

3. Recognize your inner critic:

If you are used to talking down to yourself through your thoughts, you have to identify the sources of those thoughts and delete them. It might not be easy owning the fact that you are actually harming yourself through your thoughts. One technique that has proved to be helpful is this: imagining the inner critic to be a different person.

So, in this scenario, you may just imagine that you have an evil twin or that the devil is whispering into your ears. You will find it a lot easier shutting out the thoughts if you think they are external and not internal. This is because it is (sometimes) way easier to counter negative statements about us if the statements are coming from a third party. It does almost look like we believe our own thoughts more, even when they are inherently not helpful to us.

4. Change your automatic negative thoughts into positive empowering thoughts:

You can decide to simply transform the negative thoughts into something entirely different, something a lot more empowering for you. You could make use of the process already discussed: that is the process of writing down the thoughts, confronting them and changing the outcome.

Also, there are other actions you could take. For instance, you need to learn to reframe some of the statements you make in your head about yourself. One of such is the should/shouldn't statement pattern. Instead of saying you should/shouldn't do something, you could turn it into something that isn't totally guilt driven. Of course, the truth of the statement may not even be affected by what you said but the outcome will definitely improve.

How to Lower Distress

Every adult has dealt with distressing situations in one form or the other. Distress may not necessarily include having experienced something as deeply painful as the death of a loved one. It may, however, include everyday situations such as being late for work, being stuck in traffic, or even divorce. It does not matter how trivial the case is. If it has the ability to upset your emotional balance, then it is distressing.

For people who already suffer mental illnesses such as anxiety, depression, and manic disorders, distressful situations may result in heavier consequences for them than it would for the average person. It might be slightly more complicated if the individual lacks the ability and the resources to effectively tackle that situation.

A combination of these factors has led to cases where people who are distressed hurt themselves. In certain situations, the individual can develop harmful habits such as compulsive eating or drug and alcohol abuse. Such behaviors are intended to act as a coping mechanism, but they ultimately prove to be more bad than good.

As earlier stated, distress is often a natural and universal phenomenon. The idea here is to provide you with the coping skills you will need whenever distress arises. So here are a few skills that may prove helpful in the combatting of distress.

1. Identify the need driving you

Every stressful situation is being driven by a need that is unmet. When you look closely, even though it may appear that you are freaking out for nothing or that there is no tangible cause for the feeling of helplessness that you have, the truth is that you feel that way because there is a need that is currently unmet with you. It could be an emotional need, such as the need for companionship, love, and attention. It could even be a physical/tangible need such as the lack of funds for a particular need or anything else along those lines.

The problem with this is that a lot of people do not even recognize that they have needs. They are often so focused on the immediate problem and the distress they are facing to even realize that there is a driving force to the emotion. It may also be difficult naming your needs because that would suggest that you are inadequate in some way. This is the path to recovery, however. It is at the point when you acknowledge it and the need that drives the distress that you would be able to move beyond the distress to actually solve the problem.

2. Attempt to solve the need

"Attempt" is used here because it is possible that no matter how hard you try, it may be impossible for you to solve all of your needs. Once you have discovered what it is that you need, the next step will be for you to look for ways to solve them. The responsibility may not lie squarely in you to do so, thus you may need to enlist the help of others in solving problems and having your needs met.

A lot of people do not understand or realize what they need, and they further do not often know how to communicate those needs to the people around them. But you see, when you do not let the people around you know what you need, there will be no way for them to give you the help that you require. So, first, identify the need(s), secondly, look for ways to solve them, because by so doing you will be taking care of the distress at the same time, then finally, enlist the help of friends and family in getting the needs met.

Also, in addition, while you are working on having your needs met, you should practice focusing on what you want instead of what you do not want. We often attract what we envision in our subconscious. So, instead of saying that you do not want a heartbreak, you could instead say that you need a wholesome, loving relationship.

3. Create the emotions you want

If you do not like how you are feeling at any point, you have the power to change that. You can simply do that by changing the environment around you to encourage the mood you want. If you are feeling sad you can listen to music, or watch a cartoon or hang out with friends. You alone have the power to alter the mood you are in at every turn.

How to Solve Problems Constructively

One running theme you must have observed up to this point is the fact that there are things that cannot be escaped. For example, problems will arise whether you want them to or not, and whether you are prepared to handle them or not. The thing is, for a lot of people, the problem is not with the fact that they encounter problems, the issue is usually the fact that they often lack the ability to tackle the problems in a constructive manner. This is very important because the way a problem is handled is often important in determining the rate at which the problem eventually gets solved. Here are a few tips on how to solve problems constructively.

1. Solve problems in advance

There are a lot of problems that would not arise in the first place if people take the time and initiative to watch out for them. You will save yourself a lot of trouble if you identify potential risk factors and attempt to put in place measures to solve the problems before they arise. For instance, if you live in an area that is easily flooded, or a place susceptible to volcanic eruptions, you will be doing yourself a huge favor if you can put in place measures to handle the problems if they ever arose.

Similarly, emergency situations are some of the sources of problems. Solving problems in advance would be that you will have a first aid kit handy in your home and you will know how to make use of the same. From your personal life to your normal day-to-day dealings, there are certain measures you can put in place to forestall the occurrence of specific problematic events.

2. Simplify the problem

Here, you will have to break down the problems into bits so you can view each process clearly and be able to solve it cohesively. So, ask yourself, what is the simplest way of solving this problem? Am I making use of it? Is there an alternative solution that I am not aware of? Does this problem have to be solved immediately? All of these will help you in figuring out how whether the route you are taking is the best for solving that problem.

3. Defer

Delaying/deferring is a legitimate skill that you can employ in solving problems. Deferring a problem might give you more time to handle other problems that are pressing at that moment, and it could also help you make sure that you devote the necessary time to the problem. The truth is, deferring a problem might actually be the best thing to do in any situation because when you eventually get back to the problem, you would be better equipped to handle it.

However, before you defer/delay a problem, you have to make sure that it is not something high on your list of priorities. The more urgent a problem is, the less need there will be to defer it.

4. Be innovative

In the 21st century especially, more attention is being paid to not just the solutions brought to a problem, but how innovative those solutions are. To tackle problems effectively you will need to learn how to experiment with more than one approach. Always be on the look-out for better ways of solving problems.

The nature of the situation may require that you make adaptations as they come. Thus, for instance, the problem might require you pulling an all-nighter several times within a given month, and then getting back to your regime eventually. The thing is, be ready to do what it takes to achieve the results that you seek.

Chapter 12   Fight Negative Thinking

How to Evaluate Thoughts Objectively

Thinking, in the broad sense of the word, refers to anything which goes on in the mind. In this sense, it is unconscious. There is always something one is thinking about every minute. However, when defined narrowly, thinking refers to the mental activity consciously employed to solve problems, defend a stance, etc. In this sense, thinking differs from feeling because it does not involve the emotional response to what is being considered.

When thinking, it may happen that we become biased, sometimes even without knowing so and against our best intentions. However, we will fail in the thinking process, because thinking, actually, is a skill, if we do not actively learn how to view things objectively, even in our thoughts.

Objectivity focuses on the search for the truth. It goes beyond personal biases and prejudices to discover what actually is the logical position with any issue/topic. Objectivity is the only way you can be absolutely sure you are in touch with the fact that you are viewing things thoroughly. Objectivity is a skill that you have to actively learn, especially considering the fact that there may be no defined standards to determine the outcome of any thought before an action takes place. Whatever the results of your thinking are, it is largely influenced by the thinking process through which you arrived at that conclusion.

Objectivity, in itself, can be quite hard to attain. This is because our thoughts (and actions) are often informed by biases. Some of them so hidden that we do not even realize that they exist. Biases are human constructs and thus it might be quite impossible to escape them. The intention here, however, is to help you understand the thinking process so that you may, at least, have the ability to recognize your biases and try to make sure that they do not influence your thinking, and by extension, your actions.

1.   Recognize that your biases exist

The easiest way to make sure that your thoughts are not subjective is by first admitting that you have biases in the first place. It is impossible to have found a topic where you do not have a position already. If you are to think about a particular topic and then make a decision, recognizing your biases is all the more important.

If you find yourself leaning towards a particular position ask yourself why that is so. Perhaps you already had that in mind from the start. Also, carefully consider every option available to you. For instance, if someone at work says something to you which you consider offensive while thinking about it, you should take a step back and consider your relationship with the person. Is the person a friend or just an acquaintance? Is the person a subordinate or a superior? Have you had personal issues with the person before that time? If the statement had come from someone else would you have been so offended? You could also attempt to reverse the line of thinking and check to see if you will arrive at the same conclusions.

The beautiful thing about exposing your biases is that in the end, whenever you eventually make a decision, you will not be wondering whether your actions were prejudiced or not because you would have handled the biases from the start.

2. Consider the view of others

The social value of objective thinking is based on the fact that it considers the view of others before arriving at a conclusion. It can hardly be objective thinking if the view of others is not taken into consideration before arriving at your conclusion.

To aid the objective process, ask people what their view on the topic is about. Let them honestly tell you what their views are. This will help you realize if yours comes from a place of prejudice or not. You see, objectivity means that you have to look at things from the lens of others. By its very definition, it recognizes that it is possible for a person to be wrong in their thinking, even when they are being honest with the process. Objectivity means taking a step back from the entire process to give you a better view.

For instance, in the example given above, you could simply find out from others if they found what was said rude or offensive. You could ask a colleague who was present at that time, or you could ask a third party, relaying the event to them. This latter option may produce better results because a person present at that time may be influenced by our own prejudices too.

3. Make a decision

It doesn't matter how long you ponder over any issue, eventually, you will need to come to a conclusion and make a decision. It may be harder, especially if the decision goes against what you started out with. (When you follow the points here you will come to find out that in some cases you may have to go against your preconceived notions in order to arrive at an objective answer, and that may not be pleasant at all). Eventually, when it comes down to it, make a decision and then stick to it.

- **Replace Negative Thoughts with Positive Thoughts**

  It has been said that having negative thoughts occurs randomly to people without them being consciously aware of them. This is often said in the light of negative thoughts being normal. The question then becomes, at what point do negative thoughts become harmful? This is because negative thoughts left unattended can spiral out of control and have unintended consequences not just for you but for your family, career, and several other facets of your life. In a bid to combat negative thought patterns, there are steps you can take. One of such is replacing the negative thoughts with positive ones.

  Before the steps will be listed, you have to know that trying to replace the bad thoughts with quick fixes will not work. If your brain has formulated a pattern of negative thinking, it will take studious practice for you to untangle the mass and learn to allow positive thoughts in again. Drowning the negative thoughts in alcohol, or abusing drugs will not work either. If anything, they will only act as a temporary reprieve and you will go right back to the state you were in before.

  You will need to start by recognizing and releasing negative thoughts from your mind. This crucial step is the most important and this is because it is only when you have identified the problem that you can attempt fostering a solution. After this, you

358

will need to start the replacement process. The replacement process will involve recognizing the positive aspects of the problem you are thinking about. For instance, you may have been fired from your job. It is expected that in this sort of scenario that you develop some sort of negative thinking pattern. However, you can choose to recognize that there could be some benefits from having some free time for yourself. Even though the circumstances that produced the free time may not have been pleasant, you have the power to turn what potentially could have been an unpleasant situation into a teachable experience.

Make no mistakes, it will not be a pleasant ride. In fact, chances are that because your brain might have become so used to the negative thought pattern, you may find yourself revolting against this new practice. It is for this reason that it is necessary for you to practice this process daily. In the beginning, you will have to consciously impose this new practice whenever you feel like indulging in negative thinking. To make the process better, you should say the positive confessions aloud. As you think of them, say them out loud. This will make it that not only will your mind be aware of this new routine, your auditory senses would have taken part in it also. It will be a hard journey, no doubt, but it is one you can take if you put your mind to it.

- **Replace Negative Thoughts with Coping Statements**

   One other very popular means of combating negative thoughts is through the use of coping statements. You may have noticed it before, maybe with athletes on TV or in the movies too. Coping statements are the statements you say to yourself, or are said by someone to you, whenever you feel anxious, or whenever any other such negative thoughts spring up.

   Coping statements are always positive and work to remind you of the things your brain may not be conscious of at that moment. You see, there may happen to be some sort of disconnect between the realities in your mind and what you are momentarily experiencing.

For instance, you may be failing horribly at a task but of course, that does not mean you are a failure. However, your brain might not recognize this reality at that moment. It will then be up to you to create that consciousness for yourself, and that is often done with the aid of coping statements.

Ideally, coping statements are supposed to cut off the negative thoughts and then replace them with the positive statements being made. When these statements are repeated over and over again at that moment, the brain gets used to it and automatically takes over. In the same vein, when the cycle is repeated over time, the brain gets accustomed to automatically switching to positive thoughts whenever anxiety arises.

From what has been discussed, you can see that coping statements have to be made first from the conscious part of the mind. This means that you will have to decide on the coping statements ideal for you even before the negative thoughts arise. Some of the examples of coping statements include: "I can do this." "I am better than this." "This anxiety will eventually pass." Apart from these examples, which are hardly exhaustive, you can choose the coping statements that will work for you.

You have to specifically consider the problems that you usually encounter, i.e. the negative thoughts that you usually experience, then you have to craft coping statements along those lines. You have to be deliberate and consistent with your use of coping statements. With regular practice, eventually, your brain will learn how to always swing into the positive mode at all times.

- **Replace Negative Thinking with Realistic Statements**

There is something to be said about positive affirmations and how they can act to brighten your day. However, some folks do not believe that positive affirmations work. In the first place, you cannot hope to repeat such positive affirmations every time an unwholesome thought pops up. In fact, you may not even have the ability to do that all the time.

360

Furthermore, these folks also argue that the effects of those pep-talk styled affirmations are momentary. They do not last beyond that immediate moment. It is also possible for someone to be saying one thing and for their minds to be telling them something entirely different. For instance, a person can repeat, "I am wealthy," as many times as possible yet he does not believe it.

You see, there is nothing wrong with having a deluge of negative emotions, and of course it goes without saying that if you constantly indulge those thoughts you will be harming yourself, however, like already pointed out, you may not be helping yourself by whitewashing them either. Research has even found that for people with low self-esteem, positive affirmations may not only be useless but may even be harmful to them.

In any case, if you belong to this category of persons, then replacing negative thoughts with coping statements or positive thoughts will hardly work, you may need to replace the negative thoughts with realistic statements.

In making realistic statements, the first step in the process is recognizing the thoughts weighing you down. At this point, your aim will not be to seek appeasement or for a release or anything of that sort. At this stage, you will merely be recognizing the root of the thoughts.

After this, the next step is to have a conversation with yourself. Here it is advised to follow the normal procedure you would follow if you were going to have a conversation with another person. You will not be issuing commands but merely be seeking to understand the thoughts further after you have listed them. The difference here is that during positive affirmations, people just issue commands of what they expect without querying to see if there is a legitimate cause for the feeling, here you will also be realistic with yourself in the sense of understanding what it will take to get from where you are to where you want to be. So, for instance, you are angry, can you put in the work to move from being angry to being happy? Or maybe you are sad, now that you have identified the root of the sadness, can you do what it takes to be happy? If it was a low grade that caused you the sadness, are you willing to work hard to make sure that the outcome is changed? A realist outlook on life does not just point out the problem, it further helps you do what it takes to make sure that the results you need are achieved.

Finally, in making realistic statements, the focus should be on progress and not perfection. No doubt, you may not get to where you want to be as fast as you want to but that is okay. A realistic outlook on life makes you realize that the whole process is a journey that you have to take one step at a time. so, of course, you will not expect the changes to occur in one fell swoop, and so you will make room for you to make mistakes, get up and move on.

Chapter 13 Face Your Fear

There are several ways people handle fear. Some try to ignore it, hoping that it will go away. Well, they usually discover that fear rarely goes away. When left on its own, fear can grow to such monstrous proportions and can eat one up so badly that the imprint would be left on the individual for many years to come.

Some others try to run away from their fears. It is, after all, a basic human instinct to run away from whatever we feel is capable of causing us harm in whatever form. Thus, these sets of individuals hide from confronting their fears, or they run away from any potential triggers, i.e. any situation that has the capacity to scare them. These two responses are equally unhelpful.

Firstly, you cannot take care of the root of the fear if you keep running away from it; as already stated, it will not go away on its own. More importantly however, if you run away from potential triggers then you will never grow. Developing resilience comes as a result of facing challenges as they come. That will be impossible if you do not confront the challenges in the first place.

So, having discussed some inappropriate responses to fear, what are the ways you can actually handle fear to achieve better results?

1. Identify the Sources

Before we go further, it is important to ask: is it necessary to identify the sources of your fears? And then, going further, is there even a need to confront your fears? The latter has been discussed at the beginning of this section, as for the former, the answer is still in the affirmative; there is indeed reason to confront and identify the sources of our fears. Even with that thought, a certain distinction has to be made.

This distinction is in the fact that it is possible that there are fears that do not need confronting. For instance, if you have a fear of volcanic eruptions and you do not live anywhere near a volcano, then there will hardly be any need to identify the source of that fear because it would be an exercise in futility.

It is at this point that self-evaluation comes in. You have to undergo some introspection, find out if the fear is hindering you from achieving a goal or attaining happiness. If that is the case, then you have to identify the source.

Every fear started out from somewhere. Even when it is latent, not immediately visible to you, it may have been lying dormant for a while before a trigger event occurred. Start with identifying the sources, then work your way to facing them.

2. Face your Fears Using Exposure Therapy

Exposure therapy has been hailed to be one of the most effective means of handling fear and anxiety in patients. Exposure therapy involves introducing the patient to the fear and helping them cope with it in a controlled environment. The idea is that coming face to face with the root of their fear desensitizes them to it. This technique is used as a direct opposite of flight, which is actually the response of a lot of folks when they get afraid. Avoiding the fear or actively running away from it is harmful because it teaches your brain to assume that you cannot deal with the fear on your own.

Although momentarily, you will feel some form of relief from having escaped the fearful situation, however, in the long run, you will eventually be hurting yourself and lowering the chances of handling the fear by yourself. Furthermore, flight makes it seem as though you have a genuine reason to be afraid. This is wrong because fear is a creation of the mind. In a lot of cases, there is actually no empirical evidence to support the fear that you face. But when you run away from the fear instead of facing it squarely, you give the idea that there actually is something to be afraid of.

Exposure therapy is used for specific fears and/or anxiety. Although the differences in the application of the therapy vary from one condition to the other, the differences are not much. This is to say that the technique used to treat anxiety disorders could be tweaked a little and then applied for the treatment of phobias.

Exposure therapy is mostly conducted under the supervision of a doctor. This is to ensure that there are medical personnel who are overseeing the process. However, there are situations where it will neither be wise or possible to constantly be under the supervision of a doctor. For instance, you may be requiring therapy as a coping mechanism for the rest of your life. This means that you will have to incorporate the techniques into your everyday activities, and in those situations, being under the supervision of a doctor would not be practical.

Exposure therapy is of two forms: gradual exposure and repeated exposure. The two forms are used together. Gradual exposure entails introducing the element of fear gradually. While repeated exposure entails introducing the individual into those situations repeatedly, over a period of time. The process makes it that the person becomes familiar with the stimulus that causes the fear, and so will be less likely to respond out of panic when the stimulus arises later on.

The first step in the exposure therapy system is imagining the feared object or situation. Here it is expected that you conjure up the feared object, in as much detail as possible. You may not have a specific object/situation which causes the fear, then you may have to think of something that represents the fear to you. You have to employ relaxation techniques while engaging in this process or else you will panic. This is because even though the situation/person which causes the fear may not be actively present at that moment, the brain cannot tell the difference. Thus, the same reaction -panic- which you would feel if the situation is actively present, will be what you would feel at that moment.

The next step is to stay there a little longer. You have to stay at the imagination phase for as long as it will take your brain to get used to the fear impulses and begin to realize that there is nothing to be feared about the situation.

After facing the fear in a controlled environment, the next step is to move a step further and tackle the fear outside in real life. Exposure therapy is only successful if it prepares you to handle the fear in the outside world by yourself. In the controlled environment, your hands are being held, and you are guided to confront your fears. However, in the real world, there would be no such safety harness. You will learn how to navigate by yourself and confront the fears alone.

Relaxation Techniques to Incorporate

While you are carrying out the exposure therapy, you have to keep an eye on your breathing, and on relaxation generally so that you do not get overly agitated and experience shock. Because the process of exposure therapy exposes you to your fears, it means that some level of agitation is expected. However, the idea is to create a system where you not only engage in the therapy but also learn to manage agitation at the same time.

Some of the relaxation skills you can practice include diaphragmatic breathing. This is a technique that involves breathing in and out slowly. Here, you take a deep breath with your nose, then hold it for a bit, before expelling it through your mouth slowly. The average time to hold the breath is usually one minute.

There is also the use of visualization. Here, usually, you will try to recall a happy memory, and then focus on it. Alternatively, you could imagine a place that represents peace and tranquility to you. You are expected to just focus on that thought even though you may be feeling agitated. With time, the agitation will dissipate.

Finally, you can practice meditation and mindfulness. Meditation is a lot like introspection and helps you focus on what you are thinking and feeling at that moment. Mindfulness, on the other hand, helps you become more aware of your environment. These two skills can be very important for relaxation.

Chapter 14   Relaxation Strategies

Diverse strategies/techniques exist to bring about increased relaxation and stress relief when dealing with cognitive behavioral therapy. Apart from what will be discussed in this chapter as practical techniques, muscle relaxation, mindfulness, visual creations and many more are all relaxation strategies in CBT. They are used as intense anxiety reduction treatment.

Relaxation strategies help send messages to the central nervous system. These messages are expected to calm the mind and relax it from anticipated danger, which is what induces worry and stress. We all witness anxiety at one point or the other in life, however, it becomes dangerous to one's mental health if one's anxiety level is higher than normal. Examples are anxieties that are so intense that they affect our thinking and effectiveness, like going blank during a school exam. Images of the brain have shown that people with very high anxiety levels are slow in their response and functioning of the parasympathetic nervous system. This nervous system is responsible for feelings of calmness and this system is expected to become active after the fight-or-flight system. This thread of functioning of the nervous system does not occur in people with anxiety issues. This is because of the slow response of their various nervous systems. These strategies are there since they constitute an intervention to reshape the physiological components of anxiety.

Research has shown that people who have high anxiety levels who engage in this relaxation are able to recover the normal functioning of their parasympathetic nervous system with time. However, practicing these relaxation strategies without being part of the full CBT regimen would only worsen anxiety issues. The reason for this is that, in such cases, relaxation strategies are used by such persons avoiding the full CBT regimen as techniques for avoiding feared or disappointing situations and avoidance worsens worry and anxiety. Let's look at some relaxation strategies.

1. **Practice calm breathing**: Before engaging in this strategy, it is important you find out if you have any health issues which could adversely affect you if you engaged in calm breathing. If you are aware of any such health issues already then all you need do is to consult with your doctor on how to go about this particular

relaxation strategy. Such health issues that may be adversely increased by practicing calm breathing include asthma, cardiovascular disease, and epilepsy. To practice calm breathing get a very quiet place.

This will allow you to practice and concentrate on your relaxation Strategy without being disturbed. This exercise should take at least ten to fifteen minutes. Take to mind your normal breathing pattern before the practice. You could use a stopwatch if it helps you better. If you have a measurement (the length of time it takes you to inhale and exhale) then, what you need to do is to add a second to the length of your inhale and exhale. Invariably, you would have to slow down the rate of your inhale and exhale. Do this continuously for some time then add another one second to the length of your inhale and exhale, follow the same pattern and continue for some minutes.

If you are experiencing any difficulty then it probably means that you are prolonging the exercise beyond what is required. Continue adding one second to the length of your inhale and exhale until you reach, comfortably, a breathing rate you can engage in without difficulty.

Once you have attained a comfortable level in your breathing pace then take another experiment while continuing with the exercise. Pause after each exhalation and inhalation. The length of the pauses is dependent on how long you can go. It could be a second, 2 seconds, longer than that or even ten seconds. Just do as much as you can.

However, irrespective of how long your pauses are, you will have to keep adjusting your rate of inhalation and exhalation to enable you to continue to breathe comfortably without the need to gasp for air.

The aim of it all is to ensure that fewer breaths are taken in each minute. If you have gotten the exercise and the pace at which you can comfortably move, then set an alarm and continue the practice for the next ten to fifteen minutes. After this, you will surely experience an increased relaxation and an instant drop in anxiety.

The purpose of this particular exercise is simple: you would have noticed that whenever you are anxious, the rate at which you breathe increases and you tend to take shorter breaths due to this. When you are relaxed, however, the opposite is the case. When you practice calm breathing, you are tricking your brain and nervous system into thinking that you are actually calm even though you are not yet. Eventually, all the neuro-chemicals enhancing relaxation will be released. Research has given diverse advantages to this technique. First, the effect is immediate on the brain to attain relaxation. Practicing calm breathing at least twice a day helps lower anxiety levels in people who are prone to excessive worry. The next time you do not feel up to an activity: while awaiting your doctor's news, or biting your nails before your interview, utilize this technique and get yourself out of worry.

2. **Progressive muscle relaxation**: This is another anxiety-prevention/reduction technique. It was introduced as far back as the 1930s by Edmund Jacobson, an American physician. The relaxation technique focuses on the main muscles of the body which deal with stress by alternating tension. You would likely experience occasionally tense muscles if you suffer Social Anxiety Disorder (SAD).

Progressive muscle relaxation is often practiced with other relaxation techniques such as systematic desensitization. This does not, however, imply that the technique cannot be practiced alone. Practicing progressive muscle relaxation alone gives you greater control over your body anxiety levels. Its effects go as far as making you fall asleep if the technique is properly and consistently practiced. Note that it is important that you consult your doctor before engaging in this training if you have any medical conditions.

To practice progressive muscle relaxation, ensure you are not putting on any tight clothes. Remove eye contacts and glasses if you are wearing any. Get a very quiet place to avoid any distractions and lay on the floor. Alternatively, if you have a reclining chair then this will also be perfect. Take your time and practice calm breathing as already discussed above. Do this for some time then focus your attention on the important muscles of your body which deal with anxiety and relaxation:

- **Jaw**: hold your jaw for about 15 to 30 seconds in order to tense it. Release your jaw and release the tension slowly and count to about 40 seconds. You would notice the feeling of relaxation and ensure to continue breathing slowly and evenly.

- **Forehead**: squeeze your forehead muscles until they are tight and very tense. Do this for about 20 seconds to achieve the tenseness. Then, release your forehead slowly and let the tension fade out. Ensure that the time it takes to finally release your forehead and the tension spans up to about 30 seconds. Notice the feeling of relaxation and the release of tension. Continue with the release of tension until you are fully comfortable and relaxed. Ensure your breathing is even.

- **Neck and shoulders**: you can increase the tension in your neck and shoulder region by lifting your shoulders up enough until they touch your ears. Hold your ears with your shoulders for about 20 seconds or until you can feel the tension in your neck and shoulders. Release your shoulders slowly and count until 30 seconds. You will feel more relaxed at the end of the exercise.

- **Buttocks**: increase the tension in your buttocks slowly for about 15 seconds then release the tension slowly while counting to 30 seconds. Ensure you maintain even breathing.

- **Legs**: increase the tension in your calves and quadriceps slowly. Ensure you do this for about 15 seconds then release the tension gradually and count normally for 30 seconds. You will feel relaxed. Ensure that in the course of the exercise that your breathing is even.

370

- **Feet**: tighten the muscles on your toes and feet slowly to increase the tension on that part of your body. Do this for the usual 15 seconds then release the tension slowly while ensuring that you count to 30 seconds. Your tension eases out. Ensure you are breathing slowly in the course of the exercise.

- **Arms and hands**: draw both hands into fists slowly and lift both to your chest region, slowly. Hold both hands to your chest for 15 seconds. Ensure that while holding your fists are as tight as possible. Release slowly while counting for 30 seconds. You feel more relaxation. Ensure you breathe slowly during the exercise.

Progressive muscle relaxation is very useful in the treatment of anxiety and it aids relaxation close to 98%. If you are having terrible social anxieties then you should engage in progressive muscle relaxation often. However, if the problem becomes severe then you can see a doctor for prescriptions.

3. **Listen to calm music**: From ancient Greek times, music has always been a form of healing for the body and mind. In native America, cultures exist with diverse songs numbering up to about 1,500 which were used for healing purposes. After the first and second world wars, veteran soldiers who had suffered mental and emotional trauma were healed using the diverse music available during that period.

   The soothing power of music has been established even before now. Its unique connection to our emotions and minds with the use of words is immensely important as a stress management tool. Particularly, music aids in relaxation. Oftentimes music is used to calm the nerves and induce sleep.

   Of great importance is slow and classical music which has the most therapeutic effect. Calm music can have tremendous relaxing effects on both our minds and body. It can also have a tremendous effect on the physiological functions of the body by slowing the heart rate, pulse, inducing low blood pressure and decreasing the stress hormones in the body. Basically, music is very important as a stress management and relaxation tool. Music, because it takes the mind away and absorbs feelings, can be a great tool of distraction at the same time because it explores emotions and aids meditation by keeping the mind from deviating.

Music differs just as individuals do and preference for music differ just as there are different music and different people. Only you can, therefore, determine for yourself what type of music you want to listen to depending on your mood. However, the purpose of the following list is to give you a choice instead of leaving you to the litany of the music list available outside there.

If you are having issues relaxing and concentrating, or you are having problems managing your stress level then you should consider calm music. Because people that are stressed and cannot manage their stress rarely give attention to any other activity once their stress level has skyrocketed, it might seem like a waste of time and additional stress trying to play music to relieve stress.

But, understanding that the less stressed you are the more productive you are likely to be, helps you give it a shot. You just have to take the first step which would mean getting calm music to be part of your life. Listen to calm music in your daily activities, if you have a car then play CD's, tune in to a channel where they play cool music and listen to it while in the shower. If the medical condition is a bipolar disorder or clinical depression then listening to music in your lowest mood can be very helpful.

Below is a list of calm songs I recommend you listen to:

1. Echoes of Time, by C. Carlos Nakai from Canyon Trilogy.

2. Quiet Mind by Nawang Khechog. It is the third track from Universal Love.

3. A Moment of Peace Meditation by Aneal and Bradfield, 'Heaven and Earth Spirits' track from Life & Love.

4. The Winding Path by Ken Kern from The Winding Path.

5. Classical Indian Music for Healing and Relaxing by Gayatri Govindarajan in the 'Pure Deep Meditation' track.

6. Earth Drum, Spirit Vision, by David and Steve Gordon.

7. Weightless by Marconi Union. This song has its harmonies, rhythms and bass lines carefully arranged to help slow a listener's heart rate, lower stress hormones, reduce blood pressure and reduce the levels of cortisol hormones.

8. Buddha Spirit by Aneal and Bradfield from Light and Love.

9. Sleep deeply by Dan Gibson.

10. Other songs that could aid relaxation are: In My Time by Yanni; Monkey Business by The Blacked-Eyed Peas; Songs About Jane Maroon 5; Vivaldi's Four Seasons by Music for Relaxation; A Day Without Rain by Enya; Pachelbel's Cannon with Ocean Surf; Best of Silk Road by Kitaro.

Chapter 15   How to Prevent a Relapse

There is something called a relapse prevention therapy. This was designed originally to maintain the achieved level of behavior into which one has moved from unwanted behavior. Although this process can also be used as a stand-alone treatment. In general, however, relapse prevention is used to teach individuals who are working towards maintaining a certain level of achievement in relation to their behavior with people and things, how to expect and eventually manage relapse. Relapse simply refers to a sudden (but most times anticipated) failure or breakdown in a person's decision and attempt to maintain a set of behavior and rules.

The prevention of relapse is as much work as attaining the desired set of behavior, relaxation, or reduction in stress that we have worked towards. Relapse prevention usually combines a series of self-management tools and emphasizes an approach that rejects the labeling of clients on the basis of whatever behavior they are working to avoid or stop. The relapse rate after a series of relaxation techniques can be very high.

The reasons for these are not farfetched. Individuals are used to going through a stressed life, having little or no time for the body and mind. In order to achieve a balance in the activities we engage in and in the time, we give ourselves to relax and breath, we have to practice. It takes constant practice to be able to achieve a sense of relaxation, to listen to music once in a while and to take out time to relax your stressed muscles. And, the problem with practice is that it can be unlearned unless we practice constantly as to make it a part of the body and mind.

Research has shown that the pattern that the relapse process takes is similar across all addictive behavior such as drug or alcohol addiction. In a relapse process, individuals are most usually experiencing a high level of control and self-efficacy while they are maintaining these changes in their behavioral patterns. The longer an individual stay away in successful abstinence, the greater the individual's perception of self-efficacy.

However, a high-risk situation could occur which would threaten all that the individual has practiced maintaining. This is when relapse is likely to occur, during high-risk situations. An individual could, however, be highly effective in coping with high-risk situations so that during such times the probability of relapse decreases and this has the effect of increasing a person's self-efficacy in the long run. The major case is for those who cannot withstand a high-risk situation. They are the people who are likely to constantly experience a relapse.

A relapse occurs from not having fully gained control of one's behavior and present realities. You are partly still inclined to the old ways of doing things than you are at achieving a change in your behavior. Failure to master high-risk situations is likely to throw you off balance and decrease your self-efficacy. The question however is: how do you prevent a relapse? How do you curtail high-risk situations?

1. **Continue the journey to victory**: Research has proven that our ability to continue with something effectively is limited only when we drum it into our minds that it is limited. There are temptations everywhere but it is important that you put your eyes and mind on the goal to help you achieve the desired results. Every time you let an urge pass without giving in, you are stronger the next time you feel the urge to get into depression or work yourself out.

   The point is that you are only as strong as you let yourself be. It is quite uneasy to remain positive especially when negativity hovers around but, positivity, every day and all the time is something that can be achieved just like other normal activities that we make ourselves do out of passion. There are diverse activities to engage in to draw you out of negative thoughts.

   When you are restless you could call up your friends because this means that you need their company. Call the person you have on your speed-dial if you are depressed or really need someone to talk to. It helps you maintain your positivity if you constantly remind yourself that you are surrounded by people who could help you out, and you actually reach out to these persons when you are in dire need of company and you need to relieve your stress.

   Understand that reaching out to people might not necessarily be the solution to your problem. In some situations, sitting alone and living in your own thoughts could be the therapy. Engaging in progressive muscle relaxation could just be the solutions to your stress problem for the day rather than calling out your friends or getting a massage. It is advised that you take up all the relaxation techniques already discussed above seriously.

Vigilance is crucial in this journey. You should be able to track your changes. What have I gained so far from constantly doing this? Have I relaxed in any way? If yes, how has this relaxation in my therapy affected me negatively? You should be focused on the present rather than where you have been and do not take your new-found self and habits for granted.

What overconfidence does is that it makes you want to prove that you can be fine without this and with time everything learned could be unlearned. Live in the truth of what you have learned and understand that for every time you drown yourself into the past it diminishes the power and behavior you have acquired in the present over your body and mind. It is important also that you get to your therapist once in a while. You have a world of conflicting attitudes and behavior to deal with. You may find familial, platonic or romantic situations rearing problems.

There is a need to learn how to resolve conflicts in healthy ways. Continue your appointments with a therapist at least until you are able to get a grip on high-risk situations by yourself without the help of your therapist. Another important attribute in your journey to achieving all that you have set out to do, is to be patient with the entire process.

Understand that achieving a particular behavior is not something that happens in a day. It takes patience and a whole lot of waiting to get what you want. You should, in exercising patience be slow to think that a relapse is just around the corner. Remind yourself constantly that you are doing your best to get better and that everything you have done so far is nothing short of heroic. This way, you help yourself move on and get better. Take your time. Be kind to yourself. You are on the right track.

2. **Talk kindly to yourself**: Part of this has been elaborated on above but this idea will be fully discussed under this heading. You could be engaged in an activity such as looking for your car keys on a

hectic morning or preparing for a pivotal meeting with your boss, or a presentation with the whole company or simply just turning right at an intersection, the urge to talk to oneself always happens. It is normal to want to talk to yourself and it is normal to do so.

Giving in to talking to yourself doesn't make you weird and neither does it send a red flag that you are becoming psychotic. It is a greater tool of healing and helps well in your behavioral pattern depending on which positive behavior you're trying to adopt. A research conducted by clinical psychologists showed that talking to oneself is very normal and that in fact, we talk to ourselves every day. It is enough if you merely think things through in your head without saying them out loud. The same way we seek out companionship just to share our ideas, we talk to ourselves very often.

Talking to oneself occurs mostly when one is experiencing a very deep emotion such as anger, anxiety, nervousness, or excitement. Even in some situations, those are typical emotions triggering us to speak out loud. For instance, your stress level increases when you are running late but stuck in traffic or when you are running late but cannot find your keys. When you let out your thoughts through words, you are forced to slow down and process your thoughts because you have engaged the centers of your brain that deals with language and the effects of this are that you process messages differently.

By talking to ourselves, we become intentional with our actions and this creates a slower process to actually take in our environment and emotions. It helps you think, feel, and act instead of living in your thoughts. Talking to yourself before a meeting which is making you nervous can help you calm down and process how you feel and why you are feeling that way. This could help you prepare better for the event. You are more alert when what you hear are your own words or thoughts and it helps you go through the hassle.

Talking to oneself can be a big deal, especially for people who think that talking to oneself might portend signs of mental sickness. It is however important that you talk to yourself in the right way. Talking to yourself is part of the development of language and talking to yourself in the right way is a good way to improve your cognitive and meta-cognitive skills which could improve your mastery. In talking to yourself, practice kindness. There is evidence from psychologists to prove that talking to oneself, once in a while, in a kind manner is anecdotal. There are no limits to what constant words of encouragement, drilled into oneself can do for the mind and our output in our various activities.

Research has shown that encouraging oneself continuously helps us brew optimism and gives us a positive approach to life. It, therefore, means that negative words must be avoided. It might be difficult. Like telling oneself after a series of failures that you are no good, or telling yourself that you are never going to snap out of depression or sickness because you are getting worse every day.

Try to always focus on the positive aspect of your life, read up on people who have gone through the phase you are in presently, and who have had it much worse than you are doing, but still ended up snapping out of it in the end. This is beneficial if you constantly remind yourself that since one person could snap out of this, then you can too.

This way, you are prone to encourage yourself nicely, to do better, to see your therapist, to engage in your relaxation techniques, to sleep, to put your bad thoughts in the past and focus on the present and how to get better. What you say to yourself, how you say it and when you say it matters. The focus is not that you talk to yourself regularly but on the content of what you say to yourself. Before an interview that you are nervous about, cheer yourself up and make yourself your biggest fan. A day or week before a big event that you are not sure how it is going to all turn out thereby making you all worried, take a deep rest, relax and engage in some relaxation techniques. It helps to ease out the tension.

In the middle of intense emotions, talking to oneself could also help ease out the tension. In anger, sadness, depression or confusion taking time to mutter some kind words to yourself helps you slow your activities to enable your brain to process your speech. You would realize that feeling those emotions are not worth it. Learn to listen to what you say to yourself. It matters a lot that you do not just make the content of your self-talk kind and positive, it matters too that you listen to these words. This way, the result sought will be achieved.

3. **Keep a thought journal:** Every person experiences a series of thoughts going on in their minds. Most times these thoughts are undetectable but they are definitely very powerful. It's more like working and playing music in the background but we do know that the kind of music we listen to in the background while working could affect our work level. It could make you bored, increase your thoughts or ability to work.

   These are exactly the same roles that our thoughts play. When we think, they are powerful and form part of what will make us better at what we face daily. In order to ensure that these thoughts are not just left as abstracts, we must make them adaptable and realistic. Also, to enable you to combat anxiety and worry it is important that you keep a running record of your thoughts, the time and the situation at hand when these thoughts occurred. The best way to achieve this is to pen our thoughts down. This is what keeping a thought journal is. It's quite easy to keep a journal even though it might seem demanding that you have to constantly update your journal.

   Get any book and make the following headings: situation (what are you doing presently; it could be driving, eating, studying, etc.), Thought (what are you thinking about), level of anxiety (how anxious are you?). Under each of these headings trace out every thought and the moment. Also, attach a date and the time of this thought to every entry.

   This helps you keep track of your progress. It also helps you determine how realistic your journal is at helping you snap out of anxiety. Most importantly, write down how you feel about your anxiety. What are your thoughts now? How anxious or depressed are you? You could use a scale to describe this say 1-10. Or, you could use a scale and still attach some description to your feelings. Often times, people face obstacles of having nothing to write because according to them they are just anxious or depressed but have nothing going on in their minds.

People get anxious and cannot pinpoint what triggered their anxiety. Most times, the cause of anxiety is on our minds, we just have to investigate this cause. What were you doing before you become anxious? Who did you see? Where were you going to and what were you going to do there? There is always a reason for anxiety lurking behind our thoughts.

You just have to dig it out and pin them down. Let's take for example that you are running up the stairs of your library to go get a book for your project and then you are excited because you love writing. Suddenly you become worried and anxious and realize that your excitement is no longer there and neither do you feel any enthusiasm to continue on the way to the library.

But, even with all these new feelings, you cannot pinpoint what has triggered this new emotion. Let's call this 'you', John. What if John loves reading and rarely has time to hang out with friends even though he would love to. What if what John saw on his way to the library were a group of boys, his age, who were laughing and moving together into the library and discussing how they would work together to see to the success of their project? What if John was thinking he could never have such a group of friends and that no one wanted to associate with him.

It's quite easy to conclude that we do not know why we are depressed or anxious or worried but looking at what happened before and after we began feeling a particular way and the people we saw could just about help to decipher why we were feeling that way and what we were thinking. Even if you are unsure about your feelings and thoughts, still pen something down. Tell your journal that you are feeling a particular way but do not know why you are. Your journal is a way of checking just how far you have come in achieving sound mental health.

4. **Practice mindfulness**: Mindfulness is a meditation process that involves intense processing of our environment and feelings without any judgment or interpretation. Engaging our mind in planning, and problem-solving negative thoughts and depression can be draining and can induce stress and anxiety. Taking one's mind away from these thoughts to focus on what is happening around us at the moment is a very active way of engaging with the world around us. Researches have shown that medical conditions like asthma, fibromyalgia, anxiety, stress, pain, depression and so on can be effectively curtailed with the use of mindfulness techniques. Some of the mindfulness techniques are recommended below:

   a. Live in the moment: it is difficult, often, to focus on the present without drifting constantly to events that happened in the past or that shaped our conviction about something. Try to live in the present approaching your environment and every activity in your life with an open, accepting and discerning mind. Be conscious of your environment, activities and your thoughts.

   b. Pay attention: in a world like ours, it is very difficult to take a moment and pay attention to the environment. But this is quite necessary for others to decipher the events of our anxiousness and stress or other psychological problems.

   c. Make full use of your senses daily: smell, taste, feel, listen, and be fully aware of your environment.

   d. Accept yourself just the way you are: how do you treat and advise a good friend or relative who tells you they have stress, depression, anxiety, etc. issues? Treat yourself the same way and possibly better.

   e. Focus on your breathing: take a moment each time you are having any strong emotion or stress or anxiety to engage in your breathing exercises.

5. **Connect with CBT professional organizations**: While you improve your mental health, it is vital that you keep in touch with

381

CBT professional organizations. This will help you keep tabs on the progress of your health and know if you have had any relapse that you are not aware of. There are no known rules for choosing a CBT professional organization but it's important that you ask friends or people around you who are in one or who could help you find one. The Beck Institute for Cognitive Behavior Therapy is a good one and it also provides certifications.

Chapter 16   Additional Resources

There are cognitive distortions that could equally affect the brain and the manner in which an individual reacts to activities around them. Recognizing these distortions is important to enabling the effectiveness of a therapy:

1. Filtering: This occurs when a person focuses solely on the bad and negative activities in their life while totally ignoring the positive activities in their life. This could grow from the general need to achieve a pressing need at a particular moment and not being able to achieve the same at that moment. This leads the individual to recollect other times when like events have occurred and they were unable to reach a goal and other negative activities that have occurred before then and which are not connected to the present activity. The negative effect of dwelling on the bad events in one's life is that it saps the strength of a person to focus on achieving positive things. Eventually, a person suffers more from stress, anxiety, depression which could be induced by many factors.

2. Polarized thinking: A person having this distortion believes that life should be a jack of all things. He is either having it all or nothing at all. A person having this distortion believes that failing in a certain aspect of life implies that they are no good in every other thing in life.

They want to succeed at it all forgetting that perhaps their failure in a particular field could mean that they are not talented in that field or simply that they are not giving all their best to succeed in this field. Either way, polarized thinking could breed anxiousness and stress and depression because it gives the notion of working hard and achieving nothing when in fact the work is being poured into the wrong field.

3. Overgeneralization: This occurs when a person takes a single event and it becomes the sole yardstick for measuring other events that happen subsequently. Take for example a person who goes for a job interview and failed. Instead of taking that as a bad experience which he/she did not prepare hard enough for, they take it that they are just not good at interviews and would fail in subsequent ones.

4. Personalization: This is a distortion that allows a person to believe that everything around them is connected to them. They tend to link

383

every negative event around them to themselves. For example, if there is a queue of persons receiving something from donors and the gifts finishes when they (people who suffer personalization) join the queue, they are quick to believe that it happened that way because they joined the queue and that such negative events wouldn't have occurred if they hadn't joined in the first place.

Other distortions that could counter CBT are control fallacies, fallacies of fairness, catastrophism, conclusions, etc.

Tools and Apps

Below are some top apps/tools that could be used as alternatives for treatments and for getting through distortions

1. notOK: this is an app majorly developed for people who are more exposed to the danger of suicide. The app was developed by a struggling teenager and her teenage sister. The app allows you to send a message to your close friends, relatives and relationship network that something is wrong or that you are in danger. The app contains a red button that could be clicked and it allows you to add close relatives to the list of people that could be reached out to. Once the app is clicked it sends out a message instantly to all the persons you have added to the app and it also sends your present GPS location along with the message.

2. What's up: this is an amazing app that combines two different therapy methods to reduce stress, anxiety, and depression. It combines both Cognitive Behavioral Therapy and Acceptance Commitment Therapy methods. It contains positive and negative pages that help you to keep track of the changes in your mood and also counter the unproductive thoughts you might have. The 'get grounded page' allows you to go through hundreds of questions and answer the same in order to determine your mood and thinking. You could also keep track of changes in your thought patterns and mood. Psychologists have rated the app as being amazing.

3. Moodkit: Moodkit was developed by two psychologists as a self-awareness tool. It provides a person with diverse activities that could be used to improve a person's mood. For persons suffering from depression, the journal version of moodkit is very helpful as it helps you go through diverse activities and how best to snap out of your unproductive mood. It is rated as one of the top apps in mental health that uses the background of Cognitive Behavioral Therapy to improve a person's health.

4. Quit That!: Quit That! is a tracking and recording device used to curb addictions. It helps to provide first-hand knowledge to addicts on their progress in trying to quit a particularly bad habit. It helps to beat bad habits and addiction, whether smoking, drugs or alcohol, the progress of trying to quit these bad habits can be checked. It helps you determine how the minutes, hours, days, months or years you last indulged in the habit. It also helps to remind you of the activities you want to avoid engaging in.

5. Mind Shift: Mind shift is rated as one of the best mental health apps for teens and young adults. It is used to treat anxiety in teens and youths. With a mental shift instead of hiding from your anxiety, mind shift encourages you to go out and take charge of your life and emotions. The app gives periodic updates by gauging your feelings and attitude to questions and then gives feedback on what you should rather be doing instead of lying low. Simply put, a mental shift is like the cheerleader motivating you to keep going and facing it all.

6. CBT thought record diary: the reason why we engage in CBT in the first place is to be able to identify the negative and distorted thinking patterns going through our heads. CBT thought record diary helps you to do this. Do you remember when we discussed keeping a thought journal? Well, this is what CBT thought record diary is all about and more. It helps you keep constant records of your thoughts and then outline the negative thought patterns and then helps reevaluate these negative thoughts. It is vital for curbing anxiety and depression.

7. TalkSpace online therapy: are you one of those people who wish to meet and speak with a professional therapist daily about your health issues but cannot meet face-to-face with one? Then this is about the best solution to your problem. With Talkspace and just $65 every week you can download the talk space app and send messages about how you feel and have professional therapists attend to your problems. The reply is instantaneous, more like someone is waiting for you to speak to them before you eventually do.

Other relevant apps and tools in CBT are happified, recovery record, rise up and recover, life sum, OCD and so on. All these tools are important to treat the distortions discussed above and they could also be a very good way of saving money while still getting very good mental health treatment.

Chapter 17   CBT Testimonies

CBT Clinic, one of the most popular mental health centers in the UK has diverse success stories and testimonies of clients on how CBT has helped change their lives.

1. John, a 42-year-old man who had been laid off from work had suffered severe pangs of depression and had booked appointments with the clinic. According to him, the moment he first spoke with his therapist, he knew he had made the best decision about his health. His therapist was calm, collected and was most reassuring. Therapy helped him see how his thought patterns affected his feelings and behavioral responses to things. It helped him reevaluate his thoughts while focusing his cognitive skills on things that were more fulfilling. Soon enough, he was over his old job, was cheerfully searching for other means of employment and further recommended it to two of his friends who were having the same issue of depression.

2. Julia was aged 31 when she began seeing a therapist for her low self-esteem issues. She had no friends and was very isolated. According to her, barely 6 weeks after seeing a CB therapist, she was reformed. She began to see people as not being the enemy and she began to appreciate who she was and what she had to offer. That way, she engaged with people with an open mind, increased her friend's space and got better at work.

3. Katie is just 17 and she began having panic attacks at that age. She would refuse to go to school and when forced to, she would seem really worried and stressed out upon her return. It happened that Katie had been suffering from bullies in school and this had greatly affected the way she saw herself, her confidence level and the manner in which she engaged with people. Her parents were advised to take her to a CBT center and it was quite easy for her to connect immediately with the therapist. According to her, she was taught many 'coping' techniques for bullying situations. She also learned that she could reshape her thoughts and the manner she sees herself by constantly keeping a thought journal and using this to track the changes in her perception of herself.

4. Paul is aged 55 years and he has generalized anxiety. He mostly worries about the future and the fact that he is aging. He registered with the CBT

center and he was satisfied with the manner in which the therapist had explained the science of anxiety and how it affects the cognitive part of our brain. He was satisfied at how well he was able to track his growth from worry to worry less.

Chapter 18   Conclusion

If you have come to the end of this book then it is safe to assume that you have, by now, a fairly good idea of what anxiety and anxiety disorders are, and the steps to take in handling them, especially through employing Cognitive-Behavior Therapy. We tried to demystify the concepts and also to discuss each term in detail, using the language you are familiar with. It is the intention that if you have gotten to this point, we will have achieved the aim of this book, which essentially is to help you overcome anxiety and depression using Cognitive-Behavior Therapy.

Generally, CBT involves a process where a person attempts to challenge their perceptions. The idea is to help the individual have a cohesive view of the world around them, and this will have the effect of changing their reactions to events and changing their moods generally. CBT is often done under the supervision of a licensed doctor. The parties, i.e. the patient and the doctor, work hand-in-hand, to identify specific goals and then strive to achieve them.

There can hardly be a success if both parties are not clear on the intended outcomes and agree on the mode of solving the problems that may arise. However, in this book, the focus is on the patient, with the aim of empowering the patient to be in a position to change perceptions themselves.

In this sense, this is sort of like a self-help book. Make no mistake, in the beginning, you may have to seek the help of a doctor, and also when you experience any difficulties, it will be wise to seek the help of a doctor who will help explain things better and shed light on any areas you find confusing. But, for the most part, if you stick to all you have learned in this book, you will record tremendous success on your own (As a matter of fact, if you have been putting into practice what you have been reading, you should be seeing some results by now).

Particularly in this book, we have discussed in detail what CBT is and the various forms that exist. We have also discussed how to identify problematic thoughts, how to challenge and reset automatic negative thinking. The root of most (if not all) of mental illnesses is the mind. So, we took the time to explain how you can filter what comes into your mind and what goes out. There is also a chapter on relaxation skills to practice. This is important because when you are agitated, it often leads to distress. Relaxation is a key way to prevent distress and anxiety from taking root.

Even in the instance when you are anxious or distressed, you also need to apply some relaxation techniques to take care of that situation. Similarly, in this book, you will find out how to prevent a relapse.

Granted, it may happen that you'll suffer a relapse, but that is exactly why this chapter is important. It is better to prevent, and handle a relapse when it is expected. When you create a tight system to detect when you are spiraling downwards, you will be able to catch yourself before you experience a total relapse.

At the start, the promise was that you will find the help you need if you are going through any form of depression and anxiety. This book has not only delivered on that, but has gone ahead to provide you with testimonies of persons who have been on the path that you are on right now but were able to break free totally by engaging in Cognitive Behavior Therapy. That testimony could be yours if you decide to be committed to doing all that has been said within these pages.

Do not be discouraged when you do not immediately see the results that you want, or when the results trickle in, instead of coming in waves. You have to bear in mind that progress sometimes comes slowly, and takes time. You should commit to putting in the time and effort needed. Just keep doing what you have to do, the results will eventually show up, even beyond what you intended. As a matter of fact, the transformation may already be taking place, just that you may not be seeing them.

Cognitive-Behavioral Therapy has proven to be the number one treatment for mental health. Apart from the use of psychoactive therapy to treat general mental diseases, CBT has proven to be very effective in dealing with depression, anxiety, post-traumatic stress disorder, and other minor mental health challenges. It can be quite difficult engaging the services of a therapist to help us get better for something as little as depression or anxiety but the reason why this book has been written is for you to realize that besides CBT professionals, there are diverse ways to curb your mental health issues while keeping the therapist aside as a run-to, to ensure that your path to getting better is being followed.

This book goes to show us that not having a therapist should no longer be a reason why you should wallow in minor mental health issues without seeking help. Above are diverse approaches to take to solve anxiety, stress, depression and other mental disorders. However, it is important that we do not make these tools and strategies our sole solution. Keep your therapist.

Finally, you could run into challenges not anticipated by this book. We have tried to cover every possible challenge that you encounter, however, it may happen that even with our due diligence, there could be a challenge that you cannot find the solution for. In that regard, it will be advisable to consult a doctor as well.

References

American Psychological Association. (2000). Answers to your questions about panic disorders. Retrieved from https://www.apa.org/topics/anxiety/panic-disorder

Ackerman, C. (2017). What is rational emotive behavior therapy? Retrieved from https://positivepsychology.com/rational-emotive-behavior-therapy-rebt/

Basic principles of cognitive behavior therapy. (n.d.). Retrieved from https://www.cbttherapies.org.uk/2015/06/01/basic-principles-cognitive-behaviour-therapy/

Cherry, K. (2017). How rational emotive behavior therapy works. Retrieved from https://www.verywellmind.com/rational-emotive-behavior-therapy-2796000

Cognitive behavioral therapy. (2017). Retrieved from https://www.mind.org.uk/information-support/drugs-and-treatments/cognitive-behavioural-therapy-cbt/cbt-sessions/#.XbbsU5Ao_5e

Darla, B. (2016). Panic disorder. Retrieved from https://www.healthline.com/health/panic-disorder

Facts & statistics. (n.d.). Retrieved from https://adaa.org/about-adaa/press-room/facts-statistics

Ferriman, A. (1995). The mother and father of all arguments. Retrieved from https://www.google.com/amp/s/www.independent.co.uk/life-style/the-mother-and-father-of-all-arguments-1581531.html%3famp

Laura. (2018). Cognitive behavioral therapy - ten things to expect. Retrieved from http://thebutterflymother.com/2018/06/19/5-things-expect-cbt/

Micu, R. (2018). Understanding anxiety| symptoms, causes, treatment. Retrieved from https://motivationformore.com/understanding-anxiety/

Pros & cons of CBT therapy. (n.d.). Retrieved from http://www.thecbtclinic.com/pros-cons-of-cbt-therapy

Sado, M., Shirahase, J., Et al. (2014). Predictors of repeated sick leave in the workplace because of mental disorders. *Neuropsychiatric Disease and Treatment.* 10, 193-200. DOI: 10.2147/NDT.S55490

Simmons, J. & Griffiths, R. (2008). *CBT for beginners: A practical guide for beginners.* Retrieved from https://books.google.com.ng/books/about/CBT_for_Beginners.html?id=DBtRuAd0NgAC&printsec=frontcover&source=kp_read_button&redir_esc=y

Thomas, S. (n.d.). Rational emotive behavior. Retrieved from https://study.com/academy/lesson/albert-ellis-theory-lesson-quiz.html

Part 2 : Anxiety in Relationship

Chapter 19　Introduction to Anxiety in Relationship

So you have lived happily ever after ... Or at least if only you would be more interesting or attractive; or if you were not so in need; or if you could find out what is wrong with you that never makes your relationships function well. You may have been with a partner for a long time, but you are dealing with the feeling your partner is always falling short and can never fill the void in your heart. You think you're part of the problem too.

Whether single or in a relationship, a lot of people believe that in love they will never be happy. They feel lonely and want to be a companion — not just a friend sitting next to someone in a movie, but a friend, confidante, and lover to accompany them through the greatest of all the adventures we call life. They sometimes worry that if they get to know "the real me" their partners will bolt. Often, they believe their partners appreciate the things they do. But that does not suffice. What if their success falls apart, after all? Then there is the ever-present fear that if they let themselves be vulnerable by turning to that person for support, comfort, and reassurance, will that someone will be really there for them.

As with virtually everything else in life, through experience you know about relationship. And because your first serious relationship with your caretakers began as a child, that is where you started thinking about relationships. I know that is one of the psychology clichés, but that is real, too. Your first lessons are focused on the love, acceptance, and reassurance given by your parents or those who took care of you when you needed them and how lovable you are. You have established a certain style of communicating with — and bonding to — others during the early months and years of your life.

While before puberty or adulthood you may not have been conscious of this style (or maybe it has still unclear), your current style is probably essentially the same as what was nurtured in childhood. If your early encounters left you questioning your sense of being worthy of love, afraid of being rejected, or with an unquenchable desire for reassurance, then you probably still feel this way. It may also be that later traumatic events in life increased guilt about relationships that had previously lurked beneath the surface. Yet the underlying susceptibility to this fear associated with attachment possibly evolved during childhood.

It is important to recognize that attachment-related anxiety does not need to be in response to any parenting that is necessarily coercive or harmful; in fact, it is most often not. Most people with anxiety related to attachment come from really caring families. Sadly, even though they genuinely loved their children, their parents 'own challenges or complicated or stressful situations interfered with their being able to parent effectively.

You may wonder why will my anxiety associated with attachment stubbornly stay with me through life? To answer this, think about the nearly endless amount of experiences you had during your childhood, day after day, year after year, with your parents or other caregivers. Such interactions — although not of equal weight — implicitly teach you how others are likely to react to you, and how deserving you are to be loved. Their messages layer one over the other, and fuse together, becoming part of your being's very fabric. So, it is not easy to adjust, understandably, — not convenient, but certainly possible.

One important thing I have learned from doing counseling is that making progress is a bit like gardening. I listen to people, share my impressions of them and their situations, offer sympathy and provide guidance. In turn, they (hopefully) learn to see each other differently; react to each other in fresh, more constructive ways; feel empowered to take risks (the unknown is still at least a little scary); and learn to adapt. But all this will happen at its own pace; it can be supported but it cannot be compelled to do so.

Greater self-awareness is one key factor in fostering personal development. This involves being mindful of your thoughts; knowing and feeling your feelings consciously; and realizing what makes you tick. Such activities can be challenging, particularly when you find yourself facing negative or contradictory aspects. We do give you a greater sense of your struggles, though. Such self-awareness also makes people feel a greater sense of well-being and, by itself, also encourages change — such as reducing anxiety associated with attachment and fostering healthy relationships.

As important as self-awareness, understands that it happens within the sense of your relationship with yourself is equally important. And it is too hard for the people themselves. Much like you would care about a hurt child by being nurtured; treating yourself in a caring way is extremely beneficial.

Chapter 20   Anxiety in Relationship, And How It Works

Nearly every facet of a relationship is affected by anxiety, no matter what type. When someone enters into a relationship, there are relatively simple expectations that go along with it. First and foremost, you assume the other person can fulfill the role of a partner. Being a partner involves a solid ability to communicate openly, offer companionship, contribute financially, and more.

Relationship Communication

As you should know, communication is particularly important when it comes to romantic relationships. Being able to discuss all issues freely, make plans, and set goals for the future are all vital for a successful relationship. Otherwise, how could two partners handle their responsibilities, challenges, and expectations?

However, what happens if one of you is suffering from anxiety? Any of the disorders can have a severe impact on your ability to maintain a healthy way to communicate in your relationship. Of course, it depends on how severe the anxiety is. However, no matter its level of development, a personal connection will be in some way affected. You or your partner might encounter difficulties in reacting in a healthy way when either of you expresses an opinion or an emotion. For instance, it is common to misread someone's intent or misinterpret the meaning of individual conversations. Anxiety works in many ways as a filter, and when it clouds your vision, you might act in a way that will eventually damage your relationship. Any joke, comment, or harmless critique can lead to an overreaction that will put a strain on any couple, even more than the anxiety itself.

Relationship Communication Anxiety

Anxiety has a severe emotional effect on people, and the partner is always affected in some way as a result of seeing his or her significant other suffering and going through the whole life crippling experience. Emotions carry a great deal of power, and some people find it too challenging to face them. Those who are afraid to express themselves emotionally have likely lived in a household where the behavior was discouraged.

The act of suppressing emotions is a sign that the person is trying to hold onto a semblance of control. If you find yourself behaving this way, it might be because you are scared at the thought of losing that control and allowing the locked-up feelings to overwhelm you. Naturally, the biggest issue here is when it comes to negative emotions as they have such a substantial impact on a person's life. You might think that if you let it all out, you will change your partner's feelings. And whatever good opinions and thoughts he or she has about you will be gone, causing damage to the relationship. However, while you may think of this as a solution, it leads to even more problems. Acting this way will increase the amount of anxiety you experience. You will find less and less peace of mind, until one day when it will all come out in a wild burst. It is difficult to suppress those feelings forever, and when they do come to the surface, the feeling will cloud all judgment.

Communication anxiety can also oppositely manifest itself without involving any emotion suppression. For instance, let us say your partner unloads only her most powerful feelings and emotions regularly. Some people cannot hold back on certain beliefs, so they lash out, and as a result, both of you end up feeling overwhelmed and confused, leading to another problem. Experiencing these outbursts often enough, you can start feeling that it is your job to find a solution to your partner's issues. It is not enough to notice the anxiety and the strain it is putting on your relationship. You get the feeling you are the sole savior of this partnership. Unfortunately, this usually makes things worse as your partner could start developing resentment towards you for their behavior.

Another communication problem is when you consider expressing yourself as a risky affair. Maybe you are wondering what will happen if you reveal what you honestly think. It is enough to trigger your anxiety as you are afraid of the uncertainty of the outcome. Frequently, this symptom stems from not having confidence in yourself and you are worried about an adverse reaction from your partner. In this case, you might be taking a great deal of time to rehearse what you will say and complicate things further by imagining all the possible scenarios.

Social Situations

Being in certain social situations is difficult for many people who do not even suffer from any form of anxiety. However, those with anxiety will encounter other problems that would not cross other people's minds. It is typical behavior to deny meal invitations from coworkers or friends, ignore unnecessary phone calls, and even avoid small family gatherings. While social situations are more specific and do not occur every day, there are also daily occurrences that can cause extreme amounts of anxiety. For instance, some have issues performing any task or responsibility as long as there is another human being in their presence, looking over their shoulder. Here, we are going to focus on the broader kind of social situation, referring to any environment in which other people are around.

Isolating yourself from any social situation usually leads to more than just personal social isolation. In some cases, this behavior can turn into a never-ending cycle of avoidance. The social aspects of life causing you anxiety, can, in turn, create even more tension in new situations. Avoidance reduces your ability to cope, and you will be dealing with even more fear during the next social gathering. This self-perpetuating cycle often leads to relationship problems, especially breakups, especially if one party is not suffering from any anxiety.

With that in mind, you should take note that a disorder does not necessarily cause anxiety in social situations. This problem is not limited only to those who fit that particular case. Either type of stress can manifest itself in a social setting and determine how you behave when forced to interact with other people, including your partner. For example, your behavior at home may seem normal because you are in a safe space, but in a social event, you may seem unrecognizable to your partner. Your behavior changes as soon as you are around others, especially strangers. Some common signs are stuttering, prolonged silence or pretending you are busy to avoid conversations, talking a lot more than what you may consider "normal", and relying on your partner to carry any conversations. There are also some physical signs mentioned when discussing various disorders, such as excessive sweating, nail-biting, playing with an innate object or hair, and avoiding direct eye contact. Some people feel so uncomfortable during social engagements that they leave the conversation suddenly or leave the room altogether.

How it affects your Relationship
Social interactions are more crucial than ever, and if you (or your partner) are suffering from social anxiety, your career and relationships may suffer as a result. Participating in social gatherings and popular events is essential to developing healthy relationships. Building friendships and

expanding your career opportunities can almost exclusively be achieved only in a social setting, whether it is an office Christmas party or someone's birthday.

If you are suffering from anxiety and it makes it impossible for you to socialize with anyone other than your partner, you will unknowingly isolate yourself and feel left out. In addition, your partner will start resenting you for all the pressure you place on him or her whenever you have to avoid a social event. Your partner will always have to come up with an excuse regarding your absence and feel out of place. Keep in mind that after a while some of those people will no longer send invitations to your partner as they can feel that something is wrong, or that they will only receive an excuse instead of attending. In addition, your partner will feel even worse about the entire situation as he or she listens to you blaming yourself and judging yourself over something you have little control. At the same time, if your anxiety does cause a rude overreaction during a social event, your partner will feel torn between siding with her hosts or with you. In either case, unnecessary damage is done to your relationship.

Do not forget that anxiety does not always manifest itself in obvious ways. Even if you are the one in the relationship that has it, you might not be aware of how it manipulates some of the decisions you make. For instance, let us say your partner asks you to go to a concert or a party. You do not start talking about your anxiety as you may not even be aware of it at this point. You may refuse the idea because you are just not in the right mood that day, or that you want to spend time at home watching a movie. This scenario will likely repeat itself, slowly increasing the level of frustration building up inside your partner. Why are you acting like this? You may be feeling shameful or guilty because you do not want to disappoint your partner by admitting a problem, so you make up an excuse for not wanting to go out.

Take a piece of paper or in a journal, write down everything you can remember about your behavior in social situations. Do the same thing for your partner. Here are some of the behavioral clues you may notice that are typical for anyone suffering from social anxiety:

1. **Avoiding groups of people by sitting alone at the table, standing in a corner or vanishing for certain periods.**
2. **Making excuses leaving an event as early as possible.**

3. Avoiding the conversation by never getting involved even when offered.
4. Suddenly becoming easily irritated and quick to anger.
5. Consuming more alcohol that what is your normal limit under average circumstances. Many people with anxiety feel they need alcohol to survive a social situation or that they even become more likable.
6. Never leaving the side of your more charismatic and talkative partner.

Chapter 21   Behaviors that Trigger Anxiety in a Relationship

Unhealthy anxiety can have a big impact on your life. It will hinder you from doing the things you desire. When you are anxious, you get a feeling that your life is under the control of an external force. Anxiety is a negative, vicious circle which consumes you completely and can have an effect on your wellbeing, your relationship, your hobbies, and more. It feels difficult to break this anxiety, but the possibility exists. Anxiety often makes people assume that they are no longer in charge and cannot do anything about it. This is not the case - you can learn to get your anxieties under control and find happiness.

Anxiety disorder occurs when you regularly feel disproportionate levels of worry, tension, or fear due to an emotional trigger. The ability to identify the reason behind a series of anxiety attacks is the key to successful treatment.

1. Environmental factors: Elements within your surroundings can trigger anxiety. Worries and stress associated with a private relationship, job, school, or monetary difficulty can lead to anxiety disorder.
2. Genetics: Research has shown that if any members of your family have dealt with anxiety disorder, there is high chance that you will experience anxiety as well.
3. Medical factors: Different medical issues can lead to an anxiety disorder, such as the side effects of drugs, symptoms of a sickness, or stress from a difficult underlying medical condition. These conditions could lead to significant lifestyle changes like pain, restricted movement, and even emotional imbalance. It is worth noting that anxiety can be triggered by any of these problems.
4. Brain chemistry: Experiences that are traumatizing or stressful can alter the structure and performance of the brain, making it react to certain triggers that may not have previously caused anxiety.

Relationships are amazing and very fulfilling with the opportunity for happiness, fun, interesting conversations, and exciting dates. They can, however, also be a major source of upheaval and worry. Your ability to identify the major sources of anxiety in your relationship will help you stay away from them, thus enhancing the balance and stability of your relationship.

I will now take you through some of the most common triggers of anxiety in your relationships and how to look out for them and control them.

What triggers anxiety the most is when you are vulnerable to another person. We yearn for safety and love in a relationship. If you have been hurt before, the fear of being hurt again can make you anxious.

Financial concerns of either partner are another cause of anxiety in relationships. Most times, people do not fully disclose their money related issues or financial strengths. They open up when a problem arises, and at this point it may be too late. It could be that you are not compatible with your partner when it comes to saving and spending money, or you do not even share the same money views with them. It is also easy for you to get carried away by love and close your eyes to the financial wherewithal of your partner. When real life expenses set in and you seem to be carrying the brunt of them, anxiety sets in. Money in relationships is a constant.

Another root cause of anxiety in relationships is jealousy. Your inability to trust your partner could lead to jealousy. Jealousy is also as a result of a lack of confidence in yourself and your abilities coupled with low self-esteem. In order to overcome this, build up your self-esteem and begin to think very highly of yourself. The best way to eradicate jealousy is by building up your self-esteem.

Jealousy can reveal our greatest fears and insecurities, and this can quickly lead to an unhealthy and toxic atmosphere in your relationship. When you are jealous, you become overwhelmed and begin to imagine the worst.

The fear of being abandoned and the fear of rejection are also major causes of anxiety in relationships. Whatever insecurities you have are mirrored back to you by your partner. It is only normal to worry about these things, but instead of keeping the thoughts to yourself, speak them out loud and have a conversation about them with your partner. You have to develop a stronger identity and sense of self. You have to learn to

404

be consciously aware of your state of mind and thought processes in order to keep all anxieties at bay. Most of the arguments you have with your partner over your family, work, social life, or money actually have some form of rejection as their roots. The underlying feeling and fear during these fights is that you will be rejected. For instance, if you are having a heated discussion about how much time your partner spends with his friends; it is actually about why they are not spending that time with you?

Your ability to relax into your relationship will make you feel less rejected and no longer defensive. Be present in your relationship and have no negative thoughts.

You must deliberately set clear boundaries on the type of information that gets into your head. Work to stop unwanted information and behaviors from coming in and penetrating into your mind.

When anxiety comes knocking at your door, open the door for it, address it, look at it, then inhale deeply and close the door, knowing that you have armed yourself with all the information that you need. You do not have to welcome anxiety with open arms, but you can acknowledge that it is there.

Ongoing communication with an ex is another trigger for anxiety. Communications with an ex should be handled cautiously. This is because it can lead to great anxiety, anger, and eventually a breakup in your current relationship. If you have to communicate with your ex, you should explain why to your partner and ensure all communication is strictly platonic and transparent. If you do not have to communicate with your ex, do not do it.

Distance backed up with a lack of communication can hugely contribute to anxiety between you and your partner. When your partner is not physically available for a long period of time, it can be difficult to find assurance and thus anxiety sets in. Even if you talk on the phone and video call regularly, you can still feel a void in your heart. In situations like this, you have to rely on the power of words to communicate your feelings with your partner. Feel free to tell your partner what you need from them, express yourself, and talk about any insecurities you may be going through. By so doing, your partner will be able to address this and reassure you of their love and commitment.

Another major cause of anxiety is doubt. It can be weakening to question every move and action of your partner, wondering if you made the right decision or what next steps you should or should not take. If you are in great doubt, begin to make a conscious effort to release yourself and set yourself free from doubt. Take your mind off every question that makes you doubt your relationship or your partner. Just take a deep breath, calm down, and revel in your relationship. Make up your mind to just enjoy your relationship and your partner by allowing yourself the freedom of not having to make any decisions about your relationship for a period of time.

A major health challenge can also trigger anxiety in your relationship. You or your partner may be caught off guard by a diagnosis or medical scare. This may also stress you out and cause a great deal of anxiety within yourself. If you or your partner falls ill, anxiety will naturally set in. This health challenge may cause your partner to break down emotionally. You will have to be very patient and calm with them through this process. Provide all the support you can during this time and let them be assured of your unwavering love and commitment.

Chapter 22   Why They Feel Anxious, Insecure, and Attached in Relationships

When you begin a relationship, the initial stage can get you worried and tensed up with different questions in your head, begging for answers. You begin to think: "Does he/she really like me?" "Will this work out?" "How serious will this get?"

It is sad to know that these worries do not diminish in the later stages of the relationship when you are plagued with anxiety. As a matter of fact, the closer and more intimate you get in a relationship, the higher the intensity of the anxiety displayed in such a relationship can be.

Worry, stress, and anxiety about your relationships can leave you feeling lonely and dejected. You may unknowingly create a distance between yourself and your loved one. Another grave consequence of anxiety is its ability to make us give up on love completely. That is rather devastating, because love is a very beautiful thing. It is important to really understand what makes you so anxious in a relationship and why you feel so insecure and attached. I will take you through some of the reasons in subsequent paragraphs.

Falling in love puts a demand on you in countless ways - more ways than you can imagine. The more you cherish a person, the more you stand to lose. How ironic is that? This intense feeling of love and the powerful emotions that come with it consciously and unconsciously create the fear of being hurt and the fear of the unknown in you.

Oddly enough, this fear comes as a result of being treated exactly how you want to be treated in your relationship. When you begin to experience love as it should be, or when you are treated in a tender and caring way which is unfamiliar to you, anxiety might set in.

More often than not, it is not only the events that occur between you and your partner that lead to anxiety. It is the things you tell yourself and feed your mind with regarding those events that ultimately lead to anxiety. Your biggest critic, which is also the "mean coach" you have in your head, can criticize you and feed you with bad advice which will ultimately fuel your fear of intimacy. It is this mean critic that suggests to you that:

- "You are not smart, he/she would soon get bored of you."

- "You will never meet anyone who will love you, so why try?"
- "Don't trust him, he's probably searching for a better person."
- "She doesn't really love you. Get out before you get hurt."

This mean coach in your head manipulates you and turns you against yourself and the people you love. It encourages hostility, and you soon discover that you are paranoid. You begin to suspect every move your partner makes, and this reduces your self-esteem and drives unhealthy levels of distrust, defensiveness, jealousy, anxiety, and stress.

What this mean coach in your head does is constantly feed you with thoughts that jeopardize your happiness and make you worry about your relationship rather than allowing you to just enjoy it. When you begin to focus so much on these unhealthy thoughts, you become terribly distracted from the real relationship, which involves healthy communication and love with your partner.

You soon discover that you are reacting to unnecessary issues and uttering nasty and destructive remarks. You may also become childish or parental towards your partner.

For example, your partner comes home from work and does not have a good appetite, so they politely turn down dinner. Sitting alone after some time, your inner critic goes on a rampage and asks, "How can he refuse my food? What has he eaten all day? Who has been bringing food to him at work? Can I really believe him?" These thoughts can continually grow in your mind, until by the next morning you are insecure, furious, and temperamental. You may begin to act cold or angry, and this can put your partner off, making them frustrated and defensive. They will not know what is been going on in your head, so your behavior will seem like it comes out of nowhere.

In just a few hours, you have successfully shifted the dynamics of your relationship. Instead of savoring the time you are spending together, you may waste an entire day feeling troubled and drawn apart from each other. What you have just done is initiate and enthrone the distance you feared so much. The responsible factor for this turn of events is not the situation itself - it is that critical inner voice that clouded your thoughts, distorted your perceptions, suggested bad opinions to you and, as a result, led you to a disastrous path.

When it comes to the issues you worry about so much in your relationship, what you don't know - and what your inner critic doesn't tell you - is that you are stronger and more resilient than you think. The reality is that you can handle the hurts, rejections, and disappointments that you are so afraid of. We are made in such a way that it is possible to absorb negative situations, heal from them, and deal with them. You are capable of experiencing pain and ultimately healing and coming out stronger. However, the mean coach in your head, that inner critical voice, more often than not puts you under pressure and makes reality look like a tragedy. It creates scenarios in your head that are non-existent and brings out threats that are not tangible. Even when, in reality, there are real issues and unhealthy situations, that inner voice in your head will magnify such situations and tear you apart in ways you do not deserve. It will completely misrepresent the reality of the situation and dampen your own resilience and determination. It will always give you unpleasant opinions and advice.

These critical voices you hear in your head are, however, formed as a result of your own unique experiences and what you have adapted to over time. When you feel anxious or insecure, there is a tendency to become overly attached and desperate in our actions. Possessiveness and control towards your partner set in. On the other hand, you may feel an intrusion in your relationship. You may begin to retreat from your partner and detach from your emotional desires. You may begin to act unforthcoming or withdrawn.

These patterns of responding to issues may stem out of your early attachment styles. These style patterns influence how you react to your needs and how you go about getting them met.

There are some critical inner voices that talk about you, your partner, and your relationships. These inner voices are formed out of early attitudes you were exposed to in your family, amongst your friends, or in society at large. Everyone's inner critic is different; however, there are some common critical inner voices.

Inner Voices that are Critical about the Relationship

- Most people end up getting hurt.
- Relationships never work out.

Inner Voices that are Critical about Your Partner

- He is probably cheating on you.
- You cannot trust her.
- Men are so insensitive, unreliable, and selfish.

Inner Voices about Yourself

- You are better off on your own.
- It is your fault if he gets upset.
- You always screw things up.
- You have to keep him interested.
- He does not really care about you.

When you listen to your inner voice, the resultant effect is an anxiety filled relationship, which can mar your love life in many ways. When you give in to this anxiety, you may stop feeling like the strong and independent person you were when you first started the relationship. This can make you thin out and fall apart, which further induces jealousy and insecurity. Attachment and neediness set in, and these put a strain on the relationship.

This anxiety disorder may begin to leave you feeling threatened in your relationship and you thus begin to dominate or control your partner. You find yourself setting rules for what they can or cannot do just to reduce your own insecurities. This may lead to a feeling of withdrawal and resentment from your partner.

When you allow yourself to be anxious in a relationship, you may begin to defend yourself by becoming cold and distant to protect yourself, and this can be traumatic for your partner. This distance can also stir up insecurity in your partner.

Sometimes, your response to anxiety is more akin to aggression. You may yell and scream at your partner without even realizing it. You have to consciously pay attention to how many of your actions are a direct response to your partner, and how often they are a response to your inner critical voice.

Chapter 23   Why and How Their Attachment Style Impacts Their Relationship

The evolutionary theory, in addition to its conceptual and empirical implications, is a valuable and important tool for understanding the nature of personalities, relations, and impact controls. Several growing number of research studies have been undertaken over the past two decades into the origins and associations of individual variations over adult attachment types. A significant drawback of previous studies is, however, that the effect of contexts on the speech of dependencies is not taken into consideration by many. This is surprising because evolutionary theory is essentially an interactionism theoretical framework "person by circumstance," likely deriving from the lack of methods that allow such a dynamic approach.

While substantial insights have also been obtained in the historical studies of the expression of attachment, there is currently little information as to how attachment types are expressed at the moment and how they are articulated in a real-life context.

Evolutionary theory is a philosophy that suggests that people are born with an inherent motivational mechanism (called the behavioral attachment mechanism), which is triggered in times of a real or symbolic danger, which causes the person to seek proximity in order to relieve anxiety and to gain a sense of protection. The key to the theory is, based on their accumulated story of experiences with attached personalities, that the individual constructs behavioral-affective representations or "personal working models." Such models help to analyze and to play an important role in controlling knowledge from the social environment over its entire life cycle.

The bulk of adult attachment work focuses on the forms and assessment of attachment. Overall, attachment style in terms of security and vulnerability can be conceptualized. Repeated experiences with attachment figures which are emotionally accessible and sensitive facilitate the build-up of a healthy personality type, with optimistic internal models and constructive techniques for coping with anxiety. Conversely, the risks of forming unhealthy attachment types that characterize any use of negative inner self and/or others constructs and the use of less appropriate regulatory approaches are repeated encounters with non-responsive and contradictory figures

While a large number of definitions and measures of relationship vulnerability are present, they are typically characterized in intimate relationships by high levels of concern and / or evasion. The fear regarding relationships reflects a desire for closeness and the concern to be excluded or removed from significant ones, while the avoidance of attachments indicates deep self-reliance and discomfort towards others. Both types of schemes include different secondary takeover strategies for the management of pain. People with depression with an attachment prefer to be using the hyper-activating (or optimizing) approach. In addition, previous empirical research has shown that relationship anxiety has been associated with higher negative emotional reactions, increased environmental threat identification, and negative psychological views.

In fact, individuals with stable attachment alone showed more positive effects than those with vulnerability. In addition, while the variation of their emotional status did not vary in both groups, participants with a safe style supported more severe positive mental states in all social environments, and participants with an unsecured style supported more severe negative emotional experiences, particularly when alone. The results of their research supported the idea that attachment types have a large impact on cognitive experiences, but the significant limitations of this analysis were that only observations were published that compare stable vs. vulnerable participants. Further analytical work is therefore required to investigate how stylistic relationship expressions are articulated in everyday life and how the interplay of attachment types with the environment produces specific experiential trends at the moment. Illustrating the significance of reactive attachment disorder in interactions with real-world encounters, potentially informed by the personality type of an individual, would illustrate the relevance of the attachment style form in the particular sense in which the individual is incorporated. Therefore, the recognition of changes in the style of attachments in the sense of social activities may improve our understanding of how relationship types work in the social setting.

marital satisfaction & the life cycle

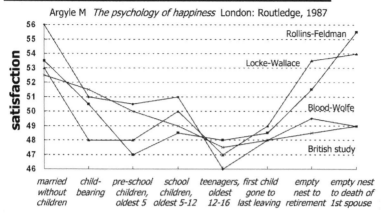

Argyle M *The psychology of happiness* London: Routledge, 1987

The emotional state of love is that researchers have known matured love over three centuries as one of the fundamental psychological needs of their absence, contributing to psychological deficits. Components of mature love are:

(1) Desire,

(2) Passion and

(3) Fellowship.

(1) Desire. Full-hearted romantic relationships build an atmosphere for development that ultimately motivates people to know more and make money. Everyone's self-knowledge, confidence, and mental wellbeing are improved during this relationship, to make a more established relationship. Instead, adolescent love appears to construct a social atmosphere that is evolutionarily adaptive. Intangible love is composed of:

(1) Strength,

(2) Possession,

(3) Security,

(4) Grace, and

(5) Immorality.

413

Such traits manifest in adolescent love as obsessive thoughts. The person whose trait of love can be called obsessive love is an individual that is finding it difficult trusting her / his partner and continuously testing him/her. This trait will surely result in negative consequences. Many psychologists claim that an addictive model of love is close to substance abuse. Obsessive love as a drug has detrimental implications for life, society, and family. In order to achieve the desired emotional impact, there is a need for a significantly increased attitude. If you try to avoid acting (e.g., feel helpless to lonely if not in a relationship, feel sorrowful and permanent, like withdrawing from alcohol), there is a subjective desire to keep up the course of your behaviors. There is a persistent inability or failure to decrease or regulate the conduct for a longer period of time than was expected.

Obsessive love can affect the dynamics and cultural effects of social learning. Developmental events, like the development of children's social attachments, can create obsessive affection. According to research, people are born in an attachment state called a psychobiological pattern. Through this program, a baby can remain close to adults and improve its chances of survival; the purpose of this program is to achieve health, trust, and security among children.

The attachments are of three styles:

- Free,
- Avoidable and
- Apathetic.

Three types are important in being attentive to children's needs in the early years of a child. Due to the theory of an antenna, a network of antenna attachment is not constrained to childhood and involves interpersonal interactions (e.g., families, romantic relationships, etc.).

You assess yourself to be gorgeous and important.

Ambivalent individuals have dysfunctional behavior and feeling. They relied heavily on others, they fear being left behind, and they fall in love with others. Misleading of individuals and less complexity relationships were recorded in avoiding subjects.

414

Both romantic couples often disagree. Even though disagreement is bound to happen, those who are extremely satisfied with the relationship vary greatly from each other. Conflict management is associated with higher happiness in relationships and greater social well-being. Greater relationship tension and reduced well-being are also correlated with a lack of dialogue.

As conflict has to do with important aspects of the interaction of families, it is essential to investigate how these particular conflict techniques occur. Annexation theory offers a consistent structure to explain how different types of conflict occur in the context of intimate relationships. While researchers have recorded clear connections between types of attachment and conflict behaviors, further clarification of the mechanisms that bind these two structures remains a significant area of study to establish explanatory procedures that may become the subject of therapeutic intervention.

Styles of attachment

Our attachment style influences everything from the choosing of our mate to the success of our relationships to the sad end. So it will help us to recognize our strengths and weaknesses in a relationship by understanding our attachment pattern.

In early childhood relationships, a sequence of attachment is developed and still works as a working prototype for adult relationships.

This attachment model affects how each one of us responds to and meets our needs. When a stable attachment pattern occurs, the individual is secure and self-confident and able to communicate comfortably and to meet his or her own desires and the needs of everyone else. However, if a person chooses a partner who fits the ill-adaptive pattern, he or she might most probably choose someone who does not have the right option to make him or her happy.

For example, if you have a nervous/obsessed attachment pattern, you must be with your spouse and be confident that you are still there to get close to him or her and have your needs met. They choose a person who is alone and hard to communicate with to support this view of reality. The individual who has a working model of discarding / evicting attachment appears to be far away, so his style is to behave like you have no one. He or she chooses someone who is more possessive or over-conscious.

The following are the four basic forms of attachment. Please note that these definitions are very general; not everyone has these features. Attachment styles are relatively smooth and can change subtly in relation to the attachment style of your partner.

Strong attachment – Adults firmly attached to their relationships tend to be better satisfied. Children with safe attachments see their parents as a stable foundation from which they can travel and discover the world on their own. A healthy adult has an equal relationship, feeling comfortable and closed with his or her spouse while allowing his or her spouse to move freely.

Chapter 24   Why They Act Irrationally

Love is just a big sprinkling of hormones in the brain which interrupt our normal way of behaving. It can feel crazy, distract us, and drive us wild. Love can be extremely tiring and awesomely beautiful all at the same time. When you are irrational, you are not able to listen to reason, logic, or apply common sense. You just want a particular need to be met, any way it can be.

Until that need is met, you act in terrific and unpredictable ways. What you must remember is that emotions form an important aspect of our lives, not only in influencing our wellness, but also in determining our relationships with people. There are times when negative emotions overwhelm you, despite how much you try to keep them in check. Emotions involve complex states of mind that affect the body as well as your external environment.

Your emotions are a perception of the events going on in and around you. These emotions cause you to portray one or more patterns of behavior. When you are upset by something or someone, you get angry and may lash out, and when something makes you overwhelmed and unhappy, you cry. In the same way, when you are experiencing the positive emotions of love, you may show affection and when something is funny, you express yourself by laughing.

The ability to both understand and control your emotional responses is an important skill that affects your relationship with others. If all you do is constantly express negative emotions, also known as negative energy, your relationships and even your health can be at great risk. Irrational behavior is a demonstration of intense emotion in a situation in which your partner does not understand why such strong emotion is necessitated.

Romantic relationships are an arena where emotions run wild, as do misunderstandings which are often caused by these emotions and their effects that lead to irrationality. The reason for this is because they are engaged in attachment relationships.

Attached relationship, if approached in the right way, can foster love, security and comfort. However, if the partners are not alive and responsive to each other's need, this kind of relationship can be a turbulent one.

When you feel that the security of your relationship is threatened, you may respond with strong emotions such as grief, loneliness, anger, and disappointment. These responses, if intensely expressed, can seem irrational.

Science might not be able to tell you exactly what love is; however, it will tell you what love will do. When in love, the sensory, molecular, and organic chemistry processes concerned as well as sexual union have the tendency to make people do foolish things.

Attraction, romantic feelings, and aroused love that sometimes happens within the first stages of a relationship are characterized by obsessive behavior, targeted attention, and intense desire. This is due to the fact that you are in high spirits when the relationship is going well - however, terrible mood swings follow when it is not.

This is the stage of affection when we see folks act the most irrational, impulsive, and emotional, showing direct similarities to the emotional mind frame of addiction.

The feeling of a real bond with somebody, or rather the sense of calm, peace, and stability that this bond causes, is attributed to the hormones that are discharged through childbirth, milk production, and orgasms.

So however sensible a couple's "chemistry" is, it will still have some rather dangerous behavioral and emotional results. Love is as natural to human life as breathing. Attempting to prevent it out of fear or discomfort is suffocating.

Irrational Behaviors that are caused by Anxiety

Anxiety alters your brain chemistry and thus triggers behaviors and emotions that under normal circumstances would never even occur to you. However, when anxiety takes over, all bets are off. Here are some of the behaviors that can occur when an uncomfortable situation or stressful trigger crops up in your relationship:

Excessive, Obsessive Worrying
We all worry - it is natural. Life is unpredictable, which is one of the reasons anxiety is so prevalent. However, when that worry begins to

overtake your mind to the extent that you cannot think about anything else, there is a problem.

You might, after seeing a suspicious text, feel a twinge of worry before thinking about the situation rationally. My partner loves me, I have complete trust in them, and I know that they will not hurt me. There is no reason to jump to conclusions.

Of course, if you are dealing with anxiety, this situation triggers more than a moment of worry. Your mind will suddenly be filled with bits and pieces of messages you've seen in the past, whether innocent or not, and you'll go over all of your partner's actions in your mind to try to identify and moments where you felt suspicious. Worry turns into panic, which leads you into the territory of the irrational. If you have seen many signs of cheating, it is not irrational to worry. However, if this is the first and there has never been a spark of an indication in the past, that is when the behavior begins to look irrational. No matter the outcome, worrying to the point of panic will not give you the answers you seek. To stop worrying, you need to let go of the things you cannot control.

Unwarranted Irritability
We get irritated as humans. That is okay! You might have had a bad day, or you are hungry, or any of a dozen other reasons. Irritability is not irrational until it is born from anxiety. The fight or flight response that kicks up all kinds of hormones can put us on edge, leading to excessive irritation from no cause other than anxiety. The unfortunate thing about irritability is that it is so easy to direct at loved ones. When irrational irritability springs up and causes you to lash out at your partner, it can be difficult to explain why you did so. You may not even know yourself where the mood is coming from, which can lead you to conclude that you are just mad at your partner for some reason and now seemed like a good time to express that anger. Your partner will not know what they did, and before you know it a rift has formed in your relationship. The cause of the initial anxiety is no longer of any concern because the resulting irritation is what did all the damage.

Physical Aggression
Again, the fight or flight response kicks into gear and triggers nearly automatic reactions, some of which are violent. When you feel threatened or in danger, your body takes over to protect you. When you are in a situation that makes you anxious, if the severity is high then you are more

likely to express that anxiety in a physical way. To protect yourself emotionally, your arm yourself physically. It may not make perfect sense to you even though you are the one displaying the behavior - that is what makes it irrational.

Moping

This might seem like a less drastic behavior than irritability or aggression, but it can be detrimental, nonetheless. Moping is characterized by sadness, depression, and a lack of energy. This comes as a result of anxiety causing a shutdown in your mind and body. Your limbs become lethargic, as does your mind, and this depression of the internal function causes sadness to emerge from seemingly nowhere. The only thought you may have is "I don't feel like it," no matter what "it" is. This depressive mood can strain a relationship, especially if your partner does not know if they did something wrong or why you are feeling the way you are. You may not even know.

Compulsive Behavior

Anxiety is often at the root of obsessive-compulsive disorder. You desire to be able to control some aspect of the world, so you develop routines and habits that offer you some semblance of order. The uncertainty found in relationships can lead to anxious thoughts about the future, so you engage in compulsive behaviors that give you a way to control a small part of your life and future. These behaviors can be almost anything, but some of the more common ones include checking the locks several times, ensuring the burner is off multiple times before leaving the house (even if the stove wasn't used), needing to keep everything straightened or in a specific order, and more.

Agoraphobia

If you never leave the house, there are fewer things that will trigger your anxiety, right? Severe anxiety can lead to agoraphobia, or the fear of going somewhere that may lead to embarrassment or cause panic. Crowded places are particularly troublesome to those afflicted. While it is irrational to always expect the worse, it is absolutely understandable. It is hard to put yourself out there, and this fear of the unknown can make you never want to leave the relative safety of home. Whether you have already met someone or would like to, it can be difficult to start or maintain a relationship when you never want to leave the house.

Chapter 25 Tips and Tricks to Resolve Disputes, Reconnect, and Address Anxiety

Here, you will learn about simple tips you can use to resolve disputes with your spouse. Usually, after years of marriage, the emotional and physical bond that partners share tends to fade away slowly. To avoid this, you must work on putting in the necessary effort required to keep the relationship going; not just going, the relationship must thrive. When you are in a happy marriage, you will be happier in general.

At times, perhaps the best thing you can do is not to say anything. Give your partner a hug or maybe even gently pat them on the back to allow them to know you are there for them. Leaving a couple of things unsaid is actually a good idea. Whenever you are wrong, you must admit it. However, there might have been times when you were right, but by merely holding your tongue and by not saying anything, you can save yourself an unnecessary fight. Once your partner is calm, test the waters before you restart the conversation.

Even the darkest cloud has a silver lining. Make it a point to look for any positive aspect of the relationship and stop concentrating solely on the negative ones. Couples who share positive communication are usually more satisfied with their relationships. It takes about five positive communications to undo the impact of one negative communication. Keep this ratio in mind whenever you are communicating with your partner.

If the bond you share with your partner is strong enough, then your relationship can withstand pretty much anything that happens to you. To do this, you must concentrate on the positive aspects of your relationship. Always look for something good you can say. If you want, feel free to use any positive affirmations you feel like. If you both are in trouble, by telling your partner everything will be okay, and you will be there to support them along the way, this works as a positive affirmation. In the midst of a fight, stop for a moment, and tell your partner how grateful you are to have them in your life. I am sure this will certainly put an end to the argument you are having.

Whenever in a conflict, you must never lose perspective. When in a foul mood, even the slightest thing can make you angry. In such times, everything may seem dull and gloomy to you. A lot of couples tend to talk about taking time away from each other or even calling it quits the minute they run into any obstacles. Well, obstacles are part of life. You cannot go through life unscathed. Your success depends on how well you handle those obstacles. There are some things you can avoid, and some you cannot. Learning to deal with obstacles will certainly save your relationship. Remember, whenever you hit a rough patch, all you must do is adapt and overcome the problem you are facing. If the issue at hand is rather petty and you know it, then merely ignore it. Some issues are just not worth losing your peace of mind over or hurting your relationship.

If you know your partner's emotional state of mind was your fault, then you must apologize. The bigger the mistake you committed; the bigger the apology you need to offer. It is not merely about saying sorry, but you must mean it as well. If you say you are sorry, and then keep making the same mistake over and over again, your apology will be worthless. You can always fix any mistakes you make in life. Do not allow your ego to prevent you from doing the right thing. If you make a mistake, own up. It is okay to make mistakes, provided you learn from them. Do not try to lie or try to talk your way out of it. If you did something wrong, then the least you can do for your partner in such a situation is be truthful and honest.

It really is not unusual for couples that are passionate to find themselves riding an emotional roller coaster from time to time. It would be better to let the past stay in the past; this will give the couple a fresh start to begin things. Letting resentments build is not really good, and even the smallest of altercations can create a really big fight. There really is no point in holding onto unnecessary fights and arguments; all it does is build resentment toward your partner. Keep short accounts of any fights you had. For the sake of your mental wellbeing and the health of your relationship, learn to let go. You do not have to hold onto everything and learning to let go of petty issues will be quite helpful. However, I am not suggesting that you must repress your emotions. If you have an issue with something, talk it out, and express yourself. That said, it will not do you any good if you hold onto the fight you and your partner had over three years ago because your partner forgot to load the dishwasher! You cannot control much in life, but the two things you can always control are the way you think and feel.

If things start getting tense and a plan that you or your partner has made isn't working out, then it would be good if you could offer alternative suggestions instead of just saying you knew the plan wouldn't work out. Give your partner some time to calm down, and then you can probably suggest that it would be good if you two can brainstorm together to come up with a solution. Make sure that in a tough situation, at least one of you is calm because this will definitely help resolve any issues. You can regroup and think things through before proceeding with a particular idea.

If you notice that any argument, you are having with your partner is getting quite heated, then it is time to take a break from the conversation. At times, merely putting some physical distance between the two of you can help. Give your partner some space and take some space for yourself. Maybe you can draw a nice path between you and your partner and even play some soft music to calm things down. Or you can go for a walk or jog if you want. Apart from this, even engaging in a sport together can help diffuse the tension in the situation.

Chapter 26   Managing Your Jealousy in a Relationship

Jealousy can unfortunately ruin even the best relationships. It can be a powerful signal that it is time for you to change or risk losing an otherwise fulfilling relationship. Jealousy can be a good checklist to better understand your underlying feelings, taking immediate action, and protect your relationship from experiencing the disastrous fallout of your jealous thoughts or behavior. Here are some of the most foolproof techniques to help you tackle jealousy and insecurity in relationships with ease.

Question Yourself Each Time

Each time you find yourself feeling even remotely jealous, question the underlying feeling behind the complex emotion of jealousy. Is the jealousy a consequence of my anger, anxiety or fear? What is it about this situation that makes me jealous? When you question your jealously critically, you are a few steps away from taking constructive steps to convert a cloud of negativity into a bundle of positivity.

Be Open about Your Insecurities

Discussing your insecurities with your partner will help you create a frank and open communication channel. Rather than doing and saying crazy things to your partner, be upfront and share your feelings. Say something similar to "I apologize for bothering you regarding your friendship with ABC, but it is not my lack of trust in you. I simply feel insecure about it."

Admitting it is you and not the other person goes a long way in resolving your relationship issues over hurling accusations at your partner. Together, you can work better on your insecurities if you both acknowledge it and take active steps to eliminate it.

Learn to Trust People

Learn to consciously get into the habit of trusting people more. Choose a trusting disposition over a distrustful attitude. Unless you have absolutely concrete evidence about someone, take their word for it. Going around snooping, stalking your partner and behaving like a suspicious maniac only harms your relationship further. Rather, if there really is no reason to be suspicious other than a feeling of insecurity or jealously, let it go.

Get to the Root of Your Feelings

It can be really hard to objectively assess why you feel pangs of jealously each time someone compliments your partner, or he/she speaks warmly with his/her colleagues. It can be highly tempting to blame another person for your emotions. However, getting to the root of your jealousy by being more self-aware is the foundation to free yourself from its shackles. Take a more compassionate and objective look at the origination of your jealousy. Think about the potential causes for feelings of insecurity.

For instance, if you find yourself being increasingly jealous of your partner; know why you feel it. Is it because you do not want to lose him/her? Is it because your previous relationship ended due to a similar reason? Do you suffer from a false sense of self-entitlement that your partner's time belongs only to you? Do you feel what you feel because of a sense of inadequacy that constantly makes you think "you aren't good enough?" Once you identify the underlying reasons causing feelings of jealousy and insecurity, it becomes easier to deal with your behavior.

Write Down Your Deepest Thoughts

Journaling is known to be one of the most effective techniques for bringing to the fore your deepest feelings and emotions. It helps you discover multiple layers of your personality to achieve greater self-awareness. For instance, you may constantly harbor feelings of insecurity because you were raised by neglectful parents or you may never feel you are "good enough" because you were raised by parents who had extremely high and unreasonable expectations of you.

People who have been neglected in their childhood often feel they are not worthy enough to be loved. This, in turn, causes them to think that their partner is seeking someone more worthy or deserving of love than them, which creates feelings of insecurity. Writing down may help you discover certain events, circumstances and facets which may directly be responsible for your irrational behavior. Once you have nailed down underlying feelings behind the jealousy, its way simpler to manage it.

Learn from Your Jealousy

Jealousy can be converted into a learning or inspiration if you channelize it productively. For instance, if your partner plays the guitar really well and finds himself/herself the cynosure of all eyes at a party, you can up your skills, too, by learning from him/her or signing up for guitar lessons. Instead of wallowing in defeatist self-pity, you have transformed your negative feelings into something positive.

Jealousy Does not Mean Something Will Actually Happen

We need to understand that our jealous hunches do not necessarily mean the act is actually occurring. Just because we fear something is going to happen does not mean it will happen. A majority of the times, our fears are totally unfounded and not even remotely close to coming true. Just because your partner is somewhere else, and you fear he/she is with someone else, does not really mean he/she is actually proposing marriage on a date. Understand the difference between thoughts and actual events. The make-believe imaginations of our destructive mind are often far from reality.

Paranoia or replaying a worst-case scenario is common among people suffering from jealousy or insecurity. They imagine things that have no basis in reality. For instance, your partner may call or visit an ex to express his/her condolences when the ex's mother passes away. This does not in any way imply that your partner is still hooked to the ex. However, you may find yourself imagining terrible things that may be the result of sheer jealousy and paranoia.

Rather than imagining negative things, try shifting the focus of how wonderful your partner is to be considerate and pleasant with an ex. This might be the very reason that made you fall in love with him/her. See what you did there? You shifted your feelings from insecurity to pride, from untrue suspicions to a positive reality.

Get Rid of Past Relationship Garbage

A strong reason why you are always paranoid about your current partner cheating on you can be traced back to a prior relationship. You may have had an ex-partner horribly cheat on you with your best friend. The betrayal may have had such a severe impact that you view every relationship in a similar distrustful light.

However, understand that your current partner has nothing to do with your relationship. He/she should not have to bear the brunt of what someone else did. Painting everyone with the same brush can be a disastrous mistake in any relationship. There is a solid reason your prior relationship did not last, and you should leave the garbage of your prior relationship where it belongs – in the trash can.

Focus Your Energies Elsewhere

Rather than obsessing over who your partner is cheating you with, try to develop interests outside of your relationship. Do not make it the nucleus of your existence even if it means a lot to you. Pursue your hobbies, be a part of local clubs, volunteer for good causes, be active in the local community, play a sport, learn different languages, take fun dance/aerobics sessions, be a part of a local club – anything that shifts your focus from overwhelming jealous thoughts to productive channelization of energy.

Surround Yourself with Meaningful Relationships

People are often so wrapped up in their romantic relationship that there is a tendency to distance ourselves from all other relationships. We believe in spending every waking minute of our lives with our partners. This only leads to a greater feeling of fear and insecurity because we realize that once this relationship ceases to exist, we have no other meaningful relationship as our safety net. We tend to develop greater feelings of insecurity and jealousy when we have no one to fall back on.

It helps to not make a single relationship the center of your universe and develop several meaningful friendships. Do not distance your close friends after getting into a relationship. Talk to them, spend time with them, do fun things together (that you probably did in school or college), have lunch dates, travel with them and more. This will give you a life outside of your and your partner's time together. Once you have a momentous life outside your relationship, you will be less likely to wallow in self-pity and self-induced sulks. You will always have someone to talk to if you are surrounded by family or friends who understand and love you unconditionally.

Mindfulness for Managing Your Emotions

Mindfulness is a great way to calm your nerves and manage runaway emotions. Tune into your physical and mental self by identifying your feelings, thoughts and emotions by taking deep breaths. Try and detach yourself from overpowering negative emotions such as jealousy and insecurity. Every time you find yourself overcome with thoughts of jealousy or insecurity, practice mindful meditation.

Find a quiet corner that is free from distraction, sit in a comfortable position, and clear your mind by eliminating all thoughts and take deep breaths. Focus only on the present and your deep breathing without allowing your mind to wander. If you find your mind drifting, gently bring it back to the present by concentrating on your bodily sensations. Daily meditation sessions can help you break free from ugly thoughts and behavior patterns.

Chapter 27   Fear of Abandonment and Conflicts in Relationships

A fear of abandonment is a complex phenomenon in psychology that is believed to originate from childhood loss or injury. This worry has been examined from a variety of perspectives. Concepts behind why anxiety of abandonment occurs consist of disturbances in the regular advancement of little ones' social and mental capacities, past connection and life experiences, and direct exposure to certain norms and also concepts.

Although it is not the main phobia, the fear of desertion is probably among the most common and most damaging worries of all. Individuals with the fear of abandonment might tend to display necessary actions and also thought patterns that affect their connections, inevitably leading to the abandonment they dread becoming a reality. This anxiety can be ravaging. Recognizing this worry is the very first step toward solving it.

The worry of abandonment is the frustrating worry that individuals close to you will undoubtedly leave. Anyone can create anxiety of abandonment. It can be deeply rooted in a stressful experience you had as a youngster or a stressful relationship in the adult years. If you fear desertion, it can be virtually difficult to keep healthy and balanced relationships. This incapacitating concern can lead you to wall surface yourself off to prevent getting hurt. Or you may be unintentionally undermining partnerships.

The first step in dealing with your anxiety is to recognize why you feel in this manner. You should be able to resolve your issues and problems on your own or with treatment. But the fears of desertion may additionally be part of a personality disorder that requires treatment. Continue analysis to explore the reasons and also long-lasting effects of a worry of abandonment and even when you ought to seek assistance.

Signs of a Fear of Abandonment

Numerous people have a problem with anxiety. Nearly 10% of individuals in the U.S. have some type of phobia. When it involves connections, its resulting habits consist of:

- You fast to affix, also to not available partners or relationships.
- You are reluctant to commit fully, as well as have had very few long-lasting partnerships.
- You might be quick to move on just to guarantee that you do not obtain also affixed.
- You aim to please. For some ladies, a study has also located an increase in the desire to have undesirable sex.
- As soon as in a partnership, you stay, despite how undesirable the relationship is.
- You are often hard to please as well as nitpicky.
- Emotional affection is hard for you.
- You feel insecure and unworthy of love.
- You locate it tough to rely on individuals.
- Being jealous of everybody you satisfy is not an odd sensation to you.
- Feelings of separation anxiousness are extreme.
- Feelings of underlying stress and anxiety and also clinical depression are very common to you.
- You often tend to overthink points and also work hard to identify the concealed significance in everything.
- You are hypersensitive to objection.
- You have quenched anger and also control issues.
- Self-blame prevails for you.

Sorts of concern of abandonment

You may be afraid that someone you like is going to leave and not come back physically. You may fear that a person will undoubtedly desert your psychological requirements either can hold you in relationships with moms and dad, partner, or a good friend.

Fear of psychological desertion

It may be less apparent than physical truancy. However, it is not much less stressful. We all have psychological needs. When those demands are not fulfilled, you may feel unappreciated, hated, as well as separated. You can feel quite alone, even when you remain in connection with somebody existing. If you have experienced psychological desertion in the past,

430

primarily as a youngster, you may reside in continuous fear that it will certainly take place once more.

The anxiety of abandonment in children

It is regular for babies as well as toddlers to experience a separation anxiousness phase. They may sob, howl, or refuse to allow when a parent or critical caregiver needs to leave. Children have a hard time understanding when or if that person will certainly return. As they begin to understand that enjoyed ones do return, they outgrow their anxiety. For a lot of kids, this takes place by their third birthday celebration.

Desertion anxiousness in partnerships

You may be frightened to let yourself be susceptible to a company. You may have depended on issues as well as stress excessively regarding your relationship. That can make you suspicious. In time, your anxiousness can cause the various other people to drawback, bolstering the cycle.

Signs and symptoms of fear of abandonment

If you fear desertion, you may recognize a few of these signs and also indications:

- overly conscious criticism
- problem trusting in others
- trouble making friends unless you can be confident, they like you
- taking severe procedures to avoid being rejected or separation
- a pattern of unhealthy connections
- getting affixed to individuals also swiftly, after that going on equally as promptly
- problem dedicating to a relationship
- functioning as well hard to please the other individual
- blaming yourself when things do not exercise
- remaining in a connection even if it is not healthy and balanced for you

431

Abandonment problems in relationships

If you fear desertion in your present partnership, it might result from having been physically or emotionally abandoned in the past. For example:

- As a teen, you may have experienced the fatality or desertion of a parent or caretaker.
- You might have experienced parental forget.
- You might have been turned down by your peers.
- You experienced a prolonged health problem of an enjoyed one.
- A charming partner might have left you instantly or behaved in an undependable fashion.
- Such occasions can result in fear of desertion.

Chapter 28   Life Cycle of Relationships, Advice and Tips for a Better Couples Relationship

One of the most important things that a spouse or partner of an anxious person has to recognize is that their role in the process is as a supporter. It may be the case that you know your significant other better than anyone else, but that still leaves the task of dealing with anxiousness primarily to them rather than to you. This does not mean that you should leave the anxious symptoms to eat away at the person until it damages their life irreparably, but it means that your place in the big picture should be recognized both by you and by your partner.

The role of the supporter is an important one. The goal here is to provide you with tips that you can use help you fulfill this role in the best way that you can. Sure, sitting on the sidelines can be frustrating sometimes, but a solid supporter is just what your partner or spouse needs right now. And if you are the one dealing with anxiousness, then these tips will help you get an understanding of the sorts of things that your partner can do for you.

Tip 1: Understand that overcoming anxiety is a process (anxiety is not something that someone will snap out of)

Anxiety is not like having the common cold. It is not something that you get and which you will experience resolution from with the snap of a finger. Anxiety disorders should be thought of as conditions that require treatment. What this means for the significant other of an anxious person is that you should be realistic about your partner's anxiety. They are not going to snap out of their anxiety, and it is more than a little unfair of you to expect them to. As a supporter of an anxious person, it is critical to recognize that you will be helping them through the long process of overcoming their illness.

Tip 2: Be conscious of your own dysfunctional thoughts or preconceived notions

Anxiousness is characterized by a cavalcade of dysfunctional thoughts that people often are not conscious that they are having. Unfortunately for the significant others of anxious persons, they can have their own spiral of dysfunctional thoughts that can impact the way that they

433

perceive and interact with their anxious partner. The meaning here is not that the partner is necessarily at risk for worry, but merely that the partner should recognize how their interaction with their partner can be colored by notions that they have about their condition (including subconscious stigma that men and women often have towards conditions of the mind).

Tip 3: Provide reassurance that things are going to turn out all right

One of the most important things that someone supporting someone else through anxiety (or any condition) can do is to provide reassurance that things are going to turn out all right. This does not mean telling a lie. If someone has a terminal illness like stage IV cancer, it is obviously important to recognize exactly what that means. But honest reassurance in the case of anxiousness is a little different. Anxiety can and does frequently get better, so reminding your partner of that can place a positive thought in their head that can be an important part of creating real change in their life.

Tip 4: Encourage your partner to get help

A difficult reality for some partners of anxious people to accept is that it is not their job to steer their partner in the direction they think they should go. We have established that anxiety disorders are conditions that typically do not get better without treatment, but that does not mean that it is your role as their supporter to force them to get treatment or to dictate to them the form that the treatment should take.

Intervention-type maneuvers can be problematic in mental health. This is especially true in the case of anxiousness, where the individual may already be inclined to have a suspicious or fearful approach to others or the world in general. Forcing or cornering your partner into treatment is not a good idea for anxious people. What you can do is educate yourself about the help that is available for their condition and encourage them to get help. That is really all that you can do.

Tip 5: Be patient as your significant other moves through their condition

It is important to be patient when dealing with a person that has a mental health condition and this is just as true of anxiety as it is of other conditions like depression. Recall that anxiety disorders include conditions as divergent as GAD, specific phobias, and obsessive-compulsive disorder. The point here is that some of these conditions can be very debilitating for the individual dealing with and very frustrating for the partner or family member who is around it. For your own sanity (and for the sake of your partner) it is important to be patient. Change will happen slowly, and it will help you to keep this in mind.

Tip 6: Provide on-going education and support to your partner

In this case, being supportive means being someone that your significant other can go to when they need help. Again, the goal here is not to force your partner to do something that they may not be ready to do but to support them as they decide to make a change and take steps towards making that change. As a supportive partner, you can provide ongoing education for yourself about anxiety and related conditions like depression and you can even find ways to pass this information along to your partner.

Anxious individuals can have exaggerated or otherwise excessive or unnecessary reactions to stimuli, so it is important that you and your partner both recognize that you are occupying a supportive role. If your partner feels that you are attempting to manipulate them or push them in a particular direction, they may begin to mistrust you and avoid you. Therefore, it is important to approach your partner's anxious symptoms from the standpoint of educating both yourself and them on this subject.

Tip 7: Recognize that no one understands your partner's anxiety more than your partner

As much as you may educate yourself about anxiousness, no one is better poised to understand your partner's anxiety than they are. Sure, you may be around them for several hours of the day and you may feel that you may see aspects of their anxiety that they may seem unconscious of, but as you are not experiencing what they are and are not inside their head to know what the triggers are, you perhaps do not understand their condition as well as you might think. Use this as an opportunity to let your partner educate you about their worries, not the other way around.

Tip 8: Be available, not overbearing

It is easy to fall into the trap of being overbearing when you are in a relationship and you notice that your partner needs help with something. You may find that you have an overwhelming desire to help them, and perhaps you feel that you are able to see matters from a vantage point that they may not see. Even if that is the case, your partner does have the ability and the right to make decisions for themselves. Loved one or not, you do not necessarily have the right to force them to do as you want them to do if they are not a danger to themselves or others. If you are interested in maintaining a loving relationship with your significant other, you should focus on being available when they need support rather than overbearing.

Tip 9: Take your partner's comments seriously

One of the ways that you learn the character of your partner's anxiousness (and gain a deep sense of what they are going through) is by talking to them. Your partner's anxiety is just that, their anxiety, and you need to leave it to them to clue you in on how they are feeling and why. Therefore, it is important as a supportive partner to talk to your partner and to exercise active listening. Just as your anxious partner may hang on to your every word, you need to learn to pay attention to your partner's words. When your partner tells you something about themselves or what they are going through, take it seriously.

Tip 10: Remember that empathy is important

Sympathy is a word that many people understand, although they do not always show it. Sympathy involves feeling compassion and tolerance for others, a feeling that comes from a deep understanding of where the other person is coming from. We can show sympathy for others through our words, our actions, or even by our facial expressions. But empathy is something different. Empathy involves sharing the feelings of others: actually experiencing what they are experiencing. Although having true empathy for someone with a mental condition may be fraught with danger, this is something that many partners are able to do, and their relationships can be improved through it.

Therefore, having empathy for your partner means that you recognize that their anxiety is not just an illness. You also need to understand that what they are dealing with in some ways may be part of them. They may have dealt with anxiousness in some way or another for most of their life and they may not understand how to live without their anxious, obsessive, or compulsive behaviors. By truly coming to experience the world the way that they do, you are able to be a real supporter: someone who is able to deal with their highs and lows right along with them.

Chapter 29   Learning How to Listen to Your Partner

Good conversation is not about just what you are doing, but when you are doing it. We all know a conversation consists of two people who talk in exchange, sharing knowledge for mutual benefit and (hopefully) enjoyment.

Unfortunately, in the hope of knowing them too many of us are not really listening to our discussion partner. Really, we continue to listen only so that we know when we can take our own place in the spotlight next time without being too rude!

This means that two people may have what seems to be a conversation, but in fact it is a simple game of "When do I get to talk next? "Obviously, this kind of" conversation "is a total waste of time because no one gets the chance to know anything new, and there is no real relationship.

Many of us are not only bad listeners, but we fail to recall what other people tell us. Speaker and communications specialist Julian Treasure states that while we spend about 60 percent of our overall speaking time listening to other people, we do not really pay attention.

On average, we retain just 25 percent of what we hear. He claims that over the years we have slowly lost our ability to listen at high quality. Why? For what? Technology has, in short, made us lazy.

Since we've become accustomed to using copies of material, books, images, and so on, we subconsciously assume it doesn't really matter if we're listening around for the first time, because we can play or read it again later.

Of course, the trouble is that you cannot just fill in the blanks for a conversation and Google it later on. In this moment you need to be listening and paying attention.

How to Practice Directing Your Attention

Luckily, you can retrain your brain to tune in, and pay attention to every sound in your world. Close your eyes and imagine how many different sounds "channels" or "streams" you can hear at any given moment.

Give them labels-" talking men," "window rain, "and so on. This strengthens the willingness to stay focused on what someone else says. Practice this exercise every day for several minutes and you will soon find a change in your ability to concentrate.

What kind of listening do you need to do?

Were you aware that there are many ways we can listen to each other? Such methods are called role listening. We may participate in critical versus empathic listening, reductive versus expansive listening and active versus passive listening while we listen.

Many of us have heard about active and passive listening – and it has been said that active listening is usually what we should be doing – but listening is a little more complicated than that. For example, you could adopt a critical, reductive, and active role in any given conversation.

When you listen from a strategic position you are evaluating the truth behind a case. For instance, if someone tells you about the new phone they have just purchased and how their features make it better than all the other models on the market, you might be able to judge their points while they're talking.

You may wonder the does the phone have the biggest screen size, the fastest processor, etc. In this sort of scenario, it scans every piece of knowledge and you draw your own conclusions.

By contrast empathic listening is the art of honoring feelings over bare reality. If you have an empathetic approach of listening, the main aim is to help others express their feelings-simply by being present and paying attention.

By focusing on the emotions of others, you get a better understanding of their thoughts and behaviors. It will come up in your facial expression, body language and tone of voice. You can also experience a sense of comfort when you are listening style is a good fit for the topic of discussion and the other person's needs.

The disparity between reductive listening and expansive listening must also be acknowledged. You will engage in a reduction listening approach by listening to others with the hope that they can get to the most important points as soon as possible.

The listening posture is useful in high pressure situations and when faced with direct facts. For example, a surgical nurse who listens at the operating room to the instructions of the lead physician will participate in reductional listening. We need to hone on the facts as quickly as possible and then act upon it.

It is not necessary to minimize listening if a speaker does not really know what he thinks, what he needs to say or even how he feels. For this sort of situation you have to take another approach. You ought to sit calmly with the speaker as they work through their thoughts and feelings, rather than waiting for the other person to get straight to the point like you would when you are doing a reductional listening.

Expansive listening is similar to empathic listening in the sense that both positions value the speaker's feelings, but the former is more focused on finding insight than on providing an emotional outlet for others.

The most famous are the last pair of positions-active versus passive listening. In brief, active listening refers to the process of deliberately trying to hear what the other person is saying and to respond in an encouraging way, perhaps by summing up and asking questions.

In contrast, passive listening takes no effort. When you adopt a passive stance, you can take some of the information in, even if you do not hear it or completely understand it, you are not too bothered. Popular wisdom holds that active listening is often the preferred option. That is definitely not a bad law to live by. No-one was ever insulted, after all, because everyone listened so well! Yet, occasionally, passive listening is all it takes.

You need to sharpen your listening skills before you even think about other people's answers. Have you ever spoken to someone whose body is there, but they are not? Amnesty, aren't they?

Bad communicators believe "listening" is merely the act of waiting for their turn to speak all while writing their answer mentally. That is a grave error. Listening is so much more than that – it is a way to give someone else the opportunity to express their thoughts and opinions, create emotional intimacy and display empathy.

Listening is not just about allowing another person the ability to vocalize what is on their minds, while that is important in it's own right. Listening also reflects the first step towards personal progress.

Psychotherapist Carl Rogers, one of the 20th century's most influential psychologists, noted that when someone gives us the opportunity to think about what happened to us and how we feel about it, we begin to understand the best way to improve our emotions and behaviors.

Although it may be helpful to take advice from someone else, if we sort out ourselves through our issues, we are more likely to improve for the better. Some of the most important ways of doing this is being able to communicate openly to an informed audience.

Keep your tongue and give them the space they need if your conversation partner rambles, or if their words do not seem to make sense. Before implementing a strategy, they may want to speak to some other people first, or they might need to analyze the problem in their own time. Do not want to get angry! Extend the kindness you wish to earn in exchange to others.

Top tips that will make you an outstanding listener

1. To encourage them to keep talking, use non-intrusive verbal and non-verbal gestures: Nodding and saying, "Uh huh" and "I see" are brief, unobtrusive gestures that facilitate more disclosure. Silence is all right too – occasionally someone needs a couple of moments to collect their thoughts before continuing the discussion. Give them some room.

2. Let them continue until they run out of steam: I was shocked to discover when I learned to listen properly that a lot of people really want someone to slow down and hear what they have to say. This is particularly true if they feel frustrated, upset or need to work through an issue.

3. Do not play the role of armchair psychologist: Everybody is a psychologist to some degree. We all want to come up with our own hypotheses as to why so-and-so is so mad all the time.

Do not worry about their personal motives or why they act in a particular way when someone shares sensitive details with you. You are going to come off as a bit too nosy at best. At worst, your partner in the conversation would feel patronized and furious. Thank you.

4. Do not disturb unsolicited advice: even though you were in the same position or faced the same issues as someone else, do not suggest your

suggestions or solutions until you have asked them to do so. There are few items that are more irritating than unwelcome feedback or advices.

Try to resist the temptation to remind them you know exactly what they are doing. You just do not, to put it plainly. Two people may have similar experiences, but their styles of personality, their culture, and past life events ensure they will not feel the same emotions.

When your conversation partner asks for your feedback, go ahead-but take a look at their answer. If they seem open to your suggestions, go ahead. If, however, they begin to frown, cross their arms, or offer some sign that your advice is not helpful or welcoming, then pause and ask if they want you to proceed.

Note, they have no duty to obey your advice. Set aside your ego. When you have invested it is up to the other person to make their next step strategic. In addition, they will not be sharing the whole story, so they may need to consider other facts so factors when drawing up an action plan.

4. Re-phrase the words of someone else, but do not parrot them again: you might have learned that repeating the words of others again to them indicates you listened. That is right-to a point. There is a fine line between expressing awareness and quoting others verbatim.

Chapter 30   Setting a Goal for a Healthy Relationship

For relationships to succeed, like in every area of life, you need to know what you want. While out of dumb luck you can come upon a successful relationship, it helps to be clear about your target. This clarification can be used to point you in the generally correct direction and guide you along the way.

Broadly speaking, what makes for a stable bond in childhood always makes for a safe adult relationship. So you should think of relationships as having the following three basic characteristics: emotional availability: Children need to be physically and emotionally close to their parents to make them feel safe, but adult relationships are more dependent on emotionally close partners. Although separations and romantic long-distance relationships can trigger a strain, they are not necessarily deal-breakers. Partners must accept each other's needs and be responsive to them. When your partner remains emotionally distant or aggressive, you are likely to feel isolated, ignored or discarded, and you may doubt your worth as an individual.

Secure haven: Just as a child runs back to his mother when threatened or upset, partners in a stable relationship turn to each other in tough times when they need reassurance or support. Since life often requires at least some pain and fatiguing challenges, it is vital to have a partner who is willing to provide support, aid and relief from those problems. The problems of life are less overcome by people who know they have this trustworthy "bridge in a storm." Unfortunately, if your partner dismisses or criticizes then you will not turn to him; or if you turn to him, you will eventually feel insulted.

Secure basis: To feel fulfilled in life and truly loved in a relationship, it is important for people to be able to pursue the desires of their hearts — or even just to be able to explore what those desires might be. Healthy partnerships are ships where partners are promoting and supporting these activities.

When you think about these attributes of a healthy partnership, note that in order to build them, all partners will work together. Partners must be able to agree that is necessary for emotional availability; security and relaxation, providing a safe refuge in times of trouble; and supportive, making the relationship a stable base from which to explore the world. While you are probably more worried about a partner being able to give you these "gifts," it is equally vital for him to be able to accept them, as an open reciprocal giving-and-take nurtures relationship. In the same way, it is important for you to be able to give and receive these items.

What to Look for in a Partner

The person best qualified to be there for you in this way technically speaking has the attributes mentioned below. I offer this with the qualification that someone whose characteristics do not match parts of this list could satisfy your needs. That is perfect. This is intended only as a rough guideline — as something to consider (though seriously considered) while you are looking for a new partner or evaluating how well the person beside you is meeting your needs. This being the case, you want a partner who is:

Securely attached and mature: Since these people are confident with themselves and their relationships, they are able to be emotionally intimate, as well as continuing to pursue independent, personal interests with themselves and with their partners. They are also able to talk about themselves and their lives in a way that is accessible, reflective and emotionally linked. This allows them to recognize their limitations and to admit to their mistakes in a non-defensive manner — all without sacrificing their positive sense of self. Understanding that other people are similarly flawed they will quickly forgive their spouses.

A successful communicator: These partners are excellent at listening and communicating, which allows them to nurture and maintain close relations. They are also able to work together through disputes. They have these skills in part because they are inherently excellent at detecting and controlling their emotions — a definite bonus when you attempt to communicate and work through the challenges that naturally occurs in an emotionally intimate relationship.

Appreciative of you: Falling in love is not enough. Since relationships are co-created, they will only make you happy in the long run if your partner loves you and supports you — and works in a way to express this. You need to give your partner an interest in getting to know you. And, while it is at first a steep learning curve, the journey to know you better should never be completely plateau. You would always be happier with guidance and motivation to pursue your personal interests and achieve your full potential.

A good fit: Enjoying the time together is crucial. Generally speaking, this means having at least some shared interests. Yet it also means doing things together, even if this actually includes participating in conversations. Sharing values of each other, or at least honoring them, is very important for a long-term relationship. And the more that influences those ideals in everyday life, the more important it is to share them.

Nurturing a Relationship You Feel Secure In

It can be completely fun to watch couples dance together. Watching two people flow up in perfectly timed motions is fascinating. Those that are most successful are apparently connected by some magnetic force. In this case, seeing them dancing offers the vicarious feeling of sharing a wonderful relation to another; what could be more seductive than this?

You will want to nurture a relationship after finding a romantic partner, which can feel like that perfectly coordinated dance at its best. The two of you would work well together in such a relationship, communicate effectively and trust each other, all while being in tune with each other as well as with each other. You would still want that to be a coordinated effort, even at its worst. You would find ways to accept and work with differences among yourselves, instead of trying to force each other to change.

 Part of the beauty of enjoying such a supportive relationship is that it helps you feel more secure within yourself and your relationship as well.

Self-Disclosure

Your initial experiences with a potential partner set the stage for how your relationship story will unfold. It will go most smoothly at the very start if the two of you open up in synchrony to each other. One of you shares something personal and the other one responds with empathy, sympathy, and a dis-closure of a similar nature. You both feel stronger and you are motivated to share more, to deepen the level of openness. You also develop a sense of security and faith in each other's company as you enjoy those intimate moments. The love and fondness that naturally

445

emerges from these relationships is necessary to sustain a healthy long-term relationship.

If you have an insecure attachment style, getting to know each other with this kind of give-and-take probably will not go smoothly. For example, you may hope that expressing a lot of your problems at once would gain your partner's attention, comfort, and reassurance. On the other hand, the need for closeness may make you feel too vulnerable to share; so then, you may stay away and near. You risk shutting your partner off in both situations. This often interferes with getting to know her and feeling empathy for her, as your attention is on whether your partner can support or hurt you.

If your relationships have been disrupted by the way you choose to communicate, perhaps it is time you approach it differently. Start by thinking about your disclosure motives-or not disclosure. So keep an eye on when and how you share when you go forward.

You will want to share your personal experiences with your wife at the right time, as a way of getting closer and helping her understand you. But, as tempting as it may be to "unpack all your luggage" and share everything in detail, be mindful about what you are sharing. In general, share enough to understand your partner, so she can be empathetic and supportive. The rest will come out with time if you so choose.

Of example, you might confess, "I'm worried about letting my guard down because my last girlfriend has been critical of me all the time." By deciding not to say anything about it for the moment, you may keep your focus on your current relationship. You give this prospective girlfriend an opportunity to talk about herself or inquire about you more. She might say, "I know how you feel ...." Or she might ask you, "What do you mean?" "This way, you can direct your discoveries and growing sense of connection to happen synchronously with your partner — leading to a sense of warmth and love that will ideally tide you over the years.

Chapter 31   Strategies for Solving Anxiety Issues

Partners/couples generally face challenges which need to be addressed as the partnership progresses. Your ability to manage issues as they come up in your relationship will ultimately determine the growth of the relationship. If a challenge is not well managed, you may find your relationship in a crisis and may need to take concrete steps towards charting a way out.

Some of the challenges that most people face in their relationships include communication, joint development as a couple, relationship needs, contentedness and autonomy of the partners, equal rights, routine, habit, sexuality, loyalty, stress, quarrels, conflicts, difference in value systems, distance, illness, and the list goes on.

How careful are you in your relationship? Being careful and considerate of each other saves a lot of frustration in the relationship. Do you live in the here and now? Can you enjoy the moment? Living in the here and now sounds easier than it is. More often than not, our thoughts slide into the past or the future.

Other questions to ask yourself about your relationship:

How intensely are you enjoying the moment? Does your partner always understand what you mean? Do you do a lot in common together? Are both of you a well-rehearsed team in all walks of life? Do you find security, tenderness and sexual satisfaction with your partner? How about division of labor - does it work well between the both of you? Do you find peace, support, and security in your relationship? Can you talk about everything very openly? Does your partner make you strong and happy?

The answers to these questions will guide you into a proper self-evaluation of the challenges you might be facing in your relationship.

In most cases, men do not like relationship talks. Nevertheless, it is necessary to exchange regularly about needs and wishes in a partnership. Especially for conflict resolution, communication strategies are needed. Firstly, you must distinguish between generally communicating as partners and communication as a result of conflict resolution. Communication about each partner's wishes, ideas, plans, and hopes is an important foundation for a relationship. Couples who are happy in long term relationships are usually able to communicate their feelings to each other, and they do not see themselves or their relationship threatened by these expressions, even if they are negative without being aware of it. They are able to develop their own, very subtle language, gestures, and facial expressions throughout their relationship.

Quarrels are normal in a relationship - it is the "how" that matters. Clashes arise when you or your partner are strained by external stress. For example a job, problems in raising children, conflicts in the family, etc. The stressed partner often communicates in a more irritated and violent tone.

It is in our greatest interest to be proactive and inventive regarding how we communicate with those closest to us.

Creating, maintaining, and nurturing relationships with friends, co-workers, and family, not just partners, is critical for our well-being.

Rather than looking to others to create relationship changes, the simplest place to start out is with yourself.

A Relationship Self-Assessment

Below is a list of some relationship statements. Go through the statements and make note of any that do not seem to be very true for you. Write these down on a separate sheet of paper.

1. I have told my spouse/partner/children, that I really like them within the previous few days or week.
2. I get on well with my siblings.
3. I get on well with my coworkers and/or clients.
4. I get on well with my manager and/or employees.
5. There is nobody I might dread or feel uncomfortable running across.
6. I place relationships first and results second.
7. I have forsaken all of the relationships that drag me down or injury me
8. I have communicated or tried to speak with everybody I may have hurt, injured, or seriously disturbed, though it may not have been 100% my fault.
9. I do not gossip to or about others.
10. **I have a circle of friends and/or family who I love and appreciate.**

448

11. I tell people close to me that I appreciate them.
12. I am completely wrapped up in letters, emails, and calls relating to work.
13. I always tell the truth, even if it may hurt.
14. I receive enough love from people around me to feel appreciated.
15. I have forgiven those people that have hurt or broken me, whether or not it was deliberate.
16. I keep my word; people can rely on me.
17. I quickly clear up miscommunications and misunderstandings after they occur.
18. I do not judge or criticize others.
19. I have a supporter or lover.
20. I talk openly about issues instead of grumbling.

Relationship Problem: Money

Many relationship problems start with money. Whether one person manages it differently than the other, or there has been mistrust due to mismanagement of finances in the past, money can strain even the strongest relationship.

Problem-solving strategies:

Be honest concerning your current monetary scenario. Do not approach the topic when the situation is tense. Rather, set aside a suitable and convenient time for both of you.

Acknowledge the fact that one of you will always be a spender while the other person is a saver, talk about the advantages of each, and try to learn from each other.

Do not keep your financial gain or debt away from your partner. If at some point you want to join finances, lay out all monetary documents including recent credit reports, pay stubs, bank statements, insurance policies, debts, and investments.

When things go wrong with finances, never apportion blame. Pieces of paper and ones and zeros on a computer are insignificant compared to your human connection.

When it comes to shared money, incorporate savings into a joint budget and decide that your payment of monthly bills is a joint responsibility. Still allow the both of you to be independent by putting aside some money to be spent when the need arises.

Make decisions concerning your long term as well as short term goals. It is normal to have personal goal, but you must not underestimate the importance of family goals.

Relationship Problem: Struggles Over Home Chores

A majority of partners work outside the house and sometimes at more than one job. Therefore, it is vital to fairly divide the household responsibilities.

Problem-solving strategies:

Be organized and clear regarding your jobs within the home. Write all the roles down and agree on who will do what, or what schedule to work off of. Be honest about what you do or do not want to do and what you have time for.

Be open to alternative solutions: If you each hate housework, perhaps you will be able to spring for a cleaning service. Or maybe you can be a bit laxer about the level of cleanliness around the house. If you are a neat freak but your partner isn't, is there a compromise to be found? Always try to meet in the middle.

Relationship Problem: Not prioritizing your relationship

If you wish to keep your relationship going, prioritizing your relationship is a must. Make it important and worth your while. Recognize the importance of it, cherish it, and nourish it so that it will stand the test of time.

Problem-solving strategies:

Go back to those things you did when you started dating. Appreciate one another, give compliments, contact one another through the day, and show genuine interest in each other.

Schedule a time to go on a date and plan it with as much consideration as when you were trying to win each other over.

Respect is very important. Learn to be appreciative. If your partner does something that makes you happy, never hesitate to show your gratitude by saying thank you. Let your partner know what matters most to you - them.

Chapter 32   Conclusion

Anxiety is a beast but without medicine you will fight the war. Overcoming anxiety and nervousness is sometimes simply a matter of modifying your attitude, thoughts and lifestyle. If your symptoms do not improve or worsen, you should start with a drug-free treatment, and then speak to a doctor. Such anti-anxiety, drug-free tactics can also help you improve your medicine regimen. Do what works for you, and know your life is not dominated by anxiety.

Probably Ways to Treat Anxiety without medication are:

1.Shout it out

Relating to a trusted partner is one way of dealing with anxiety. Yet something much better than shouting is there: yelling at the top of the lungs. You have always been taught as a child not to yell and be told to use your "inside voice," but as an adult you can make your own rules. And if you are grappling with anxiety and pent-up emotions, let it out.

2.Get Moving

Having yourself going is probably the last thing you want to do while you are in overdrive. You may be concerned about soreness from post-workout and being unable to walk or sit for the next two days. Or maybe your mind walks into the worst-case scenario and you are scared to over-exert yourself and have a heart attack. But in fact, exercise is one of the best possible solutions for natural anti-anxiety.

Physical exercise increases the levels of endorphins and serotonin to make you feel physically better. And if inside you feel better, the whole outlook is changing. And because your brain cannot focus equally on two items at once, exercise will also take your mind off your problems. Three to five days a week, strive for at least 30 minutes of physical activity. Do not think that you have got to suffer through a tough workout. Any kind of movement is good, so get your favorite jam on and dance around the house. Or grab a mat and split your favorite poses in yoga.

3. Break Up With caffeine

A cup of coffee, chocolate or an ice-cold coke might make you feel better. However if caffeine is your favorite go - to medication, then your anxiety could get worse.

Caffeine gives a jolt to the nervous system, which can raise energy levels. But the nervous energy can cause an anxiety attack when under pressure. Now, the thought of giving up your favorite caffeinated coffee may increase your heart rate and cause anxiety as you read this, but you do not have to quit cold turkey or give up caffeine altogether. It all comes down to balance.

Reduce back to one or two regular sized cups a day instead of four cups of coffee a day — regular as in 8 ounces, not 16 or 32 ounces.

4. Grant yourself a bedtime

There is no time for sleep with your busy schedule, right? Many workaholics complain that they only need three or four hours of sleep a night, as if they were saying, "I'm more dedicated and devoted than anyone else." But no matter what you might say to yourself, you are not a robot. Human beings need to sleep to function properly, and that also applies to you unless you have beamed in from some neighboring planet.

5. Feel OK saying no

Your plate is just that big, and if you burden yourself with the personal issues of everyone else, your anxiety will escalate as well. We have all heard the adage, "Giving is more satisfying than receiving."

6. Don't miss meals

The idea of consuming food is as tempting as eating dirt if fear triggers nausea. Yet missing meals will heighten anxiety. If you do not eat, your blood sugar drops which causes a stress hormone called cortisol to be released. Cortisol can help you work better under pressure, but if you are still prone to anxiety it can also make you feel worse.

The fact you have to eat does not justify just stuffing something in your mouth, so that is not an excuse to overindulge in sugar and fast food. Sugar causes no anxiety, but a sugar rush may cause physical anxiety symptoms, such as nervousness and trembling. So if you start obsessing over a sugar reaction, you might get a panic attack out of it.

Incorporate into your diet leaner protein, fruits, vegetables and healthy fats. Eat five or six small meals all day long and avoid or reduce your sugar consumption and refined carbohydrates.

7. Grant yourself an escape plan

Often, feeling out of control is due to anxiety. You cannot always be in your life's driving seat, but you should act to recognize your causes and deal with anxiety-causing circumstances.

But what if there was an escape plan in place before you left the house? For example, you could drive yourself, instead of carpooling with your party animal mates. This way, if your anxiety starts rising and you cannot take another minute of uncomfortable experiences, you can leave. The more that you feel in control, the less anxiety you may have.

8. Live in the moment

What do you think about right now other than the words on this page? Are you aware that you have a meeting next week? Have you been worried over meeting your financial targets? Or maybe you are concerned about whether you are going to be a good parent — even though you have got zero kids and do not have any plans to conceive early.

If you replied "yes" to all of these questions, you just discovered a part of the problem. Like several others suffering from anxiety disorders, you are having trouble living right now. You are already worried about the concerns of tomorrow, instead of stressing about today. And depending on the extent of your anxiety, maybe you are remembering the errors of yesterday.

You cannot monitor the future, and you cannot borrow a time machine and reverse the past, so here is a thought: Take it as it comes every day. Not to say that you cannot be cautious and head off issues. Yet do not dwell too much on what is been, and what is going to be causing fear for yourself. Mindfulness and meditation are embedded in the moment of living, and anxiety has been shown to ease. Aim to train for a few minutes a day and increase the amount of time. Better part? Anywhere you can do it: in bed, at your work desk, or even on the home commute.

Do Not Go Yet; One Last Thing to Do

Your help makes a real difference and I actually read all the comments so I can get your input and develop this novel.

Just a little break to ask you something that means a lot for me: Are you enjoying this book? If so, I'd be really happy if you could leave a short review on Amazon. I'm so curious to know your opinion! Don't forget to add a photo of the book if you can, thank you.

Part 3 : Empath

Chapter 33   Introduction to Empath

If you check the word "empathy" in a dictionary, the definition will explain this state of emotion in a rather simple way by describing empathy as the ability or capacity to feel and understand what other people are feeling or going through within the frame of the other person.

It is the ability to place oneself in place of the other person and completely experience what the other person is feeling – empathy thus describes the capacity of being able to experience emotions of others the way they do, while empaths often take these emotions rather personally. Ultimately, extreme empathy may lead to psychological and mental exhaustion, suffering and may lead to increased sensitivity alongside the existing sensitivity in the form of empathy. Empaths may feel exhausted, unable to protect themselves from picking up every and any emotion they manage to sense and pick up from other people, to the extent at which this ability may as well become a burden for empaths. Even though empaths may have a hard time managing to create a "bubble" around their "empathy receptors" so to speak, it is very important to note that empathy actually represents a sign of high emotional intelligence. Just as the capacity of your intellect can be measured by IQ tests and the way you are presenting reality, the way you understand math or logic, emotional intelligence can be measured based on the capacity to empathize with other human beings alongside various and different determining factors that affect one's emotional intelligence.

Empathy allows us to realize that we are not that different from other people, as in the end, we all feel same emotions, although we may experience these emotions in a different way; anger, happiness, joy, sadness, jealousy – these are all the feelings that make us human. Even though the definition of empathy describes this ability in a simple way, empathy has more layers than it may appear, which is why there are several types of empathy that you can develop as you are maturing emotionally and intellectually.

However, before we focus on the anatomy of empathy and explain what types of empathy there are and how to handle them, we would like to reflect on one of the most common questions asked by empaths: How do I feel this way and Why do I feel this way?

Empathy: Why Do I Feel This Way?

As an empath you may know a lot about other people's emotions and even be rather emotionally invested in other people's distress, however, you may be clueless about the origin of your feelings and the ability to place yourself "in other people's shoes". This state may make you wonder: 'Why am I feeling these emotions? Why do I empathize with others? Why do I feel this way?'.

Actually, you might be happy to know that you are not the only person puzzled by the nature of empathy – researchers, psychologists and philosophers have also embarked on a journey to find out why do empaths feel the way they do, and what empathy actually represents – what is the defining factor of these emotions and what triggers increased emotional sensitivity or extreme compassion if you will, in some people?

The answer might not be as simple, as there are neuroscientific explanations as well as theories that imply that empathy is in human nature, and in the end represents a channel that allows empaths to fully experience feelings that they otherwise wouldn't be able to.

For starters, let us turn to practical examples for explaining the emotional aspect of empathy; for instance, empaths may feel an array of different emotions, some of which are triggered by rather specific circumstances that not all people will find themselves in. An empath may open any newspapers and find a page filled with crimes, pain, misdeeds and sorrow. The empath personally is not emotionally related to any of these news stories, but is emotionally invested. How come?

The increased feeling of compassion and sympathy transforms into empathy where empaths are able to feel the same way other people do, even having the ability to imagine exactly what it would feel like in case they were the ones to be personally involved in those sorrowful, crime-packed, painful news. That way, the exact feelings that the people who are actually involved in these cases may feel and are probably feeling are likewise triggered and created in the mind of empaths. That way, an empath is able to experience emotions that are otherwise created based on specific circumstances.

But, why do empaths feel this way?

Neuroscientific theory suggests that the state of empathy is narrowly connected to neurobiological processes where mirror neurons present in the brain may mimic any emotion once activated and triggered, while researches suggest that there are specific areas in the brain that are directly responsible for the ability that empathy represents. Thanks to these neurobiological components, the brain of an empath may reproduce the same emotion that the other person is feeling, that way creating the same response that would naturally be generated in case the empath was in the place of that other person.

The sociological point of view suggests that empathy makes a valuable part of social intelligence and social relationships. According to the theory, the feeling of empathy has a role in helping human beings' bond, creating strong social connections and the feeling of unity, which is a basic unit of any type of community, whether the community is as small as a family or as complex as a country. After all, we are all social beings by nature and have found socializing and creating communities as a crucial part of our survival and evolution.

Empathy, thus, even though it may sometimes feel like a burden, is actually a clear sign of emotional intelligence and social skills, as long as the emotional flow you are getting from other people as an empath can be controlled without overwhelming you emotionally and physically.

You should also note that as well as it is the case that some people may have increased compassion for others, interpreted as empathy, some people are faced with a complete lack of the ability to empathize or even sympathize with others, which is how these groups of people may often be isolated from social interactions and usually feel distant from other people, having problems with the inability to feel or connect. As the opposite, empaths may at times become overwhelmed by other people's emotions, drowning in uncontrolled feelings that are triggered by the ability to feel the exact way someone else feels. In case you feel that way, you need to know that there are ways of diminishing the harmful side effects of empathy by learning how to survive increased sensitivity and prevent your empathy from affecting you mentally, spiritually or physically.

To simplify the answer on why do you feel the way you do as an empath, it might be suitable to say that it is in the very human nature to be able to feel what others feel, that way creating strong bonds and connections with other human beings.

However, the reason why empathy might be even dangerous at times is the fact that there are all kinds of selfish and inconsiderate people who are more than willing to take advantage of those who are able to empathize with anyone and place themselves in other people's shoes. Before we get to tips that should help you protect yourself from the downfall that empathy may bring, we need to learn more about the three types of empathy.

Chapter 34   What Is Empathy and Why It Is Important to Be an Empath

An empath is a person with the special gift of perceiving the emotions and feelings of other people as though they were their own. They don't even try. They are naturally tuned in to the energies floating around them. If an empath walks into a room and sits next to a person who's quietly mourning, the empath will pick up on the sorrow and experience it as though it were their own. An empath who lacks awareness of their gift can be deeply conflicted, as they cannot tell apart their own feelings from those of others.

Ask yourself the following questions to find out if you're an empath:

- Can you perceive people in some way?

- Do you feel people's emotions and mistake them as yours?

- Can you think along the same line as other people?

- Do your feelings change as soon as you meet a particular person?

- Do you sometimes wonder whether you're co-dependent, neurotic, or even crazy?

- Can you read peoples' minds?

It can be awesome having the ability to pick up on other people's energies, but on the downside, it can be a real struggle when the said energies are of the dark nature and especially if the empath in question knows nothing of their ability.

As an empath, these are some traits that you're bound to display:

Highly Sensitive
People keep on telling you that you're too sensitive. This is because what they say or do can affect you quite easily. You can read into their unsaid messages when they talk or do something. This sensitivity can make you susceptible to things that don't hurt well-adjusted people. Your high sensitivity makes you give a lot of thought to what you do or say. This pattern always leads to self-inhibiting tendencies. You end up customizing yourself too much so that the world can fall in love with

you. The habit of suppressing your true emotions comes with a cocktail of challenges.

Soak Up Other Peoples' Energies

You could be having a fantastic day with your spirits high, and then you go to Starbucks and sit next to a family who unbeknownst to you just lost one of their members. Nothing is said. All are sipping at their coffee with quiet faces. Ever so slowly, the joy you first had begins to fade away, and in its place, sadness takes over. You have no reason to be sad, but you experience this sadness anyway. Soon, the family gets up, troops out of Starbucks, and then your sadness fades away. You had just absorbed their energies.

Introverted

Being introverted is not the same as being shy. A shy person might loathe being alone and feel rejected for lack of human contact, but on the other hand, an introvert gets drained when they stay too long with other people, and they cherish being alone. A shy person has self-inhibiting tendencies, but an introvert has a strong sense of self and stays true to it. Empaths are more likely to be introverted than extroverted. They don't shun all human contact but prefer socializing on one-on-one terms, or within small groups.

Highly Intuitive

One of the most effective weapons in an empath's hands is their gut feeling. They have this ability to sniff out the true nature of a situation. This makes it a bit hard to play games with an empath. They will see right through your tricks. As an empath, if you meet someone, you tend to have a gut feeling of what that person is really like. You are always in tune with your surroundings and can tell when there's danger. This ability is obviously one of the main advantages of being an empath because you're less likely to be taken for a ride.

Overwhelmed By Relationships

Conventional relationships put emphasis on partners spending as much time together as possible. An empath cannot thrive in this kind of arrangement because they constantly pick up on their partner's emotions and mistake them as their own. This is not to say that empaths cannot form any relationships. However, the traditional arrangement of a relationship needs to be deconstructed. For instance, they can have a

462

room of their own that they may retreat to when their urge to be alone kicks in, and also, their partners should be patient with them.

Take Long To Process Emotions

The average person has laser attention to their emotions. Whether sadness or joy, it kicks in suddenly. Their emotional reflexes are fast too. An empath takes the time to understand the emotions that they are currently feeling. For instance, if something terrible goes down, the sadness won't register immediately. They will first try to process the situation, going over the details time and again, and then the sadness will accumulate inside them. They can experience emotions in such a powerful way. Thus, whether it's sadness or joy, they feel it completely.

Love Nature

For most empaths, they are at their happiest when surrounded by nature. Whether it's the sunlight kissing their skin, the rain falling on them, or taking in a gulp of fresh air, no other activity restores their balance as being surrounded by the natural world. They feel a deep sense of connection with nature. When an empath is experiencing a tsunami of emotions, one of the restorative measures would be taking a stroll through an open area beneath the sky.

Strong Senses

An empath boasts of very developed senses. They can catch the slightest whiff of an odor, can see into the shadows, can hear the tiniest sound, and can feel the vibrations of various other things. These developed senses make them so good at noticing the small stuff. Empaths seem to notice what would ordinarily escape the attention of most people. For this reason, they tend to flourish in careers that demand close attention and the exploration of the abstract.

Generous

There isn't a more selfless person than an empath. They don't have to have something in order to help. They are willing to go the extra mile and be of help. For instance, when an empath comes across a street child and sees their suffering, it tugs at their heart. They not only want to give them some food but also find a way of removing them from the streets. The majority of the world doesn't care about street children and sees them as an annoyance. We can assume that the empaths of the world play a critical role in helping street children and other people who are experiencing hardship.

Creative

Empaths tend to be very creative. This is aided by the wealth of emotions that they are always experiencing. Their creative nature manifests itself in almost every aspect of their life — food, relationships, homes, and most importantly, career. An empath is likely to do well in a career in the arts. They have tremendous potential when it comes to drawing, writing, singing, or making films. They tend to portray their emotions unambiguously and can capture the emotions of other people just as intended.

People Are Drawn To You

If an empath isn't aware of their special gift, they are likely to hide away from the world. They would rather hide and be safe than stay among people and experience every emotion imaginable. This can make the society grow suspicious of them and even hate them. However, if an empath is self-aware and knows of their ability to soak up the energies floating around them, then people will be drawn to them. People know that empaths have a tremendous capacity to understand them and helping them get through whatever challenges they are facing.

Empaths Fall Into The Following Distinct Categories:

• Geomantic empaths: These empaths are attuned to a certain environment or landscape. Geomantic empaths are connected to specific sites like buildings, lakes, oceans, and mountains. These empaths can feel the historical emotions of these sites. For instance, if an empath visits a site where people were slaughtered many years, they can still feel the sorrow. Empaths attach feelings to different environments so that each environment evokes certain emotions. Such empaths tend to carry souvenirs to remind them of various environments.

• Physical empaths: Also known as a medical empath, they can pick up on the condition of someone else's body. They would instinctively know what ails another person. In extreme cases, they can pick up on the symptoms so that they share in the pain of the other person. Physical empaths also have healing abilities. They tend to take careers in conventional or alternative medicine. Physical empaths are great at taking care of ailing people. Those who have ailments trust them instinctively because they can feel that they care.

464

- Emotional empaths: They are sensitive to the emotional energy floating around them. As an emotional empath, you will absorb the emotions of other people and think that they are yours. This can be deeply distressing if you're constantly around negative people. An emotional empath should increase their self-awareness so that they can tell apart their emotions from those of others. Emotional empaths tend to withdraw from other people so that they can spend time alone and recharge. An emotional empath should protect their energy by following various healing practices.

- Animal empaths: You have certainly seen someone in your neighborhood which is more interested in keeping company with animals than human beings. They have a certain pet or even various pets that mean the world to them. There's a high likelihood that such a person is an animal empath. An animal empath feels a deep connection toward animals. They can sense what the animals want or feel and the animals love them back. The connection is so deep that they have a way of communicating with each other. An animal empath answers to their intense desire to connect with animals by domesticating their animals of choice. Also, they tend to be passionate about animal rights and make contributions to funds that advance animal welfare.

- Plant empaths: A plant empath shares a deep connection with a certain plant or plants in general. The plant evokes certain emotions when they touch it. A plant empath can communicate with the plant and can know its condition. They like hanging out near the plant in a natural environment, bringing it into their house, or planting it in the garden.

- Precognitive empaths: Are you the type of person that can always tell the future? And this is not down to your future alone, but also the future of other unrelated people or events? You're certainly a precognitive empath. You tend to "see" things before they actually come to pass. Your visions are made manifest in various ways such as dreams or feelings. Having this ability to foresee the future is both rewarding and distressing. It can help you brace for the future, and at the same time, it can amplify your misery knowing the pain that awaits you.

Chapter 35   Characteristics of Empathic People

As an Empath you get an understanding rather well of certain things that have a strong influence on your being. Whether it is your emotional state, your health, your physical wellbeing, or your overall energy levels, Empaths are sensitive to a variety of things, people and places that can have a negative impact on their health and happiness.

As you become more familiar with your role as an Empath, consider some of the following possibilities:

1.   Are you sensitive to other people's voices or odors to the point that it is hard for you to be around them?

2.   Do bright lights or overcrowded rooms or spaces cause you to feel anxiety or fear?

3.   Are you imbalanced around certain people in your home or work life?

4.   Do you have a sensitivity to certain foods or beverages, more than other people you know?

5.   Do you easily get sick, including allergic reactions, or flu-like symptoms and wonder how you could possibly be that sick all of the time?

6.   Do you live with someone who makes you feel uncomfortable whenever you are close to them physically or emotionally, whether they are a roommate, friend, spouse or child?

7.   Have you ever felt the urge to immediately leave a building, house or venue because you didn't like the way it felt inside?

8.   Do you have an "allergic reaction" to other people's energy?

9.   Have you often found yourself feeling unwell after a party or a group meet up?

10.   Are there important moments in your life that you had to cut short or walk away from because of anxiety, panic, of fear?

These questions and many others can help to shed light on exactly WHAT Empaths are sensitive to. It varies from person to person and many Empaths share similar qualities in how they react to certain stimuli in their lives. Here are some examples of what an Empath may be sensitive to on a regular basis:

- Harsh or hateful words

- Attitudes of contempt, rage, anger, jealousy and ego

- Other people's repressed emotions that are projected

- Crowds, whether small or large

- Energy vampires, or someone who drains you of your own energy because of their own emotions, drama, or excessive energy around your empathic energy

- Physical discomfort coming from another person or animal, and sometimes even plant life

- Major changes in the environment, or living situation, including career changes, office movement, large moves to new cities and anything involving having to leave a comfort zone

- Travelling, especially in large airports and to large cities

- Foods that are highly processed and generic and have low nutritional value

- Caffeine, sugar, alcohol, drugs

- Medications, especially prescription drugs instead of herbal and natural remedies

- Various forms of energy from emotional states represented through shouting, yelling, crying, laughing, sighing, pacing, sweating, shifting, and fidgeting

- Subways, buses, and all forms of public transportation that involve being in close quarters with many strangers

- Sensitivities that come from allergic reactions to beverages, food or drink that are high in unnatural ingredients or that have been manufactured in industrial machinery

- Many people all at once, even for enjoyment or entertainment, such as in a movie theater, concert, lecture hall, march or parade, ceremony, or event

- Nervous tension, anxiety, or depression, brought on by other people or circumstances

- Hidden emotions that are raw and fresh from other people

- Strong aromas, such as perfume, decay, body odor, breath, unhealthy internal body odors of another (some Empaths can smell cancer or terminal illnesses coming from a person who may or may not has been diagnosed)

- Strong feelings on either side of the spectrum, from happy to sad, from one person or a group of people

- Relationship drama from someone else's experience that can be carried into your own

- Other people's deceitfulness or lack of honesty in various situations

The list goes on and it is possible that you have felt some, none, or all of these. You could still be an Empath and have none of these specific sensitivities but may have an awareness of other things, people or places that you are sensitive to. It is important to keep in mind that as you learn more about Empaths, you recognize that it is each person's journey and that no two people are exactly alike. All Empaths have a different experience in uncovering their gift and have to really listen in and develop a strong personal awareness with their own experience.

You may already know that you are an Empath and how you are sensitive to a variety of things and it is always good to remember other ways you can be sensitive. The closer you get to your empathic gift, the more sensitive you can become to receiving and processing the energy that is all around you.

Part of understanding the sensitivities of the Empath is to make sure that you can discover what you are sensitive to so that you can learn how to change that experience. If you are sensitive to strong odors and bright lights, you may try to avoid these kinds of things in your own home, but may have to find ways to accept them or ground yourself well when you go out in public places or spend time in other households.

You may be sensitive to the energy of large groups and find yourself feeling overwhelmed and anxious in those situations, so you may have to enjoy your concert experiences through a television broadcast or from a higher balcony seat where you can have some separation from the main crowd.

You may be sensitive to certain people's energy in your close circle of friends and find it hard to stay in their company for very long because it feels physically and emotionally draining for you to be around them. You might have to limit your friendship with them, or even step away from them all together until you can safely build better boundaries and grounding techniques so that you can spend time in their close company with more internal balance.

Whatever you are sensitive to as an Empath, there is always a solution that can help benefit your journey toward embracing your gift and becoming more empowered as a healing soul. You do not have to live the life of a hermit because of your sensitivities; however, it is beneficial to know your sensitivities so that you can provide yourself with the proper tools to maintain a balanced, healthy and happy life as an Empath.

Chapter 36   The Dark Side of Being an Empath

There is no doubt that empaths have been blessed with a unique gift; but unfortunately, it can become a curse if you don't understand it and know how to control it. As I am sure you are aware, constantly feeling the stress and pain of others can leave you feeling drained and lifeless. Since your neurological and biological makeup absorbs the emotions of others on a large scale, a lot of empaths experience serious health problems including:

•   Headaches

•   Back pain

•   Digestive issues

•   Anxiety

•   Chronic depression

•   A weak immune system

•   Chronic fatigue

On a social level, empaths are extremely compassionate. This trustworthy trait is very appealing to people who are suffering. Unfortunately, many empaths are taken advantage of because of this, and they tend to attract the worst kinds of people—sociopaths, narcissists, and people with a general manipulative character. It has been argued that one of the reasons sociopaths are attracted to empaths is because they don't have any emotions, and so they look to others to fill that void. Empaths are highly emotional people, and sociopaths instinctively know this. They lure the empath in through eye contact, subtle gestures, mannerisms, and body language. Empaths are drawn to this because of their attraction to special feelings.

Empaths find it difficult to make personal choices because they pay so much attention to the emotions of others. They are always worrying about how their decisions might affect the people around them. This leads them to create an image of perfectionism, and there is always a conflict between pleasing others and pleasing themselves.

Empaths are very in tune with their instincts, which makes it easy for them to read people immediately. However, being aware of other people's difficulties can become problematic. There is often an overlap between their feelings and the feelings of others, which can have a negative effect on the confidence of an empath. Empaths often find it difficult to understand why they feel the way they do. They often ask themselves, "Am I personally experiencing anxiety or is it coming from someone else?" Some empaths don't know how to handle the emotional overload and will turn to drugs and alcohol as a coping mechanism.

Empaths are often mistaken as being overly sensitive and weak, which can have a negative effect on their self-esteem. Additionally, they find it difficult to watch violent or graphic content and will avoid watching the news or TV in general. They also feel uncomfortable discussing misfortune, cruelties, and injustices.

CHALLENGES FOR EMPATH MALES AND FEMALES

Male and female empaths experience some of the same, but also different challenges. Empaths are sensitive people—females can show this side of them openly, but males find it difficult because of the social stigma attached to overly emotional men. Boys are raised not to cry, to be strong and macho, and to display their sensitivities is seen as a sign of weakness. Boys with such characteristics are often bullied at school and labeled as "sissies" and "cry babies." Therefore, empath males find it difficult to talk about how they feel in fear of being judged as not masculine enough. They are not interested in sports like basketball, baseball, and soccer; neither are they interested in aggressive contact sports such as rugby and wrestling, and so they may feel isolated and rejected by their peers. As a result, male empaths tend to repress their emotions and act as if they don't exist. They often suffer in silence feeling that no one understands them, which can have a negative impact on their health, relationships, and careers.

Alanis Morrissette, a known empath, wrote a song entitled "In Praise of the Vulnerable Man." Men must embrace their sensitive nature because it is nothing to be ashamed of. This does not mean being overly feminine, it means being balanced, owning both your masculine and feminine sides. It means being secure enough to be vulnerable and strong enough to be sensitive. Men of this nature have high emotional intelligence. They do not fear their own or other people's emotions, which makes them attractive and compassionate partners, leaders, and friends.

Females, on the other hand, don't experience the same challenges when it comes to emotional sensitivity. Girls are raised to express their emotions—it's okay for them to cry and feel sad. The notion of female intuition is also socially acceptable, but the idea of females being powerful is still frowned upon in Western society. Historically, women have had to and are still fighting for equality. Females have experienced horrendous struggles because of their gender. More than 200 women were arrested and approximately 20 were slaughtered during the Salem which trials because of their sensitivities.

Even though it is somewhat acceptable, women today are still afraid to express their sensitivities in fear of being judged or misunderstood. This is especially true in relationships because overly emotional women are often deemed as being needy and insecure. It's important that female empaths learn to be authentic in their relationships and openly discuss their needs. They should know how to set boundaries with their time and energy so they don't get overwhelmed and experience burn out. Male or female, an empath who knows how to give and receive in a balanced way holds a lot of power.

Chapter 37   The Importance of Energy and How to Protect from Energy Vampires

Types Of Energy Vampires

Victim Vampire

The victim vampire is the type of person who thinks that they are at the mercy of the world. They have a long list of people who did "wrong them wrong", and they believe that were it not for these people, their lives would have been better. Everyone is scheming against them. When you come into contact with a victim vampire, they will make it seem as though your actions or words have affected their lives that you are the villain.

Innocent Vampire

Not all energy vampires are malicious people. Some energy vampires can be people you care about. In most cases, they are people that have valid reasons to depend on you. For instance, if your spouse suffers an accident and they have to rely on you, or your little sibling hasn't stopped being needy, or your parents are always checking after you. It is okay to help these people with whatever they demand of you, but at the same time, you should put plans in place to ensure that they become self-dependent as soon as humanly possible.

Narcissistic Vampire

A narcissist cannot show empathy. They tend to sneak up on you by wearing a mask, a false identity, and when you drop your guard, their true nature comes out. A narcissist only cares about their own needs. They will stop at nothing to ensure that they have snatched whatever they wanted from you. A narcissist gets very delighted whenever they spot an empath because they know empaths are easy to exploit. They will drain you of energy, thanks to their parasitic nature. Once a narcissist is done using you, they will get rid of you.

Dominator Vampire

This kind of vampire tries to get involved in every aspect of your life by being overbearing. They want to influence your life down to the smallest detail. When you leave them out on any decision that you make, they act angry toward you. Their intense desire to dominate others stems from a point of insecurity. They are afraid of being seen as weak. Empaths are

473

easy targets because of their sensitive nature. A dominator vampire will suffocate you with their presence and a never-ending desire to be the architect of your life, and for this reason, they will drain you of energy.

Melodramatic Vampire
Melodramatic vampires are great at creating scenes. They always drag you into trouble that would have been avoided easily by observing basic rules of decency. You could be out having a fun time, and then they will start a fight with someone random and put you into danger. What's happening with a melodramatic vampire is that they feel empty in their souls. They have nothing to live for and thus creating drama becomes their second nature. Melodramatic vampires are very determined, but if you want to get rid of them, you have to be particularly ruthless.

Judgmental Vampire
These kinds of vampires thrive on passing judgments on everything that you do. They intend to make you feel bad about your decisions or actions. For instance, if you buy a present for your loved one, the judgmental vampire might spread malicious rumors about you having to buy love. They are intent on tarnishing your reputation and making you seem bad. Empaths are sensitive, and when someone judges their deeds, they feel underwhelmed. An empath should stay away from judgmental people to avoid getting their feelings hurt, and by extension, suffering energy drain.

Blamer Vampire
The blamer vampire can never accept personal responsibility for what is wrong in their life. For instance, if you accompany your friend to apply for college and their application fails, and then they blame you for somehow making their application fail to get through, they are certainly blamer vampires. A blamer vampire refuses to take charge of their own life and finds people to blame for what's wrong with their life. A blamer vampire will not do things alone. They delegate work to victims. If things go to the dogs, they whip out the blame card, but should their plan pan out — they will bask in the glory.

Jealous Vampire
The jealous vampire will never be happy for anyone. It doesn't stop there either. They will try to hurt anyone that they think is doing better than them. The jealous person will try to devise a plan to harm a person, and they leave that person devastated. For instance, if you get someone to

agree to become your significant other, a jealous person might contact them and say some untrue things and end up tarnishing your name, making your significant other see you in a suspicious light. The jealous vampire relishes seeing people in pain.

Whining Vampires

It is not only tiring being around these people but annoying as well. When they encounter the least challenge, their knee-jerk reaction is to whine and cry about it, rather than take helpful actions. When you stay close to a person who's eternally whining, their negativity eventually closes upon you and causes your vibrations to go down. Whining vampires influence you into developing negative thoughts and this stifles your ability to make progress. Empaths should note people who have a tendency of whining and eliminate them from their lives.

Insecurity Vampires

Some people are so insecure about themselves that they end up becoming energy vampires. The problem with being insecure is that it makes you look for ways to overcompensate. For instance, if a short man is insecure about their height, they might develop a queer habit of making themselves look bigger. They will come across as a try hard, and this behavior will hinder them from having normal interactions with other people. When a person reeks of insecurity, other people tend to be wary of them. This leads to the parties engaging in wars and counter wars at the emotional and physical level.

How To Protect Yourself

Have you ever gone somewhere feeling vibrant and after spending time around that place, you felt drained of energy? Or have you ever met someone and after spending time with them, you felt an energy drain? Both of these situations point to an encounter with an energy vampire. Most energy vampires are only interested in their own desires, lack empathy, and are incredibly immature.

An energy vampire will leave you feeling exhausted, irritated, and overwhelmed. An energy vampire can be anyone – friends, family, coworkers, etc. Once you realize that someone is a vampire, you should do yourself a favor and cut them off from your life. Getting rid of an energy vampire is not a self-serving deed; it is an act of self-preservation. The vibrations of energy, vampires are incredibly low. As a coping

475

strategy, they have to suck energy from others through the following ways:

• Gossiping: An energy vampire knows that people want to hear a good story; therefore, they say anything in an attempt to earn the attention of their victim. They resort to telling lies about people. If an energy vampire tells you about other people, you can be sure that they will tell other people about you as well. They also start slow wars between factions by telling each side antagonizing news.

• Manipulation: An energy vampire is a master manipulator. Before they approach anyone, they already have a script to play by and have rehearsed how to take advantage of that person. They have no remorse about manipulating people into doing their bidding, as their capacity to empathize is incredibly limited. Energy vampires get a high out of manipulating people and getting their way.

• Complaining: No one is more "wronged" in the entire world. An energy vampire believes that the world is out to get them. They can take advantage of someone and yet find a way of twisting the story so that they appear to be the victims. An energy vampire is good at weaving stories together, and they have the experience of passing themselves off as victims. Due to this habit of complaining, an energy vampire tends to be slack in their work, knowing too well they can find something to complain about or someone to throw the blame at.

• Massive ego: An energy vampire has a massive ego, and it comes with delusions of grandeur. An energy vampire sets himself extremely ambitious goals. The goals are unrealistic because they lack the wherewithal of achieving these goals. Their massive ego also manifests in how they treat other people. Energy vampires think that they are special people and are above everyone else. Thus, they act self-entitled and expect everyone to bow down to them. When an energy vampire comes into your life, they will normally have an agenda of taking something away from you, before they move on to the next victim.

• Not being accountable: An energy vampire will hardly ever be accountable for anything. They want easy things and hate responsibility. Due to this hatred of accountability, energy vampires make the worst candidates for doing any serious task. They will usually disappoint you. If you have to rely on an energy vampire for the completion of a task, they will frustrate you with their subpar performance and an unwillingness to be accountable. Energy vampires will develop a hatred toward anyone that expects them to be answerable, but when the shoe is on the other foot, they are extremely ruthless.

• Neglecting the needs of their dependents: Energy vampires are only interested in their own needs and woe unto anyone that depends on them. For instance, if the energy vampire in question has a family, they may spend their earnings on vain things like sex and alcohol at the expense of their family. The people that depend on an energy vampire lead very sad lives because of both the cruelty and humiliation that the energy vampire metes out at them.

When an energy vampire is around you, you will feel uneasy, and soon your energy levels will take a massive dip. The following are some things that take place when attacked by an energy vampire:

• Nausea: After an interaction with an energy vampire, you can be left feeling nauseous. This feeling may be accompanied by a stomach ache. This happens because your body is going through a lot of stress because of losing energy. Once you get rid of the energy vampire, both the nausea and the stomach ache will go away.

• Headache: An energy vampire will also make you experience a terrible headache. Once your energy levels go down, there's not enough energy for your brain. The brain reacts by trying to create awareness of the fact that the body has run out of sugars. The brain consumes a significant portion of the total energy of a person, and if the energy suffers a drop, a person's ability to use their mental faculties is severely affected.

Chapter 38   How to Stop Absorbing Negative Energies?

How to embolden yourself from the emotional effects of others

The transference of energy from other people is a real challenge in today's world. Highly sensitive people are often plagued with this phenomenon and wonder what to do about it. Signals carrying the energy from those around us is often involuntary. It just happens. Sometimes we can gain from these encounters but most often, they are a weight that can drag us down and ruin a perfectly good day.

When we absorb other people's feelings and emotions, they become mixed up within our own similar inclinations and thoughts. When this happens, things can get a bit more involved and interrupt the natural flow of our own lives so that things don't get done or become halted altogether. For this reason, we must guard against the potential for misinterpretations of these bundles of feelings in order to have an actively progressive flow of our own information and forward motion.

When you find yourself in a room with a very negative individual, their "bad" energy can actually very quickly be activated in you. In order to prevent this from happening, the first step to take is to take a moment and look inwards, try to identify the true source of the negative energy. Is it you and was it always there inside you, or is it the other person's energy invading your otherwise happy system? In most cases, you will be able to learn that it is indeed not yours and was not present in your immediate feelings and emotions until that other person walked into the room. You must then take steps to let it go. Close your eyes and visualize who you are. Embolden yourself with the strength that you know you have always had within you and hold on tightly to that which you believe. Since you are a positive life form, this will manifest in those negative energies leaving your body and your mind. Remove yourself from surroundings containing negative thought patterns and feelings. Just walk away from it and do everything you can to avoid repeating this type of situation and condition in the future.

Another trait empath all exhibit is that they are all hyper-sensitive to the effect of their surroundings. When an empath is in a space where harmony abounds, they are most at home, as they will always mimic the happy and harmonious qualities of the room. Consequently, when they are in an environment where there is negative and dark energy, the opposite happens and they must remove themselves as quickly as possible which is exactly what they usually do. Actually, this is something all normally energized people should also do. Nobody should have to put up with those who simply drag us down with their whiny grievances.

Here are some things that you can do in order to protect and embolden yourself from the negative and nonproductive energy of those around you:

• Set your limits and boundaries. Negative people will recognize this in you and will generally move away from you.

• Be selective in where you go, who you are willing to speak with and always be sure to be in control of you.

• Don't get sidelined. Keep your antenna's up and use your special awareness to stay clear of others' bad behavior and negative energies.

• Stay positive. Don't let anyone or anything drag you down. It is much easier to stay positive within yourself than to have to battle your way back up after being dragged down unnecessarily.

• Remember who you are and how much you love being you. You are above the fray when it comes to bad energy. Use your own "intact" systems to stay strong.

So, if you've thought it over and wondered to yourself just how to stay positive when your find yourself in a negative environment; stick to the rules set out here and things will gradually begin to smooth out and become much easier for you. If these are people you just cannot avoid, and would really rather avoid, you must have a protection program in place or you will suffer and they will drag you down.

There is really no sense in letting this happen if you already know that it is a "given," with a certain person or set of people, that it has already formerly been proven to be so. You can do this. Know the parameters, set up your own system in your mind when you know you must face them again, and keep it up!

You may want to think of it in the abstract; be creative. Think of your next meeting with these low energy people as a heading. The heading tells the reader what is coming, and then the data pours out and is indeed, "as advertised." The heading predicted it because it knew for a fact what was coming next, and the data had to work closely with the heading because they work in tandem with each other. They are a team!

Now, breaking this theory down, you are the heading and the "people" in the group are the data. If your heading says, "Do not try to mess with me because I am protected, and it won't work!" They will take one look at you and immediately back off. Problem solved.

As stated, toxic people, whether they are consciously aware of it or not, do not do well with boundaries or "rules of engagement." These would be "your" rules so you are in charge. When going into battle, be armed and dangerous. Be ready for the enemy.

I know that sounds a bit terse but it gets the point across and the alternative is having to sit through hours of soul destroying and painful negativity that you know within yourself that you don't like and you don't need. Just do your homework and take control. It will be easy once you understand how to do it.

And there is more; again, while you know that you must see them, be with them, and interact with them, keep it short and concise so that there is no room for "small talk" or any unnecessary banter. Keep the communications brief and keep the material light whenever possible. Remember, toxic people will search for key areas in your speaking on which to pounce. This will create a scenario where they look better. This is their MO. If the conversation is by telephone, set a timer so you have control.

Weigh out the consequences of new topics that may arise in conversation and know which are worth dealing with and which are worth tossing into the circular file as soon as possible. Observe others' intention in their speaking. Where are they attempting to take the conversation?

You really do need to protect yourself from what could be called "second hand stress." Just being around people who operate out of drama can be very draining and as everyone must know by now, stress is not just a bad thing, it is a killer. You must come up with ways to avoid it at all costs. Research has shown that stress can be a bit like a yawn, it can actually be contagious. In an earlier part we consider "mirror neurons" that are signals produced in the brain that provide some degree of ability for us to absorb and comprehend other people's feelings and emotions.

In the same way that we might understand others, we can also be a huge "antenna," for receiving those around us who may send us all their bad stuff. Negative energy and stress can be incoming in this way. Science tells us that even as we observe another's anger, our stress hormones may rise up to twenty-six percent in our bodies. Stress conveyed to us through other people can show up in a variety of ways. When we spend time thinking about the problems that someone else may be experiencing or getting nervous or afraid because that is the emotion that another person close to us is feeling is a stress maker for all of us.

Also, sustained stress can give us all sorts of extended health issues which means we must find a way to protect ourselves from the "outside" sources of errant stress. The following are a few suggestions that may help to immunize you against second hand stress:

1.   Do not let stress spread into your body! As social individuals, we see and we feel. Prevent unfavorable "other peoples" stress and negativity by focusing on your own current feelings. This will contain your emotions and show you that these new apparent "inputs" are not yours. Thereby keeping tabs on your good feelings.

2.   Empathize without swallowing the entire pill yourself! We are in charge of us and they are in charge of them and this focus can be a great deal of help as a filter or boundary locator. Put up your fence and play on your side, let them play on their side. This is actually a good time to do a lesson within yourself and know your passions and your own empathy. It's okay to substantiate their situation and do listen to their words if they need to "get it out," but remember, don't jump right in and share the agony. This is just not necessary.

3.   Monitor your own stress levels on a regular basis and don't let them rise up! Get the endorphins going and observe your breathing. Utilize your mindfulness and meditate daily and if you can, multiple times a day. Any kind of exercise is also a great way to keep tabs on yourself. Your body will thank you when you pump up the body machine now and then.

4.   Monitor your sense of boundaries! In a way, checking in on your boundary patrol is a healthy thing to be doing. Simply be vigilant and always know when to step away from an individual or a situation.

5.   Boosting your sense of self, staying vigilant on boundary patrol, and monitoring your own feelings are all tools that can help to keep secondhand stress under control.

For the past few years, there has been a relatively new psychological theory in the works called "Emotional Intelligence." The idea is that just as people have an array of intellectual abilities, they also have a range of emotional abilities and skills. These emotional "tools," can be of immense assistance in the area of our thinking and what we do from day to day. The bottom line here is that utilizing this theory makes you a better person and can help you grow in ways that you want to grow and not where ever the wind may take you.

Chapter 39 Manage Emotions and Thoughts to Overcome Stress and Shyness

Think of your emotional intelligence as a muscle. To strengthen that muscle and build it up to where you want it to be, you need to exercise it consistently, just as you would with physical exercise.

Reflecting on Your Feelings

The first exercise that you can begin working to develop and improve your emotional intelligence is to begin by observing your feelings and reflecting on them. It is easy to fall out of touch with ourselves in this hectic world that we live in. From the moment we wake up each morning our lives seem to be constantly on the go. Trying to manage one thing after another, taking care of ourselves often falls by the wayside and we lose that connection to our innermost feelings. Instead of learning to focus on our emotions when they arise, we choose to do the easier, more convenient thing. We either brush it aside, ignore them or deny them completely. Maybe even distract us from those feelings by doing something else. The more you deny your feelings though, the harder it becomes to manage them later on. Bottling up your emotions and hoping they will just go away on its own has never proven to be an effective strategy. If it were, there wouldn't be quite so many people walking around lashing out emotionally or reacting impulsively. From now on, whenever you experience an emotion (no matter what it may be), observe it, acknowledge it, and reflect on how it is making you feel.

Make a Note of Your Triggers

This is something new because you've probably never done this before. Take your exercises towards building emotional intelligence one step further by writing down the triggers that cause you to become emotional each time you observe your feelings. What caused you to get worked up? What caused you to feel stressed? What's responsible for creating this feeling of happiness you now feel?

Whenever you make a note of every emotion you experience, write down and make a list of the things that triggered it. Examine that list a couple of times a week. Do you notice any patterns? What is a recurring theme that you can spot? Learning how to identify the triggers that cause extreme emotional reactions are the key to learning how to manage your emotions. After all, you can't manage something that you don't know. You need to know what you're dealing with before you can start making moves to remedy it.

Keep track of the emotional triggers!

Once you have found out the reasons behind the occurrence of every emotion, write down those reasons on your list. For instance, if there is a certain person or a certain event that invokes the emotion of anger in you then you must write down this reason under the heading of anger.

Making use of those emotions

We must never underestimate how emotions affect our thoughts. Whenever we think about a certain thing, our emotions control our reactions to that thing.

Emotions don't just tend to occur on a sudden basis. They occur due to reasons that have been supporting them for a certain period. For instance, you are getting late in the morning while driving to work. You see a car with a flat tire standing in the midst of the road. You start angrily shouting at the driver of that car to move his car away from the road. This anger didn't just occur as a sudden reaction to the flat tire of that car, but it occurred because you woke up late that morning due to which you were already late for your work.

At the end comes the task of managing your emotions. For some people, this task is known to be the biggest challenge in their life. Managing your emotions is not just a one-day task, but it requires a continuous struggle. However, once you master this task, managing your emotions might turn into the easiest thing on this planet.

Take a Timeout When You Need It

An emotionally intelligent person does not let their feelings overwhelm them. They always remain, cool, calm and collected. They always respond appropriately. More importantly, they know when to take a time out and come back to the situation with a better solution. It is easy to let your feelings overwhelm you if you're not careful.

As much as you want to resolve a conflict there and then, sometimes you need to take a time-out or a five-minute breather to just clear your head whenever your emotions are starting to get the best of you. That is the intelligent thing to do. Instead of ploughing through your emotions, forcing yourself to resolve a conflict for example, observe the way you're feeling and if you need a break, speak up, let the other person know, walk away for a couple of minutes and come back to it when your head is clearer and you're thinking straight.

Start Practicing Responding

 Where prior to this you may have been more prone to reacting impulsively each time you had an extreme emotional reaction, now you need to adopt a new exercise. You need to learn how to respond first instead of reacting. You now need to make response your first default mode, and you do that with self-awareness and self-regulation. By paying attention to your emotions, especially the ones that tend to trigger an extreme reaction in the past; you can then learn how to regulate yourself. You can make a conscious effort to choose the next move you will make instead of letting your emotions drive you. You will do the intelligent thing by leading with your head, not your heart. This is why it is so important to emulate the steps above, especially learning how to identify your triggers. If you know something will trigger an extreme emotional response, take measures to that put a stop to that through self-regulation.

No Room for Superiority

An emotionally intelligent person is that way because of one thing – they are humble. It simply won't do to think that you may be better than everyone, or that someone is not on par with you and that makes you more superior. You will never achieve a leadership position if you inflict an air of superiority because no one will ever respect a leader who makes it difficult to be likable. When you choose not to be humble, you make it very difficult for yourself to achieve self-awareness, because you will be blinded to your own faults. It's no problem for you to immediately point out the flaws in others, but you won't be able to see the things that you are doing wrong. See everyone as an equal, not a subordinate. No matter what background they come from, everyone deserves to be treated respectfully. Display emotional intelligence by always choosing to be humble, approachable, likable and pleasant.

Avoid Overthinking

One of the reasons that we sometimes become more emotional than we should is because we tend to overthink a lot of things. A simple matter which could be resolved easily could potentially get blown out of proportion because someone was reacting to it in a highly emotional way. To start exercising better emotional intelligence on your part, what you could do is to stop overthinking situations and just see things for what they are. You do that by looking at the facts in front of you. If something is not a tangible fact, then don't think about it. Observe the situation in front of you and see things as they are. Don't embellish, don't assume, and don't add on facts of your own. This is how things get more complicated than they should, and emotions get fired up when there was no need to be.

Writing Down Your Feelings

Take a paper and a pen. Note down the emotions that you feel on a regular basis. Point out your physical reactions to each type of emotion under the heading of that emotion. For instance, you have written down the emotion of HURT which you feel now and then. The next thing you need to do is to point out your bodily reactions that occur as a result of feeling hurt. Whether you cry or feel a sense of loss, just write it down on your list. Once you have completed the first emotion and its symptoms, move on towards the next emotion.

Pour your heart out, open the floodgates of emotion and just let it flow until you're done. When you've finished, read what you've just written down. Assess your thoughts, observe the way that you're feeling and reflect upon why and what triggered such an emotion within you. Once you've finished and felt better, you can always tear up or shred the paper. The point of this exercise is to provide you with an outlet for your emotions, to give you something that helps you regulate the way that you're feeling instead of just letting the emotion fester within you. Do you notice how you sometimes feel better after talking about your feelings with someone? It works the same way, except that by writing it down you ensure that you always have an outlet for your emotions, even when no one is available.

Chapter 40   The Mind-Body Connection

Head Movement

Head movement is one of the simplest body languages to decode. However, for someone who has no clue of what this nonverbal communication signal means, hardly will they be able to make sense of it. To explain the head movement, I have here two scenarios:

As part of the exercise to get a job, a candidate is required to make a presentation on why he is the best candidate for the job. During the presentation, his audience, the hiring manager, nods in quick succession while the candidate desperately keeps trying to sell him. Obviously, he is unaware of the message of the hiring manager, which clearly shows he is wasting his time.

Consider another candidate giving the same presentation. As he goes off trying to sell himself, the hiring manager leans back with his head tilted. Oblivious to the meaning of this body language, the candidate does not try to shed light on the point, which triggers the manager's body reaction. He is ignorant of the body language; hence, he keeps on blabbing.

Below are some common head movement signals and their meanings:

When a person gives quick, successive nods, they are probably fed up with the interaction. Had the candidate in our first example know this, he would have tried harder to impress the manager or end the interaction, saving him time.

A slow nod is a sure sign of interest in the interaction. This is what the candidate should be after, had he any knowledge of nonverbal communication and body language. It is also the same when the person you are with tilts their head sideways.

A slight, backward tilt of the head is a sign of suspicion, uncertainty, or confusion. This, at times, might be accompanied by a slight change in facial expression. This is a cue to clarify the last point that triggered such an expression. The candidate in our second example could have cashed in on this point and clarified his statement.

If you are having a discussion with a group of people and one of them starts scratching their jaw, there is a big chance that the person is not in agreement with the subject of discussion. Be sure to allow the person to voice out their view.

Reading The Face

There are many expressions we can reveal with our faces. Even babies and toddlers are smart enough to decode this body language cue. A smile reveals happiness or satisfaction. A frown shows dissatisfaction or sadness. There are times as well when the facial expression could give insight into what is really going on with a person. A person who says he's fine with a slight frown, for instance, could be lying.

The facial expression can help you know if someone is worth our trust or not. According to research, "a trustworthy facial expression involves a slight smile with a gentle rise of the eyebrow" (Duenwald, 2005). This conveys friendliness.

It is a universal form of expression that conveys a wide range of emotions, such as sadness, fear, panic, anxiety, worry, disgust, distrust, happiness, and many others. The best part is that this expression does not change or vary with people.

Many people, in a bid to hide their true intention, desperately try to control the face. A careful study of the face, however, can give you a clear glimpse into the message someone is trying to pass across. There are times when someone might hide obvious body language, such as raised eyebrows, smiles, frowns, etc. Be sure to watch out for the following:

A warm and genuine smile does light up the whole face. It indicates happiness. It is also a sure indication that the other party is enjoying your company.

A fake smile, on the other hand, is a polite way of showing approval, even if the person does not enjoy the conversation or interaction. For you to detect a fake smile, take a look at the side of the eyes. The lack of crinkles is all you need to pass a smile off as fake.

The Eye Window

The eyes reveal a lot about a person. This explains why the eyes are referred to as the window to the soul. Besides, in all forms of interactions, it is an important and natural communication process for you to take note of the eyes.

In communicating with people, it is normal to take note of eye contact, whether someone is averting your gaze or not, the rate of blinking, and the size of their pupils.

The following explains some nonverbal clues from the eyes:

Eye gaze: A person interested and paying attention to a conversation will look directly into your eyes while having a conversation, although they might break eye contact once in a while because prolonged eye contact is rather uncomfortable. A distracted and uninterested person, on the other hand, will often break eye contact and look away. This person might be uncomfortable or is trying to hide their true feelings.

Blinking: While blinking is a completely natural process, the frequency matters. A person uncomfortable or in distress will blink more often. Infrequent blinking, on the other hand, means that a person is intentionally trying to control their eye movements.

Pupil size: Pay attention to the pupil size as it is very subtle and is affected by the level of light in the room. However, emotions also do affect pupil dilation as it can cause small changes in the size of the pupil. This explains why someone with highly dilated eyes is either aroused or interested in a person.

Hand Movements

There are some cues that can be easily found from the position and pattern of movement of the hand. We explain this in detail:

When someone has their hands in their pockets, they could lack confidence, is hiding information, or just being defensive.

In a group or meeting, when a person unconsciously points to another person while making a speech, there might be some common ground they share.

In communicating with someone, the presence of an obstacle in the form of an object between you and the person translates to the person trying to block you out. In this case, your aim should be to build rapport and gain the trust of such a person.

A person talking with the palms facing up is probably being honest. Such a person is not hiding the palm since they most likely have nothing to hide.

The Mouth

The expressions and movement of the mouth are pretty vital in decoding body language as well. This is why a person who is worried, anxious, or insecure will likely chew their lower lip. Some forms of nonverbal communication cues from the mouth will be examined below. A person, in an effort to be polite, might cover the mouth if the other party is yawning. Be watchful, as it can be done to cover up a frown as well.

Pursed lips: When a person tightens up their lip, it could signal objection, disapproval, or distaste.

Lip biting: This is common when a person is anxious, worried, or stressed.

Covering the mouth: This could be done in an effort to hide emotional reactions like smiles or smirks.

A slight change in direction: A person's feeling can be seen through the direction of the mouth. As a result, someone happy or in a good mood might have their mouth slightly turned up. A slightly turned-down mouth, on the other hand, could signal sadness or displeasure.

Body Mirroring

This happens when you consciously or unconsciously mimic the body movement or speech pattern of another person. Take note of the following:

There is a big chance that a person who mirrors you is into you. You can confirm this by slightly adjusting yourself and see if they will follow suit.

Avoid mirroring negative body cues. If the person detects this, there is a big chance they will desist from associating with you.

Try not to mirror a fellow woman you intend to build rapport with. Women do not appreciate this.

Men, on the other hand, love this. In fact, mirroring each other, even their dressing style, can be seen as a chance to seal a friendship.

Posture And Composure

In meeting anyone, one of the first things that strike you about them is the way they hold themselves. It could be sitting, standing, or walking. There is a message it passes across that could be open, loose, defensive, welcoming, closed, poor, confident, charming, aggressive, dominating, etc.

From someone's posture, you can deduce a whole lot of information about them, as well as a glimpse into their personality.

Sitting up straight, for instance, points to a focused person who is paying attention to the interaction. A bored or indifferent person, on the other hand, might sit with the body hunched forward. In reading body language, be sure to consider the signals coming from the posture as well.

A person who is open to interaction, friendly, and interested will have their body exposed.

On the other hand, a person with a closed posture who is hostile, unfriendly, or anxious might sit with either the hands or legs crossed and the body hunched forward.

The Orientation of the Body

In decoding body language, orientation matters as well. This is because the direction of the body will help see what catches their interest or what they are trying to avoid.

The legs reveal this a lot. This explains why a person who wants to leave a room or a meeting will likely have their body and their legs facing the door, the very direction where their mind is.

The Gestures

While you might not pay attention to hand gestures, you can still learn a lot and try to read the person from how they use their hand gestures.

Gestures depend on cultures, but there is a general rule: a person who makes fewer gestures could be more calculated and reserved and might be of a higher social status.

We can associate gestures with the saying that an empty barrel makes the loudest noise. In other words, the strong, indeed, will not really make much noise about it. People of authority and influence who are confident in their ability will see no need to express and explain themselves in the form of gestures.

In understanding gestures, the body level where the gesture occurs matters as well.

If the gesture occurs at the waist level, it shows the person is calm, calculated, and more in control with a high level of self-control.

The gesture becomes pretty emotional as we proceed higher. For instance, gestures at chest level are pretty sincere and expressive. Gestures at a higher level, say the head, refer to strong emotions, such as anger, sadness, and spirituality.

Chapter 41   Emotional Intelligence

You might already know someone who is a very good listener. This person, no matter what type of situation you are in, knows how to listen to you till the end and then respond in a positive way. He knows what say and when in a way that does not upset or offend you. Even if this person doesn't know how to fix your situation, you still feel better after talking with them because of their caring, optimistic and hopeful approach. Well, this is the work of someone with high emotional intelligence.

Also, you probably know someone who is a master in controlling and managing their emotions even in stressful situations. That person knows how to stay calm and doesn't burst with anger. Instead, they keep cool, stay calm and work to find the solution. With the ability to make decisions by listening to and trusting their intuition, they climb the ladder of success faster and more confidently.

A positive attitude against criticism is key. For these people, their world doesn't come apart when they hear someone criticize them. Taking the criticism calmly, they use it in their favor to improve their performance.

Sounds amazing right? And it might even seem impossible. But this is a big part of what emotional intelligence is about. So how can we define EQ?

- Manage, Understand and Recognize our Emotions

- Understand, Recognize and Influence other people's emotions

This means that being aware of emotions can influence our behavior and then impact people (both negatively and positively). Learning to manage the emotions of others and ours, especially under pressure, is what EQ all about.

EQ is about the ability to use, understand and manage emotions, not in a negative but positive way to defuse conflict, overcome challenges, empathize with other people, communicate effectively and relieve stress.

You'd think that people who have higher IQs have a higher chance of being more successful in life and work. However, it has been proven that EQ is more important than IQ. It takes more than just being 'smart' to become successful.

Why is it Important?

Let's get one thing straight; Emotional Intelligence is not the rival of IQ. In fact, you can have high IQ and EQ levels. But life is constructed of social situations. Without knowing how to function in this environment, you won't get far only relying on IQ. It's not just about what you know; it's also how you care.

The ability to have EQ as a reserve helps in many different ways, from the ability to lead and inspire to taking care of our well-being, mental and physical health. It will be there when you manage relationships and will act as a shield when there is conflict on the horizon. Seen from a different perspective, it is the basis of success.

EQ is not only essential to having a happy personal life, but it is also important in the workplace. Did you know that people who have an average IQ tend to be better at their jobs than those with a higher IQ? What is the reason? Is it EQ? While they are not enemies or rivals, 75% of people with low career performance can thank their lack of control of their emotions, especially when it comes to being unable to handle problems between a coworker and the team during conflict or other difficulties, easily adjust to change, or earn trust from others.

Why do you need EQ in Your Workplace?

No matter what you do for a living, your career and work life are hugely affected by emotional intelligence. The workplace is, in fact, the center of relational environments. It is the point where different emotions, strengths, skills, and personalities meet.

Therefore, emotional intelligence is melded into every action and decision in the workplace. It is in the instructions for the team and even in big organizational change. So, those who possess higher EQ more successfully navigate through the workplace. Plus, it enables them to drive and build teams with an amazing success rate while being responsive and agile as needed.

So, what happens when your workplace is driven by low EQ levels? At the worst point, it can lead to low morale, harassment, and bullying. It might be present as volatility, aggression, and arrogance. So, while high levels will result in flexibility, low levels will present as rigidity and inflexibility, which is very dangerous for any type of business.

Areas Affected by EQ

Emotional Intelligence leaves a big imprint in your life. Not only does it affect your personal and work life but your health, too. Here are the 4 areas affected:

1 – Work Performance – As I told you before, EQ affects your work performance greatly. This is because it will help you navigate social complexities. You will be able to motivate and lead others. Plus, when applying for a new job many companies notice the emotional intelligence before IQ. In fact, some companies have started to require emotional intelligence testing before they hire.

2 – Physical Health – Yes, even though we are speaking about emotions, physical health is also impacted. After all, everything is connected in different ways. It goes like this: when you are not able to manage the stress levels it might lead to a low immune system. The risk of stroke and heart attack also increases. Plus, stress speeds up aging. That is why the first step to improving emotional intelligence is to learn and understand the best way to relieve your stress.

3 – Mental Health – Uncontrolled stress not only impacts physical health but also mental. It makes you vulnerable to depression and anxiety. Being unable to manage and understand your own emotions means that you are always a target for mood swings and changes. This will make it hard to form a stable and strong relationship and it might leave you with feelings of isolation and loneliness.

4 – Relationships – Once you understand your own emotions and learn how to be in control, you know how to express your feelings understand how other people are feeling. This will help in building stronger relationships because you will be able to communicate effectively, both in your personal and work life.

What Defines EQ?

Now, there are many different thoughts about what truly defines emotional intelligence. Usually, it is defined with 4 to 5 characteristics. However, if you truly want to achieve high levels, we will need to look even deeper. This means even the slightest characteristic can affect how high you can reach. After all, my goal here is to help you better understand emotional intelligence. Once you understand it and start working on the important parts it won't be long before you become one of the most successful people in the world. Yes! EQ will help you become successful.

However, remember one thing: everything requires work, practice, time and patience. You can't acquire the skills you need overnight. You will need to work on them constantly. Don't worry; it is not difficult at all, but it is important in order to have EQ as a reserve and by your side all the time.

Chapter 42   Maintain Mindfulness and Self-Balance by Relating to Stressed, Depressed or Anxious People

You will always find people telling you that every single person on this planet has a unique set of skills and abilities. Everyone is special. From childhood tales to history books and even the web series and films of the modern era speak about life's purpose and that everyone is meant to do something specific. But do you know what your purpose is?

With time, you will find that you are more attracted to certain activities. You will also find that there are some things which you prefer more than others and you resonate with their energy. This is how you will be able to identify your special gifts.

Everyone has qualities that have some role to play in society as a whole. Some people love painting while others love writing. Whatever it is that you love to do, it makes you whole as a person and it adds flavor to your overall character. And when this realization dawns upon you, you will realize that you do matter as a person. The main struggle that everyone faces with self-worth and finding their abilities is that they fail to recognize the importance of their qualities. It might seem simple now but it is often complicated to realize that you might be meant to do something in life which you have a natural flair for.

Your sense of self-worth is most affected by your limiting beliefs. You might never have considered yourself to be good at doing something in life because all your friends and siblings have been outshining you since childhood. In such scenarios, society forces the person to ignore their strengths and focus more on their weaknesses. Your negative view of your self-image might be blinding you from seeing your strengths but that does not mean that you do not have strengths. You have them but the only thing you have to do is find them. You need to dig what is present beneath the surface to understand your self-worth and this part will tell you about the ways in which you can do so and identify your unique abilities.

Mindfulness

Mindfulness is considered to be a very effective tool when it comes to understanding your self-worth. It is very normal for people to suffer from low self-esteem and it is even more common in empaths. No matter how hard they try, they often find themselves in a situation where they are not satisfied with what they are doing. They often find their actions to be inadequate. They spend countless hours thinking that the problem is with them and they need to be fixed. But this is just a case of low self-esteem. Constructive criticism is only good when it is healthy.

As an empath, you will constantly be evaluating everything that is present in your surroundings and during this, you will also have several negative thoughts which will make you feel low. But you will not be able to do anything about it until and unless you realize that you need to do something about it. At the end of the day, you need to understand that your thoughts are nothing more than just thoughts. But a dose of negative self-talk on a daily basis will shatter your sense of self-worth. That is where mindfulness comes in. Being mindful means that you are carefully assessing every thought and moment in your life. You will let your thoughts come into your mind but you will remind yourself not to get affected by them.

Whenever you find yourself engaged in self-criticism, you need to keep reminding yourself that these are your thoughts and they have nothing to do with the facts.

Don't Stick to Limiting Stories

Whatever your present state of mind is, it completely relies on your thoughts. But have you wondered whether you are telling yourself a limiting story? Because if you are, then it is going to lower your abilities and along with that, your self-esteem as well. Thus, in simpler terms, an individual's perception of reality is based on all the stories they tend to tell themselves. What you need to keep in mind is that these stories are not real although the individual believes them to be. The way you respond to your life and your attitude towards every situation is determined by these stories.

So, your first step will be to identify whether you are telling yourself any limiting story or not. If you are, then you have to come up with an empowering one that will replace the limiting story from your mind. If you want your new story to stick with you, then you will have to empower it with emotions. These emotions have to be positive. One of

498

the best ways to do this is visualizing all the positive things and this will make you look forward to it.

Once you change the story in your mind, you will see new opportunities coming your way. It is not that they were not present before but the only difference is that you did not have the courage to try new things. But now, you will see everything from a new and positive perspective. You also need to have patience because changes don't happen in a day and if you don't see changes as fast as you wanted them to, don't beat yourself up for that.

Stop Comparing Yourself to Others

In this world, you will always find people who do things better than you, so what is the use of comparing yourself to others? It will only make you feel less qualified whereas that is not the truth. The only question that you need to ask yourself is whether you are improving or not. Although this is not as easy as it sounds, you should keep trying.

The situation becomes worse because of the numerous advertisements shown on the television and the web that are designed to prey on the insecurities of the people. This keeps happening all the time with empaths, especially those empaths who consider themselves to be an outsider in every setting. When they scroll through social media platforms, they feel even more depressed because they start thinking that others are living a better and happier life. But you should not fall for that illusion. Everything you see on social media is not so bright and happy. Everyone has their own problems. The only difference is that they do not show that on social media.

The first step to stop this comparison habit is to acknowledge whether you are jealous of someone or not. If you are then you need to find what thoughts lay beneath that facade of jealousy. For example, if you saw your friend's posts on Instagram where she posed in front of the Eiffel Tower, you should start budgeting on your own so that you can also visit Paris.

You need to stop comparing yourself to others because it will only hold you back. If you want growth in your life, then you need to compare yourself with what you were a couple of years back. Have you improved? Yes? Then that is what matters and nothing else.

Recognize Your Inner Strengths

Every successful venture is standing tall on its foundation. If the foundation is ragged and not strong, the venture will eventually collapse. So, you need to understand what your inner strengths are. If you start building your world on the wrong qualities then you are bound to feel frustrated after a certain point of time because you do not love what you do. In order to truly love what you do; you need to figure out what you are good at.

Take a table for an example. The tabletop stands on the four legs and that tabletop is your confidence and legs are your inner strengths. Identify them and focus on them. In order to make your tabletop solid, you need to first make these legs strong.

Another important thing that you should do is keep all your shortcomings aside and stop focusing on them. Shift all your focus on your strengths. Do not listen to the world. They might force you to look at your shortcomings but you shouldn't.

Chapter 43   Compassion and Mirror Neurons

The words "empath" and "empathy" both stem from the Ancient Greek term "Empatheia," which is a hybrid of the words "en" meaning "in" or "at" and "pathos" which means "passion" or "feeling" but can also be interpreted to mean "suffering." This etymological root is perfectly illustrative of empathy as a double-edged sword. Humans crave deep interpersonal connection and often find joy in shared passions, but when we open ourselves up to the blessings of those around us, we also open ourselves up to their sorrows, fears, and furies.

Within the past few decades, the fields of psychology, neuroscience, and many others have made enormous strides in research towards understanding the minds of those who do not display the "normal" amount of empathy. There are some conditions, such as autism or Asperger's syndrome, wherein a person seems able to detect the emotional energies of those around them, but simply lacks the necessary cognitive tools to interpret them or determine an appropriate reaction. These people often feel attacked or overwhelmed when the emotions of others resonate within them—which is a form of empathic sensitivity— but they often react by shutting down or self-isolating rather than trying to find a way to harmonious coexistence. It is not a struggle for these people to put their own needs first in interpersonal connections, even if it is at the expense of other people's feelings, but this isn't a malicious sentiment; it is primarily a self-preservation instinct in hyper drive.

Alternatively, there are empathy-deficient personality disorders, such as narcissism, sociopathy, and psychopathy, wherein a person is capable of recognizing the emotions of others but feels personally detached from them. This is why we often describe psychopathic criminals as "cold" or "calculating." It is unsettling to imagine that a person could decide to take action, knowing that their behavior will cause pain or suffering in others and that they might remain unbothered by that fact or actually derive pleasure from it--but that is the thought process of an empathy-disordered individual. The feelings of others are considered unimportant because they do not impact their personal emotional sensations.

The general population holds a lot of misconceptions about people with these personality disorders, which are most evident within the criminal justice system. Many of us convince ourselves, for instance, that these people commit crimes of passion, temporarily losing their sense of right and wrong in the blinding heat of rage, or alternatively, that they are so mentally skewed as to be incapable of understanding how much pain and suffering they are causing. Unfortunately, neither of these possibilities proves true for these individuals. They do understand the impact of their actions and are capable of determining right from wrong, yet they choose to ignore these factors, hurting other people to serve strategic needs or for the sake of personal gain. In fact, people with these personality disorders generally display impressive skill with cognitive empathy, which you might think of as theoretical empathy; this allows them to theorize or predict the emotional reactions of others and makes them masterful manipulators.

When discussing those who struggle to display or feel empathy, it's important to remember that empathic abilities are fluid, not fixed in stone. Anyone who is willing to put in the effort can improve their empathic capabilities, even those who have been diagnosed with an empathy deficient condition or disorder. Physical empathy is often accessible to those who do not display emotional empathy, which may be a function of evolutionary development. Humans can better protect their physical bodies by recognizing physical pain in others and are biologically driven to mimic pleasurable behaviors (whether that means eating good food or enjoying sexual stimulation) by watching others and empathizing with their enjoyment of such activities. Since this form of empathy is often observable in scans of empathy-disordered brains, we must embrace the notion that empathy exists as a complex and fluid and scale. It is not like a light switch that is either flipped on or off.

Empathy is important because it allows you to simulate the cognitive and affective mental conditions of other people. Neurobiological research studies have proved that empathy is a sophisticated encounter or phenomenon that can be explained in detail using a model consisting of top-down and bottom-up processing.

Top-down processing is also called the theory of mind or cognitive perspective-taking. This is a phenomenon where you fully imagine and understand the feelings of other people. It is centered on inhibition and control mechanisms. Available evidence shows that empathic brain responses are usually affected by distinct modulating factors.

I hope you are still with me! Researchers have come up with a new model that provides an explanation of the origins of empathy and other things such as contagious yawning and emotional contagion. The model demonstrates that the origin of a wide range of empathetic responses can be found in cognitive simulation. The model shifts attention from a top-down approach that starts with cooperation to one that begins with one cognitive mechanism.

According to a post-doctoral researcher in Max Planck Institute called Fabrizio Mafessoni, standard models of the origin of empathy concentrate on situations in which cooperation or coordination are the favorites. Michael Lachmann, a theoretical biologist, together with his co-author, looked at the possibilities that cognitive processes have a wide underlying range of empathetic responses including contagious yawning, emotional contagion, and other feelings such as echopraxia and echolalia. Echolalia is a compulsive repetition of other people's speech, while echopraxia is the compulsive repetition of other people's movements. Echolalia and echopraxia can evolve in the absence of mechanisms that directly favor coordination and cooperation or kin selection.

Lachmann and Mafessoni asserted that human beings and animals could participate in the act of stimulating the minds of other people or animals. You cannot read other people's minds because they are like black boxes to you. But as Lachmann put across, all agents have the same black boxes with members of their species, and they constantly run simulations of what other minds may be doing. This ongoing process or as-actor simulation is not always focused on cooperation. It is something that animals and human beings do as a result of a sudden impulse or in other words without premeditation.

A good example of this process can be shown using mirror neurons. It has been discovered that the same neurons that take part in planning a hand movement are also responsible for observing the hand movement of others. Lachmann and Mafessoni tried to figure out what would happen if the same process of understanding would be extended to any social interaction. After modeling outcomes rooted in the cognitive simulation, they discovered that actors responsible for as-actor simulation produce different systems typically explained in terms of kin-selection and cooperation. They also realized that an observer could once in a while coordinate with an actor even when the outcome is not beneficial.

Their model is of the opinion that empathetic systems do not evolve only because animals or people simulate others to envision their actions.

According to Mafessoni, empathy must have originated from the need to understand others. For Lachmann, their discoveries have completely changed how people perceive and think about human beings and animals. Their model is based on a single cognitive mechanism that unites a wide set of phenomena under a single explanation. It consequently has theoretical import for a broad range of fields such as cognitive psychology, evolutionary biology, neuroscience, anthropology, and complex systems. Its power emanates from its theoretical interest and unifying clarity in the limits of cooperation.

Electromagnetic Fields

The subsequent finding depends on the way that both the mind and the heart produce electromagnetic fields. These fields transmit data about individuals' musings and feelings. Empaths might be especially delicate to this info and will, in general, become overpowered by it. Correspondingly, you frequently have more grounded physical and enthusiastic reactions to changes in the electromagnetic fields of the earth and sun.

Enthusiastic Contagion

The third discovery which upgrades everyone's comprehension of empaths is the wonders of the enthusiastic virus. Research has shown that numerous individuals get the feelings of people around them. For example, one crying newborn child will set off a flood of weeping in a medical clinic ward. Or then again, one individual noisily communicating nervousness in the work environment can spread it to different laborers. Individuals generally get other individuals' emotions in gatherings. Ongoing research expressed that this capacity to synchronize states of mind with others is vital for proper connections. What is exercise for empaths? To pick constructive individuals in your lives, so you are not brought somewhere near pessimism. Or then again, if, state a companion is experiencing a hard time, play it safe to the ground, and focus yourself.

Expanded Dopamine Sensitivity

The fourth discovery includes dopamine, a synapse that expands the action of neurons and is related to the joy reaction. Research has

504

demonstrated that contemplative empaths will, in general, have a higher affectability to dopamine than extraverts. Fundamentally, they need less dopamine to feel cheerful. That could clarify why they are increasingly content with alone time, perusing, and reflection and need less outer incitement from gatherings and other enormous get-togethers. Conversely, extraverts long for the dopamine surge from happy occasions. Indeed, they cannot get enough of it.

Synesthesia

The fifth discovery, which is very convincing, is the original state called "reflect contact synesthesia." Synesthesia is a neurological condition wherein two unique faculties are combined in the cerebrum. For example, you see hues when you hear a bit of music, or you taste words. Be that as it may, with mirror-contact synesthesia, individuals can feel the feelings and impressions of others in their very own bodies as though these were their own.

This is an excellent neurological clarification of an empath's involvement. "Sympathy is the most valuable human quality." During these upsetting occasions, it is anything but difficult to get overpowered. All things being equal, compassion is the quality that will get you through. It will empower you to regard every other person, regardless of whether you oppose this idea. Sympathy does not make you a wistful softy without wisdom. It enables you to keep your heart open to encourage resistance and comprehension. It may not generally be successful in breaking through to individuals and making harmony but always believe that it is the most obvious opportunity you have.

Chapter 44   Understanding Body Language

How To Read Body Language — Poor Body Language

As we mirror body language, it is equally important to understand just what we are mirroring. Reading body language is important because even before we speak, body language is our first line of communication. Even before you dialogue, eye contact and body language interact to set the pace for the rest of the conversation. That is how we gain first impressions of people, and they gain a first impression of us. Unfortunately, once these assessments have been made, it can be difficult to adjust them to reflect another side of you. It is, therefore, important that you understand how to read body language best. Below, we expound on some aspects of body language:

Finger-Pointing

Picture a scenario where you get into a home, and everything is everywhere. The children are not clean, and there is a general air of dissatisfaction with the current status of the house. The mother searches frantically for the television remote before angrily pointing to her eldest daughter, who is approximately 14 to tell her that the problem in that house is that nobody can return anything to its place. You are perturbed, but the daughter seems to be just fine, or maybe used to that kind of scenario.

From the scenario above, you can understand the message that the mother is trying to send, clearly. She could not find the remote, and she believed that her eldest daughter was responsible for misplacing it despite the entire house being a mess. However, what is more, evident is the mother is what we would term-a blamer. Something went wrong in the house, but she was placing all the blame on her daughter. Her language is suggestive, and you would be tempted to wonder where 'around here' refers to and what she means by placing things back in their places. In short, she is trying to pass a message to her daughter that she is irresponsible and careless.

There are some body language signs that also depict weakness. An example is placating. Placating is by definition, putting the hands at your side with your elbows bent and palms up. It may not seem obvious to you, but when you place your hands this way, you appear to be portraying yourself as a person that is in a position of weakness. As such, you are giving in to the situation, and you have no choice left. If you are a leader in any capacity, this is the kind of gesture you will want to avoid, especially when you need to assert something among peers.

Interestingly, placating can sometimes work to your advantage. For instance, imagine you have a difficult message to portray. When you use this gesture, it may send a signal of the kind of message you intend to send. Do not, however, overindulge because generally, it elicits the self-pity attitude.

Even though you may expect a different kind of response when such allegations, the daughter remains quiet—as mentioned above, she is probably used to this kind of flare-up. Nonetheless, this is not the kind of reaction you would expect in every other situation. In fact, pointing fingers is looked down upon in many cultures, and once someone takes such an action, it is the kind of body language that will lead to tempers rising and language becoming stronger. This is because pointing fingers sends a message of hostility and is intimidating. You should, as such, be careful how you use your fingers. If you are a parent or teacher, or if you deal with children in any capacity, understand that pointing fingers at them when trying to pass a message may be deleterious. Pointing fingers can be a sign of bullying, and as such, it should not be done to your partner either.

You see, the problem with pointing fingers is that it is the surest way to distract your audience from the message you are trying to pass to them. Even when people do not speak, pointing fingers is usually pretty reflective of what they want to say and elicits feelings of being intimidated and bullied.

Notice that even lawyers use their fingers when speaking. However, it is very rare to see them using their hands. Instead, they gesticulate-talk with their hands. If they do point, you can be assured that any of the people being pointed at-including witnesses, or even the jury, do not like it. Such behavior in places such as the courtroom only serve against your favor and may show that you want to push the blame on anyone else but yourself. This is not a courageous act because it may lead to conflict outwardly and is a sign of bullying. However, it may point to a lack of success or confidence or isolation at a personal level.

Snapping Fingers

Just like pointing fingers is considered rude, snapping fingers is taken in the same way. Imagine someone trying to get your attention by snapping their fingers at you. It would be a horrible scenario. For instance, in a restaurant, it may be really embarrassing to sit at the same table with a person that snaps his fingers to get the attention of a passing waiter, only to complain about trivial matters. In the end, they will certainly not get better services. Neither will his companions be impressed with his lack of manners and respect for the waiter. The chances are that his friends will avoid dining with him in the future. It would not come as a surprise that such a person is also a finger-pointer and, by extension, a blamer, too. Sometimes, you may feel like these behaviors impress, but honestly, the only person being pleased is you!

Distracting

Distracting is the haphazard use of arms such that the speaker is often switching between different hand positions almost all the time. While this may seem harmless sometimes, it may have implications on how you are perceived, for instance, by your audience if you are a politician. Switching hand gestures rapidly gives your body a weird angle when viewed. Worse still, it creates confusion. As such, your audience will not understand whether you want to stay where you are, or you are uncertain. When people cannot trust your motives, it is highly unlikely that they will listen to you.

How To Read Body Language — Confident Body Language

Just like there are poor body language signs mentioned above, there are also things that when you do with your hands, you come out as more confident and even calm-which in many cases, adds to your credibility. Below we discuss some of the body language strategies that you may use to your advantage:

Computing

In body language, computing involves placing the elbow of your hand in the other arm then cupping your chin in the free palm. While this is not a technique that is written in many books, it can be useful for you in many scenarios and circumstances. For instance, when coaching, or during a consultation or even when you simply want to lend an ear to the next person. The reason why computing is so powerful is that it creates the impression of a calm and confident person. It may not be easy to adopt such a position when you are in the thick of things, but when used at any time possible, the outcomes are likely to be positive.

Apart from depicting calm and confidence, computing shows that you are willing to listen to another person or their point of view. If you want to prove the efficiency of computing, try and see how much more people open up to you when you use it.

Another effective technique that can be used with the hands is known as leveling. If you observe most magistrates, they adopt a stance much like placating, but this time, their palms do not point upwards. Instead, they point downwards. The palms pointing downward conveys the idea of stability. As such, it represents the idea that a speaker is presenting facts as they are and is honest and accurate. If you are trying to reinforce your position while speaking, you can use it alongside other body language techniques such as using the voice to emphasize your point. When you place your hands in this manner, your message is likely to be received positively. However, be careful and ensure that your words and actions are congruent. You will always notice that when someone speaks, and their hands are not in sync with the message, they risk having themselves misinterpreted.

Talking With The Hands

While snapping and pointing fingers can have negative connotations, it is important to realize that using hands to talk may not be so bad after all. Sometimes, you find that there are individuals that are naturally talented at communicating with their hands and never point fingers or snap. If, however, you have not yet fully grasped the concept when it comes to speaking using the hands, all hope is not lost because you can still train yourself to use your hands effectively.

Have you ever observed that when photographers take pictures, especially those of children, they mostly include the hands?

The reason is simple: the hands add some life, warmth, and comfort to the picture—and they tend to have the same effect in a conversation. The hands are an important tool of communication. However, if not used well, they appear as a tool for bullying and project hostility. In order to use your hands effectively, just ensure that you avoid pointing and snapping as this is the biggest cause of the feeling that you disrespect someone during a conversation and balance the use of your hands with the conversation.

Chapter 45   How to Use Your Empathy to Help Others?

Being an Empath is a gift and how you use that gift is determined by your acceptance of it and how it affects your whole life.

It isn't about what causes you to become an Empath in the first place; it's all about why you want to exist with such a gift. Some people don't have a choice and are raised in conditions or circumstances that cause them to innately understand the world in a different and more powerful way. Others will choose to dedicate their time to researching and studying ways to become an Empath because of a desire to help others, to become more psychic, and to enhance their perception of the world around them.

Whatever brought you to this path must have something to do with the powerful benefits of living in this way. Often, Empaths are looking for professions that support these talents and abilities, while others are wanting to empower their partnerships and relationships by honing in on other people's needs in deeper ways.

The ways that people are naturally gifted as Empaths will usually come from a challenging or difficult early life and childhood experience, stemming from family dynamics, abuse, or addictions that can exist, as well as mental programming and attachment styles. Other people are born with sensitivities that naturally exist or occur because of their personalities and what they have inherited from their family tree. It really depends on so many factors, including nature vs. nurture.

As an adult, if you weren't naturally developing your Empath skills at an early age because of environment and family dynamics, you may have evolved to have these skills because of a certain career choice, personal relationships, or life events that challenged your perception of reality and identity.

You could have pursued a degree in medicine, working under stressful conditions in emergency rooms and patient care for hours and hours every day, naturally learning the gift of reading people, not just their medical charts. Or you could have chosen a partner with serious or debilitating issues that forced you to live with their problems, slowly and indefinitely making them your own, teaching yourself how to read your partner in a different capacity.

511

Many people are not actively trying to pursue becoming an Empath; it can simply be the natural result of life experience and circumstances, as with the two examples listed above. And of course, there are so many different ways that this can manifest for you, so don't limit your thinking to just a career choice or a relationship challenge. Everyone has a different story to tell, and whatever your story is, your gifts are valuable to this world, no matter how they were arrived at.

As it turns out, there are a lot of people in the world today who are studying the benefits of being an Empath and are looking for ways to enhance their own abilities through other means. For some, the spiritual path will lead them to a deeper sense of knowing as they pursue enlightenment and for others, going on a profound healing journey and recovering from intense illness cause them to want to become healers themselves. Some people are just curious about it and want to have a greater understanding and so they will pick up a book like Empath: The Complete Healing Guide to Develop Your Gift and Finding Your Sense of Self, to learn how to broaden their Empathic scope.

It really is a unique experience for anyone who is coming to terms with having such a special gift or desire. If you are already working to embrace the gift of being an Empath, this book is a great resource to offer you the guidance and support that you need. If you are someone who is looking for ways to enhance their empathic skills and become more sensitive as an Empath, this book will also give you an understanding of what to expect along the journey.

If you are looking at ways to help empower your gift and make it a bigger and better part of your life, then you may want to consider some of the following benefits associated with this gift.

Empaths:

• Give hope and help to others

• Provide support on a deeper and more sensitive level

• Can help people overcome great adversity and life challenges

• Experience the world in a more sensual way because of naturally heightened senses

- Are often very creative through a variety of artistic expressions like painting, dancing, drawing, music, etc.

- Have a strong capacity to heal wounded feelings and emotions, including in group situations, acting as mediator and counselor

- Are promoters of growth and transformation

- Can bring peace and harmony to dysfunctional dynamics and relationships

- Are very open-hearted and open-minded to all races, religions, and cultural backgrounds

- Are accepting of all people, most of the time

- Are very good at nurturing and caregiving and make very loving and attentive partners, friends, and parents

- Are gifted at working one-on-one to help with problem-solving, as well as in group settings

- Are advocates and activists for a variety of meaningful causes

- Are naturally kind, generous, and compassionate

- Are especially gifted in healing professions including talk therapy and counseling, massage and bodywork, pet and animal services, birth assistants and doulas, hospice and palliative care, nursing, medicine, life-coaching, and more

- Benefit from working with children, animals, and elderly people and can be very healing and helping caregivers in return

- Are capable of psychic awareness, spiritual growth, and enhancing clairvoyant abilities with practice

- Develop incredibly strong and powerful senses and can live more exciting and passionate lives as a result

- The list goes on!

What you choose to do with your empathic gifts is up to you and depends on your personality, interests, and what type of Empath you are. It can affect your career path, relationships, creative expression, and how you explore the world when you are living in balance with these benefits.

People will tell you all of the time what a great friend and good listener you are and it goes so much further and deeper than that. When you are an Empath you are experiencing your whole life in a more sensitive way and will be able to offer more sensitivity to any person in need as a result.

There are also important personal benefits to being empathic at this level that will revolve around your ability to take good care of yourself the way you are able to take care of others. When you are in alignment with your intuition and true self, you are able to live the life of your dreams. As an Empath, you may find it easier to hone in on what you need to do to reach your goals because of your own heightened perceptions. Some of the great personal benefits of being an Empath are:

- Enhancing intuition

- Developing and improving self-esteem and self-worth

- Overcoming your fears, doubts, and worries

- Spiritual awakening and enlightenment

- Kundalini Awakening (long-term healing and balancing of the chakras)

- Overcoming addictions and chemical, food, or substance abuse

- Healing wounds of the past and karmic past lives

- Sensing and feeling your own feelings and well-being to a greater extent

- Forming deeper love bonds with yourself, your passions, desires, pursuits, and personal needs

- And more!

The benefits to the self are as powerful as the benefits to others. It isn't just about how you are able to help other people with your gifts; it's about what it can also do for you and your ability to live a happy, fulfilling, healthy, and carefree life!

The key is to let yourself have your own feelings, separate from other people's so that you are able to clearly identify what it is that YOU want versus what other people make you feel like you want.

Being an Empath will open a whole world of possibility for you if you are able to manage it carefully. You can gain in self-confidence, use your gift to help yourself and other people, make a big difference in your chosen career and in the world, and find who you truly are.

As you are getting closer to learning about all of the ways that this ability can influence your life in more positive ways, you will also have to identify some of the ways that it can bring challenges into your life. Many Empaths will struggle, as you already learned here, and looking at the downsides of being an Empath will help you learn to understand what has to be resolved in order to help you thrive and find your sense of self.

The next part will give you more information and input about what some of those downsides are and how to monitor them when they are starting to get out of hand. Your gift requires a bit of maintenance and a look into the issues of being a strong Empath will only help you improve your skills and abilities.

Chapter 46   The Pros and Cons of Being an Empath

Depending on how long you've known that you are an empath, you may be quite familiar with the pros and cons of being one. We've already covered that one of the downfalls can be the way it is a heavy burden to bear due to the outside energies and emotions you are surrounded by. However, most things in life come with both negatives and positives. The experience of feeling those emotions around you can be wonderful and helpful in many different ways.

The pros and cons can't really be separated as they are often intertwined with one another.

Empaths are listeners. They can be all sorts of joy, being outgoing and enthusiastic and generally bubbly. Let's not forget the heyoka empath literally known for being humorous when you least expect it. Their journey can be one of emotional bliss, but it can also be one of emotional turmoil since empaths can be weighed down with mood swings galore. This is because their moods are not always their own. If empaths don't fully understand and differentiate their own thoughts and feelings from those of others, they can have fluctuating mood swings that literally change with the speed of flicking a switch on and off.

As with the good, being an empath can come with feelings of depression, anxiety, panic, fear, and sorrow. Without having any control over these feelings, you can be experiencing the suffering of others. It's a very difficult thing to have to handle and shouldn't be done so alone.

This is where compassion comes in. An empath should have at least one person they can turn to in the throes of these mood swings because being left alone can be detrimental to mental and physical health. Find someone, be it a friend or a partner or a family member, who you can turn to when things get too overwhelming for you. Whoever you find, make sure to tell them that all you really need from them is empathic love—the ability to show compassion without judging you. This may help you in recovery from these overwhelming moments.

Most empaths, unless they have gone on their own journeys of self-discovery and self-acceptance, don't actually know or understand what's going on within. They don't know that they're feeling another person's emotions like they are their own emotions. This can quite obviously lead to a myriad of feelings such as confusion, particularly if things were grand in one moment and terrible in the next. Understanding their empathic connection is a part of the journey.

It's easier for an empath to withhold their feelings and emotions than it is for others. They want to do their best not to be barraged by the feelings and emotions of others. In doing so, they often become reclusive and learn to block out these feelings. The downside of this is that they can end up bottling up their own emotions or building walls so high that they don't ever let anyone else in. This can definitely be bad for an empath—or anyone for that matter—because the longer you allow these feelings and emotions to build up inside yourself, the more power they build up. Eventually, they can explode and leave behind a lot of damage to both the empath and those around the empath. This can create an unstable environment, a mental/emotional breakdown, and/or actual disease.

Expressing yourself honestly is a choice, but it is a great form of healing.

Cons of Being an Empath

Some of these can count as pros depending on how you look at them. You'll notice how short this list is compared to the list of pros. This is because being an empath is truly a positive blessing if you understand your gift properly.

•   You are easily overwhelmed. Wherever there are lots of people, you can be overwhelmed with the feelings and emotions emanating off of those that surround you. Sometimes you can be in a room with one person and still feel this way. This is why it is so important not to bottle things up.

•   Addictive personalities. Empaths are prone to looking for ways to escape or block out the emotions of others. This means that they sometimes turn toward addictive substances such as sex, drugs, and alcohol. Learning to protect yourself and your energy means that you won't be struck with the need to escape these things. Instead, you will know how to cope with them properly.

•   Media can be devastating. Some empaths turn away from media altogether. They can feel the emotions of others so strongly that even reading a newspaper is too much for them. It is a harsh world out there.

- Empaths can pick up both mental and physical ailments that others may suffer from. This can happen even if you don't come into contact with the other person, depending on how strong your gift is. Needless to say, no one wants to suffer this way.

- Intuition can be hurtful when you know that someone you care about is lying to you or keeping secrets from you. The ability to know and feel these things can be difficult, particularly if you can't prove such things. Try to surround yourself with people who are like minded to prevent feeling this way on a regular basis.

- We don't really have a home. Empaths are natural wanderers. After a certain amount of time, we can often feel foreign in places we once cherished. Our intuition implores us to explore the great big world. Due to this, we're rarely ever satisfied with one place, but it does mean we make brilliant travelers.

Pros of Being an Empath

Well, we covered the cons, which I admit were pretty bad. Now we get to look at the reasons why being an empath truly is a gift. Bear with me here, because it's a pretty long list of reasons.

- Empaths are natural healers in many different forms: emotional, physical, environmental, animal, you name it. They can use their touch, their voice, and their creativity to do so. Most empaths end up on a path of healing because they simply have that pull toward their profession.

- As tough as crowds may be for an empath, the small circle they often end up building for themselves is a strong one. Once an empath makes a connection with someone, they are incredibly loyal and loving. We hold onto our loved ones tightly because we don't want to let the good ones go.

- Okay, we already know this one, but empaths love an insane amount. Their hearts are just bigger than most. Being so overloaded with all these feelings makes faking them difficult.

- That gut instinct is extremely strong and if you listen to it, I'm pretty sure you could conquer the world if you wanted to. Listen to that sixth sense of yours because it could save you from potential dangers if it hasn't already.

•   Along with having an extremely strong sense of intuition, we also have amazing senses. It isn't only emotions and feelings that are heightened. If you find yourself enjoying a myriad of sensations with a lot more intensity than those around you, you can chalk that up to being an empath. We have heightened senses that allow us to better enjoy our food, beverages, flowers, essential oils, touch, and so forth. Admittedly, these can sometimes overwhelm us, but they could also help save lives. How, you might ask? Well, if you work on increasing a certain sense, such as smell, you could be able to track down death or disease in animals, people, and/or nature.

•   I know we said that the weight of other people's emotions is a burden and we're really prone to lows, but we've also got the other end of the spectrum. We have great highs, too. Most empaths actually have a deep enthusiasm for life, and when we are enjoying it, we experience joy intensely.

•   Empaths have an abundance of creativity! We think and see things differently. Our art is not the only creative aspect of our life, but so are our experiences, situations, and prospects. Now, you've probably had the misfortune of being told that the way you think about and/or do things is wrong, but it's a capacity all your own. Don't let anyone take that unusual creativity away from you, and let it shine brightly instead.

•   This Is yet another con that also turns out to be a pro, but we can't be lied to. We are good at reading people's thoughts, feelings, and emotions. This means that we can tell when people are lying, we can tell when people aren't okay, and we can tell when people are bad news.

•   Empaths can read emotional and nonverbal cues really well. It's a talent in numerous places. Due to our good senses, we can even sense the needs of those who do not speak, such as animals and plants, but also the body and babies.

•   An empath generally has a craving to make the world a better place. This isn't a desire that you should ever feel ashamed of. We are capable of bringing plenty of positive changes to this world, and when we can, we should. There are already too many people turning blind eyes. Let's work on correcting the wrongs happening around us—together.

519

•   It's especially important for us to change the world considering our pull to it. We are children of nature. It's one of the best ways to de-stress, and it can provide peace and comfort.

•   To some, this might seem more like a con, but we find that it's pretty cool to be able to recharge on our own. We require a certain level of alone time to recuperate. It is because of this that we are self-aware, and we think it's great to be self-aware.

Chapter 47   Overcoming Social Anxiety

The following methods are tailored to help empaths with social anxiety; however, with slight modifications, they can also benefit non-empaths. If you choose to seek therapy for your social anxiety, please let your therapist know that you're an empath or have qualities of an empath. This will help them to adjust your cognitive behavioral therapy to best help you. You may even find that your therapist is an empath too! Many empaths are drawn to this line of work.

Imagine the worst-case scenario. When you have come up with an extremely negative outcome, analyze the likelihood that this could happen. If you have a presentation coming up at work, your worst-case scenario could be that you would open your mouth to begin, regurgitate your last meal, and be fired. When you think about it in this manner, you will realize that the actual likelihood of this happening is absurdly low. Now that you considered and rejected the extreme, rationally think about the most likely outcome. You may stutter a few times or not keep eye contact; nothing that will get you fired or even reprimanded. Keep in mind that this is your area of expertise. People are attending the presentation to hear what you have to say for a reason, and it is not to see you fail. To take a pessimistic view of people, they would consider it a waste of their time.

Use your nervous energy to prepare. Practice your upcoming presentation. Do it in front of the mirror. Give the presentation to your spouse. Use your self-care techniques the morning of your presentation so that you are as relaxed as possible. Before the presentation, try to get some alone time, when you can separate the emotions you are feeling through other people from your own. Your nervousness is enough to deal with; don't compound it with the negative emotions of others. If you have a coworker who's consistently happy and confident, try to spend some time with them right before the presentation. Embrace their emotions and positive energy. Avoid negative people, if possible.

Change your thought patterns. People with social anxiety tend to have a negative, cyclical way of thinking about social situations. For example, the more stressed you are, the more likely you are to have physical symptoms. This gives you even more to worry about. You may begin the conversation already stressed, but then, as you analyze everything you are saying in a conversation, you reprimand yourself and think of how you could have said it better. Try to stop and think rationally. You may have stuttered a couple of times during a conversation. Would you judge someone for stuttering? Is it really a big deal? Remind yourself that as an empath, you are naturally a good listener. Try to concentrate on being a good listener, rather than focusing on judging yourself. This should come naturally to you!

It can be helpful to remember that as much as you are judging yourself, the people you are interacting with are likely doing the same thing. Unfortunately, for an empath, this means that they are absorbing this energy from the people around them. This is an instance in which getting in the habit of practicing separation of your emotions from the emotions of others will be important.

Are you only thinking about what you did wrong? Perhaps you were blushing when you told a funny joke that got a great reaction. Stop thinking about the blush and think about how people enjoyed the joke!

Are you focused too much on the past? Were you made fun of in school? Well, you're an adult now; you are no longer that awkward preteen. You don't judge others by how they were when they were younger, so why would they judge you like that? More importantly, why would you judge yourself like that? Think of all you have accomplished and how much you have changed.

People often say that you should treat others the way you would treat yourself. But, as an empath, you should treat yourself the way you would treat others—with compassion, kindness, and generosity.

It takes time and patience to change your negative thought patterns. You don't have to be completely positive at all times. Just try to be rational and logical in the way you are thinking.

Change your behaviors. Do you have certain crutches that you use in social situations? Maybe you are always checking your phone. You might have a couple of friends that you cling to when you are at an event. Take the time to reflect on what you do in social situations. You probably use a crutch and don't even realize it. Write them down. Make a journal about how you could stop using them altogether or alter them. Most importantly, begin implementing these ideas.

Desensitize yourself. Gradually expose yourself to more situations that give you social anxiety. Do this slowly, so you don't become overwhelmed. If one of your social crutches is a group of friends that you don't branch out from, start by trying to socialize with other people at an event while they are there. You still have your support system to fall back on if necessary. Eventually, you can go to social events that your support group is not attending. Ridding yourself of this crutch doesn't mean you have to give up your friends! You are simply expanding your comfort level with others.

You may never like large social events. There is nothing wrong with that, but you can handle attending them when necessary or beneficial. There's no reason for you not to have an active and healthy social life. Take the initiative and plan smaller events with your close friends and family.

Our goal is to go against your inclination to avoid social situations. You may never feel completely comfortable with certain social groups and situations, but you will be better equipped to handle them when they arise. You may never enjoy large, loud, meetings at work. But if other than those meetings you love your job, you can teach yourself to be able to handle it.

Use visualization. Empaths tend to be daydreamers. Harness that natural inclination, visualize the social situation you are dreading, and how you will handle yourself. Visualize yourself giving a fantastic presentation at work. Visualize yourself socializing with people you don't know at a party. Think about the insightful comments you will make and the interesting topics you'll bring up.

Your skills as an empath will make overcoming social anxiety harder for you than the average person. Remember that you are not average—you have an exceptional skill! Conquering your social anxiety will make you an even stronger person. If you and your trained medical professional decide that an anti-anxiety medicine is right for you and your social anxiety, this is nothing to be ashamed of. You are using the tools you have at your disposal to help yourself live a more healthy and well-rounded life. Consider this: would you judge someone else for taking anti-anxiety medications? Of course not. Don't judge yourself either.

Chapter 48   Stay Empathic Without Burning Out

Accept Yourself

The notion that empaths are too sensitive is a common theme throughout both your life and the collective societal mindset. Yet, our thoughts hold great power and it is the belief and continual projection that can create the "weight" associated with this belief itself. It is not wrong to be and feel sensitive, nor is it something that you should feel ashamed and guilty for. You also don't have to change who you are or be any lesser to accommodate, or appease, other people. Appeasement and people-pleasing is a key theme throughout your life. Your innate drive and desire to be "everything for everyone" can leave you feeling drained and depleted of energy. Although not a direct form of non-acceptance, this leads to a sort of non-self- acceptance as you literally sacrifice parts of yourself and own self-worth and identity to appease or please others. You become 1 hundred different things and versions of yourself to various people, or you could very well fall into the trap of feeling like you have to play chameleon and change your personality accordingly. This can have its benefits, taking on a chameleon-like role can lead to much growth and connection, and further allow you to access your inner empath; but, on the whole, adapting so frequently inevitably makes you lose parts of your true self and personal identity.

Being so adaptable is both a blessing and a curse. With regards to the topic of non-acceptance, however, you need to understand that your self-esteem, strength, self-worth, health and gifts are closely connected to the people around you, or to those you choose to give your time and energy. We are all one, interconnected and unified in a subtle way is a good thing to be mindful of here. Your empathy is deeply entwined with your emotions and the emotions of those around you. Merged with your inherent pull towards emotional melding and bonding and your genuine desire to use your empathy, to heal, inspire, uplift or provide comfort, your vibratory state of health and well-being affects those closest to you. Let's look at a few examples.

1.   You are happy, inspired, positive and upbeat. This actively ripples out to make those around you optimistic and upbeat. You can change the tone or mood of a room or social scenario simply through your own feelings and energy alone. Others around you may become inspired,

stimulated or connect to their artistic gifts and creative self in your presence.

2.   You are mellow, perceptive and wholly connected to your inner empath. This means that others around you are silently but powerfully influenced. Being in such a receptive and introspective space enables the people around you to be more in tune with their own emotions and femininity. Receptivity and passivity are feminine qualities- and this has nothing to do with being male or female. The physical manifestations can include others being energized and inspired by changing the topic of conversation or suggesting to watch a compassion-based documentary, or educational video. Or, they may themselves begin to shift and initiate empath-like qualities reflecting into the group dynamics.

Never Ignore The Small Hole In The Boat!

Figure out what drains you, what causes you to burn out and "how many holes there are in your boat." Imagine yourself as a ship sailing gracefully across the sea... The ocean and waters of the world are seen to represent our subconscious, the vast and deep infinite waters where all of our beliefs, identity, thoughts and impressions arise. Our emotions are also birthed from water and emotions themselves are said to be watery in nature, or of the water element. In terms of being equated with a "ship," we enter into relationships every day, and we also have a relationship with ourselves. We are essentially the masters of our own lives and our own destiny, so recognizing your capacity and capability for steering your own ship, so to speak, is what will allow you to live your best life. You should see yourself as a ship or boat with many lives on board. You are the captain and you are therefore responsible for the people on ship; yet, what happens when there's a hole or many holes? Everyone risks the chance of drowning, of course. One small hole could lead to everyone's demise and could even sink the entire ship.

This may sound extreme but the truth is, as an empath you hold considerable responsibility. Your emotions and mood influence everyone around you. Your subtle intentions radiate outwards to affect the overall mood and "vibe" of the room, gathering or physical environment. Your thoughts, intentions and feelings are powerful and you are connected to everyone through a subtle and invisible realm. But this unseen and "invisible" realm is very real, it shapes, creates and influences physical reality as we know and define it. It is our experiences that are manifested through emotions and the subtle powers of thought and mind. Therefore, embodying such an evolved and supercharged emotional frequency and intelligence means that you are naturally powerful and influential. You don't seek to gain power or control over others, like some narcissistic or overly dominating characters; you do it naturally and almost effortlessly. The power of your mind, heart and emotions are enough to leave those around you feeling loved, comforted and empowered, or low, distorted and less than joyful and optimistically inspired. In short, your mood influences others' moods.

Get Plenty Of "Me Time"

Spending time alone is essential for your health and well-being. This is possibly one of the most important and fundamental things to be aware of as an empath, next to the points expressed below in the next portion of this part. Due to your giving, selfless and helpful empathic nature you frequently find yourself depleted in energy. People and excessive social interactions and situations can drain you, much more so than the average human or extroverted person. You pick up on the thoughts, emotions, subtle impressions and projections of others, and this leaves you feeling drained, depleted and low. You are the fuel to everyone's fire! This is not being spoken from an egotistical, self-delusional or self-absorbed way- the truth is that you are a guiding light, and you further hold the light and energetic frequency of a room or space. Your family may recognize this too and turn towards you, when older, when they need some compassionate and empathic advice. Friends and peers certainly know that you are the one they can always rely on for words of wisdom, and kind and gentle support and a listening ear. But all of this means that you can burn out and give too much of yourself away...

It is only when you are whole and balanced within, with inner happiness and harmony, that you can reflect and project empathy outwards.

Me time is a chance to recharge your batteries and replenish your energy levels. It is only when you are whole and balanced within, with inner happiness and harmony, that you can reflect and project empathy outwards. Spending time alone, eating alone, taking sufficient time for rest and rejuvenation, and setting time for introspection and creative/artistic activities, are the best ways to recharge your batteries and replenish your "inner empath." Remember that your inner empath is a blueprint- a unique and specific coding of information responsible for

526

the way you think, feel and interact with others. How do you expect to be the best version of yourself for others, and heal, inspire and influence through your kindness and compassion, if you are not taking care of yourself? Sacrificing your own needs is not healthy or beneficial for anyone. It is actually extremely detrimental and destructive. So, committing to the things listed is a sure way to succeed and achieve the personal harmony you deserve and desire.

1.   Spend time alone: Eat alone, meditate, go for nature walks, watch inspiring documentaries, read, or simply be and relax with your favorite music. We are human beings- not human doings, so taking the time to be is incredibly powerful for your energy levels and self-esteem. Creating the belief or mindset that you need to constantly do and engage in mental activity, or perpetually hold and embody a certain emotional frequency for the benefit of others (or the world as a whole, as many empaths do!) is not good for you, to put it simply. It can diminish feelings of self-worth and contribute to the decrease in your self-confidence and self-empowerment. Furthermore, it is through mindful solitude; i.e. not succumbing to escapism or self-destructive habits and behaviors, where your light can truly grow and shine. This then allows you to be an empath for when you do choose to socialize and interact with family, friends or peers.

2.   Take time for rest and rejuvenation: Create a vision board or mind map with effective solutions and self-help strategies that will help you to be able to relax better. Also, the self-love and self-care tips in the next part apply directly here.

3.   Introspective activities: Introspection is very important as an empath. Introspection should not be confused with introversion, however. To be introverted is to be shy and reserved or concerned with one's own thoughts and feelings, as opposed to external environments and situations (and other people). Introspection is a form of self- analysis and examining your own mental, emotional and psychological (or spiritual) processes. Introspective activities, henceforth, help to align you and connect you with your own true essence and self. Soul-searching and spiritual alignment can be achieved through introspection, as can self-development in many aspects of life.

4.   Immerse yourself in creative and artistic expression: Everything that was expressed in the first part should be remembered and reassessed

here. There is nothing more restoring and healing to an empath than creative and artistic self-expression. Your imagination is advanced and fine-tuned, and this means that you should perpetually energize it. Dance, art, photography, craft ship, music- do it all dear empath! Creativity energizes your soul and lifts your spirits. It can help to overcome anxiety, depression and any of the daily struggles. It also assists in powering your empath nature as a lot of your empathy is connected to your capacity for ingenious thinking. Your mind and emotions are attuned to a higher frequency, a realm and dimension where subconscious influences and subtle thought forms are rich. You are infinite with infinite potential and creativity is the source of creation.

If ever in doubt, repeat this mantra: "By giving quality time to myself, I am better able to give my time and energy to others. My sensitivities are a strength and a superpower- but only when channeled wisely and when in harmony with my own best interests, needs and wants. Self-love is not selfish, nor is it bad. When I give myself space to shine, I allow others to do the same. We are all one and interconnected!"

Chapter 49   Learning to Trust and Listen to Intuition

The inner voice is very important to psychics. They train their minds to be able to cut out all of the interference that comes with modern day living and are able to hone in on intuitive thoughts that will help a client. We have already stressed how important intuition is, but if it is not listened to, it serves very little purpose.

Meditation – As we have already explained, meditation makes you more self-aware. It also links body and mind and people who meditate are better able to tap into the power of intuition. They do not let other things get in the way and see things in a much clearer way than those who choose to ignore intuition. Meditation trains the mind to be able to see things in a clearer way. Thus, the first piece of training that you need to do is taking time out and learning to meditate correctly. You will need to put time aside for regular practice and even when you are giving psychic readings to people, you should keep this practice alive with daily sessions, making sure that you are able to continually get clear signals that will help others who may consult you.

Using your senses to the fullest – This is important because it places you in the moment and that's exactly where you need to be when consulting clients. It also helps you to be able to pick up telepathic signals from others. We have talked in some small measure about how mindfulness helps you and this is all encompassed in being in the moment. If your mind is wandering to the past or worried about the future, you lose the opportunity of being in that moment and your psychic abilities will be impaired by that lack of cohesion. Thus, make the most of scent, sounds, tastes, sights and emotions and be aware of others. Your observation of the world is affected by how you use these senses. Your intuitive senses are improved when you are able to drop all the tension and simply "be" in that moment in time. It helps you to open the "Third Eye" which in turn assists you in being able to see things with clarity.

Be creative – Creativity is a great gift. You may not think that it applies to training to be a psychic but in fact it does because it puts your intuition to work. If you give a child pens, paper, stones or other basic items, the child will instinctively use his intuition to create something. As we get older, we forget about how important creativity is. Perhaps you can find creative solutions for the home. Perhaps you need to be creative with your hands or your mind. Whatever it is, enjoy it and know that you are exercising your intuition by demanding that it helps you to find solutions to creative problems.

Testing your hunches – Intuition told me to bring the washing in from outside, though I ignored it because I was enjoying doing something else. The problem is that situations such as this come up every day and yet people ignore intuition and prefer to be doing something other than what they are being told to do. The way to test your intuitive nature is to listen to yourself as you go through your daily activities. If common sense tells you to do one thing, but you have a gut feeling about doing something else, follow the gut feeling. Test your hunches and you will get more accustomed to finding the right answers. Psychics need the ability to follow hunches and this is vital to your chosen trade. If you are able to do this, you will also be able to hone in on inner thoughts that will help you during the course of your work.

Use your feelings, rather than your thoughts – If you sit on a hill above a wonderful beautiful spot, stop thinking and start feeling. This helps you to pick up on the feelings of others and makes you much more aware of their thoughts and feelings as well as being able to use your telepathic skills. The exercise that you need to do in this case is simply to close your eyes and stop being distracted by what may cause you to think. Then soak in the atmosphere. You will feel the energy in the air. You will also be able to pick up on negative and positive vibes and be able to change routines so that you can create positive vibrations. Your feelings are there for a reason and psychics need to learn to trust those feelings. Unfortunately, in this day and age, we are taught almost rote fashion to think in a set way that doesn't include allowing the intuition to work. If you switch off the thoughts and hone in on the feelings, your intuition will speak to you and will be a powerful tool in being able to help others.

Try actions that do not require thought – Whether you find pleasure in creating a supper dish or scrubbing floors, do the things that you need to do routinely without letting thoughts get in the way. This trains your intuition to kick in when you need it to. You learn humility and that's vital for someone who wants to hone the craft of becoming a psychic. People who are not this sensitive find it hard to actually allow intuition to work correctly. All of these mundane tasks can help you drive your intuition in a way that will be useful to you as a psychic.

Get your intuition honed by doing the above and you will find that it will help you considerably. Keep a diary of intuitive messages that will help you to see your progress. If you acted on a hunch, write it down and then gage the results because this will show you if you are heading in the right direction.

Chapter 50   Finding Peace

Regardless of our empathic abilities or lack thereof, we all aim to fill our lives with as much joy as possible. Using the tools and strategies outlined previously, the empath should find that their overall level of happiness generally increases. As it becomes easier to recognize and manage the different types of energies that surround them, it will also become more comfortable to be selective and make consistently positive choices.

Still, even for those who have mastered these skills and choose to focus all of their energy on positivity, constant and everlasting joy is an unrealistic goal to strive for. We all have our blind spots, vulnerabilities, and weaknesses. Sooner or later, the empowered empath will encounter a source of negativity that they cannot (or just do not wish to) ignore, compartmentalize, or remedy.

It is in those moments, where joy is not accessible, that the empath must learn to find a way to inner peace instead. Imagine, for example, that someone you love and deeply respect has passed away. It would be ludicrous for anyone, even an empowered empath, to expect to find their way to true joy during the funeral services, or at any point within the mourning period. Whatever your views on death and the possibility of an afterlife may be, a loss of this magnitude is always painful. If the empath wishes to attend a wake or funeral, they'll certainly need to prepare themselves for the experience, utilizing whatever strategies they need to avoid taking on pain of other mourners in the room. However, the empath who is focused exclusively on seeking joy may run the risk of ignoring their genuine feelings of pain, thereby distancing the self from emotions and feelings that belong to no one else. This is a dangerous practice for any empath to grow accustomed to, as it can be seductively pleasant at first; but much like the alcoholic who avoids the pain of a hangover by consistently consuming the hair of the dog that bit them, the empath will find that they can never outrun their own emotions, even if they aim to shut them out in the same way that they shut out the feelings of negative people.

Balance, ultimately, is a superior goal. An empath with a strong sense of inner balance can attend a funeral, commiserate with others, honor their sadness, and process feelings of grief without being consumed by them. Their balance allows them to recognize that sorrow is not an opposing force to happiness, but preferably that it is a functional part of joy; that without misery, we would never feel bliss, or perhaps anything at all.

Over time, the empath will learn that this state of equilibrium is indeed their most heightened state of being and the place where they will find their real self.

Embrace Discomfort

Here's a revolutionary idea that can take your yoga, tai chi, or mindfulness practice to the next level: discomfort is just an emotion. It isn't real. It isn't a threat, but it is a motivator.

Embracing discomfort isn't the same as numbing yourself to it. When you accept cognitive dissonance or moral injustices, you numb yourself to discomfort, embracing apathy and encouraging the distortion of the truth. When you allow yourself to experience discomfort without immediately reacting, however, you can learn to make empowered choices, overcome fears and anxieties, and reach towards emotional growth. For empaths, discomfort is often a sensation of uncertainty or anticipation of conflict. If you can learn to recognize the feeling without letting it trigger your fight or flight response, you can instead focus on taking productive action, making yourself the true master of your universe.

That is an enlightened position that very few humans take. If you can start to use your discomfort as a tool, rather than avoiding it at all costs, you may find yourself able to overcome challenges that leave others destroyed. Once you've mastered this technique, do your best to pay it forward to another empath.

Live An Authentic Life

One thing that can throw any empath off balance and block the pathway to inner peace is a lack of authenticity in your lifestyle. Empaths often carry lies or dishonesty inside for long periods, haunted by them, even allowing the memory of them to block their throat, heart, and solar plexus chakras. That being the case, it's best for empaths to avoid lying whenever possible--even white lies can cause disruptions in your energy field.

533

You can work towards this goal through both addition and elimination. For addition, make a point to invite positive energy flow into your life by aligning your career, personal relationships, eating habits and hobbies with your value system. For example, if you have come to realize that environmentalism is deeply important to you, then pursuing work in green planning would be a fantastic first step. You could also reach out to foster new friendships with people who are passionate about the same causes; you might alter your diet to favor organic, locally sourced produce, and make a heightened effort to buy from environmentally conscious companies.

For elimination, you'll want to start purging anything from your life that puts you in a position of moral conflict. If your job or social circle is not environmentally-conscious, you'll be under constant pressure to swallow your truth and project dishonesty, which will ultimately leave you feeling dissatisfied and ungrounded. Any relationship wherein you feel the need to lie to keep everyone happy is a bad relationship for you, and you should feel free to let go of it.

You'll also want to stop using your money to support brands whose values contradict your own, and give up any habits that have a negative impact on the things that matter most to you--for instance, if you love poetry, song, and other forms of vocal expression, it's may be time to quit smoking cigarettes once and for all. You might be pleasantly surprised to notice your physical body and spiritual energy shift in a tangible way once you release the cognitive dissonance you once held inside yourself. You'll feel lighter, taller, more dynamic, and more capable.

I'll include another reminder here to be careful with social media use. Sometimes, these applications can do a lot of good to bring people together and inject dynamic momentum into progressive movements-- but most often, they are cesspools of inauthentic energy. Aim to use these platforms sparingly, if at all, and to post honestly and responsibly.

Choosing Humility And Respecting The Unknown

No matter how empowered one may become, and regardless of how well one has honed their empathic power, it is crucial to embrace humility and keep the mind open to unexpected possibilities. The self-righteous empath who develops a hermetic view of the world, unwilling to entertain ideas that do not strongly resonate with their interior knowledge, is likely to be deeply discontented or anxious, and struggle with communication and loving relationships, as others will perceive them to be arrogant and standoffish.

This type of attitude is also likely to weaken your empathic powers. Truth is multifaceted and always changing. To grasp even a sliver of it, the empath must maintain a balanced connection between their interior and exterior worlds. Shutting either out, or favoring one over the other, will eventually lead the empath to receive misleading messages, or drive them to misinterpret messages that would otherwise be clear and easy to decipher. Empaths are privy to knowledge that often goes unseen, unheard, unacknowledged, but from time to time, they can be flat out wrong--especially if the information they're receiving from the exterior world is limited, it can be skewed to support an incomplete hypothesis.

There is an ancient Indian parable, of possible Buddhist origin, that has become popular in discussions of philosophy and religion, spreading to cultures throughout the world and retold in several different versions, about a group of blind men who encounter an elephant in the jungle. (Perhaps this parable is due for a modern update to include an equal number of blind women--please bear in mind, men are not the only gender susceptible to the pitfalls this proverb warns us.) In this story, each of the blind men must use only their hands to try and comprehend the elephant's size, shape, and overall nature; however, one man's hands find only the elephant's tusks, while another finds only the rough skin of a hind leg, and another still can only feel the animal's full, thin ears. When they compare their experiences, they are each convinced that the others are wrong or insane; in some versions of the story, this inability to agree on their sensory perceptions leads the men to resort to violence. Ultimately, the point of the story, which only the audience can see, is that each of the blind men is right, describing his experience accurately and honestly; the only problem is that they fail to acknowledge the perspectives of others as equally valid.

This is human nature, though the parable aims to inspire us to evolve past it. The truth can never be fully comprehended from one fixed vantage point--it is far too vast for any single person to hold alone. Still, the enlightened empath will be more successful than most at gathering contrasting perspectives and finding a way to incorporate them all into a single philosophy or belief, untangling knots of cognitive dissonance and drawing connections between seemingly disparate concepts--if, and only if, they are willing to stay humble and open to uncomfortable experiences. This pursuit should be handled with care--again, there is a difference between mild discomfort and decisively negative energy, and it's important for the empath to stay guarded against the latter. Don't force yourself to endure an experience that is depleting rather than charging you, but don't let yourself fall into the habit of avoiding the challenging and unpredictable opportunities life offers you, either. As an example, many empaths learn early in their journey to self-empowerment that large crowds can quickly cloud or drain their energy fields; they may have had one particularly difficult or painful experience at a party, concert, funeral, wedding, or rally, and quickly decide that it would be best to avoid large gatherings from that point on. This might be a mistake, though, as joining large groups that are unified in honest intention (a faith-based service, or performance that is effective at steering the emotional path of every audience member, for example) can be one of the most positive and energizing experiences available to the empath.

Though it may be tempting to stay cocooned in whatever emotional spaces feel safest, the empath must make a point of continuously expanding their perspective by trying new things, meeting new people, and seeking out challenges for the sake of growth. The most important thing for an empath to know is just how much the universe has yet to teach them.

Chapter 51 Learning to Control Empathetic Abilities

An empath is not created, but born. This trait is just as much a part of you as your DNA. You cannot learn to be an empath.

•   You are born one or you're not. However, you can learn how to manage and use this skill.

The dictionary definition of empathy is a person's ability to feel, perceive, and recognize another person's emotions.

All of us have this ability to a certain extent since it's part of being human.

We can understand the way other people feel. For the empath, though, it's a different matter entirely.

Emotions of others are literally shared and taken on as the empath's own.

Empathy is not Sympathy:

Contrary to what many people think, empathy is a different thing than sympathy. Sympathy is the reaction we take when we know another person is going through something difficult.

We may feel sorry for them, which is still our feeling and not theirs.

This is not related to the empath experience, which feels the other person's pain in a literal sense.

It's easy to lose sight of your own needs when you spend a lot of time handling the emotions of others.

•   Learning to Handle Emotional Input:

People will, and often do, share their negative emotions with you without being asked. They broadcast them in a way that you cannot ignore.

•   You must either handle their pain or suffer yourself.

Since this flow of input often cannot be shut off at will, learning how to handle it the right way will keep you from going crazy.

Selective Ignorance:

Selective ignorance can be your greatest asset, as an empath. This means erecting a protective shield around yourself and keeping out other people's emotions.

This mental shield can help you select when you want to notice other's feelings or not.

Ask your mind for help:

These types of techniques are not only imagination. When you ask your mind to help you, it will. Ask yours to help you be more selective with what you allow into it.

Knowing Yourself:
Knowing yourself deeply and being able to recognize your own internal states of being is a must.

This will help you easily decipher which feelings are yours and which are not. The better you get at this, the easier it will be to discard the feelings you don't want to deal with.

When you aren't aware of what you're feeling and thinking, you can't tell up from down. Make it a habit to monitor what's going on inside of you until you can do this at will, any time.

- Constructing Healthy Limits:

You have the ability to heal and help when someone else is suffering, but this doesn't mean you have to do so, or even that you should.

Many times, people are suffering for a specific reason. They might need to learn something or handle something better.

When you instantly try to take away the pain from people who have made mistakes, you might be holding them back from learning something important.

- Cleansing your Emotional body:

Empaths draw emotions and feelings to them like a magnet. If you don't take the time to clean this out every so often, the stress will continue to build.

Eventually, it can drive you crazy or seriously detract from your happiness.

538

If you don't take the time to cleanse your emotional body every once in a while, you can become anxious, neurotic, depressed, narcissistic, or worse.

This isn't an exaggeration!

How to do this:

This can be done by meditating regularly, going back to your light shield, and staying conscious of what you're feeling at all times.

When you are in this deeply aware and conscious state of mind, you will know what to do to solve your problems.

- Limit Negative Influences:

Negative feelings, whether they are someone else's or your own, should be limited or avoided when possible.

It's easy to get lost in this side of things without being able to find a way out.

In extreme cases, this can feel as though everyone disrespects you, as though you're always under attack, or that you cannot relax.

This will eventually make you vulnerable.

Keep Positive Friends around:

The first thing you can do is to surround yourself with positive people who make you feel good and empowered.

You should also cut out negative influences and spend as little time as possible with those who drag you down or make you feel stressed out.

Of course, you don't always have a choice who you will spend time around. But this just makes it all the more important to take advantage of the times you can choose.

Choose wisely! As an empath, you are more impressionable to people's influence.

- Can Empath turn you Distant and Cold?

Many empaths are considered distant and cold to other people.

This can happen for a couple of different reasons, the first one being that some empaths are actually distant and cold, having shut off emotional input from the outside world.

Emotional Disconnection:
When an empath doesn't have any knowledge or guidance on their true nature, this can happen quite easily. They shut off their ability to empathize as a form of self-defense.

The Controlled Empath:
The second category of the distant and cold empath is the controlled, trained empath.

Outwardly, they might look like someone who is emotionally disconnected, but on the inside, there's something else happening.

These types have developed a more logical way to view life in defense against feeling too much.

On the outside, they appear emotionless…

but they just have a lot of discipline mentally. If this type of empath isn't careful, they might grow distant from the people around them.

• Standing up for yourself:

Don't allow people to use you as a place to vent.

Almost every empath knows that unless they consciously put up boundaries, they will be the ones that people come to with their complaints or negative feelings.

This is because people sense that you will understand and have the ability to make them feel better.

Even strangers might start telling you all of their most personal problems hoping that you will help them.

Saying "No" sometimes:

Of course, you do have this ability, but letting this happen to you without putting up boundaries will run you into the ground, eventually.

The shielding techniques we talked about do help, but you also have to know how to say no.

You can't help Everyone:

An important realization every empath must have in order to live a healthy life is that you cannot help everyone. Actually, there are more people that are beyond your help than you probably think.

Once you realize and accept this, it can be very freeing for you.

How can you Tell the Difference?

Of course, you still want to help people, because you thrive on being the nurturing type and, on some level, are meant for this.

But you need to know how to discern those who can be helped from those who cannot.

Let's look at this in greater detail.

• Type 1: This type can be helped and lays all of their issues out there. They have already attempted to handle their problems in their own way in a logical way and are venting to you to get some peace of mind.

• They want to be listened to so they can hear themselves and find their own answers.

• This is the type that you should be able to actually help in a meaningful and lasting way. In addition, helping them will not drain you but will give you energy.

• Type 2: This type is unfortunately a lot more common than the first. They will be very upset over some issue.

• Instead of attempting to look for reasonable answers in a logical fashion, they will be seeking distraction from their own inner turmoil.

• Oftentimes, they have their issue buried deep inside and want to put it onto you. Although this feels good for them, it can harm you, so be cautious.

With type 2, in this type of interaction, what has happened is that they have dropped off a heavy load they were carrying.

But they didn't do anything to fix the issue that caused it in the first place.

They will perpetually create problems, find temporary relief by putting them onto someone else, and then move on to repeat this cycle.

Learn how to recognize this type and avoid them. You cannot help them, with the exception of a situation where you can help them face their issues in a healthy way.

Chapter 52   Empath at Work: Being A Better Leader

Sympathy is the capacity to experience and identify with the considerations, feelings or experience of others. Compassion is more than basic compassion, which is having the option to comprehend and bolster others with sympathy or affectability.

Basically, sympathy is the capacity to step into another person's point of view, know about their sentiments and comprehend their needs.

In the work environment, sympathy can show a profound regard for associates and show that you give it a second thought, rather than simply passing by rules and guidelines. An empathic authority style can make everybody feel like a group and increment efficiency, spirit and dependability. Compassion is a useful asset in the initiative belt of a popular and regarded official.

We could all take an exercise from medical caretakers about being compassionate. On numerous occasions, medical caretakers' rate as the most confided in calling. Why? Since they utilize appropriate sympathy to make patients feel thought about and safe.

Empathic individuals feel to such an extent. This doesn't imply that it's excessively, despite the fact that we're regularly informed that we're over-delicate. Being an empath at work isn't a shortcoming. It's frequently a quality. It for the most part improves us at our work. For those in deals, empaths are regularly ready to cause the correct associations with individuals to create deals, naturally detecting what individuals need and how to approach them. In client care, it's a benefit in light of the fact that empaths are normal issue solvers. In each industry, what gets focused as a shortcoming is normally our superpower.

In any case, that doesn't mean it's not testing to explore a working environment with all its various energies. We basically need to feature out how to all the more likely protect ourselves from that vitality so we're utilizing it to help without hurting ourselves all the while. At the point when we feel solid negative emotions, we have to address in the event that they are originating from ourselves or from an appalling circumstance that we're disguising. We're not off-base for making the best choice, and we have to hold quick to that reality. Being valid is rarely simple, yet it's imperative to respect our most noteworthy selves as opposed to assenting to a lethal corporate culture.

Throughout the years it was found that the vast majority who score high on evaluations for sympathy have no clue why. They don't totally comprehend what it is they really do that makes others consider them to be sympathetic. They can just express that they:

•Like individuals.

•Enjoy working with and helping other people.

•Value individuals as people.

So as to encourage a more profound comprehension of the significance of sympathy in the working environment, four inquiries with respect to the nature, job and advantages of compassion.

1. For what reason does it make a difference for us to comprehend the necessities of others?

By understanding others, we grow nearer connections. The radar of each great official just went off when they read "connections." This is certifiably not an awful thing since the vast majority comprehend the issues that happen when ill-advised connections are created in the working environment.

This being stated, the child can't be tossed out with the shower water. All together for a group of laborers and their pioneers to work effectively together, appropriate connections must be fabricated and extended.

At the point when this occurs through compassion, trust is worked in the group. At the point when trust is constructed, beneficial things start to occur.

2. What attributes/practices recognize somebody as compassionate?

Sympathy requires three things: tuning in, transparency and comprehension.

Sympathetic individuals listen mindfully to what you're letting them know, placing their total spotlight on the individual before them and not getting effectively diverted. They invest more energy tuning in than talking since they need to comprehend the challenges others face, all of which gives everyone around them the sentiment of being heard and perceived.

Sympathetic officials and chiefs understand that the main concern of any business is just come to through and with individuals. Along these lines, they have a demeanor of receptiveness towards and comprehension of the sentiments and feelings of their colleagues.

3. What job does sympathy play in the work environment? For what reason does it make a difference?

At the point when we comprehend our group, we have a superior thought of the difficulties in front of us.

To commute home the above point, further consider these:

Compassion enables us to have a sense of security with our disappointments since we won't just be accused for them.

It urges pioneers to comprehend the underlying driver behind lackluster showing.

Being sympathetic enables pioneers to help battling workers improve and exceed expectations.

Sympathy assumes a significant job in the working environment for each association that will manage disappointments, terrible showing and representatives who really need to succeed. As pioneers, our job is basic—manage our group and watch them construct a solid and prosperous association.

4. So for what reason aren't we being progressively compassionate at work?

Sympathy takes work.

Exhibiting compassion requires some serious energy and exertion to show mindfulness and comprehension.

It's not in every case straightforward why a representative think or feels the manner in which they do about a circumstance.

It means putting others in front of yourself, which can be a test in the present focused work environment.

Numerous associations are centered around accomplishing objectives regardless of what the expense to representatives.

Every one of these reasons can be viewed as evident.

Give me a chance to pose an inquiry however: What recognizes normal to fair pioneers from the individuals who exceed expectations?

As I would like to think, the qualification gets through the capacity of the pioneer who effectively neutralizes all the alleged "reasons" and fuses a frame of mind of sympathy all through their association. That sort of pioneer will exceed expectations.

By investing more energy finding out about the necessities of their workers, pioneers can establish the pace and approach taken by their representatives to accomplish their association's objectives.

9 Reasons Empaths Are Great Leaders

Empaths can show sympathy and offer a sentiment of comprehension of someone else's understanding. In some cases, this is the most significant ability that can ensure achievement and transform one into an incredible pioneer. How can it influence your odds of being an incredible pioneer? Compassion is significant in business and life's dealings as it causes you associate and communicate better. With compassion you can comprehend the necessities and addition point of view of different gatherings associated with a relationship. These are a few things that drive the practical achievement of empaths to getting to be extraordinary pioneers.

1. They need to better the world

An empath's formerly thought regarding a matter or a circumstance is on how it tends to be improved to cultivate a positive picture of the human soul. They need to contribute instead of simply take. By improving human relations and offering backing to other people, empaths show they have something lighting up to idea to the world.

2. They bear other individuals' weight

It shows initiative and solidarity to worry about the concern of others, yet empaths realize that achievement can't be practiced alone. Worrying about other individuals' concerns doesn't veer them away from their objectives yet rather pushes empaths towards their objectives.

3. They can manage difficulties

As indicated by an examination, "The degree of understanding between a pioneer's appraisal of herself and the representatives' evaluation of a similar authority is a declaration of the pioneer's self-knowledge. Pioneers with a solid self-knowledge exhibit their very own decent comprehension needs, feelings, capacities and conduct. In addition, they are proactive despite challenges." Being sympathetic makes you mindful and meet with any mishap or negative circumstance.

5. They can adjust

Driving among firm challenge can be testing. Empaths can flood through troublesome territories since they center around understanding their condition personally and transcending them. They are responsive to upheavals and know about what is happening in their associations both inside and remotely.

6. They can impact others

As indicated by an examination representative discovered it enabling when they worked under humble directors who could relate with them and get them included. Such representatives saw their directors from an alternate perspective and were eager to be progressively creative and work better.

7. They don't segregate

Empaths are available to working with a differing scope of individuals. They don't separate and are worried about how they would all be able to work to give positive arrangements. As per Richard Branson who stresses the factor of this quality, "over 40 years of building our organizations at the Virgin Group, [we have seen] that utilizing individuals from various foundations and who have different aptitudes, perspectives and characters will assist you with spotting openings, foresee issues and concoct unique arrangements before your rivals do."

8. They anticipate towards what's to come

Empaths look toward the future on noteworthy objectives. They don't extend towards the future as far as benefit yet rather in searching arrangements and showcasing their arrangements to achieve objectives.

9. They can break hindrances

Fulfilling time constraints and arriving at achievements may accompany its misfortunes. Empaths do realize how to reach even troublesome individuals by enabling them to express their considerations. Despite the fact that there will be contradictions, you can take something from the vocalist musician Leonard Cohen who concedes that our breaks let the light in.

10. They can oversee achievement

While others may crash after an underlying achievement, empaths can deal with each achievement they accomplish. To the empaths, they remain humble after an achievement and ensure their prosperity stays economical.

Chapter 53   Awakening and Embracing Your Inner Empath

Empathy is not something you should seek to cure – it is a power that can be embraced. Give yourself the opportunity to flourish your natural abilities and allow yourself to awaken your deepest powers.

You have gone through so many situations where others did not give you the opportunity to flourish. You have likely experienced deep pain that made you feel bad about yourself or even shameful.

These feelings aren't guidelines for how to live your life. They are simply thoughts that others have placed in your mind.

Thoughts And Feelings

Our thoughts and feelings are constantly changing. One day you might feel like you have the best life ever, and everything is perfect. Then the next day, you feel like you wish you hadn't ever been born. These thoughts and feelings can be extremely different from one another.

But One Thing Is For Certain: They Will Always Be There.

When breaking down your thoughts and feelings, there are a few things that we should remember. First is that our brain will play a lot of tricks on us. We are animals at the very end of the day, so the intention of our brain can mostly be traced back to survival. Everything in between is built by our society. You want that fancy car because it makes you feel like you have a higher status, and that could help you gain more respect from peers. That can boost you up in your career. You can then become more successful, therefore securing more of your financial future. You want to feel confident, so you put on some makeup and a cute new dress. You want this confidence so that you can socially interact with friends, and maybe even a romantic partner. You need that social interaction for survival. It's rather bleak if you view all your thoughts and feelings in this scientific or animalistic nature, but it will remind you in your deepest darkest and most anxious moments that there's usually an unconnected reason why you're feeling so awful. When it comes to evaluating your thoughts and feelings, there are a few steps you want to take. These are important steps because it's how you're able to embrace your abilities. An empath is always going to have more thoughts and intense feelings than other individuals. They have to not only process their own feelings, but also what they're picking up from others.

The better you can evaluate these thoughts in a healthy way, the easier your life will be in general. The first step you need to ask is whether or not what you're feeling is true. This is the quickest way to get rid of some of the more negative thoughts that you might be having.

For example, let's say you look in the mirror after getting ready to go out for a fun day.

Then you think to yourself, "Gosh, I'm so hideous." You don't even want to look at yourself. You feel so down about the way you look that you consider changing your outfit, or not even going at all. To overcome these feelings, first ask yourself, "Is this true?"

You can quickly realize that it is absolutely untrue.

It doesn't always feel that way because our brain is really good at validating our perspective. However, it is false, because there's no way that you could actually prove that. Even if you were to take 500 people, and you ask them all, "Am I hideous?" and 499 said yes, that's still not true because it's based around perspective.

It's an opinion. The only truth in that situation is that you feel that you are ugly. That is a truth that you have power over changing. The truth is one thing that's completely undeniable. There's no way to prove otherwise, and you don't have the ability to have factual evidence to back it up.

If you can change the belief and have that alternative still be true, then neither aspect is the core truth.

For example, let's say that you have a problem with a friend. They're very dismissive, and they haven't really been there for you lately. You tell your friend, "You're a bad friend."

It seems like the truth to you, but it's not the core truth. However, you could also shift your perspective and realize that they're not a bad friend, they're just a person going through a difficult moment. Even when all of your thoughts can seemingly validate something, ask if there is an alternative perspective. If so, then it is not the truth, and it is something that we are able to control.

You must remember this, because we let our feelings become our reality. We buy into the same kinds of patterns of thinking on a consistent basis and this keeps us trapped in an unhealthy mental cycle.

Once you have a thought that might be untrue, question what the feeling involved with that is. Does that make you feel one way or the other? Do you feel good or bad?

If it's making you feel bad, that's when you especially have to question the legitimacy of this belief. Thoughts that make us feel good don't need to be questioned because they are providing us with something. The important differentiation here is knowing whether they are legitimately making you feel good or if they are temporary relief from a singular moment.

If somebody gives you a compliment, like, "You're so gorgeous," you might sit there and try to prove them wrong in your brain, over and over again.

This is only going to keep you in an unhealthy place where you're unhappy with who you are.

Whenever you have these challenging thoughts, question them. Put them up for debate with yourself. Look for evidence to prove them wrong in any way possible.

Be your own lawyer, jury, and judge in the situation of your thoughts. They do not have to define you. Ask yourself what value the thoughts are having, and what feelings they're invoking that make you more productive. Of course, a thought like, "I'm overweight and I need to lose some of those pounds," isn't always the core truth, but it could have some legitimacy behind it.

This could be beneficial as long as you're not making yourself feel terrible about it. You might have some excess weight that is making it hard to fit into your clothes or giving you trouble doing basic functions, like walking around.

If you look in the mirror and say, "I'm so disgusting and fat I need to starve myself to lose weight," that's not healthy.

If you look in the mirror and think, "I've gained a few pounds, and it would be better to make healthy choices so I prevent other health conditions," that can feel bad, but it can also be twisted to help be motivational. It can be the positive that you need for a healthy change.

To help you recognize what is healthy and what is not, say your thoughts out loud. This can be another way to help validate them or help make you realize just how silly they are. Let's say that you keep looking in the mirror and thinking to yourself, "My nose is so big I look like a bird."

That's an easy thing to think right when you look in the mirror, but if you say it out loud, it can be ridiculous. You could even try taking that thought and singing it. By singing it with a silly tune, or a song that you already know, you'll realize just how ridiculous it is. Imagine singing, "I'm so ugly I look like a bird," to the tune of "Twinkle Twinkle Little Star." That would sound so silly! Doing something as simple as this makes you realize just how meaningless, goofy, and over the top some of the most negative things we say to ourselves are.

Awareness

As you begin to grow and flourish your empath abilities, it's important to know how to properly evaluate these emotions. There are usually five steps to breaking apart a thought or feeling that you're having.

The first step is to look at it from a cognitive standpoint. What happened? What did your brain just process? What experiences triggered the thoughts and feelings that are occurring in your head? Find the cause. It's not going to be another person, and it won't be an actual event.

The cause will be the response to that event. If somebody were to make fun of you, and hurt your feelings, they did not cause the emotion. Their words caused the emotion. They were responsible for stating those words, but it's still your brain that processed it in a way that made you offended.

Next, look at it physiologically. How did your body respond to this? Did you get defensive? Do you feel your muscles tense? Are you sweaty? Are you weak? Are you scared? What was it that occurred within your body, overall, that helped you process the feeling that you're having?

After this, you want to look at it as your motor expression. This is where you will communicate and express the feelings that you had afterwards.

What did you choose to do to express these emotions? What did you say to others at that moment, or what are you planning to say to people later on?

Next, look at the motivation. This is your passion associated with that thought or feeling. Is it intense? Is it consuming your life? Is it not really that big of a deal and you're going to move on from it?

Finally comes your subjective feeling. After you've looked through all of the other aspects, you want to go back and question within yourself, what did I feel, and what triggered this emotion? How can I react to it properly?

Red Flags For Empaths

There are a few red flags that empaths will want to look out for. These are things that can be rather triggering. They might be responses and other people that you should avoid. We're going to take you through a few different variations.

The biggest warning signs an empath needs to be prepared for is the language that others use against them. An empath will want to avoid any sort of insulting remarks, name calling, or rude comments from other people.

An empath can take these things especially hard. Somebody might call you dumb one time in your life, but you can hang onto that for eternity. If an individual in your life is consistently calling you names, you will want to do your best to either avoid them altogether or have a discussion about why they shouldn't be calling other people names.

Remember, however, that it is not your responsibility to change somebody else. You are not the sole person in charge of healing or educating those who seek to hurt others.

Chapter 54 Guarding Your Energy

One of the biggest reasons why being an Empath can be considered a "curse" is because many people are not educated in how they can protect themselves from the harsher symptoms, such as carrying too many energies, stepping into someone's experience without being able to step back out, or not knowing how to refrain from stepping in overall. Knowing how to protect yourself can have a powerful impact on empowering you to elevate from the wounded healer to the empowered Empath. Here is what you need to do.

Recognize Red Flags And Walk Away

One of the gifts of being an Empath is that you can quickly detect red flags in situations or people. It is easy for you to identify compulsive behaviors such as lying, exploiting others, or otherwise being abusive or negative toward those around you. Being an Empath means that you can identify these and can then walk away. For some Empaths, the walking away part is particularly challenging. If this is you, learning to walk away is important.

Walking away from situations that do not serve you is not selfish. Many Empaths mistakenly believe that they need to "save" other people. This leads to them getting caught in situations where they perpetually feel responsible for someone else, despite this not being true. Your gifts were not given to you so that you could live in a world of abuse and experience direct damage as a result. They were given to you so that you can save the world. That is likely why you get caught up in your desire to save individual people: it is your nature to "save." However, many Empaths are not taught to understand what this actually means.

You come here to save the planet from a lack of empathy and compassion, but not with the personal responsibility to take on the energy of every individual you meet. Instead, you can help by empowering, uplifting, and inspiring other people to do better in their lives. Those who desire to do better will follow your example and find themselves being saved by themselves. You are not here to save them: you are here to show them how to save themselves. This means that your only responsibility is to save yourself and lead by example. Through this, you will inspire others to do the same.

Recognize And Protect Yourself From Energy Vampires

Energy vampires are people who can drain a great deal of energy from you. They tend to have problem after problem, and they constantly come to you, asking for more than a reasonable amount of support. As an Empath, you feel into their position, empathize with them, and find yourself feeling personally responsible for providing them with the energy required to do what is needed from you. This quickly turns into a treadmill, where you are constantly running to meet the energy needs of the person but you are never able to fulfill their needs. This is because they are an energy vampire.

In order to protect yourself from energy vampires, you need to teach yourself how to say "no." Learning to say no and stand behind it is important. This is how you can support yourself in feeling confident and protected in saying no. When you say no to an energy vampire, make sure that you consciously say no with your energy as well. Some people will envision their protective shield blocking out the request, preventing the energy from coming into their space altogether. Keeping out the energy of the energy vampire is important. If you let it in, it can begin to create empathic sensations within you that might cause you to change your mind. This is less of a worry when you become stronger in protecting yourself, but early on you are susceptible to changing your mind as a result of this energy.

Recognizing energy vampires and learning how to say no to them will also require you to protect yourself from shouldering any further responsibility. Affirming to yourself that it is not your duty to fulfill other people's needs beyond what you feel is reasonable is important. If you are not doing it out of love for yourself and the other person, you are not doing it for the right person. If you are doing something that extends more of your energy than you can reasonably give, then you are giving too much. Make sure that you educate yourself on saying no and that you consciously clear your energy field from the request as well. This will protect you against the energy, the request, and the energy vampire. You also want to minimize the amount of time you spend around the energy vampire as much as possible and practice setting stronger boundaries with them in regards to what you are willing to listen to and engage with in order to create a stronger sense of protection against the energy vampire. This way, you do not feel like you are constantly in protection mode and you give yourself space to breathe and enjoy life.

Save Yourself From Time Vampires Too

In addition to energy vampires, there are also time vampires. Frequently, an energy vampire may also be a time vampire. However, not all-time vampires are energy vampires. Time vampires are people who take up far too much of your time. You may find yourself constantly doing things for them, spending excessive time with them, or investing a great deal of time worrying about them. As a result, they end up taking up far too much of your precious time.

The best way to deal with a time vampire is to limit the time that you are willing to share with them. Decide what your boundary needs to be, set it, and stand behind it. Begin reinforcing it by only giving them the allotted amount of time and then saying no when the boundary is reached. This also counts when you are thinking about them. If you find yourself worrying about the person, say no to yourself and set a boundary with yourself as well. Reducing the amount of time, you are willing to spend on a person, especially one that is toxic toward you (whether consciously or unconsciously) can support and protect you.

Even though it is nice to help people and you want to help others feel good in their lives, it is not your responsibility. Have an honest conversation with yourself about why you feel personally responsible for others and then begin to enforce boundaries with yourself as well. Creating these personal boundaries will make it easier for you to prevent yourself from feeling personally responsible for everyone else's needs and feelings. Then, it will become easier for you to say no and protect your time. When you do say no, make sure that you fulfill that time instead with something that is a genuine act of self-love. The more you take good care of yourself, the easier it is to understand why you deserve your time, energy, and attention even more than anyone else. Even if that does not feel natural or "right" to you in the beginning. Soon, you will understand that it is a necessary protection and self-care practice. Not only does it help you feel great, but it will also amplify your ability to help others.

Preserve And Protect Your Energy

It is important that you learn to preserve and protect your energy as an Empath. Knowing how to "tune out" of the world from time to time to give yourself the space to recharge is important. One great way to do this is by getting a high-quality set of noise-cancelling headphones and putting them on when you go out in public or when you are in noisy environment. While you may not be able to do this every time, using them in certain circumstances can support you in staying focused on the energy of the music rather than the environment around you. Consider using music that is uplifting and upbeat so that it actually amplifies your energy, rather than you going out and coming home feeling depleted.

Another way to protect your energy is to begin practicing energetic boundaries. This means that you make yourself unavailable to tune into the energies of those around you unless you give yourself permission to do so. Set the boundary with yourself that you are not going to tune into any energy.

Learning to switch your gift "on" and "off" can take practice, and the best way to do it is just to start. Soon, you will learn to be firm and consistent, and your boundaries will be effortless to uphold. This means that you begin gaining power and control over your Empath gift so that you no longer feel like you are being ruled by it. Instead, you can rule the gift and use it as you need to in order to support you in your life and soul purpose, as well as in leading a quality life.

Shield Your Aura

Shielding is a powerful practice that Empaths use to protect themselves from external energies. This is a form of creating an energetic boundary that can stay in place and keep you feeling protected without you always having to be consciously working toward it. In the beginning, your energetic shield may need continuous conscious reinforcement. Once you become more skilled with it, however, it becomes a lot easier.

The best shield to consider using when you are going out in public, or anywhere that your gift may be overly activated, is called a bubble shield. This shield is created by you envisioning a white light glowing in your solar plexus. This light then grows and grows, purifying your body and energy field and filling it with white light. Let this light grow until it forms a bubble that extends four feet away from your body in either direction, including down into the Earth. This shield is one that, once built, will stay in place as long as you desire. If you feel that your shield is down or you have taken it down by accident, you can always recreate it using the same strategy. Some people even choose to create a new one every morning to support them in staying protected throughout the day. Any time that you feel your energy is being threatened visualize your shield to reinforce it and keep unwanted energies out.

Leave Abusive Relationships

This can be challenging, but leaving abusive relationships is essential if you want to protect yourself as a human and as an Empath. If you are in an abusive relationship, whether it is with a family member, house-mate, friend, spouse, or coworker, you need to take all measures possible to leave this relationship. These people are robbing you of your valuable energy and you need to do everything you can to protect yourself. Removing yourself completely from these people is the best solution.

Chapter 55 How to Declutter Relationships

The Negative Impact Of Bad Relationships

The first step to breaking out of any toxic relationship is to identify the signs around you, acknowledge and then accept them as a truth that is negative to your health and needs to be amended. Everyone's relationships are different, but here is a closer look at some of the most common signs connected to toxic relationships:

• Emotional manipulation is one sign that is prominent in any kind of toxic relationship or connection

• The definition of this symptom varies because it can include a wide range of actions and behaviors that vary from case to case

• At its core though, emotional manipulation refers to the intentional alteration of behaviors or way of speaking in order to avoid or manage the emotions of someone else

• In the case of the toxic person, this can refer to an intentional intensification of tense emotions and responses when their friend or partner is talking in order to get them to leave the room or feel powerless in their current situation

• In the case of the victim, they know that when their friend or partner is in this mood that their tense emotions will only intensify if they try to talk to them so instead they intentionally find something to do in a different room to avoid talking to their friend or partner until they are in a better headspace

• Isolating oneself from other close connections with family or friends to spend more time with their toxic friend or partner

• In many cases, this isolation is directly linked to and even the result of their friends and family seeing the way their loved one has changed in this relationship or connection and confronted them about it

• This confrontation is seen as an act of aggression by the individual and they get defensive, siding with their toxic friend or partner and hindering their relationship with their supportive loved one

- Being dismissed as overly emotional or overreacting to things whenever you voice your feelings or opinions (particularly if they are counter to the toxic friend or partner)

- In some cases, the individual is not dismissed but rather teased and ridiculed making them feel even worse about speaking their mind

- They can be accused of imaging problems that do not exist if there is an issue the toxic friend or partner does not want to deal with

- Some toxic partners might try to make the individual feel selfish or guilty if their thoughts, opinions or desires are centered around anything they need or want

- A variety of controlling behaviors have been associated with toxic relationships and connections

- Calling a person names and speaking with a sarcastic tone in situations where it is inappropriate or hurtful

- Endless and harmful criticism that is meant to damage their self-esteem and confidence so that they are easier to control and manipulate

- Using intimidation and fear tactics when the person becomes too bold or exploratory for their liking

- Blaming the person for things they had no control over or were not even connected to and throwing out unnecessary accusations in an attempt to make their partner feel guilty about something that may not even have happened

Whatever the specifics are with toxic people, they are unhealthy influences on men and women of any age or profession. The more toxic people that are around and the longer or more connected their relationship with the individual becomes, the more power and negative influence they will have on the person. These types of relationships are often neglectful and even dangerous, and they can be some of the most difficult to break free from.

Remove Negative Influences

Identify where your negative self-talk comes from if you want to truly beat it. Many times, it is people around us who condition us into thinking or believing something as the truth. Even seemingly harmless or subtle negative comments or pieces of criticism can impact our sense of self-worth. The voice of others slowly and insidiously becomes our inner voice of critical self-talk. Never let someone else's perception about you define your reality or become the foundation of your critical self-talk.

Are there people around you who view their or your life in a predominantly negative light? Are you an unwilling victim of someone else's negativity? While it isn't uncommon for the negative self-talk to originate within us, it can often be traced back to our conditioning or beliefs/actions/words of the people around us. Negative critical talk originating from another person's low confidence or self-esteem is highly challenging to deal with. Run miles away from such negative and destructive people to change your outlook on life, and view it more positively and constructively.

Avoid slipping into the trap of negativity laid down by others. Stay away from chronic, habitual whiners and complainers. Don't validate other people's complaints by chiming in or playing a willing party. According to a Warsaw School of Social Psychology study, people who are always complaining experience reduced life satisfaction, greater negative emotions, stunted positive thinking and lower moods.

Chapter 56   Spiritual Purpose of Empath.

For some, they really wish that they never were an empath in the first place. This typically happens after they have given their all for someone but their feelings were crushed in return. Being an empath can be quite difficult at times, and it can be even worse if you have not become aware that you are an empath and if you have not worked on any of your skills. It is never fun being taken advantage of or hurt terribly. First and foremost, you need to recognize and analyze yourself from within. Find out what makes you the way that you are, then find out ways to use your abilities for a positive impact.

Every empath is different. There is no one model for all of us, nor should there be. We all are unique individuals who feel deeply for those around us and what happens to us. Our life purpose is to help and heal others in one way or another. We are here to catch people when they fall; however, we need to make sure we are well first. It is like the airplane example. You are no good to your child if they have their mask on first and you end up having medical problems because you chose to help your child before yourself. Take care of yourself first so that you can then be there to help and heal others.

Empaths and the Spiritual Awakening Process

It is said that we all start as empaths; it is just that most lose their ability to tune in to other people's feelings. We have basically become immune to emotions. When a spiritual awakening does occur, it awakens our consciousness to our own feelings. That is how it all begins. We regain the ability to analyze our internal operations.

Spiritual awakening can arrive in a few forms. It typically comes in a variation of seven stages:

1.   Unhappiness and feeling empty

2.   Change in perspective

3.   Seeking answers and meaning

4.   Figuring out answers and having breakthroughs

5.   Feeling lost again

6.   Analysis and deep inner work

7.   Joy from integration and expansion

Unhappiness and feeling empty. This could stem from something terrible that has happened in your life. Sometimes you may not even know exactly what is causing the depression or confusion. This typically comes about during a life crisis or out of a spontaneous state, such as a divorce, trauma, death, illness, or a life-changing event. Regardless of how it has come about, you may find yourself isolating from the rest of the world, which will not help you at all.

Change in perspective. In this stage, you may wake up a bit, and you will start to recognize the lies that have occurred around you. You will still be unhappy and will get into a feeling of disgust with what is going on around you. In this stage, you will be angry at times and then sad — it may seem as you are on a roller coaster of emotions. That is your mind working through what is happening.

Seek answers and meaning. You will start to ask questions at this point. You will wonder what is going on and how you can fix it. If you were cheated on, you will try to research every aspect of why people do such things. You want all of the information you can get in order to fix the situation.

Figuring out answers and having breakthroughs. After doing some research, you will find many teachers who can provide answers to the questions you were wondering about. You will then experience moments of enlightenment and will regain some joy and happiness.

Feeling lost again. As with any set of stages, there are ups and downs. You will then search for more from other teachers and try to figure out how to connect with others. This stage can be due to boredom with oneself or your teachers. You will seek a deeper meaning.

Analysis and deep inner work. This is when you basically rely on yourself as you want to eliminate any pain you may be feeling. Grounding will become the forefront in your life as you will find a way to reconnect with yourself in different forms of meditation. You will try to find inner peace in this stage.

The stages are something many go through before they have a spiritual awakening. Some may recognize when that occurs; however, some may not. Here are five signs of spiritual awakening:

1. You avoid negative people.

2. You have increased intuition.

3. You have increased inner peace.

4. You have a surge of positivity and compassion.

5. You have an enhancement of authenticity.

You avoid negative people. If someone is gossiping, judging, and engaging in other dramatic behavior, you tend to avoid those people. You get to a point where you will find that petty.

You have increased intuition. You tend to focus on others' actions more so than listening to what they are saying. Actions do speak louder than words. Just make sure you are watching, and never take anyone's word over what you have observed. People who are manipulative will try to alter the situation.

You have increased inner peace. You do not need validation. You will crave quiet time and alone time more often. Social media will start to take a back seat in your life. You will find that you do not need to post on social media in order to see how many likes you get; you will feel content in your own body.

You have a surge of positivity and compassion. You will find yourself wanting to uplift others instead of hoping they fail. You wish everyone the best because you recognize that, in one way or another, we are all connected and have the same struggles.

You have an enhancement of authenticity. Instead of being in the spotlight, you would rather take a back seat and let others shine. You need less and less attention when in crowds or party situations. In fact, you may dread going if the attention will be placed on you.

Spiritual awakening can be an amazing experience when you receive it. A spiritual awakening can cause someone to transform their life, happiness, health, and abundance at a very fast rate. This type of situation is not always easy to handle; however, when a spiritual awakening does happen, it will make your life better permanently. Once you get through the ups and downs, you will see how amazing the experience can be, and you will never want to lose it.

Chapter 57   Avoiding Other Energy Drainers

Apart from energy vampires and narcissists, there are other categories of people you will need to protect yourself from. They necessarily do not fall into any defined category. This is not to damage your relationships with people because as you must have noticed, there are a lot of people around you who tend to drain you of energy. An empath unlike every other person, gets drained easily and that is why you need to be extra careful of your relationships. Most times your intuition prompts you to avoid certain persons. You need to learn to trust your guts. You can also double check with a friend that is sincere as we have said earlier. When you see people exhibit the following tendencies or tend to show any of the following characters I am about to explain, you should know it is time to protect yourself from people like them.

Empaths tend to be burden bearers and this makes you prone to needy people who do not relent in seeking your help any day and anytime. This kind of person will do any and everything to get your attention. They are always asking for your help and consulting you for advice. Worse still, they never make use of the advice that you give them. You have to limit the time you spend with such people to avoid draining your energy. These are also the kind of people you should know when to say "no" to.

Similar to needy people are people who always get into trouble. There is always something wrong going on in their lives and they keep running to you for solutions. These people are always faced with serious problems that get you bothered every time and leaves you restless until you solve their problems. Every time you solve their problems, they are already presenting the latest dilemma of their life. This is where setting boundaries and discerning your feelings come to play. Being around this kind of people, will always cause you emotional and even physical pain leaving you with little or no energy left. You will need to figure out your energy Centre and source.

Empaths themselves can be their own energy vampires because they are prone to be people pleasers. It can be very overwhelming when you are making an attempt to please everyone. This is because it is impossible to succeed at such endeavors. You should attract people who have the same mind-set with you or people with positive energy. However, you should not try to please everyone because you will end up draining yourself of your energy.

Noises and bright light can be exhausting for empaths too. In your home, you can always furnish your room with dim light. Candles are also good for meditation. You can always stay away from noisy or crowded places too. At your workplace, you should position yourself in places where you can avoid noises to enhance productivity. If you cannot avoid noise, you can use headsets or earphones to listen to sounds with calming effects. Stay away from blasting sirens.

From all we have considered in this part, empaths must take note of their relationships and the energies around them. You will need to find people who are positive, secure and confident to relate with. You should build solid and rewarding relationships with people who are mentally and emotionally balanced. You do not have to worry about attracting the right people because empaths have a unique and extremely enchanting personality. Empaths are lovely and lovable.

Never forget that you pose as a unique gift to the world so don't waste time with people who will put out your light and deprive you from shining. Avoid people who are too negative. Shut your ears and hearts from people who will drain you of your energy. You can give people a second chance and when a person keeps behaving in a way that is detrimental to you, steer clear. Know when it is alright to let people into your life. Learn how to say "no" when you should. You don't need to be angry with people. You just have to set boundaries and be firm with it.

Chapter 58 Emotional Potential

Empaths are able to recognize what they feel. They are well aware of their feelings. Empaths feel everything. When it comes to emotions, empaths have no choice but to feel. Once an empath feels what the other person is feeling, they think about it, try to figure out why they are feeling the way they are feeling, and try to find ways to help it's a process every empath is familiar with. an empath can be naturally born or become an empath as one grows up. Most empaths come from abusive households or are raised by parents who neglected them and were hard to tell their mood. They felt empathy as a means of survival.

This doesn't always come from abusive homes; it might be as a result of going through a traumatic experience. People who have lost their legs and are now in wheelchairs can develop empathy because they know how to feels to be there. They can also do it so they can know who to ask for help. It helps them to read people and have a preview of what to expect. This is the same with kids who have been through a bad childhood. They develop empathy to feel the energy around them. It helps them to know how to act or even who to talk to. It's a survival means for them.

Empathy is something anyone can learn or adapt to. Natural empaths are able to see below the surface. They feel more than those who have taken empathy as a skill. Those who fall in this category have, at some point, felt the weight of the world on their shoulders.

Having this gift of empathy can be burdening to every empath.

The fact is that an empath feels emotions sometimes too much; it's important they learn to regulate and deal with their emotions. Here are four ways to help an empath navigate through the emotions;

1.   You are a priority. There is a proverb that says one cannot pour from an empty cup. You can be of help if you are feeling good yourself. Putting you first may go against many empaths who believe in putting others first, but it's the only way to be a better person or even a helpful person. You have to make sure you are taken care of first. Your cup has to be filled at all times; otherwise, other people will fill it for you. find ways that make you better in every way possible. Some of the things you may try are; yoga classes, meditation in your sacred place, using art as a way to awaken your creativity, do physical exercises, hang out with your

favorite person, or loved one, rest enough and many more. Always do what works for you.

2.   Let things go. Let loose and celebrate with your loved ones whenever you can. Choose people who are in great moods since you are able to pick up energies you wouldn't want to be celebrating with moody people; they will ruin the mood. It will feel incredibly good to share happiness and just good vibes. In cases where one is going through grief, you can be there and help them through it, but don't make it your own. Recognize the fact that those are their emotions that they need to go through and experience. Let them know they are loved and you share the pain; do what you can to help then let it go. In other words, feel it and let it go. Find ways to offload the second-hand emotional junk you are carrying. Find someone to talk to and release it. Chances are you will have plenty of tough emotions of hurt, grief and many more to deal with within your own life, no need to hold on to someone else's.

3.   Process emotions. The only way to get rid of emotions is to process them. Some say feel them until there is nothing else to feel. Your body will then return to its natural state and you will be fine again. The chances of you neglecting your own emotions are high because you are too busy helping others process theirs. You are likely to numb your own feelings or even neglect them. This cycle can be addictive if not addressed early enough. You have to be brave enough to process your own emotions first. Just because you help people does not mean you don't need processing. It's important to make a habit out of this. Some of the ways to process emotions are; seeing a therapist once a week or so, joining a support group, hire a life coach, spend some times alone like take yourself on a coffee date, talking to a spiritual leader, having a diary that you update on a daily basis. You get to choose what works best for you. once you start it gets easier with time. Habits are not easy to quit; it will be a lifelong endeavor.

4.   Celebrating. An empath knows the burden that comes with feeling negative emotions like sadness and many more. It's only fair that you practice celebration just to balance the emotions. It is important to come up with a way of creating a rhythm of celebration. Even when everything is falling apart, there is always something worth celebrating. It could be your co-worker, your spouse, just anything good that is going on around you.

569

Empathy is a powerful tool to help others. You, however, should not neglect yourself in the process. it is vital that you care for yourself. This gives you the confidence to share empathy without regrets or holding back.

Empaths feel drained when they been through an emotional rollercoaster. It's okay and normal to feel exhausted. It's not every day that you will feel drained. The intensity varies from day to day and it's important that you figure out what drains you the most. Some days an empath may feel drained to an extent they would prefer if they took days off to recharge and, on other days, it just takes a day or an hour to be recharged. For everything that makes you feel revitalized, there will be something else that will drain you. It's just how being an empath is.

Identifying what drains you will help you prepare for that in cases where you know what to expect. You will be able to plan activities that nurture your energy back after the draining experience.

Empathy relates directly to the emotional potential of empaths. Empaths feel everything, but the intensity differs. This is where emotional potential comes in. Empaths make great leaders due to their emotional potential. They recognize their emotions and emotions of those around them. Empaths learn about their emotions and their intensities before they can identify the emotions of others.

The emotional potential is the ability of an empath to identify their emotions as well as those of others distinctively.

Besides the fact that empaths need to learn how to deal with emotions, they need to develop their emotional potential. Here is how they can do it;

• Self- awareness

Practicing self- awareness is important. Dealing with emotions is okay, but can you find out what they are in the end? How can you say you have felt all the emotions to the latter, and you prepared for the next time with knowledge of what they are? Self-awareness is basically understanding yourself as a person. This happens in three stages:

1. What you are doing. It may sound easy, but the truth is, most people don't even know what they are doing most of the time. We all do what is expected of us like, waking up, check email, Instagram, and all the

570

other social media platforms. It's like we are all set in an autopilot mode. These addictions act like distractions. They keep us from feeling some uncomfortable emotions. You can know what you are doing by taking away these distractions and taking time to be without your phone, music, or the tv on for a while. This will help you get to the next level. Do what you want to do without those distractions.

2.   Feature out what you are feeling. What you will feel may come as a surprise to you. you will notice a lot of emotions that you hide from. Don't be afraid or too hard on yourself. Feel what you are feeling, it is going to be alright. Notice things about you that were not aware of before. You have to manage the emotions using the methods explained before.

3.   Learn to channel emotions. Emotions are just signs that bring something to your attention. You choose how to react to your emotions. making someone suffer because you are angry is a bad way of dealing with emotions.

•   Use the do something principle

This is used to motivate yourself to do something. Sometimes you do have the motivation to do anything. Well, honestly motivation doesn't come from thinking about doing something it catches up with you when start to do something. Thus, is called the do something principle.

Do something that is related to what you want to do and motivation will find you. Trying to motivate yourself without doing anything may never work. It feels good when the feeling eventually catches up with you.

•   Recognizing emotions in others.

This will help build healthier relationships with others. The whole idea of learning about your emotions is to be a better person and to build healthier relationships with others. Whatever the kind of relationship you have with others, acknowledging and respecting other people's emotions will be the beginning of healthy relationships. This can only be achieved by letting yourself empathize and connect with others on an emotional level. Letting yourself be vulnerable. Vulnerability helps create strong and long-lasting relationships. The other person feels needed and that's a good incentive for one to stay in your life. No one wants to be around people who act self- sufficient and make others feel useless. Empathy allows you to accept people for who they are. You allow them to be themselves while at the same time you acknowledge their pain as your own.

- Emotions and values

Emotions are meaningless without values. One has to learn to combine emotions with their own values. Being emotionally intelligent isn't a virtue. Emotional intelligence without virtue can be a bad thing. Take the case of a conman. He is very much emotionally intelligent about himself and those around him. Yet he uses that to manipulate others. Our emotions carry our values and motivate us in the way that our emotions are directed. One has to be clear about their values in order to live fully since that's where our energy is directed.

Chapter 59   Reasons for Not Healing

Empaths often overlook the significance of their personal choices and actions in life. They even mistake some of their customs as effective to help them heal their core wounds yet the truth is, they are not. So, instead of having their inner wound healed, it just gets worse and worse each day. It would take a lifetime to discuss all the reasons that are possibly hindering the healing of an empath's core wound. So, I've come up with a list to present to you some of these reasons that are particularly important, as they are the ones that empaths normally do every day.

Living the People-pleaser Personality

You try so hard to be accepted when acceptance is not something you force in the first place. When people ask you to change, you'll more or less change yourself unhesitatingly. You project your false self in front of other people because you think it suits the society. You keep on trying to change what's on the outside without realizing that you are already hurting inside.

Letting Someone's Behavior Destroy You

With your desire to please people, you try to endure everyone's behavior. You let them hurt you, bully you, make fun of you because you think that is how you make friends with people. You think that getting used to their destructive behavior will eventually lessen your sensitivity and make you stronger but unfortunately, it won't.

Doing Others' Workload

You take "helpfulness" to the next level. You try to do others' tasks, works, or assignments because you think it will increase your chance of being accepted. You overwork, stress yourself out, and exhaust yourself just to find out that you are being treated as a pet and not as a friend.

Scapegoating Yourself

You keep on taking the blame on behalf of your friends, your family, or other people. Your guilt toward things makes you feel like you are responsible for everything and that it is just right to put the blame on you. You think catching the damage for others would help them cope with the situation and would help your relationship with them get stronger.

Tolerating Abuse

You keep on giving other people chances regardless of how much they wasted your time and your feelings. You often disregard the bad things that people did to you. You are afraid of losing them because you think your life will be empty once they leave. So, you keep on chasing after them at the cost of your own self-worth. Your core wound is getting worse and worse but you can't feel it because your martyrdom is making you numb.

Depending on Drugs

You are so damaged that you think drugs are your safest escape. You take endorphins, antidepressants, anxiolytics or anti-anxiety drugs as they are the easiest way to drop down your sensitivity level. Yes, these drugs can temporarily provide relief and comfort but they are not the only solution available. At the end of the day, none of them are making things better.

Codependency

You rely so much on other people, particularly to your partner. You think things are always better when you have a companion around you. It may be true to some extent though; but relying your life, your actions, and your decisions solely on other people can ruin you. You are barely living your own life and you are losing your self-worth, piece by piece.

Empath Healing Techniques

Empath healing can be done in two ways: prevention of further infliction and taking measures to heal yourself. The first way is to let time alone heal it. The second way on the other hand, is done by healing the wound by yourself, using the following tools and practices:

Meditation

Meditation is the key to peace of mind and peace of mind is one of the keys to your healing. Meditation helps you clear all the chaotic and toxic thoughts that are poisoning your mental energy. It aligns the thoughts in your mind that are in complete disarray, as these are the reason you cannot come up with proper decisions in life.

Meditation comes in many types like the "mindfulness" meditation, originating from the Buddhist tradition, which is done by closing your eyes while sitting on crossed legs, with your back straight. The relaxation comes from breathing in and out, and is meant to release depression. You can also try the visualization method of meditation that is a more modern technique. It is a guided meditation done by watching a sequence of scenes or images, along with a voice guiding you throughout the process. There are actually a lot of methods to perform meditation. You just need to choose which among them suits your needs.

Laughter

You release all the negative vibrations inside you when you laugh. Laughter serves as your personal vibe converter because it can transform negative energies inside you into positive ones. Laughing is the simplest method of healing yourself and the best thing about it is that, it does not cost anything. Brighten up your life by laughing every day as it accelerates your healing process.

Discovering Your Outlets

The good news is, you can actually use your outlets to help yourself heal. Discover your hidden talents or in case you have already discovered them, nourish them. You may choose to paint, draw, write, sing, dance, compose, cook, or anything that could distract you, whenever you feel like you are starting to get covered by an unwelcoming atmosphere of varied energies. Use your talents to serve as your outlets for unreleased emotions like joy, gloom, hatred, or love. What's better than having an instant outlet to vent your feelings is the fact that you can also improve your talents through it.

Nature

An empath's spiritual energy is naturally linked to nature. This is the reason why some empaths possess the talent of geomancy in their subconscious. Provide yourself at least a weekly dose of nature interaction. Stay under a tree, swim in the fresh waters, or go into nature adventures. Your sensitivity allows you to absorb more of the positivity of nature so avail yourself of this healing method if you need a deeper contact with serenity.

Water

Dehydration does not only happen when you literally lack water in your body. It also happens to your soul. Fortunately, water doesn't just relieve physical dehydration but also the body's spiritual thirst. Water is your ultimate ally. It has a lot more function and importance to you than you think.

According to Dr. Masaru Emoto, a Japanese researcher, author and the photographer behind the volume "Messages from Water," emotional vibrations and emotional energies could change the water's physical structure. The conclusion was based on Doctor Emoto's water crystal experiment. Different water from different sources like river, lake, and water facilities, were frozen into crystals. The structures of crystals were observed to be different from each other. Frozen crystals from water that came from sources that are near industrialized areas didn't show beautiful crystals. On the other hand, crystals from fresh, virgin lakes and rivers developed beautiful crystal formations.

The experiment was further developed when Doctor Emoto started experimenting with the effects of different actions to water as they are being frozen. Doctor Emoto tried playing music to water, showing letters and pictures to water, and praying to water.

Based on Doctor Emoto's experiment, water can be considered as an element that absorbs energies that come from its environment. Let the water release the negative energy in you through cleansing and urination. And let clarity and positivity flow into your spirit through rehydration and refreshment.

Sea Salt

Seawater has a potent wound-healing factor. Sea salt, which is basically the solidified version of sea water and its minerals—can actually be an empath's healer. Since it is easily transferred into the bloodstream, it immediately helps clear out unwanted energy and dissolves negativity from your body.

Among the thousands of choices, the best one for an empath is the Himalayan sea salt. If the usual table salt has only four trace minerals and elements, the Himalayan sea salt contains 84 of them. You can pair your water intake with this salt to accelerate healing. Just dissolve a small amount on your tongue before drinking a glass of water.

Oils

Essential oils particularly target the skin, as well as the olfactory senses, to relax and balance emotional energy within your body. You can also inhale the vapors from essential oils. The limbic system is the part of the brain that is known to have a significant impact on one's emotions. Also, the oil's therapeutic benefits can be easily absorbed by the skin once the oil is applied on it. Oils are more into balancing the hormones and uplifting the spirit with its smooth texture and relaxing fragrance.

Lavender oil is the most versatile oil for an empath; it has tonic effects, and a relaxing aroma. Plus, it has antibacterial and antiseptic agents. Basil and jasmine oils are perfect mood enhancers. Geranium and chamomile oils, on the other hand, are best for relaxing your mind state. Don't hesitate using oils as there will always be at least one that can address your current needs.

Chapter 60   Empathy Ongoing: Your Tools at A Glance

All you have to do now is put all of these tools and techniques into practice. You are ready! If you have accepted your gift as an empath, then you can really get going with changing the way you process your own feelings and the feelings of other people. There are so many important things to remember from what you have read in this book, and this part will give you the information in a distilled format so that you can quickly reference all of the pointers and steps you need to set you up for empath success.

Anytime that you feel like you need a quick reference, you can fast forward to this part to give you the resources that you need to feel supported and capable of any situation.

Step 1: Know Your Sensitivities

Ask yourself what you are the most sensitive to. Value your knowledge about your sensitivities, whether it is to noise, smells, certain places or people, certain foods or beverages, and so forth.

Whatever you are sensitive to can be either avoided or mastered. If you are prepared to explore your sensitivities more, then you can have a better handle on any situation you are involved in.

Find ways to work with your sensitivities so that they don't prevent you from enjoying the world around you, but allow them to guide you in healthier ways (ex: enjoying the first part of a rock and roll concert, but leaving half an hour early to avoid your sensitivity to thick crowds; or bringing an essential oil with you in your pocket, if you are stuck in an airplane for two hours next to a really "loud" perfume someone is wearing).

Your sensitivities are not a bad thing and can actually be incredibly helpful and useful in a lot of ways. Know what they are so that you know how to work well with them in the big, wide world of people, places, and scenarios.

Step 2: Know Your Gifts

Knowing what your gifts are can help inform you of what kind of empath you are. You may be an empath who needs to work in a certain profession as a healer or a diplomat so that you can express your gifts to the world. Other empathic gifts are about the home, children, and family life. Some empaths become teachers to guide other people on their paths throughout life.

Whatever your gifts are, they are helpful for you to know so that you can be more in touch with how you want to develop your gifts in your daily life. Some of the gifts mentioned in this book are not limited to, the following:

- Natural healers

- Human lie detectors

- Counselors

- Artistic and creative

- Passionate

- Problem-solvers

- Advisors

- Mentors

- Etc.

Only you can truly understand the depth of your gifts. Take time to identify what they are so that you can improve upon those specific qualities to help you align with your skills better.

Step 3: Remember Who Is Most Challenging for You

Empaths have a lot of connection to other people. You can absorb anyone's feelings and have a knack for reading a person from the moment you lay eyes on them. There are problematic people for empaths to be around because of the nature of that person's energy and emotions. The two main personality types to be more protective around are the energy vampire and the narcissist.

- Energy vampires don't mean to be challenging or difficult; they don't have a filter, and they control the situation with their energy and emotions. It can often feel like they are draining you of your energy, even when your goal is to be a helpful friend. Know your limits and set healthy boundaries with this personality type.

- Narcissists are all charm, ease, and pleasure when you first get to know them and then fall into the patterns of being unconsciously and creatively manipulative in order to gain more of what they want and need from you. They are not capable of empathy and cannot be healed of this by you. You may think you can affect change in the narcissist, but you are mistaken. They will always want you to help them without giving you anything in return unless it is an act of manipulation to get something from you.

Be wary of certain types of people who are looking for someone just like you to latch onto so that they can get their needs met by someone good at feeding people empathy, empowerment and the courage to feel their feelings. Look for those who are more like-minded. You don't have to reject energy vampires and narcissists from your life; you simply need to be aware of their tactics and create boundaries to better support your emotional energy when you are around them.

Step 4: Good Listening and Boundaries

Developing your good listening skills and healthy boundaries will help you be a better empath. If you are helping someone feel better about a situation in their life, it is important that you are paying close attention to all that they are saying and not let your mind wander. You also want to be careful not to personalize their experience by taking in their emotional baggage and claiming that energy as your own. You have to state clearly to yourself that you know your limits and where they end and you begin.

Good listening means being open and available, but not a human energy sponge. You create personal, internal boundaries that help you stay focused and grounded in your own sense of self as you receive input from another person.

A boundary can be as simple as an affirmation, meditation, or a pact with yourself that you will be clear with a person when you are available to listen and when you are not.

Step 5: Empowerment

Empowerment is the focus of a lot of empathic work you do. All of us need someone to talk to, to listen to us, and to help us reach perspective in our life qualms and experiences. As an empath, you have the power to help someone feel in charge of their experience, that it is okay for them to be going through what they are going through, and empower them to feel good about whatever decisions they are making.

Lack of judgment and criticism leads to successful empowerment. The last thing you want to do is tell someone that what they are thinking, feeling, or choosing is wrong; that is actually incredibly disempowering. In order to offer a sense of empowerment to another, empathizing with their journey is what will help them the most, and showing them that you know exactly how they must be feeling.

The act of empowering someone else to feel good about their experiences and their choices can be directly empowering to you, the empath. When you are helping others, you feel empowered because it is in your nature to offer support. Offering good support—and not critical, judgmental advice—is the best way to empower yourself and others as an empath.

Step 6: Grounding, Clearing, Realizing

581

These three basic steps to developing your empath skills are significant and important to your self-awareness, empathic gifts, and emotional intelligence. When put into a regular life practice, you can find ways to exist in and engage with any situation and any person, no matter how intense the personal energies and emotions may be.

•   Grounding connects you to your own energy. It is centering, balancing, stabilizing, and creates a sense of security within yourself as you relate to other people and their emotions. You don't have to practice grounding constantly, but it can be helpful right before a meeting with someone, and directly afterward. It is a technique that can involve a simple meditation, a conscious act of connection to the earth, or even as simple as several deep breaths in and out, to help you relax, calm your mind and energy and bring you more deeply rooted into your own presence.

•   The clearing is a way for you to release and let go of any unwanted energies that are infiltrating your very existence. Sometimes, it isn't possible to completely avoid absorbing someone else's emotions, and your only choice is to clear them afterward. Clearing can involve setting up a boundary with someone at the moment, either verbally, or internally in your thoughts, changing the subject, removing yourself temporarily and returning after some grounding, and so on.

•   Realizing is an important step that occurs throughout a situation. As you begin to get comfortable in a situation, as soon as your feelings or energy shifts into something else, something that feels "off" with how you are feeling, realize why and where it came from. Pay attention to the cues all around you so that you know when to clear and ground yourself.

These simple tools are an effective method for helping you manage your empath skills so that you don't lose sight of your own energy and emotions. This developmental tool, combined with your emotional mastery formula, is a great key to success.

Step 7: Intuition

Trusting your intuition is a huge step and can afford you with your greatest tool yet. Many people are guided and taught by their families, society, culture, and life experiences to ignore, or not trust their personal intuition. We don't even realize how much advertising teaches us not to trust ourselves and instead to trust the brand name or the tag line. It's everywhere.

Your intuition is powerful, and it has been since you were born into the world. An empath's intuition is highly sensitive, and when you train yourself to trust your inner guidance system, you will be less fearful and more confident about your skills and abilities to help and heal people.

Ask yourself how to get in closer touch with your intuition and just listen for an answer. I guarantee that the first thing that pops into your head is the right choice for you, right now. Stop second-guessing yourself and use your intuition to benefit yourself and others along the way.

Chapter 61 How to Protect Your Energy Reservoir as An Empath?

Empaths are more susceptible to expending more energy than they are receiving. Thus, it is common for empaths to have an energy deficit.

The negative consequences of severe energy deficit make it imperative for empaths to device ways and means to protect their energy reservoirs from getting dangerously low.

To be able to protect your energy reservoir from leaks, you need to know potential leakage points.

Potential Leakage Points

As we have indicated, empaths are likely to suffer from the chronic energy deficit. This is due to the higher likelihood of more outflow than inflow.

The following are potential leakage points:

* Crowds

* Pollution

* Clutter

* Humanitarian crisis

* Eerie spaces

* Energy vampires

Crowds

Empaths are generally signal recipients. Thus, they probe, receive, synthesize and respond to signals from others. Like any other signal receiver, signals from multiple sources result in higher energy consumption, confusion and at times some signals obfuscate others. This makes the signal receivers to be overwhelmed and even break down.

The same is the case with empaths. Empaths like one-on-one encounters. They are great at dialogue. They are active listeners. Active listening requires higher energy concentration. When different sources compete for the active listener, the energy gets overdrawn. This is why empaths become more anxious, irritated, and stressed by the mere presence of crowds.

Thus, it is natural for empaths to avoid crowds and crowded places. However, sometimes situations, especially certain kinds of jobs, forces them to be in crowds or work with crowds.

How to protect oneself from being drained by crowds

• Get yourself distracted – you can get yourself distracted from the crowds. You can achieve this by putting on an earphone. You can also pick one person whom you decide to engage in a deep one-on-one conversation and that puts all your attention away from the crowd and to the conversation.

• Make yourself busy – one of the ways to avoid getting too much absorbed by the sensitivity to the crowds is to get yourself busy. Being physically busy will obviously drain your physical energy but not as much mental and emotional energy that you would lose when you focus on listening to the crowds. Seek an opportunity to serve the crowd. For example, you can choose to be an usher, a waiter, or even an errand person.

• Avoid unnecessary crowds – be selective about the social events you attend. Those that are not important, turn down the invitation or delegate if possible.

• Make your attendance as brief as possible – If you happen to attend, find ways to excuse yourself so that you do not spend a lot of time with the crowd to such a level that you feel bored and irritated. Endeavor to leave the crowd while you still feel good. Don't stay to that point that you no longer feel happy. Leave at the climax of things.

Environmental Pollution
Noise pollution, water, and air pollution are the two common irritants to empathetic persons. They easily push an empathetic person into thinking so much about them. For example, an empathetic person will be so concerned about the welfare of children in such an environment, the welfare of the sick, different kinds of risks, etc. Even bad memories about the effect of such pollution can be triggered and thus drain the empaths mental energy.

The empath will be thinking about what to do about it. And if the empath feels incapable of doing anything, he/she will feel stressed, discouraged, and overwhelmed.

Clutter

Most empaths are highly sensitive to clutter. The presence of a cluttered space disorients them. This is because the clutter sucks energy from them. They end feeling exhausted. To react to this exhaustion, most empaths become irritable, moody, stressed and more aggressive.

The following are some of the clutters that can have a profound negative effect on the empaths:

- Trash clutter

- Color clutter

- Motion clutter

- Scent clutter

- Mind clutter

How to protect oneself from being drained by clutter:

- Tidy and organize your space – be it the bedroom, living room, study room, or office.

- if possible, keep off cluttered public space that you have no means of tidying or rallying people to do so.

- In case you are in an untidy place where you may not have the power to tidy – for example, when you are someone's guest, try to draw your attention away from the clutter until you leave. You can excuse yourself to leave or if inappropriate, find ways to take a walk away from the clutter. For example, if it is the living room that is cluttered, you may draw your attention towards a flower outdoor and request your host to explore it.

Humanitarian Crisis

Most empaths are driven into action mode whenever a humanitarian crisis happens. Unlike non-empaths, most empaths are deeply involved. They go beyond physical and invest a lot of their emotions and thinking into a given crisis. Even after leaving the crisis scene, they can't switch off their minds and emotional attachment to the scene.

This makes empaths feel extremely drained.

Eerie Spaces
Eerie spaces are those spaces that make you uncomfortable due to the negative energy that is contained in them. They could be a crime scene, ruins of war, shrines for satanic rituals, among others. Such places are like a giant suction pump.

If you are a psychic empath, then, such places will drain your energy since you will be exposed to psychic forces eager to suck off your energy.

Energy Vampires
Energy vampires are those people who, when you encounter them or interact with them, you end up losing a lot of your energy to them.

Energy vampires have a way of sucking off your mental and emotional energy through devious means of dark psychology. It may be deliberate or even unknown to them that they are sucking off your energy.

Whenever you detect energy vampires, keep off them.

Chapter 62   The Process of Empathy

The process of empathy has six very distinct phases and are said to overlap each other. They can be a bit confusing at times when trying to differentiate them. However, it is good to note that all six phases can be grouped into two categories. The first category is the cognitive level, while the other is the emotional level. Within the scope of the cognitive level, the three major phases include the theory of the mind, cognitive empathy, and perspective-taking. For the emotional level, we have Identification, true empathy, and emotional contagion.

In this part, we are going to discuss each facet of the empathetic process in detail. I will also analyze why each phase is considered unique from the others.

The Cognitive Level

a) Theory of the Mind

The Theory of the Mind is said to be the ability of an individual to attribute mental states, including the intents, beliefs, pretensions, desires, knowledge and the like either in oneself or those of others. It is also the ability to understand the beliefs, intentions, and desires of others which are different from yours. In research conducted by Simon Baron, he described the theory of the mind as "being able to infer the full range of mental states such as beliefs, desires, imaginations, intentions, emotions, and so on.

b) Perspective Taking

This has been defined as the ability of one to see things from a point of view that is very different than that of one's own. We will be able to find a different number of traits that fit this description.

To begin with, we must first acknowledge the fact that we all have varying perspectives on the same situations and phenomena. So, even if we "agree", it is very likely that we will all have a different perception. This leads to a type of relativism in what we tend to perceive as "reality". As a result, we cannot assume that everyone completely agrees with us especially if the object in questions does not have a clearly defined aspect. For example, love has a plethora of definitions. So, even if there is a consensus on what feeling love entails, there is not clear consensus on a definition of the word. Hence, the perception of love is very personal to every individual. Ultimately, attaining consensus can be a monumental task.

c) Cognitive Empathy

This term can be defined as having awareness of the needs of others. As such, it is one thing to empathize with others, that is, to feel what others feel, and it is another completely different thing to be aware of what others need. Consider this situation: you are taking care of a sick person. This person is going through pain and discomfort on both a physical and emotional level. So, you empathize with them. You feel what they feel. This can happen at a subconscious level in which there is a connection, but the empath is not fully aware of this connection. As a result, empathy takes place, but both parties are not conscious of what is actually occurring.

When cognitive empathy takes place, the empath is fully aware of what they are feeling and will use that to "sense" what the other person is feeling. After a while, the caregiver knows when the other person is in pain or is feeling depressed as a result of their illness.

The Emotional Level

d) Identification

Identification occurs on a deeper, emotion level. While the cognitive level creates a level of awareness in the empath, the emotional level creates the actual feeling and sensation of empathy. This is a gut-level reaction that occurs any time there is an empathetic reaction. Consequently, the empath is able to absorb what others are feeling. The end result of this situation is the empath imbibing their surroundings. This is one of the fundamental reasons why empaths tend to become overwhelmed when faced with large groups of people especially in situations of despair and suffering. Imagine yourself, as a finely tuned empath, working as a relief worker in the zone of a natural disaster. The feelings of the affected people will certainly cause you to feel a great sense of despondency. This can lead to a great sense of loss and suffering, as well.

e) True Empathy

True empathy happens when a person, not just an empath, is able to truly put themselves in the position of someone else. This usually happens when the empath has been through the same, or similar situation. For instance, the empath will pick up on feelings of sadness from someone else as a result of the loss of a loved on. This is empathy. However, true empathy will occur when the empath has also been through the loss of a loved one. This maximizes the empath's ability to fully immerse themselves in the emotions of others.

f) Emotional Contagion

As stated earlier, this is when a person, basically anyone, ins influenced by the circumstances surrounding them. For instance, when a person goes to a sporting event, they may be influenced by the reaction of the crowd even if they have little interest in the sporting event itself. Yet, it is the reaction of the collective group of individuals that leads to an emotional response in the individual attending the event.

Also, emotional contagion is very common in the workplace. When the environment in a place of work is tense, this rubs off on even the most of cheerful employees. This is why psychologists strive to understand what motivates employees and what can lead to creating a positive atmosphere within the workspace. While the link between positive workspace atmospheres and high levels of productivity is clear, what is not fully understood is what drives workers as a collective group. Of course, we have a clear understanding of what motivates individuals, but not as a collective group. As such, if a person works in a toxic environment, it is quite probable that they will end up becoming influenced by this environment to the extent that it affects their life outside of work, as well.

Emotional Contagion vs. Empathy

So, the debate rages on: are emotional contagion and empathy the same thing? The short is answer is no. Emotional contagion is a part of a greater system known as empathy.

Now, the long answer is that emotional contagion is simply a perception of someone else's feelings based on their environment whereas as empathy is the process by which the individual is transported to the same state as others.

Let's consider this example: a caregiver is tending to a terminally ill patient. It is obvious that the patient is suffering. Emotional contagion would occur when the caregiver is affected by the patient's despondent state, but the caregiver wouldn't really care less if the patient died the next day. In fact, they would be glad if they did. This callous and inhuman attitude highlights how emotional contagion is not necessarily the same as empathy.

An empathetic caregiver is not only noticeably affected by the suffering of the patient but is actually in pain along with the patient. Then, when the patient finally passes away, the empathetic caregiver would most like become shattered at the loss. This is one of the reasons why the health care profession takes such an emotional toll on doctors, nurses, caregivers and paramedics.

The Mirror Neuron System

Mirror neurons are a specific class of visuomotor neurons, initially found in territory F5 of the monkey premotor cortex, that release both when the monkey completes a specific activity and when it watches another individual (monkey or human) completing a comparable activity. These cells empower each one to reflect feelings, to sympathize with someone else's torment, dread, or euphoria. Since empaths are thought to have hyperresponsive mirror neurons, we profoundly reverberate with other individuals' sentiments.

Furthermore, the mirror neurons have been said to be triggered by external events. For instance, when our spouse gets hurt, we also feel this kind of pain. When we have a happy friend, the same feelings rub off on us, making us happy. As a result, mirror neurons provide us with physiological evidence that allows us to explain the reasons behind empathy. Research has also shown that individuals who have brain lesions in the parts of the brain which house mirror neurons tend to feel a lack of empathy. This is one of the tell-tale signs of psychopathic behavior. Since psychopaths are unable to feel empathy, they have no trouble inflicting pain on their victims. As a result, they are able to commit unspeakable acts without feeling any kind of remorse.

Evidence of this system in the humans emanates from neuroimaging studies and noninvasive neurophysiological investigations. Neuroimaging further brought about an understanding of the two main networks that exists with the mirror properties: one resides in the parietal lobe together with the premotor cortex and the caudal part of the inferior frontal gyrus.

The other is formed by the insula and the anterior medial frontal cortex (limbic mirror system). In this type of system, there is the involvement of the recognition of behaviors that can be said to be highly effective.

Mirror-Neuron System and Communication

Gestural Communication

The mirror neurons represent a neural premise of the systems that make the immediate linkage between the message sender and the beneficiary. One study has suggested that the mirror neuron framework speaks to the neurophysiological component from which language developed. Its functioning is comprised of the way that it shows a neurophysiological instrument that makes a typical (equality prerequisite), nonarbitrary, semantic connection between imparting people.

Chapter 63   Daily Exercises

You should know more about your gift than you did when you started this book. You should feel proud about your gift and are happy you have it. Many different exercises have been explained throughout this book that you could use to hone your skills and make living an empathic life easier. Here are a few more exercises that you can do daily if you would like.

Because you can be constantly bombarded by the world's negative energy, it is hard to stay grounded. Trying to stay home can be hard if you keep your empathic antennas on all the time. Due to all these problems, you can easily become drained, be consumed by apathy, and become distracted from your roles.

To work against all this, you need to protect yourself to keep yourself grounded. Everybody is different, so what might work for your friend will not work for you. With that being said, the best way to remain grounded and protect yourself is to build up resilience, strong energy fields, a healthy body, and a quiet mind.

1.   What is Earthing?

This might just be the most beneficial thing that you can do to help you stay grounded. Earthing simply means to put your naked feet on the ground. This means you need to walk around outside, if it is safe to do so, barefoot. Mother Earth's healing power is usually taken for granted but it is the easiest way to connect and find balance.

2.   Using Essential Oils

Essential oils work similarly to crystals for their healing powers. They have been used just as long as crystals, too. The benefits of essential oil are obtained through our olfactory senses. You should be able to find an oil that will help you with whatever you need.

3.   Healing Crystals

Many cultures have used crystals to heal for many generations. Ancients would have a room full of crystals where they would go to heal their physical, spiritual, and energetic ailments. Crystals can be used with the chakras to help balance and remove any blockages. Because empaths can always sense their vibrations, they are instinctively drawn to crystals for their grounding and protective abilities.

4.   Laughter is the Best Medicine

Adults spend an excessive amount of time being solemn, serious, and not enough time having fun. Can you even remember the last time you enjoyed a good belly laugh? The kind of laugh that makes you cry. Children laugh all the time at the smallest of things. I remember my daughter laughing every time I would sneeze. She just thought that was the funniest noise coming from her mommy. Children do not take life as seriously as we do. They play and have fun and this keeps them grounded. It is important that we adults try our hardest to be like children. We need to be able to see wonder and amazement in the world around us. We need to have some fun and laugh as often as possible. Anything that makes you laugh will boost your spirits.

5.   Get Out in Nature

Being in nature is very grounding and healing for empaths. As an empath, if you do not spend a lot of time in nature, you will struggle to stay balanced and grounded.

6.   Get Creative

We live in a world of rules and routines. Many people do not have the time to get creative but this is the best way to get into your feel-good time. When you feel good, then you are grounded. If you are able to create things you are passionate about, it uplifts your psyche. If you are engaging in the things you love, it keeps your mind away from dark thoughts and feelings.

7.   Get Some Exercise

Many people like to exercise in order to get their bodies toned and to lose weight but exercising can do much for an empath. It is a great way to release pent-up emotions, improve moods, increase happiness, gets rid of impurities through sweat, energizes, can help ground, and creates an energy field.

You might be thinking you are going to have to go out and buy a gym membership but you are wrong. The good thing is you get to do whatever you like. If you like walking, go for a walk. If you like hiking, go for a hike. If it is too hot to be outside, put on your favorite music, crank it up, and dance like nobody is watching.

8.   Healing Powers of Sea Salt

Many people think that Hippocrates, the father of medicine, was one of the first people to discover that sea salt has the ability to heal after he noticed how fast seawater healed a wound on an angler's hand.

Sea salt does not just heal, it can also purify. It has the ability to pull out and dissolve negative energies from our emotional and physical bodies. This is wonderful if you interact with others on a daily basis, where it is easy to pick up their stress and anxiety.

9.   Watch Your Diet

Another thing that empaths can do is to eat grounding and nutritious foods and to get rid of foods that are drug-like. Wheat is the worst offender. Empaths are very sensitive to vibrations. Everything that is in the world will vibrate at different frequencies and this includes drugs, food, and alcohol. Things that have low vibrations can affect empaths negatively. Most drugs and alcohol have low vibrations and could bring an empath down.

If you have a hard time remaining grounded, even if you are trying everything, take a close look at what you eat daily.

10.   Drink a lot of Water

The human body is made up of about 75 percent water and most of our body tissue is 95 percent water, so it should not be surprising that water is the best thing to help us heal ourselves. Most people do not realize that they are dehydrated and not drinking enough water can cause problems on the ways our energetic and physical bodies function. It can also affect your overall well-being and can advance the aging process.

Water protects empaths and it is important to drink a lot of it both for the inside and outside of our bodies. Many people should try to get at least eight glasses daily to replenish what you excrete when you urinate, sweat, and so on. If you are on the heavier side, you need to drink more than eight glasses a day.

Water is also good at washing away things. Washing your body in water is not just good hygiene but water can also cleanse your body's energy fields and get rid of all the negativity you have picked up. If you do not think this is true, the next time you come home from a hard day at the office, run a warm bath rather than going for that glass of wine. You will thank me.

That is, it. You can do all of these exercises daily to help keep you connected and grounded. Do some experimenting and figure out what is best for you. Once you have found what you like, just stick with it.

Chapter 64   Conclusion

The gift of empathy is such a beauty, the people who possess this gift initially seem weird and a bit anomalous, but their sensitivity and connectivity are what the world around us needs. The empath who does not understand what this is about may keep burning out and not understand why they bring so much relief to others and are always blue. They might not understand why they always feel drained or why they even feel overwhelmed by crowds. Some of them seem to find it weird to love solitude and nature or even animals compared to other human beings. It is terrible as an empath not to have an understanding of yourself because you would cause more harm than good to the people around you and what's worse, you will destroy your own mental health.

This book has taken a step by step journey on who an empath is and their traits, we looked at the different kinds of empaths and their abilities. We have moved further in teaching the empath how to cope with the stress that comes with being an emotional dump site. We also took time to see how the abilities of an empath are not a curse and to help the empath see from another paradigm and understand that they are gifted and accept their gifts. In addition to all these we looked at the empath as leader; how to lead with empathy! How can an emotional sponge lead effectively without upsetting the balance between executing the project and feeling for people? All these and more elucidated in this book and of course would be of great benefit to you.

If you are an empath, and you are beginning to feel overwhelmed by your gift, then reading this book is the first great thing you have done. So, we mirror this unknown jailer into anyone we see and begin to fight whatever represents authority. The battle is actually within, but we have missed the terrain for the fight and have begun to fight one another; everyone has this fight also to win – the fight for meaning."

A joke is told about a patient that went to see a physician. The physician asked him to give his complaint, he began to point at every part of his body with his index finger; his forehead, nose, kneecap, jaw, etc. with each touch comes a groaning of pain. The physician was a bit perplexed and began to map in his mind what could be causing pain all over. So him decided to take the case history again. The physician now, using his own hand, began to point at the parts of the body the patient formerly pointed at asking him, "do you feel pain here?" to all the parts, the patient answered "no". After thinking for some time, the physician asked the patient "tell me again, where do you feel pain?" the patient began to point again, with groaning again. The physician stopped him and said, sir, you do not feel pain all over your body; you feel pain only on your index finger! This story might be explaining you; your problem might not be that you have bad relationships, or your boss, or your job – your problem might just be one and simple; you have not understood yourself and how to harness that greatness in you. This book has done a good job in revealing this.

As earlier stated, empathy is an in born talent; it is not something you just learn, no! Empathy is a gift; you are either an empath or you are not. But you can go on and develop your skill and even channel the skill into a profession and monetize your gifting.

This book has provided step by step information on how to survive and do well as an empath for yourself and the people around you. It is a how to book, and much thought should be given to it as to follow it. Following the steps and instructions given here is the only way to maximize the thoughts in this book. Study carefully, apply them and become a better empath for yourself and the whole world around you.

If you enjoyed this book, please let me know your thoughts by leaving a short review on Amazon. I will personally read it…Thank you!

Printed in Great Britain
by Amazon

50521154R00346